THE MEMOIRS AND MEMORIALS OF SIR HUGH CHOLMLEY OF WHITBY 1600–1657

Hon. General Editors
SYLVIA THOMAS
C.C. WEBB

RECORD SERIES COMMITTEE
Mr G.C.F. Forster (*Chairman*)
Mr W. Bentley
Dr L.A.S. Butler
Dr R.M. Butler
Dr W.R. Childs
Professor M.C. Cross
Mr P.B. Davidson
Professor R.B. Dobson
Mr T.W. French
Ms J. Heron
Professor D. Palliser
Dr G. Redmonds
Dr E. Royle
Professor D.M. Smith
Dr R.T. Spence
Dr J. Taylor

To my granddaughters,
Emma and Rebecca

Sir Hugh Cholmley (1600–1657), *c.*1640, artist unknown,
by kind permission of Major G. Cholmley.

THE YORKSHIRE
ARCHAEOLOGICAL SOCIETY
FOUNDED 1863   INCORPORATED 1893

RECORD SERIES
VOLUME CLIII
FOR THE YEARS 1997 AND 1998

THE MEMOIRS AND MEMORIALS OF SIR HUGH CHOLMLEY OF WHITBY 1600–1657

EDITED BY

JACK BINNS

YORKSHIRE ARCHAEOLOGICAL SOCIETY

THE BOYDELL PRESS

2000

Editorial matter © Jack Binns 2000

All Rights Reserved. Except as permitted under current legislation
no part of this work may be photocopied, stored in a retrieval system,
published, performed in public, adapted, broadcast,
transmitted, recorded or reproduced in any form or by any means,
without the prior permission of the copyright owner

First published 2000

A publication of the Yorkshire Archaeological Society
in association with The Boydell Press
an imprint of Boydell & Brewer Ltd
PO Box 9, Woodbridge, Suffolk IP12 3DF, UK
and of Boydell & Brewer Inc.
PO Box 41026, Rochester, NY 14604–4126, USA
website: http://www.boydell.co.uk

ISBN 0 902122 83 5

A catalogue record for this book is available
from the British Library

This publication is printed on acid-free paper

Typeset by Joshua Associates Ltd, Oxford
Printed in Great Britain by
St Edmundsbury Press Ltd, Bury St Edmunds, Suffolk

Contents

Illustrations

Acknowledgements

My heaviest debt is to Percy Burnett, for many years librarian of Whitby's Literary and Philosophical Society. Without his skill, stamina and dedication little of this work would have been possible or worthwhile. He alone rescued the original holograph of Sir Hugh Cholmley's Memoirs from oblivion and probable destruction; his fair copy of it – before further deterioration made parts of it unreadable – was indispensable; and his meticulous manuscripts of the Cholmley property papers in some cases are all that survive of these records. My regret is that he did not live long enough to receive the recognition and gratitude he so richly deserved.

I should also record my indebtedness to Mr Gordon Forster of the School of History at Leeds University. He nursed me through the Ph.D. thesis from which much of this work is derived. Without his advice and encouragement I might have abandoned the project some years ago.

I must also thank Mrs Sylvia Thomas and Mr Chris Webb, Honorary General Editors of the Record Series, for their unfailing patience with my carelessness and inexperience and the many hours of painstaking work they have done to make this volume presentable. Whatever errors it still contains are my responsibility, not theirs.

The expense of publishing this volume was greatly assisted by the continuing help of the Elisabeth Exwood Memorial Trust for the work of the Record Series.

Finally, a work of this kind necessarily owes much to the conscientiousness of the staffs of many libraries and record offices. In particular, I wish to record my thanks to those of the record offices of North Yorkshire and Humberside at Northallerton and Beverley, the libraries of Scarborough Central, York City and York Minster, and those of the universities of Cambridge, Hull, Leeds, Oxford and York.

Abbreviations

The following abbreviations have been used in footnotes. Unless stated otherwise, place of publication is London.

Alum. Cantab.	J. and J.A. Venn, *Alumni Cantabrigienses*, pt 1, 4 vols. (Cambridge, 1922–27).
APC	J.R. Dasent *et al.* (eds.), *Acts of the Privy Council of England*, 46 vols. (1890–1964).
BIHR, PW	Borthwick Institute of Historical Research, York, Probate Wills.
BIHR	*Bulletin of the Institute of Historical Research.*
BL	British Library.
Bod. Lib.	Bodleian Library, Oxford.
Brooke, thesis	T.H. Brooke, 'The Memoirs of Sir Hugh Cholmley', B.Litt., Oxford Univ., 1937.
CJ	*House of Commons Journals*, I–IV.
CFR	*Calendar of Fine Rolls.*
Clarendon, *History*	Clarendon, Edward, Earl of, *History of the Rebellion and Civil Wars in England*, ed. W.D. Macray, 6 vols. (Oxford, 1888).
CPR	*Calendar of Patent Rolls.*
CRO	County Record Office.
CSP	R. Scrope and T. Monkhouse (eds.), *State Papers Collected by Edward, Earl of Clarendon*, 3 vols. (1767–86).
CSPD	*Calendar of State Papers, Domestic Series.*
CSPV	*Calendar of State Papers, Venetian.*
DC/SCB	Scarborough Borough Corporation Records.
DCY	Cholmley of Howsham MSS.
DNB	*Dictionary of National Biography.*
Dugdale, *Visitation*	J.W. Clay (ed.), *Dugdale's Visitation of Yorkshire*, 3 vols. (Exeter, 1899–1917).
EHR	*English Historical Review.*
EYLHS	East Yorkshire Local History Society.
Foster, *Pedigrees*	J. Foster (ed.), *Pedigrees of the County Families of Yorkshire*, 4 vols. (1874–75).
Gardiner, *Civil War*	S.R. Gardiner, *History of the Great Civil War 1642–1649*, 3 vols. (1886–91).
HUCRO	Humberside County Record Office, Beverley.
HUL	Hull University Library.
LJ	*House of Lords Journals*, V–VI.
L.andP. Hen. VIII	J.S. Brewer (ed.), *Letters and Papers of the Reign of Henry VIII*, 23 vols. (1862–1932).
Memorials(Scarborough)	Sir Hugh Cholmley, 'Memorialls tuching Scarbrough', Bod. Lib., Clarendon 22, MS 1669.

Memorials(York)	Sir Hugh Cholmley, 'Memorialls touching the battle of Yorke', Bod. Lib., Clarendon 23, MS 1764.
MIC	Microfilm edition.
NH	*Northern History.*
NRQSR	*North Riding Quarter Sessions Records.*
NRRS	North Riding Records Series.
NYCRO	North Yorkshire County Record Office, Northallerton.
Observations(Hothams)	Sir Hugh Cholmley, 'Some Observations and Memorialls touching the Hothams', Bod. Lib., Clarendon 23, MS 1809.
ORN	P.W. Thomas (ed.), *Oxford Royalist Newsbooks*, 4 vols. (1971).
PB	Percy Burnett collection.
PRO	Public Record Office.
r.	recto.
Rushworth, *Collections*	J. Rushworth, *Historical Collections . . . in five Parliaments*, 8 vols. (1680–1701).
SP	State Papers.
SRL	Scarborough Reference Library, Scarborough Room.
TERAS	*Transactions of the East Riding Antiquarian Society.*
TRHS	*Transactions of the Royal Historical Society.*
TSHAS	*Transactions of Scarborough Historical and Archaeological Society.*
TT	*Thomason Tracts.*
v.	verso.
VCH, YNR	W. Page (ed.), *The Victoria History of the County of Yorkshire, North Riding*, II (1923).
WWM	Wentworth Woodhouse collection.
Whitby LPS	Whitby Literary and Philosophical Society Library, Pannett Park Museum, Whitby.
Whitelocke, *Memorials*	B. Whitelocke, *Memorials of English Affairs*, 4 vols. (1732).
YAJ	*Yorkshire Archaeological Journal.*
YAS	Yorkshire Archaeological Society.
YASRS	*Yorkshire Archaeological Society, Record Series.*
YML	York Minster Library.
YRCP	*Yorkshire Royalist Composition Papers.*
ZCG	Cholmley miscellaneous MSS.
ZPK	Cholmley estate papers.

Bibliography

Primary sources

I MANUSCRIPT

Bodleian Library, Oxford (Bod. Lib.)
  Clarendon MSS
  Firth MSS

Borthwick Institute of Historical Research, York (BIHR)
  Archbishops' Visitation Books
  Probate Wills in the York Registry

Hull University Library (HUL)
  DCY Cholmley of Howsham MSS

Jesus College, Cambridge
  Bursar's Book

North Yorkshire County Record Office (NYCRO)
Mainly, DC/SCB Scarborough Borough Corporation Records
  ZPK   Cholmley estate papers
  ZCG   Cholmley miscellaneous MSS
  ZF   Hackness estate papers

Public Record Office (PRO)
  AUDIT OFFICE   Declared Accounts (AO1–3)
  CHANCERY   Patent Rolls (C.66), Inquisitions Post Mortem (C.142)
  EXCHEQUER   Hearth Tax returns (E.179), Lay Subsidy Rolls (E.179)
  STAR CHAMBER   Proceedings, Elizabeth I, James I, Charles I (StaC 5–8)
  STATE PAPER OFFICE   State Papers Domestic (SP2/5, 12, 14, 16)

Scarborough Central Library
  Chapman MSS
  Scarborough Wills

Sheffield Archives
  WWM Wentworth Woodhouse MSS: Strafford Papers

Skipton Library
  Petyt Collection

Whitby Literary and Philosophical Society Library (Whitby LPS)
  Bagdale Old Hall MSS
  Farside MSS
  Percy Burnett MSS
  Shaw Jeffrey MSS

York Minster Library (YML)
 Civil War tracts
 Memoirs of Sir Hugh Cholmley (Add. MS 343)

Yorkshire Archaeological Society Library, Leeds (YAS)
 Fairfax Evidences
 Scarborough Parish Register (Bishop's Transcript) 1602–82

2 PRINTED

Acts of the Privy Council (*APC*).
Armytage, G.J. (ed.), *Marriage Licences Issued by the Bishop of London, 1611–1828*, Vol. II (1887).
Atkinson, J.C. (ed.), *Cartularium Abbathiae de Whiteby* and *Ministers' Accounts 31–38 Henry VIII*, Surtees Society, LXXII (1881).
Atkinson, J.C. (ed.), *North Riding Quarter Sessions Records*, North Riding Record Society (*NRQSR, NRRS*), I–V (1884–7).
Audrey's Book of Whitby (NYCRO, Northallerton, 1987).
Bell, R. (ed.), *Memorials of the Civil War*, 2 vols. (1849).
Brigg, W. (ed.), *Yorkshire Fines for the Stuart Period*, Yorkshire Archaeological Society Records Series (YASRS), LIII, LVIII (1915, 1917).
Calendar of the Letters and Papers of Henry VIII (*LP*).
Calendar of Patent Rolls (*CPR*).
Calendar of State Papers, Domestic (*CSPD*).
Calendar of State Papers, Foreign (*CSPF*).
Calendar of State Papers, Scottish (*CSPS*).
Calendar of State Papers, Venetian (*CSPV*).
Calendar of the Proceedings of the Committee for the Advance of Money, 1642–56, (*CPCAM*), 3 vols. (1888).
Calendar of the Proceedings of the Committee for Compounding, 1643–60, (*CPCC*), Part III (1891).
Camden, W., *Britannia* (1695 edn.).
Cartwright, J.J. (ed.), *Chapters in the History of Yorkshire* (Wakefield, 1872).
Chapman, J. (ed.), *Scarborough Records*, 3 vols. (Scarborough, 1909).
Cholmley, Sir Hugh, *The Memoirs of Sir Hugh Cholmley* and *An Account of Tangier* (privately printed together in one volume, 1787).
—— *The Memoirs of Sir Hugh Cholmley* (Malton, 1870).
Cholmeley, Richard, *Memorandum Book, 1602–23* (NYCRO, 44, 1988).
Clarendon, Edward, Earl of, *History of the Rebellion and Civil Wars in England* 6 vols. (Oxford, 1888).
Clay, J.W. (ed.), *Yorkshire Royalist Composition Papers*, YASRS, XV, XVIII, XX (1893, 1895, 1896).
—— (ed.), *Dugdale's Visitation of Yorkshire*, 3 vols. (Exeter, 1899–1917).
C[okayne], G.E., *The Complete Baronetage*, 5 vols. (1900–06).
—— *The Complete Peerage*, 13 vols. (1910–59).
Coates, W.H. (ed.), *The Journal of Sir Simonds D'Ewes, 12 October 1641–10 January 1642* (New Haven, 1942).
——, Young, A.S., Snow, V.F. (eds.), *The private Journals of the Long Parliament, 3 January–5 March, 1642* (New Haven, 1982).
Collins, F. (ed.), *Feet of Fines of the Tudor Period*, YASRS, II, V, VII, VIII (1887–90).

Commons Journals (CJ), I–IV.

Cope, E.S. and Coates, W.H. (eds.), *Proceedings of the Short Parliament of 1640*, Camden Society, 4th series, 19 (1977).

Craven, W.F. and Hayward, W.B. (eds.), *The Journal of Richard Norwood* (New York, 1945).

Croker, T.C. (ed.), *The Autobiography of Mary, Countess of Warwick*, Percy Society, XXII (1848).

Dugdale, Sir William, *The Visitation of Yorkshire, 1665–66*, Surtees Society, XXXVI (1859).

Firth, C.H. (ed.), Margaret, Duchess of Newcastle, *The Life of William Cavendish, Duke of Newcastle* (1886).

—— and Rait, R.S. (eds)., *Acts and Ordinances of the Interregnum, 1642–60*, 3 vols. (1911).

Fisher, F.J. (ed.), Thomas Wilson, *The State of England A.D. 1600*, Camden Society Miscellany, XVI, 1 (1936).

Fletcher, R.J. (ed.), *The Pension Book of Gray's Inn, 1569–1669* (1901).

Foster, J. (ed.), *The Visitation of Yorkshire in 1584–85 and 1612* (1875).

—— *The Register of Admissions to Gray's Inn, 1521–1889* (1889).

Fuller, T., *The History of the Worthies of England* (1811 edn).

Gentleman's Magazine, LVIII (July, 1788).

Green, M.A.E. (ed.), *Letters of Queen Henrietta Maria* (1857).

Historical manuscripts commission:

  Bouverie MSS, *Tenth Report*

  Braye MSS, *Tenth Report*

  Coke MSS, *Twelfth Report*

  De L'Isle MSS, II

  Hastings MSS, I, II

  Portland MSS, *Thirteenth Report*

  Salisbury MSS, IX, X, XI, XII

  Stewart MSS

  Strickland MSS, *Fifth Report*

  Various Collections, VII, VIII.

Hodgson, J.C. (ed.), *North Country Diaries*, 2nd series, Surtees Society, CXXIV, (1915).

Howell, J., *Familiar Letters* ed. J. Jacobs (1890).

Hutchinson, J. (ed.), *Memoirs of the Life of Colonel Hutchinson* (1905).

Jackson, C. (ed.), *The Autobiography of Mrs Alice Thornton of East Newton, Co. York*, Surtees Society, LXII (1873).

Johnson, G.W. (ed.), *The Fairfax Correspondence. Memoirs of the Reign of Charles the First*, 2 vols. (1848).

Kemble, J.M. (ed.), Roger Twysden, *Certain Considerations upon the Government of England*, Camden Society, XLV (1848–49).

Kenyon, J.P. (ed.), *The Stuart Constitution 1603–1688* (1966).

Knowler, W. (ed.), *The Earl of Strafford's Letters and Despatches*, 2 vols. (Dublin, 1739–40).

Lords Journals (LJ), V, VI.

Maltby, J.D. (ed.), *The Short Parliament (1640) Diary of Sir Thomas Aston*, Camden Society, 4th Series, 35 (1988).

Maseres, Baron Francis (ed.), *Select Tracts*, 2 vols. (1815).

Meads, D.M. (ed.), *The Diary of Lady Margaret Hoby 1599–1605* (1930).

Newsbooks, I, *Oxford Royalist* (*ORN*), i–iv (1971).

Norcliffe, C.B. (ed.), *Flower's Visitation of Yorkshire 1563–64*, Harleian Society, XVI (1881).

Notestein, W. (ed.), *The Journal of Sir Simonds D'Ewes, from the beginning of the Long Parliament to the Trial of the Earl of Strafford* (New Haven, 1923).

Parsons, D. (ed.), *The Diary of Sir Henry Slingsby of Scriven, Bart.* (1836).

Peacock, E. (ed.), *A List of the Roman Catholics in the County of York in 1604* (1872).

——*Army Lists of the Roundheads and Cavaliers* (1874).

Pennyman, J.W. (ed.), *Records of the Family of Pennyman of Ormesby* (1904).

Powell, J.R. and Timings, E.K. (eds.), *Documents Relating to the Civil War, 1642–48*, Navy Records Society, 105 (1963).

Purvis, J.S. (ed.), *Bridlington Charters, Court Rolls and Papers* (1926).

Rushworth, J., *Historical Collections* 8 vols. (1st edn. 1680–1701).

Scott, E.J.L. (ed.), *Eikon Basilike* (1880).

Scott, W. (ed.), *Lord Somers' Tracts* 13 vols. (1809–15).

Scrope, R. and Monkhouse, T. (eds.), *Clarendon State Papers* 3 vols. (1787–86).

Smith, L.T. (ed.), *The Itinerary of John Leland 1535–43* 5 vols. (1906–08).

Snow, V.F. and Young, A.S. (eds.), *The Private Journals of the Long Parliament, 7 March to 1 June 1642* (New Haven, 1987).

Stanewell, L.M. (ed.), *Kingston upon Hull: Calendar of the Ancient Deeds, Letters and Miscellaneous Documents 1300–1800* (1951).

Sturgess, H.A.C. (ed.), *Register of Admissions to the Honourable Society of the Middle Temple* vol. 1 (1949).

Sutherland, J. (ed.), *Memoirs of the Life of Colonel Hutchinson* (Oxford, 1973).

Testamenta Eboracensia, v, vi Surtees Society, LXXIX (1884), CVI (1902).

Thomason Tracts (*TT*) microfilm edition.

Turton, R.B. (ed.), *The Honour and Forest of Pickering*, NRRS, NS, I–IV (1894–97).

Twysden, Sir Roger, *Journal*, ed. L.B. Locking, *Archaeologia Cantiana*, II (1859).

Valor Ecclesiasticus Hen. VIII vol. 5.

Vicars, J., *England's Parliamentary Chronicle 1640–46* (1646).

Walker, J.W. (ed.), *Hackness Manuscripts and Accounts*, YASRS, XCV (1938).

Whitelock, B., *Memorials of English Affairs*, 4 vols. (1732).

Whiteman, A. (ed.), *The Compton Census of 1676, Records of Social and Economic History*, New Series, X (1986).

Wildridge, T.T. (ed.), *The Hull Letters, 1625–46* (Hull, 1887).

Woodward, D. (ed.), *The Farming and Memorandum Books of Henry Best of Elmswell, 1642, Records of Social and Economic History*, New Series, VIII (1984).

Yorkshire Parish Register Society: Registers of Hackness, Scarborough, Thornton Dale and Whitby.

Secondary sources

I GENERAL

(a) *Books*

Aylmer, G.E., *Rebellion or Revolution? England 1640–1660* (Oxford, 1986).
Beales, D.E.D. and Best, G. (eds.), *History, Society and the Churches* (1985).
Bence-Jones, M., *The Cavaliers* (1976).
Bone, Q., *Henrietta Maria* (1972).
Boynton, L., *The Elizabethan Militia 1558–1638* (1967).
Brunton, D. and Pennington, D.H., *Members of the Long Parliament* (1954).
Carlton, C., *Going to the Wars. The Experience of the English Civil Wars, 1638–1651* (1992).
Carte, T., *The Life of James, Duke of Ormonde* 2 vols. (1851).
Clark, P. and Slack, P., *English Towns in Transition 1500–1700* (1976).
Cliffe, J.T., *The Puritan Gentry* (1984).
Cooper, J.P., *Land, Men and Beliefs: Studies in Early Modern History*, eds. G.E. Aylmer and J.S. Morrill (1983).
Coward, B., *The Stuart Age* (1980).
—— *Social Change and Continuity in Early Modern England 1550–1750* (1988).
Cowper, F., *A Prospect of Gray's Inn* (1951).
Cruickshank, C.G., *Elizabeth's Army* (2nd edn. 1966).
Cust, R. and Hughes, A. (eds.), *Studies in Religion and Politics 1603–1642* (1989).
Dictionary of National Biography.
Fletcher, A., *The Outbreak of the English Civil War* (1981).
Fletcher, A. and Stevenson, J., *Order and Disorder in Early Modern England* (1985).
Fox, L. (ed.), *English Historical Scholarship in the Sixteenth and Seventeenth Centuries* (Oxford, 1956).
Fraser, A., *The Weaker Vessel: Woman's Lot in Seventeenth-Century England* (1984).
Gardiner, S.R., *History of the Great Civil War 1642–49* 3 vols. (1886–91).
Gruenfelder, J.K., *Influence in Early Stuart Elections 1604–1640* (Columbus, Ohio, 1981).
Hasler, P.W., *The History of Parliament: The House of Commons 1558–1603*, III, M–Z (1981).
Hexter, J.H., *Reappraisals in History* (1961).
—— *On Historians* (1979).
Hill, C., *The Century of Revolution, 1603–1714* (rev. edn. 1980).
Houlbrooke, R., *The English Family 1450–1700* (1984).
Howarth, D., *Lord Arundel and his Circle* (1985).
Hutton, R., *The Royalist War Effort 1642–46* (1982).
Ives, E.W. (ed.), *The English Revolution 1600–1660* (1968).
Jessup, F.W., *Sir Roger Twysden 1597–1672* (1965).
Keeler, M.F., *The Long Parliament, 1640–41. A Biographical Study of its Members* (Philadelphia, 1954).
Knowles, D., *The Religious Orders in England*, III (1959).
Macfarlane, A., *Marriage and Love in England, Modes of Reproduction 1300–1840* (1986).
Manning, B., *The English People and the English Revolution* (Peregrine edn. 1978).
Morrah, P., *Prince Rupert of the Rhine* (1976).

Morrill, J.S., *The Revolt of the Provinces* (pbk edn. 1980).

—— (ed.), *Reactions to the English Civil War 1642–1649* (1982).

Nef, J.U., *The Rise of the British Coal Industry* 2 vols. (1932).

Newman, P.R., *The Old Service: Royalist Regimental Colonels and the Civil War 1642–1646* (Manchester, 1993).

O'Day, R. and Heal, F. (eds.), *Princes and Paupers in the English Church 1500–1800* (Leicester, 1981).

Oman, C., *Henrietta Maria* (1976 edn.).

Parry, R.H. (ed.), *The English Civil War and After, 1642–1658* (1970).

Porter, S., *Destruction in the English Civil Wars* (Stroud, 1994).

Prest, W.R., *The Inns of Court under Elizabeth I and the Early Stuarts 1590–1640* (1972).

Powell, J.R., *The Navy in the English Civil War* (1962).

Reinmuth, H.S. (ed.), *Early Stuart Studies* (Minneapolis, 1970).

Richardson, R.C., *The Debate on the English Revolution* (1977).

Richardson, W.C., *A History of the Inns of Court* (Baton Rouge, 1979).

Ridley, J., *The Roundheads* (1976).

Ridsdill Smith, G. and Toynbee, M., *Leaders of the Civil Wars* (1977).

Routh, E.M.G., *Tangier: England's Lost Atlantic Outpost 1661–1684* (1912).

Russell, C. (ed.), *The Origins of the English Civil War* (1973).

—— *The Crisis of Parliaments. English History 1509–1660* (1971).

Savine, A., *English Monasteries on the Eve of the Dissolution* (Oxford, 1909).

Sharpe, J.A., *Early Modern England. A Social History 1550–1760* (1987).

Shaw, W.A. (ed.), *The Knights of England* 2 vols. (1906).

Simpson, A., *The Wealth of the Gentry 1540–1640* (1961).

Slack, P., *The Impact of Plague in Tudor and Stuart England* (1985).

Stone, L., *The Crisis of the Aristocracy 1558–1641* (Oxford, 1965).

—— (ed.), *The University in Society* vol. 1 (1975).

—— *The Family, Sex and Marriage in England 1500–1800* (1977, pbk edn. 1979).

Thirsk, J. (ed.), *The Agrarian History of England and Wales* IV, 1500–1640 (1967); V, 1640–1750, i (1984).

Timmis, J.H., *Thine is the Kingdom: The Trial for Treason of Thomas Wentworth* (Alabama Univ., 1974).

Tomlinson, H. (ed.), *Before the English Civil War* (1983).

Trease, G., *Portrait of a Cavalier: William Cavendish, First Duke of Newcastle* (1979).

Tucker, J. and Winstock, L., *The English Civil War: A Military Handbook* (1972).

Upton, A.F., *Sir Arthur Ingram c.1565–1642* (Oxford, 1961).

Venn, J. and J.A. (eds.), *Alumni Cantabrigienses* 4 vols. (1922–27).

Warburton, B.E.G., *Memoirs of Prince Rupert and the Cavaliers* 3 vols. (1849).

Webster, C. (ed.), *Health, Medicine and Mortality in the Sixteenth Century* (Cambridge, 1979).

Wedgwood, C.V., *The King's Peace, 1637–1641* (1955).

—— *The King's War, 1641–1647* (1958).

—— *Thomas Wentworth, First Earl of Strafford 1593–1641. A Revaluation* (1964).

Willan, T.S., *The English Coasting Trade, 1600–1750* (Manchester, 1967).

Wilson, J., *Fairfax* (New York, 1985).

Woolrych, A., *Battles of the English Civil War* (1961).

Woodward, G.W.O., *Dissolution of the Monasteries* (1966).

Wrightson, K., *English Society 1580–1680* (1982).

Young, P. and Emberton, W., *Sieges of the Great Civil War, 1642–46* (1978).

—— and Holmes, R., *The English Civil War 1642–1651* (1974).

(b) *Articles and Pamphlets*

Aylmer, G.E., 'Collective Mentalities in Mid-Seventeenth-Century England', *TRHS*, 5th series, 36, pp.1–25; 37, pp.1–30; 38, pp.1–25; 39, pp.1–22 (1986–89).

Aylmer, G.E. and Morrill, J.S., *The Civil War and Interregnum, Sources for Local Historians* (1979).

Collinson, P., *English Puritanism*, The Historical Association, G. 106 (1983).

Cooper, J.P., 'The Fortune of Thomas Wentworth, Earl of Strafford', *EcHR*, 2nd series, XI (1958), pp.227–248.

Everitt, A.M., *The Local Community and the Great Rebellion*, The Historical Association, G.70 (1969).

Gordon, M.D., 'The Collection of Ship Money in the Reign of Charles I', *TRHS*, 3rd series, IV (1910), pp.141–162.

Holmes, C., 'The County Community in Stuart Historiography', *JBS*, XIX, 2 (1980), pp.54–73.

Hoskins, W.G., 'Harvest Fluctuations and English Economic History 1620–1759', *AgHR*, 16 (1968), pp.15–31.

Hughes, A.L., 'The King, the Parliament and the Localities during the English Civil War', *JBS*, XXIV (1985), pp.236–63.

Kerridge, E., 'The Movement of Rent 1540–1640', *EcHR*, 2nd series, VI (1953), pp.16–34.

Malcolm, J.L., 'A King in Search of Soldiers', *HJ*, 21, 2 (19768), pp.251–73.

Morrill, J.S., 'The Religious Context of the English Civil War', *TRHS*, 5th series, 34 (1984), pp.155–78.

Pennington, D.H., 'The Cost of the Civil War', *History Today* (Feb 1958), pp.126–33.

Porter, S., 'Destruction of the Civil Wars', *History Today* (Aug 1986), pp.36–41.

Routh, E., 'The English Occupation of Tangier 1661–1683', *TRHS*, 2nd series, XIX, (1905), pp.61–78.

Russell, C., 'Why did Charles I fight the Civil War?', *History Today* (June 1984), pp.31–34.

Wanklyn, M.D.G., 'Royalist Strategy in the South of England, 1642–1644', *Southern History*, 3 (1981), pp.55–79.

2 LOCAL

(a) *Books*

Atkinson, J.C., *Memorials of Old Whitby* (1894).

Aveling, H., *Northern Catholics: The Catholic Recusants of the North Riding of Yorkshire 1558–1790* (1960).

Baker, J.B., *The History of Scarbrough* (1882).

Beswick, D., *The History of Gristhorpe* (n.d.).

Binns, J., *A Place of Great Importance: Scarborough in the Civil Wars* (Preston, 1996)

Boyle, J.R., *The Lost Towns of the Humber* (Hull, 1889).

Bridges, J., *The History and Antiquities of Northamptonshire*, 2 vols. (Oxford, 1791).

Browne, H.B., *Chapters of Whitby History, 1823–1946* (Hull, 1946).

Charlton, L., *The History of Whitby* (York, 1779).

Clarke, L., *Family Chronicles* (Wellingborough, 1911).

Cliffe, J.T., *The Yorkshire Gentry from the Reformation to the Civil War* (1969).

Daysh, G.H.T. (ed.), *A Survey of Whitby and the Surrounding Area* (Windsor, 1958).

Foster, J. (ed.). *Pedigrees of the County Families of Yorkshire*, 4 vols. (1874–75).

Gaskin, R.T., *The Old Seaport of Whitby* (Whitby, 1909).

Gent, T., *History of Hull* (Hull, 1735).

Gillett, E. and Macmahon, K.A., *History of Hull* (Oxford, 1980).

Gooder, A., *The Parliamentary Representation of the County of York 1258–1832*, II, YASRS, XCVI (1938).

Hey, D., *Buildings of Britain 1550–1750: Yorkshire* (Ashbourne, 1981).

—— *Yorkshire from AD 1000* (1986).

Hinderwell, T., *The History and Antiquities of Scarborough* (1798, 1811, 1832).

Howell, R., *Newcastle upon Tyne and the Puritan Revolution* (Oxford, 1967).

Hughes, A.L., *Politics, Society and Civil War in Warwickshire 1620–1660*, (Cambridge, 1987).

Ingram, M.E., *The Manor of Bridlington and its Lords Feoffees* (Bridlington, 1977).

Jeffrey, P.S., *Whitby Lore and Legend* (3rd edn., 1952).

Jeffrey, R.W., *Thornton le Dale* (Wakefield, 1931).

Legard, J.D., *The Legards of Anlaby and Ganton* (1926).

Marchant, R.A., *The Puritans and the Church Courts in the Diocese of York 1560–1642* (1960).

Marshall, W., *The Rural Economy of Yorkshire* 2 vols. (2nd edn., 1796).

Newman, J., *The Buildings of England: West Kent and the Weald* (1976).

Newman, P.R., *The Battle of Marston Moor 1644* (Chichester, 1981).

Oliver, G., *The History and Antiquities of the Town and Minster of Beverley* (1829).

Ord, J.A., *The History and Antiquities of Cleveland* (1846).

Pevsner, N., *The Buildings of England: Yorkshire, the North Riding* (1966).

Poulson, G., *Beverlac* (1829).

Reckitt, B.N., *Charles the First and Hull, 1639–1645* (Howden, 1988).

Reid, R.R., *The King's Council in the North* (1921).

Ridsdill Smith, G., *Without Touch of Dishonour: The Life and Death of Sir Henry Slingsby 1602–1658* (Kineton, 1968).

Roebuck, P., *Yorkshire Baronets 1640–1760* (Oxford, 1980).

Rowntree, A. (ed.), *The History of Scarborough* (1931).

Schofield, J., *Guide to Scarborough* (York, 1787).

Stirling, A.M.W., *The Hothams*, 2 vols. (1918).

Tickell, J., *History of Kingston upon Hull* (1796).

Torr, J., *The Antiquities of the City of York* (York, 1719).

Trotter, E., *Seventeenth Century Life in the Country Parish* (1968).

Tuke, J., *A General View of the Agriculture of the North Riding of Yorkshire* (1794).

Turton, R.B., *The Alum Farm* (Whitby, 1938).

Victoria County History:

    A History of Northamptonshire, 4 vols. (1902–37).

    A History of Yorkshire, 3 vols. (1907–13).

    A History of Yorkshire: North Riding, 2 vols. (1914–23).

    A History of Yorkshire: The City of York (1961).

    A History of Yorkshire: East Riding, 6 vols. (1969–89).

Wenham, L.P., *The Great and Close Siege of York 1644* (Kineton, 1970).

Whellan, T., *History and Topography of the City of York and the North Riding of Yorkshire*, 2 vols. (1857).

Whitby Panorama, Vol. 2 (1828).

Whittaker, M., *The Book of Scarborough Spaw* (Buckingham, 1984).

Young, A., *A Six Month's Tour through the North of England*, 4 vols. (1771).

Young, G., *A History of Whitby*, 2 vols. (Whitby, 1817).

—— *A Picture of Whitby* (1824).

Young, P., *Marston Moor 1644: The Campaign and the Battle* (Kineton, 1970).

(b) *Articles and Pamphlets*

Binns, J., 'Scarborough in the 1640s', *Transactions of the Scarborough Archaeological and Historical Society*, 24 (1982), pp.11–19.

—— 'Scarborough and the Civil Wars, 1642–51', *NH*, XXII (1986), pp.95–122.

—— 'Captain Browne Bushell: North Sea Adventurer and Pirate', *NH*, XXVII (1991), pp.90–105.

—— 'Sir Hugh Cholmley: Whitby's Benefactor or Beneficiary?', *NH*, XXX (1994), pp.86–104.

—— 'Sir John Lawson: Scarborough's Admiral of the Red', *NH*, XXXII (1996), pp.90–110.

Boddy, G.W., 'Players of Interludes in North Yorkshire in the Early Seventeenth Century', NYCRO, *Journal* 3, No.7 (1976), pp.95–130.

Brown, H., *A Walk Around Whitby* (Whitby, 1988).

Carroll, R., 'Yorkshire Parliamentary Boroughs in the Seventeenth Century', *NH*, III (1968), pp.70–104.

Clapham, Sir Alfred, *Whitby Abbey, Yorkshire* (HMSO, 1952).

Clay, J.W., 'The Gentry of Yorkshire at the time of the Civil War', *YAJ*, 23 (1915), pp.349–94.

Cliffe, J.T., 'The Royalist Composition Papers and the Landed Income of the Gentry: a Rejoinder', *NH*, XIV (1978), pp.164–68.

Cross, C., *Urban Magistrates and Ministers: Religion in Hull and Leeds from the Reformation to the Civil War*, University of York, Borthwick paper 67 (1985).

Dickens, A.G., 'Romanist Recusancy in the Diocese of York', *YAJ*, 35, (1943), pp.157–81; 37 (1951), pp.24–48; 38 (1952), pp.524–28.

Firth, C.H., 'Marston Moor', *TRHS*, 2nd series, XII (1898), pp.17–79.

—— 'Cholmley, Sir Hugh (1600–1657)', *Bulletin of the Institute of Historical Research*, III, 9 (1926), p.189.

Forster, G.C.F., 'Elections at Scarborough for the Long Parliament 1640–1647', *Transactions of the Scarborough Archaeological Society*, 3 (1960), pp.3–8.

—— *The East Riding Justices of the Peace in the Seventeenth Century*, East Yorkshire Local History Society, 30 (1973).

—— 'The North Riding Justices and their Sessions', 1603–1625', *NH*, X (1975), pp.102–25.

—— 'Faction and County Government in Early Stuart Yorkshire', *NH*, XI (1976), pp.70–86.

Gruenfelder, J.K., 'Yorkshire Borough Elections, 1603–40', *YAJ*, 49 (1976), pp.101–114.

Holiday, P.G., 'Land Sales and Repurchases in Yorkshire after the Civil Wars, 1650–70', *NH*, V (1970), pp.67–92.

Hughes, A.L., 'Warwickshire on the Eve of the Civil War: A "County Community"?', *Midland History*, 7 (1982), pp.42–72.

Isham, G., *Easton Mauduit and the Parish Church of SS. Peter and Paul*, (Northampton, 1974).

Kendall, H.P., *The Streets of Whitby* (1938; rev. edn. 1976).

—— *Whitby in the Civil War* (Whitby, 1938).

Leadman, A.D.H., 'The Battle of Marston Moor', *YAJ*, 11 (1891), pp.287–347.

Long, W.H., 'Regional Farming in Seventeenth-Century Yorkshire', *AgHR*, 8 (1960), pp.103–14.

Morrill, J.S., 'The Northern Gentry and the Great Rebellion', *NH*, XV (1979), pp.66–87.

Morrison, A., *Alum: North-East Yorkshire's First Chemical Industry* (Birmingham, 1981).

Newman, P.R., *Marston Moor, 2 July 1644: The Sources and the Site*, University of York, Borthwick paper 53 (1978).

Ollard, S.L., *Notes on the History of Bainton Church and Parish* (n.d.).

Pearson, F.R., *The Abbey House Whitby under the Cholmley Family* (Whitby, 1954).

Pettit, P.A.J., *The Royal Forests of Northamptonshire, A Study in their Economy 1558–1714*, Northants. Record Society, XXIII (1968).

Phillips C.B., 'The Royalist Composition Papers and the Landed Income of the Gentry: A Note of Warning from Cumbria', *NH*, XIII (1977), pp.161–74.

Pickles, R.L., 'A Brief History of the Alum Industry in North Yorkshire, 1600–1875', *The Cleveland Industrial Archaeologist*, 2 (1975), pp.1–7.

Rimington, F.C., 'The Early Deer Parks of North-East Yorkshire', *Transactions of the Scarborough Archaeological Society*, 17 (1974), pp.5–11.

Ryder, I.E., 'The Seizure of Hull and its Magazine, January 1642', *YAJ*, 61 (1989), pp.139–48.

Sim, H.D., *The Church of All Saints, Bisham* (Marlow, 1967).

Wenham, L.P., *The Siege of York and Battle of Marston Moor 1644* (Skipton, 1969).

Willan, T.S., 'The Parliamentary Surveys of the North Riding', *YAJ*, 31 (1934), pp.224–89.

Woolrych, A., 'Yorkshire's Treaty of Neutrality', *History Today* (October, 1956), pp.696–704.

(c) *Unpublished Theses*

Binns, J., 'Sir Hugh Cholmley of Whitby, 1600–1657: His Life and Works', Ph.D., Leeds Univ. 1992.

Brooke, T.H., 'The Memoirs of Sir Hugh Cholmeley', B.Litt., Oxford Univ. 1937.

Hall, B., 'The Trade of Newcastle and the North-East Coast, 1600–1640', Ph.D., London Univ. 1933.

Holiday, P.G., 'Royalist Composition Fines and Land Sales in Yorkshire 1645–1665', PhD., Leeds Univ. 1966.

Jones, S.K., 'A Maritime History of the Port of Whitby 1700–1914', Ph.D., London Univ. 1982.

Mcintyre, S.C., 'Towns as Health and Pleasure Resorts', D.Phil., Oxford Univ. 1973.

Newman, P.R., 'The Royalist Armies in Northern England 1642–45', D.Phil., York Univ. 1978.

Newton, J.A., 'Puritanism in the Diocese of York, 1603–40', Ph.D., London Univ. 1962.

Rudsdale, J., 'History of the Alum Trade', M.A., Leeds Univ. 1932.

Sheail, J.D., 'The Regional Distribution of Wealth in England as indicated in the 1524–25 Lay Subsidy Returns', Ph.D., London Univ. 1968.

Townsend, D.A., 'Scarborough in the Civil War 1642–45', B.A., Manchester Univ. 1966.

Editorial method

FOLIATION

Folio references are given in the margins, with the end of each folio indicated by a vertical mark.

SPELLING

The spelling of the manuscript has been retained, but Cholmley's abbreviations have been extended. Modern pound signs have been used.

PUNCTUATION

Though minimum revision has been done to Sir Hugh's punctuation, full-stops have been substituted or added to make his meaning clearer.

CORRECTIONS

Except in trivial cases I have reproduced Cholmley's mistakes, corrections and second thoughts because they often provide interesting insights into his mentality.

BLANKS

The word 'blank' in square brackets indicates words and passages left blank in the manuscript.

SQUARE BRACKETS

Letters and words which are now illegible or lost but were almost certainly in Cholmley's original manuscript have been printed in square brackets.

PREFACE

The Life and Works of Sir Hugh Cholmley

I ANCESTRY AND INHERITANCE

Hugh Cholmley was born in the family home, Roxby castle, at Thornton-on-the-Hill on 22 July 1600, and baptised five days later in the nearby parish church of Thornton Dale. The parish register reads: 'Mr Hew Cholmelaye sonne to Mr Richard Cholmelaye was chistened the xxvij daye of Julye 1600.'[1]

The Cholmondeleys had shortened their name to Cholmeley or Cholmley soon after they came into Yorkshire from Cheshire, where the main branch of the family remained. As Hugh noted in his Memoirs, his great-great-grandfather, Sir Roger, was the first of the Cholmleys to settle at Roxby, between Thornton Dale and Pickering, but he owed his estate there largely to the successful career of his elder brother, Sir Richard.[2] This Sir Richard was rewarded for his faithful service to the first two Tudor monarchs with appointment to many offices of profit and power in the north-east of England. At times, he was treasurer of war at Berwick-on-Tweed, controller of customs at Newcastle, Hull and London, and steward of a long list of castles in Yorkshire which had once belonged to Richard III.[3] In particular, as constable of Pickering castle and steward, receiver and master forester of the royal honour and forest of Pickering, effectively he displaced the Hastings hegemony in that area. Finally, in 1519, when Francis Hastings failed to redeem the mortgages on his manors of Kingthorpe and Roxby, they were purchased by Sir Richard.[4]

This first Sir Richard Cholmley had no legitimate children and one of his two brothers was a priest, so that when he died in 1521 the other, Roger, his deputy in Yorkshire, became his heir there.[5] Sir Roger's contribution to the Yorkshire Cholmleys was twofold. He established what became a long-term family tradition of winning royal favours by fighting against, and usually beating, the Scots: his knighthood was gained on Flodden field. Secondly, not only did he marry well but he saw to it that his many offspring by their marriages connected the Chomleys with some of the highest in the kingdom. Katherine, his own wife, was granddaughter of the famous Sir Marmaduke Constable of Flamborough, who was also an English captain at Flodden.[6] His eldest son and successor, the second Sir Richard, was married first to the daughter of Lord Conyers of Hornby, and after her death, to Catherine Clifford, daughter of the first Earl of Cumberland and widow of the eighth Lord Scrope of Castle Bolton. Two of Roger's daughters were in succession wives of the Earl of Westmorland.[7]

---

[1] Memoirs MS (YML, Add.MS 343), ff.14r.–v. (see below, p.80); NYCRO, Thornton Parish Register, PR 806.

[2] Memoirs MS, f.2r. (see below, p.61).

[3] CPR, 1485–94, pp.176, 299, 454, 478; Ibid., 1494–1509, pp.213, 233, 269, 312; CFR, 1485–1509, p.378.

[4] R.B. Turton (ed.), 'The Honour and Forest of Pickering', NRRS, New Series, I (1894), pp.xxv–xxvi; NYCRO, ZPK 1, 2.

[5] NYCRO, ZPK 3; Turton, 'Honour and Forest of Pickering', pp.227–8.

[6] Memoirs MS, f.2r. (see below, p.62); Monument to Sir Marmaduke Constable, who died in 1520, in St Oswald's parish church, Flamborough.

[7] Memoirs MS, ff.2r., 2v. (see below, p.63).

Sir Richard (II) carried on his father's precedent by also winning his spurs in Scotland; and this most powerful and distinguished of all the Cholmley's known as 'the great blacke knight of the North', was the one who founded the family's Whitby estate.[8] On 1 March 1540, less than three months after the closure of the Benedictine house at Whitby, the young Richard took out a twenty-one-year lease of the former abbey buildings and demesne from the crown – altogether about 500 acres on both sides of the river Esk.[9] Five years later, now knighted but still in his twenties, Sir Richard (II) purchased first the land and buildings of the former priory of Grosmont in Eskdale, then more of the Whitby abbey estate in Eskdaleside (Sleights), Aislaby and Ugglebarnby.[10] His major investment, however, took place during the reign of Mary between 1555 and 1557. For £5,000 he bought 22,000 acres, consisting of the properties he had on lease since 1540 and the manors of Whitby, Whitby Laithes, Larpool, Stainsacre, Hawsker and Fyling, the last including the abbot's grange and deerpark.[11] Finally, in 1565, Sir Richard added the remaining piece to complete his compact estate in Whitby Strand by paying over a thousand pounds to the crown for Robin Hood's Bay, Fyling Raw, Fyling Thorpe, Normanby, Thorny Brow and Stoupe Brow.[12]

Though the great black knight's great-grandson was aware that Cholmley lands in Kent had been released to raise money for these purchases, Sir Hugh failed to reveal in his Memoirs that in fact most of the ready cash had come from the sale of Sir Richard's inheritance in Ryedale and his second wife's portion in Wensleydale. Consequently, from this time onwards, the centre of gravity of Cholmley power began to move from Roxby castle to Abbey House at Whitby.[13]

If the dissolution of the monasteries had provided Sir Richard (II) with a unique opportunity to accumulate a vast estate at bargain prices, the religious Reformation also nearly ruined him and his family. At first the radical religious changes in state policy seem not to have troubled him: under Henry VIII he was knighted, named commissioner of the peace for the North Riding and chosen sheriff of Yorkshire.[14] As reward for these services, Edward VI granted him Scarborough castle for life and a life-long lease on the adjacent manor of Northstead for a rent of only £24 a year.[15] In return, Richard appeared happy to take an active part in the closure of religious guilds and chantries in the North Riding.[16] When Catholic Mary succeeded her Protestant half-brother, the great black knight still showed no lack of devotion to the monarch. Again he was pricked to be Yorkshire's sheriff; again he took a leading role in the sacking of more Scottish towns; and finally he was returned as one of the county's members to Mary's last Parliament.[17] As confirmation of her favour and trust, the Queen ordered him either to reside in Scarborough castle or put his son in there 'for the better garding of the same', after it had been seized briefly by Thomas Stafford and his fellow rebels.[18]

[8] Memoirs MS, f.2r. (see below, p.62 and n.18); f.4r. (see below, p.66).
[9] L and P, Hen. VII, xv, p.565; L. Charlton, The History of Whitby (York, 1779), pp.292–4; G. Young, A History of Whitby, 2 vols (Whitby, 1817), ii, pp.930–1.
[10] L and P, Hen. VIII, xx(i), p.128; Ibid., xxi(i), p.244.
[11] CPR, 1554–5, pp.257–8; Whitby LPS, PB, MS 2018.
[12] CPR, 1563–6, p.206; Charlton, pp.300–2.
[13] F. Collins (ed.), Yorkshire Feet of Fines in the Tudor Period, i, YASRS II, (1887), p.190.
[14] L and P, Hen. VIII, xxi(i), p.222; CPR, 1547–8, p.92; Ibid., 1547–53, p.316.
[15] CPR, 1548–9, p.133.
[16] Ibid., p.136; Ibid., 1550–3, p.394.
[17] APC, 1556–8, pp.49, 396; S.T. Bindoff (ed.), The House of Commons, 1509–58 (1982), i, pp.642–4.
[18] APC, 1556–8, p.254.

However, though Richard was never seduced into open treason against Queen Elizabeth, his refusal to adopt Protestantism inevitably brought him into conflict with the state. In 1565 he was described as Scarborough's leading 'papist'; in 1572 he was on Thomas Gargrave's list of Yorkshire's principal Catholic gentry, though only one of the 'meane or lesse eyvell' kind; and in 1580, his last appearance in recusancy documents, he was recorded as the head of the family of 'recusants' at Thornton.[19] Since Richard's formidable second wife, the Lady Catherine, also remained a Roman Catholic, their eldest son, Henry, was brought up in the same faith and subsequently married Margaret Babthorpe, a member of one of Yorkshire's most stubborn recusant families, not surprisingly the Cholmleys came under increasing suspicion.[20] When Abbey House became a refuge for continental Catholic missionaries, Scarborough castle was placed in the safe Protestant hands of Sir Henry Gate of Seamer.[21]

In 1565 Sir Richard was summoned before the Privy Council to answer a charge that he had conspired with the Earl of Northumberland to advance the claims of Lord Darnley to the English succession. Richard not only denied the allegation but rashly counter-attacked by accusing his detractors in the Council in the North of dishonesty and corruption. For his defiance and slander he spent several uncomfortable months in York castle.[22]

Nevertheless, when the rising of the Northern Earls took place in 1569, fortunately for Sir Richard and his family he was not one of them. Perhaps on this occasion he was wisely advised by his wife Catherine whose eldest son, the ninth Lord Scrope, remained actively loyal to Elizabeth, and later was custodian of Mary, Queen of Scots, in his castle at Bolton.[23] As a result therefore of Sir Richard's passive loyalty the whole of Whitby Strand and Pickering Lythe, in contrast to other parts of the North Riding, were unaffected by the rising, so that when the great black knight died in 1583 he was no longer so great in power and royal favour, but he was still great in wealth and estate.[24]

Four years before his death Sir Richard (II) had made a settlement regarding the Cholmley estate which had momentous consequences. Francis, the eldest son by his first wife, was to be his immediate heir, but should he die without issue then the estate was entailed to Henry, Catherine's son.[25] In effect, when Francis died prematurely in 1586, Sir Richard's will disinherited his second and third sons, Roger and Richard, in favour of his fourth, their half-brother, Henry. Neither Roger nor his sons, Marmaduke and Richard, were reconciled to their loss: even after Henry had tried to buy them off with annuities they still insisted that the whole of the Cholmley territory was theirs by rightful inheritance.[26] As late as 1620, after the death of his father and elder brother, Richard Cholmley of Brandsby was still asserting annually his claim to all his grandfather's lands.[27]

Francis was the first Cholmley to make Whitby his principal residence. Unhappily, however, he was not the first or the last of that family to be dominated by an overbearing and foolish wife. According to Sir Hugh's own account, it was Joan Bulmer who convinced her husband Francis that, though there was an abundance of

---

[19] J.J. Cartwright (ed.), *Chapters in the History of Yorkshire* (Wakefield, 1872), p.67; H. Aveling, *Northern Catholics* (1966), pp.418, 426, 427.

[20] Aveling, *Northern Catholics* pp.182, 194. cf. n.118.

[21] *CSPD*, Addenda 1547–65, p.567 (for 'Chamberlain' read 'Cholmley'); *Ibid.*, Addenda 1566–71, p.96.

[22] *APC*, 1558–70, pp.231, 233, 301.

[23] Aveling, *Northern Catholics* p.68.

[24] *Ibid.*, p.81

[25] PRO, Inquisition Post Mortem, C142/214/157; NYCRO, ZPK 4.

[26] Memoirs MS. f.5r. (see below, p.67).

[27] *The Memorandum Book of Richard Cholmeley of Brandsby 1602–23*, NYCRO, 44 (Northallerton, 1998), p.192.

good building stone already on the site, a timber house in the grounds of the former abbey would be sufficient for their needs.[28] It was therefore left to Sir Hugh himself to convert Abbey House into an entirely stone dwelling half a century later.[29]

If Francis's early death without heirs was, in Sir Hugh's view, an act of divine providence because it opened the way to the succession of his grandfather, it also proved nearly fatal to the family's fortunes. Henry was the most worthless of the Cholmleys. Even his own grandson could find nothing to write in his favour except that just when it seemed he would be bankrupted and disgraced by recusancy he and his wife Margaret had the good sense to declare themselves Protestants.[30]

During the thirty years, from 1586 until his death in 1616, that Sir Henry was head of the family, the Cholmley estate went downhill with alarming speed. At a time when raging inflation was destroying the real value of long-term, fixed rents, Henry continued to live extravagantly and well beyond his income. He wasted his life in hunting and racing and his money on hounds and horses. He was too vain to live frugally and foolishly tried to emulate the style of his very rich and even more profligate cousin, George, third Earl of Cumberland. Debts mounted and the estate shrank as more of it was sold to raise ready money and pay off creditors.[31] For example, in 1596 the manor house and lands of Stakesby on the west side of Whitby town were sold for £605.[32] Six years later, Lease Head farm in Iburndale raised another £200.[33] As early as 1607, after a succession of sales culminating in the largest of that year, Henry effectively divested himself of the Cholmley lands in Pickering Lythe and Ryedale, at Kingthorpe, Roxby, Thornton, Farmanby, Ellerburn, Pickering town, Lund and Kirkby Overcarr (now known as Kirby Misperton). Altogether these properties yielded well over £2,000.[34]

Apart from his own folly, Henry suffered from two other handicaps: his eldest son and heir, Richard, and his vindictive, powerful neighbour, Sir Thomas Posthumous Hoby of Hackness. Though handsome and intelligent, in other respects Richard was not much of an improvement on his father. At the too-early age of sixteen he chose to stay with his new wife, Susannah Legard, rather than resume his studies at Trinity College, Cambridge.[35] His violent temper and rash actions soon got him into serious trouble: he was imprisoned and fined £200 (not £3,000, as his son later wrote) for alleged involvement in the Essex rebellion of 1601;[36] he was fortunate not to lose the offending hand when he struck an opponent in Star Chamber;[37] and, worst of all, in August 1600, Richard was one of a party of five local gentry who abused Hoby's hospitality by acting outrageously under his Puritan roof.

Richard and his companions did all they could to annoy and insult their hosts, Sir Thomas and Lady Margaret; but, as they eventually discovered, it was an expensive blunder to target this formidable pair.[38] Not content with heavy financial

---

[28] Memoirs MS, f.4v. (see below, p.67).

[29] Ibid., ff.22r.–v. (see below, pp.94–5).

[30] Ibid., f.5v. (see below, p.68).

[31] Ibid., f.5r. (see below, p.68).

[32] Whitby LPS, PB, MSS 814, 2889.

[33] Ibid., PB, MS 872.

[34] Collins, Feet of Fines, iv, pp.29, 47, 144; W. Brigg (ed.), Yorkshire Fines for the Stuart Period 1603–14, YASRS, LIII (1915), pp.31, 69; Whitby LPS, PB, MS 885.

[35] Memoirs MS, f.6r. (see below, p.69).

[36] Ibid., f.6r; HMC, Salisbury, xi, pp.39, 214; APC, 1600–1, pp.160, 261, 488.

[37] Memoirs MS, f.6r. (see below, p.70).

[38] HMC, Salisbury, x, pp.302 et seq., 325, 391; Ibid., xi, pp.11–12, 38, 456, 546; Ibid., xii, pp.32, 105; PRO, StaC 5/H22/21; D.M. Meads (ed.), The Diary of Lady Margaret Hoby 1599–1605 (1930), pp.197–8.

damages awarded by Star Chamber, Sir Thomas now pursued a relentless vendetta against the Cholmleys, Sir Henry and Sir Richard, his heir. When it was no longer possible to bring charges of recusancy against them, Hoby made a direct attack on their right to hold the hereditary stewardship of the Liberty of Whitby Strand. Supported by his cousin, Robert Cecil, Earl of Salisbury and Lord Treasurer from 1608 until 1612, Hoby tried to extend his control of Hackness to cover the whole of the Liberty.[39] However, even if Salisbury had lived longer, it is doubtful that he would have been able to rescue Sir Thomas from defeat in a case which dragged on from 1609 until 1613. The Barons of the Exchequer finally ruled in favour of the Cholmleys: Hoby was obliged to surrender all his claims beyond the boundaries of Hackness lordship. The parties to the quarrel were ordered to be 'loveing friends and with all good respect each of them use and entrust each other at all tymes hereafter.'[40]

However, resentment on both sides was now too strong for anything more than a temporary cease-fire. Richard Cholmley was no less aggressive than Thomas Hoby: contrary to his son's partial memory, it was he, not Hoby, who was complainant in a second Star Chamber confrontation in 1609.[41] Though the Cholmleys appear to have lost this round, the pendulum swung back to their advantage in 1619 when the eleventh Lord Scrope became President of the Council in the North.[42] After several years of political retirement, Sir Richard now unwisely re-entered public affairs. Almost immediately he was given a place at the Council in York, and in 1622 he resumed his seat on the North Riding Bench. By that time, thanks to the Lord President's 'friendshippe and kindness', Richard had also been elected one of Scarborough's Members of Parliament.[43] Finally, in 1624, he was chosen sheriff of the county and his son Hugh took over his parliamentary seat.[44]

However, this was to prove disastrous for Sir Richard. First, he attempted to drive home his advantage by bringing another bill of complaint against Hoby in Star Chamber in 1623.[45] Sir Thomas was temporarily out of favour because of his open slanders against Scrope whom he accused of harbouring papists;[46] but Cholmley's charges were weak and unconvincing. For instance, he accused Hoby of poaching deer from the royal forest when it was common knowledge that he disapproved of all sports except fishing.[47] Though the outcome of this third conflict in Star Chamber is not known, it seems that neither party gained from it.[48]

Moreover, Sir Richard could not afford the cost of offices or fulfil their responsibilities. Emmanuel Scrope was no better example for Richard to follow than George Clifford had been for his father.[49] Richard would have been wiser to stay in Whitby and to try to save his crumbling estate rather than to incur more expenses and debts. His seat in Parliament cost him dearly because he took most of his family to live with him in the capital. His year as sheriff proved to be even more expensive:

---

[39] CSPD, 1603–10, pp.502, 516; Memoirs MS, f.7v. (see below, p.72).
[40] Whitby LPS, PB, MSS 1460–6; NYCRO, ZF 1/12/5, 6, 8, 9.
[41] Memoirs MS, f.7v. (see below, p.72); PRO, StaC 8/110/23; G.C.F. Forster, 'Faction and County Government in Early Stuart Yorkshire', NH, xi (1976), pp.77–9.
[42] Memoirs MS, f.8r. (see below, p.73).
[43] Ibid., f.8v. (see below, p.73).
[44] NYCRO, DC/SCB, B1, General Letters, 27 Jan. 1624.
[45] PRO, StaC 8/104/15.
[46] CSPD, 1620, p.168.
[47] Meads, Diary, pp.121, 123.
[48] Forster, NH, xi, pp.80–2.
[49] Memoirs MS, f.9v. (see below, p.75).

according to his son, it cost him a thousand pounds.[50] It also nearly cost him his liberty and certainly tarnished his reputation. In the conduct of the county election of 1625 for the first Parliament of Charles I, Richard was accused of gross partisanship. After Sir Thomas Wentworth and Sir Thomas Fairfax were returned and Sir John Savile defeated, a petition signed by more than a thousand Yorkshire freeholders claimed that the sheriff had closed the poll prematurely when it was beginning to go Savile's way. Sir Richard was described as 'wholly Wentworth's'. Though in the end a second poll confirmed the result of the first, Cholmley was not vindicated. When summoned before the Commons to explain his behaviour Sir Richard arrived two days late and without a single witness to support his case. Sir John Eliot told the House that no trust should be placed in such a man or his words and the election was declared void. In this particular instance, as in others concerning Sir Richard's career, Sir Hugh's version of events represents the triumph of filial affection over regard for the truth.[51] Sir Richard's public life ended abruptly and ignominiously in 1625.

Meanwhile the Cholmley estate continued to shrink. Like his father, Sir Henry, who seems to have retired to York in 1613, Richard sold farms for cash. Carley House in Eskdaleside had already gone in 1610 for £320; Normanby Hall, a capital messuage with 15 closes attached, fetched £560 in 1621; a few weeks later, four farms in Hawsker were sold to their tenants for £845; and just at the moment when Hugh succeeded his father in 1626 they released 240 acres in Fyling and Robin Hood's Bay for £1,020 to a London fishmonger.[52] Sir Richard's only sound investment during these years of mounting debt was in Whitby's rectory which cost him £1,500.[53]

As far as Sir Richard's accounts were concerned, money nearly always flowed outwards. His second marriage to Margaret Cobb in 1613 brought in a dowry of £1,500 and '500 more upon death of a sister', but the financial relief was only short term.[54] Like his father and grandfather before him, Richard had too many children to support. If his daughters married well, they also married expensively. Margaret, his eldest, married William Strickland of Boynton with a dowry of £2,000.[55] Ursula, his second daughter, who married George Trotter of Skelton castle, cost him only a little less. Fortunately for the family fortunes and the integrity of the estate, all but one of Richard's four children by his second wife died young. The only survivor, another Richard, had to be satisfied with Grosmont as his inheritance.[56] As for Henry, Hugh's younger brother, born in 1608 the last of Susannah Legard's children, he was obliged to settle for an annuity of £50.[57]

II ESTATE MANAGEMENT

Hugh succeeded Sir Richard as manager of the family estate in the spring of 1626 because by then it was practically bankrupt. Thirty years later, Hugh estimated that his father had owed more than £11,000 when at the most his annual income was only £900. Since he was paying 10 or 11 per cent interest on this huge debt and much of the estate was charged with the jointures of his mother, his wife and his daughter-in-

---

[50] Memoirs MS, ff.9r.–9v. (see below, p.74).
[51] Memoirs MS, f.9r. (see below, p.74 and n.127).
[52] NYCRO, ZPK 8; Whitby LPS, PB MSS 666, 875, 878, 1773.
[53] Memoirs MS, f.8r. (see below, p.73).
[54] *Ibid.*, f.12r. (see below, p.79).
[55] *Ibid.*, f.8v. (see below, p.73).
[56] *Ibid.*, f.11r. (see below, p.77).
[57] *Ibid.*

law, there seemed no way to avoid foreclosure. Moreover, inflation had devalued rents, and these were usually on long-term leases and could not be increased.[58] Sir Richard's creditors were now pressing hard and two of them in particular, both London scriveners, Robert Harrison and John Betts, who each held bonds of £1,000, were on the point of taking over the Cholmley lands.[59]

At the age of 25, Hugh Cholmley's past record was far from promising. Up to this moment he had done nothing to indicate that he had any more ability than his father or grandfather to run the estate successfully and live within its income. By his own admission, Hugh's education had been privileged and prolonged but largely wasted. At Jesus College, Cambridge (1613–17) and at Gray's Inn (1618–21) he had misspent his time in drinking, gambling and 'all sports and recreations'. Where he described himself as 'allwayes inclynable to play', his tutors might well have been blunter with 'bone idle'.[60] Not even the responsibilities of marriage at the age of 22 and subsequently fatherhood of two sons, Richard and William, had yet converted him to a life of frugal care and serious preoccupation. He was still gambling, and, out of increasing desperation, more recklessly than ever. His own personal debts now amounted to £600 or £700. Though he had been living with and at the expense of his Twysden in-laws in Kent and London for the past four years, his wife's dowry of £3,000 had been frittered away.[61]

However, this new and onerous responsibility proved to be exactly what Hugh needed: from now on he allowed himself no diversions, frivolous or otherwise. He carried out his duty as Scarborough's Member of Parliament in 1626, and was knighted in May of that year, but when the next election came up in 1628 he withdrew his name.[62] He also kept out of county politics and steered well clear of Sir Thomas Posthumous Hoby. The recovery of solvency and the rescue of his encumbered estate were now his overriding priorities.

According to his own account, Sir Hugh seems to have been remarkably successful within a short time. Only five years later, in September 1631, when his father died, he inherited from him manageable liabilities of only £4,000. According to his own explanation, the estate was saved by a happy combination of 'gods providence and direction', his 'owne wits', and the welcome intervention of his uncle John Legard of Ganton and his dear friend and cousin, Sir John Hotham of Scorborough, who together stood surety for debts of £2,500. To maximise its financial yield, Hugh had let out as much as he could of the demesne land; but apart from the sale to Hotham of Fyling Old Hall and its adjoining deer park for £4,400 in 1634, the integrity of the Cholmley estate in Whitby Strand had been preserved. By 1636 Sir Hugh's fortunes were so improved that he was able to enlarge and greatly enhance Abbey House and its grounds and move his family there from the cramped quarters of the Gatehouse. Only eight years earlier he had been hiding from creditors; ten years earlier he had been ready to flee abroad to escape them; and now he had mastered his debts and lived handsomely as head of a large and distinguished household.[63]

However, as on other sensitive subjects, such as family recusancy and the feud with Hoby, when dealing with his management of the estate Sir Hugh's Memoirs mislead by omission. Though surviving documentary evidence does confirm that Hugh owed

[58] Memoirs MS ff.9v., 17v., 18r., 18v. (see below, pp.75, 86, 87, 88).
[59] NYCRO, ZPK 12, 13.
[60] Memoirs MS, ff.15r., 15v., 17v. (see below, pp.81, 82, 86).
[61] *Ibid.*, ff.16v., 17r., 17v. (see below, pp.84, 85, 86).
[62] NYCRO, DC/SCB, B1, 1 Feb. 1626, 17 Jan. 1628.
[63] Memoirs MS, ff.18v., 19r., 20r., 22v., 23r. (see below, pp.88, 89, 90, 94, 96).

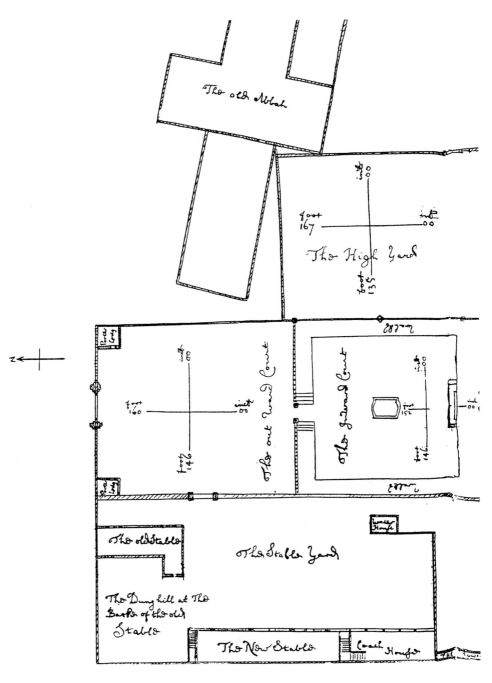

The old Abbah

The High Yard

foot 167

foot 135

N

The out Guard Court

The inward Court

foot 160

foot 142

foot 152

foot 146

2.887

2.887

The old Stable

The Stable Yard

The Dung hill at The Backe of the old Stable

The New Stable

Coach House

Plan of Abbey House and grounds, *c.*1700 (NYCRO, ZCG (MIC 1343/272); Whitby LPS, PB 5939). Original measures 2′ 7″ × 2′ 4″.

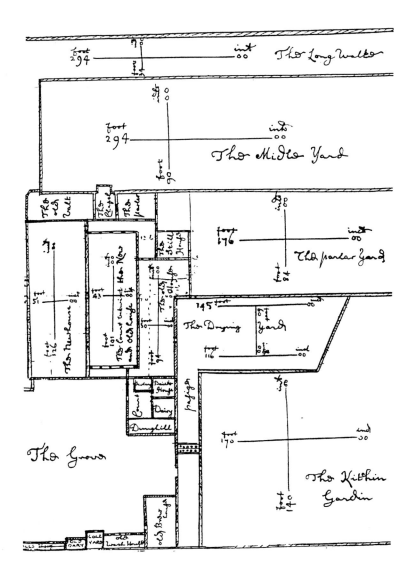

foot 428 — inch 00

foot 160

The Grove for fir Trees

The Long Walter
foot 294 — inch 00

foot 294 — inch 00

The Midle Yard
foot 90

The parlar Yard
foot 176 — inch 00
foot 24

The old Walk
The Chapel
The parlor

The Nursery gat

The New Hall

The Court intended to be built

145 foot — 00
The Drying Yard
foot 116 — inch 00

foot 170 — inch 00

The Grove

Parlor Brick House
Coal
Dairy
Dunghill

The Kithin Gardin
foot 140

Old Bakers

COLE YARD
OLD DAIRY
Old Wash House

his rescue largely to the generosity of John Legard and Sir John Hotham, it also reveals that these two were not his only benefactors. Of the two creditors' securities or 'statutes' of £500 each referred to in the Memoirs, that held by Robert Harrison was in fact bought by Henry Wickham in 1627. Since Wickham was not only archdeacon of York but also Hugh's uncle by his marriage to Annabella Cholmley, Sir Richard's youngest sister, his purchase was presumably a means of preventing a writ of assignment being executed.[64] Hugh also failed to record in his Memoirs that in March 1627 he and his father sold 316 acres of mostly good arable land in Hawsker to Alice Cobb, widowed sister of Sir Richard's second wife Margaret for £915.[65] All these farming lands were held on seven year leases granted only a year earlier, but dire necessity and the ready money of the Cobbs made their sale inevitable.

The Fairfaxes of Denton also helped to bail out the Whitby Cholmleys. Of Sir Richard's seven surviving sisters by 1626 only Mary Cholmley was left a spinster. Though she and the Reverend Henry Fairfax, second son of Sir Thomas Fairfax of Denton, were deeply in love, without a dowry from her family there was no prospect of a marriage. Happily, in February 1627 the Fairfaxes bought a portion for Mary for £600 out of part of the Cholmley estate in Fyling and Lockton which enabled the couple to marry.[66]

In this general movement towards liquidation of his Whitby estate, Sir Hugh was also obliged to several of his richer tenant farmers who provided him with the cash he so urgently needed to pacify the money-lenders. George Conyers was one such tenant who had formerly occupied Fyling Old Hall and who was clearly a trusted and valued friend of the Cholmley family.[67] He must also have been a well-to-do friend. In 1626, with two other local men, he paid the Cholmleys £120 for land, shops and houses in Fyling and Whitby; the following year, he found £337 for two Cholmley farms in Fylingdales; in 1633, he bought the principal mansion of Middlewood Hall in Fylingthorpe for £420; and in 1638 for £64 he purchased more land near his new home there.[68]

On a smaller scale, another successful tenant of the Cholmleys, Thomas Taylor, provided them with much ready cash when they needed it. In 1638, when he bought two acres from them in Fylingthorpe for a mere £6 13s. 4d., Taylor was then described as a local fisherman. Ten years later, when he put down £128 for four cottages in Robin Hood's Bay and a close in Fylingdales, he had become 'Thomas Taylor of York, kidger als panyerman'. By the time he died at York in 1675 he had made a small fortune out of buying, carrying and selling fish.[69]

Other significant sales of farm land during this period included that of Poskitt's at the north end of Fyling Raw to John Harton, a yeoman from Wykeham. He paid the Cholmleys £270 for it. There was also Wragby farm, an extensive holding of moor and pasture in the south-west corner of the estate, which went to another outsider from neighbouring Staintondale for £350.[70]

Land losses to outsiders were exceptional: usually Sir Hugh sold to sitting tenants leases of anything between 900 and 2,000 years, reserving only a nominal rent and

[64] Memoirs MS, f.18v. (see below, p.88 and n.238); NYCRO, ZPK 13.
[65] Whitby LPS, PB, MS 879.
[66] G.W. Johnson (ed.), The Fairfax Correspondence (1848), i, pp.62–4; YAS, Fairfax Evidences, MS 41 (I am grateful to Mr John Rushton for this reference).
[67] Memoirs MS, f.20r. (see below, p.89 and n.246).
[68] Whitby LPS, PB, MSS 1772, 1779, 1788, 1800.
[69] Ibid., MSS 12, 5946, 5969.
[70] Ibid., MSS 739, 869.

lordship rights such as suit of court. If there was any logical purpose behind these sales
other than to raise money immediately it might have been to sell off the more remote
moorland parts of the estate on Eskdaleside and Fylingdales; but it seems more likely
that if any tenant or neighbour offered him a cash payment he would take it.
However, far from having solved his financial problems by 1636, from October 1638
until April 1639 Hugh conducted a new series of property transfers which collectively
were far more substantial than those just described. In little over six months he raised
nearly £2,000, more than half of it on houses and shops in Whitby town, and the rest
on properties in Fyling and Robin Hood's Bay. A deed of recovery, dated
5 September 1638, authorising the sale of 150 houses, 30 tofts or wastes, 10 shops,
20 acres of arable and eight of meadow, has survived.[71]

Against this 'diminution of the esstate', Hugh's only purchases were of Daletown
and Aislaby. As he noted in his Memoirs, Daletown proved to be a sound investment.
Two months after his death, it was sold by his trustees to Lord Fauconberg for the
princely sum of £2,950, more than enough to cover his daughter Elizabeth's portion if
and when she married.[72] In contrast, Aislaby in Eskdale was a small, poor settlement
which he lost almost immediately and recovered only at the end of his life.[73] The only
piece of land initially sold by Sir Hugh but subsequently recovered by him was 24 acres
of Fyling Ness, the coastal promontory north of Robin Hood's Bay. In 1638 Cholmley
paid George Conyers £64 for what he had been compelled to sell a decade earlier.[74]

Contrary to the misleading impression given in his Memoirs, Sir Hugh's heavy
sales in 1638 and 1639 suggest that, like his father and grandfather before him, he was
living beyond his mostly-rental income; but whereas they were obliged to borrow
much, he was able to sell freely. The truth is that Hugh Cholmley had become the
indirect beneficiary of Whitby's success as the kingdom's chief alum port and, to a
lesser extent, of the growth of the hinterland's butter trade. From Charlton, who
called him 'the father of Whitby' and 'its continual benefactor', down to Pearson,
who praised his 'civic foresight and philanthropic zeal', all Whitby's historians have
regarded the first Sir Hugh Cholmley as their town's greatest asset.[75]

However, closer and less partisan examination of the extant evidence indicates that
Sir Hugh owed at least as much to Whitby as the town and port owed to him.[76] In the
first place, Cholmley's Memoirs are a deceptive guide to his part in Whitby's history:
they should not be accepted, as they often have been, at face value. Sir Hugh would
have his readers believe that his motive for petitioning the Privy Council for a new
west pier at Whitby was entirely altruistic. According to his account, without such a
protective stone barrier the town would have been swamped and its harbour made
untenable. However, the selfish and short-sighted townsmen refused to cooperate
with him and he was left to pursue the matter alone. Fortunately, his good friend, Sir
Thomas Wentworth, had recently entered the Privy Council and with his powerful
support Cholmley was given permission to gather subscriptions throughout the
kingdom to pay for the pier. Even so the men of Whitby would still do nothing to

[71] See below, Appendix C, pp.172–3.
[72] Memoirs MS, ff.21r., 22r. (see below, pp.92, 94 and n.270; HUL, DCY/19/2.
[73] Memoirs MS, ff.21r., 22r. (see below, pp.92, 94 and n.271).
[74] Whitby LPS, PB, MS 1783.
[75] Charlton, p.318; F.R. Pearson, *The Abbey House under the Cholmley Family* (Whitby, 1954), pp.15–16. See
    also Young, ii, pp.830–8; R.T. Gaskin, *The Old Seaport of Whitby* (Whitby, 1909), pp.129–48; P.Shaw
    Jeffrey, *Whitby Lore and Legend* (Whitby, 3rd ed., 1952), pp.78–9.
[76] For a fuller examination of Cholmley's debt to Whitby and Whitby's to Cholmley see J. Binns, 'Sir Hugh
    Cholmley: Whitby's Benefactor or Beneficiary?', *NH*, xxx (1994), pp.88–104.

help him, and it was thanks only to two 'honest neighbours' of Fylingdales, John Farside and Henry Dickinson, that £500 was collected and the pier finally built.[77]

In fact, the circumstances concerning Whitby's great west pier were rather different from what Sir Hugh claimed. As his son later explained in his 'Account of Tangier', the main purpose of the pier was to protect the east side of Whitby which was vulnerable to flooding and silting;[78] the west side of the river was already well sheltered by the natural heights of Burtree Crag and West Cliff. Also, whereas the undeveloped east side of the river Esk, consisting largely of mudflat and sandbank, was almost entirely Cholmley territory, the west bank, with its shipbuilding yards, coal garths, alum houses and landing staithes, serving the alum works at Mulgrave and Sandsend, belonged to Whitby men involved in that industry and trade. Not surprisingly, therefore, the Newtons, Wigginers, Bagwiths and Shiptons saw no need for an expensive west pier, whereas Sir Hugh and his east-side tenants had much to gain from one. In his anxiety to enhance the economic and rental value of his side of the river, as lord of the manor he transferred the town's main market from the west to the east side as soon as the pier was under construction.[79]

The principal weakness of Cholmley's Memoirs with regard to Whitby is that of omission rather than distortion. Whitby's spectacular growth as a shipbuilding, cargo-carrying and exporting harbour was directly due to the successful foundation of Cleveland's unique alum industry in the second decade of the seventeenth century. Nevertheless, though this industry transformed his home town and port during his lifetime, he made only one reference to it in his Memoirs: in 1649, on his return from exile, he opened up a new mine on his own land at Saltwick, which proved to be immediately profitable. There is no hint here that by this time alum-making in the locality was forty years old.[80]

Indeed, Sir Hugh was himself a major beneficiary of the local alum industry. As lord of the port as well as the manor of Whitby, he reaped a handsome return without risking a penny of his own money. All ships entering the harbour, all goods landed there, and all vessels taking shelter there had to pay dues to him. What had been worthless mudbanks became sought-after sites for warehouses, coal-yards and shipbuilding berths. Even the rocks off the shore became seaweed gardens harvested to supply kelp to the alum works. Above all, unlike his father and grandfather, Sir Hugh was able to convert much of his inheritance in Whitby town and its hinterland into ready money by selling very long leases with high entry charges. By 1638 he was receiving good prices for Whitby tofts and half tofts because by then the town's prosperity had pushed up their market value and provided tenants with the cash and the credit to afford them. When Sir Hugh returned home after the first Civil War, he was able to clear his debts and fines and restore his pre-war life-style by the same method. Between 1649 and 1658 more than 21 town properties were sold for a total of £728, and about 30 cottages in Robin Hood's Bay and Fyling yielded another £381.[81] The Cholmley family's concern for their own east side and their indifference to the opposite bank might also explain why both Sir Richard and his son allowed Whitby bridge to fall into decay.[82]

---

[77] Memoirs MS, f.21v. (see below, p.93).
[78] Sir Hugh Cholmley, The Memoirs of Sir Hugh Cholmley (1787), p.50.
[79] Charlton, p.314; Young, ii, pp.573, 589.
[80] Memoirs MS, f.29v. (see below, p.111).
[81] See Appendices D and E.
[82] NRQSR, ed. J.C. Atkinson, NRRS, i–v (1884–7), i, p.124; iii, p.46; iv, p.16; v, p.72; Whitby LPS, PB, MSS 1532/3.

On the other hand, in fairness to Sir Hugh, as a North Riding justice between 1632 and 1638 he does appear to have drawn attention to the deplorable state of public roads in the Whitby area and to have insisted on their immediate improvement.[83] Also, though he made no such claims himself, by others he has been given the credit for enclosing part of his demesne in the Great Park, north of Spital Vale, and planting an orchard there in 1652. Whether these so-called New Gardens were intended to provide fruit for the people of Whitby or the residents of Abbey House cannot be determined.[84]

It is certain, however, that Sir Hugh was directly responsible for the radical improvement of Abbey House and its grounds, as he describes in his Memoirs. Though his trees have long since disappeared, much of his levelling and terracing, stone walls, new well and conduits and outhouses, including the restored brewhouse, have survived. His new stables in the south-west corner of the outer courtyard have become accommodation for the Youth Hostels Association.[85]

Finally, whether Cholmley was the mainspring of public charity in Whitby remains debatable. Clearly, he took pride in continuing the monastic custom of dispensing 'bread and gud pottage mad of beefe' at his gates twice a week;[86] but there is no reference in his Memoirs to the foundation of Whitby's first House of Correction. Again, Sir Hugh's motive in setting up this institution in his own property on the north side of upper Flowergate is impossible to define. The official record explains that in the summer of 1636 a 'multydute [sic] of poore' had been created in the Whitby area by the failure of the fishing trade, but it is much more likely that a visitation of the plague coinciding with the Dutch-Spanish naval war in the North Sea had interrupted normal seafaring activities. Little is known of Whitby's House of Correction; it flourished briefly and then went out of business. Its fate had probably more to do with local politics than the state of the local economy. After the Civil War had destroyed Sir Hugh's power in the region, a new House of Correction was opened at Pickering under the direction of Luke Robinson, who had effectively replaced him as the dominant figure in this part of Yorkshire.[87]

By taking up arms for the King in March 1643 Sir Hugh might well have forfeited his estate. Fortunately for him and his heirs, in June 1640, in anticipation of forthcoming 'trobles', he had transferred the bulk of his property into the care of trustees, reserving only Fyling for himself. Subsequently, since Fyling was estimated to be worth only £170 a year, the Committee for Compounding let him off lightly with a fine of £850. Moreover, since two of the trustees, Sir Henry Cholmley and Sir William Strickland, became staunch parliamentarians who put blood ties above political differences, Sir Hugh's wife Elizabeth and her four children, William, Hugh, Ann and Elizabeth, were well cared for by them during his exile in France. By 1650, within a year of his return to England, the Cholmley estate was secure from sequestration and the composition fine paid in full.[88]

A deed of 1658, by which William Cholmley placed his inheritance in the hands of

---

[83] NRQSR, III, pp.324, 326; IV, pp.16, 31, 88, 91.

[84] Charlton, p.68; Gaskin, p.166.

[85] Whitby LPS, PB, MS 5939: Plan of Abbey House and Grounds c.1700 (see above, pp.8–9).

[86] Memoirs MS, f.23r. (see below, p.96).

[87] NRQSR, iv, pp.55, 67, 75, 85; v, p.55; NYCRO, ZCG, MIC 1286, DN 184; Whitby LPS, PB, MSS 4199, 554.

[88] Memoirs MS, f.28v. (see below, p.109); J.W. Clay (ed.), Yorkshire Royalist Composition Papers, ii, YASRS xviii (1895), pp.221–2; M.A.E. Green (ed.) Calendar of the Proceedings of the Committee for Compounding, iii (1891), p.2062.

family trustees, described his part of the estate less than a year after his father's death. Despite the heavy losses of 1648–39 and 1653–54, the estate still yielded a good return in rents because a smaller number of tenants now paid much more than their predecessors. For example, the 13 burgage tenants in Whitby town now had to find four times as much money as the 36, who in 1626 had paid only one shilling each every year.[89] It was also clear from this deed that one of Sir Hugh's permanent legacies had been the development of Whitby's east side.[90] To serve his mine and works at Saltwick he had built a new riverside wharf at Spital Bridge, and where previously there had been waste land there were now salt pans, roperies and lime-burners. In their new market place the Cholmleys had now about 20 shops and stalls on lease.[91]

From his father William had inherited the bulk of the enclosed demesne, now known as the Great Park, which ran south-east from Abbey House to Stripes farm, and from Stainsacre Lane in the west (now the A171) to Hawsker Lane in the east. Twenty years later it was valued at £300 per annum, though by then it was let and stocked with deer.[92] But the most valuable asset in this area was undoubtedly the new alum mine and works at Saltwick. For his one third share Sir Nicholas Crispe was obliged to pay £200 a year in rent and a further £150 a year for a sixth share given to Sir Henry Cholmley by his elder brother 'in retorne of all his kindnesses'.[93] By the time of his death, Sir Hugh had raised Sir Nicholas's rent to £300. Alum had been Cholmley's best ally: by coming to the industry late he had avoided the many costly failures incurred by its pioneers. Even now he made a minimum investment by deciding not to build a boiling-house at Saltwick; instead the liquor was shipped to South Shields for the final process of evaporation into crystals.[94]

Thanks to the influence at Court of his powerful patron, Sir Thomas Wentworth, Sir Hugh had been able to prevent the Whitby alum lobby from gaining a charter of incorporation from Charles I. If granted, a petition of 1630 would have taken the control of Whitby's port, river, courts and market out of Cholmley hands and into those of an oligarchy of self-elected burgesses.[95] As a result, though the extent of the Cholmley estate in Whitby Strand had much diminished since 1565, the seignorial rights once held by the abbot and then bought by Sir Richard (II), remained intact at Sir Hugh's death in 1657.

III POLITICAL CAREER

If Sir Hugh wrote much less than all of the truth about his management of the family estate, he failed to maintain even this standard when relating his political career. About the imperfections of his ancestors he was sometimes remarkably frank; about his own record in public affairs he was almost silent and often wilfully misleading. For instance, Sir Hugh was less than honest about his relations with Strafford, and chose to omit entirely his own vindictive part in the Earl's trial and conviction. When he wrote his Memoirs he was still an unrepentant Royalist and clearly much troubled in

[89] NYCRO, ZPK 11; Ibid., ZCG IV, 5/2.
[90] The Hearth Tax return for Michaelmas 1673 (PRO, E179/261/32) shows that by then there were 150 occupied houses on the east side and 184 on the west.
[91] Whitby LPS, PB, MSS 1162/1181, 6374.
[92] Ibid., PB, MSS 650, 1552, 1162/1181; HUL, DCY/18/3. The best cartographic guides to this area are: J. Wood, Plan of Whitby (1828); Ordnance Survey, 25″ (1913), sheet xxxii.11; Ordnance Survey, 25″ (1928), sheet xxxii.7.
[93] Memoirs MS, f.29v. (see below, p.111).
[94] Young, ii, p.814.
[95] PRO, SP16/159/43.

his conscience by a Parliamentarian past which he deeply regretted. Indeed, he was so ashamed of his political behaviour between 1640 and 1642 that he drew a convenient veil over much of it.

That Sir Hugh was a late convert to the opposition to Ship Money is hardly surprising considering his past experience of North Sea piracy and his personal appreciation of the urgent need for English warships to guard shores and merchant-men. As he related in his Memoirs, in 1626 he lost household furnishings and plate to the value of four or five hundred pounds and his wife her whole wardrobe to a Dunkirker privateer.[96] Not reported in the Memoirs, however, was an incident in 1632 when at Whitby Cholmley announced the presence of a French pirate ship which was said to have robbed many English vessels at sea.[97] The worst outrages took place in the summer of 1635, only months after the first writ for Ship Money was directed to seaport towns. Both Scarborough, which suffered two attacks, and Whitby discovered how vulnerable they were to Dutch men-of-war as well as Dunkirkers. Sir Hugh's own detailed account of what happened at Whitby is the only one that seems to have survived.[98]

A well-to-do Buckinghamshire landowner and landlubber like John Hampden might well contend that Ship Money was illegal, but Yorkshiremen like Sir Hugh, who lived on the North Sea coast, must have welcomed the extension of the tax to cover the whole country, and were more than willing to pay it themselves if it protected the lives and livelihoods of their tenants. There is no evidence that Sir Hugh refused to pay Ship Money until the sixth and final demand for it in the winter of 1639–40; and by that time the purpose of the tax had changed: instead of paying for warships in the Royal navy it was now being used to finance the Bishops' War against the rebel Scots.[99]

Yet Cholmley was not at first obstructive to the King's determination to suppress the Scottish rebellion by force. On the contrary, Sir Hugh appears to have been one of the most active and conscientious justices and deputy lieutenants in the county during the first Bishops' War. When the deputies were summoned to York in July 1638 to discuss the King's order to call out the trained bands, he was the only one there from the North Riding. Sir William Savile refused to bring his cavalry to York and Sir John Hotham would not muster his East Riding men until after the harvest was brought in.[100] Two months later, when Wentworth wrote to Cholmley from Ireland, his letter, signed 'your very sure affectionate friend and servant', makes it clear that he regarded Sir Hugh as one of his few remaining allies in Yorkshire.[101] At the time Wentworth's trust seemed well placed: the two were related by blood and marriage; Cholmley still depended on the Lord Deputy to finish Whitby's new west pier; and, ever since his father had risked his own honour in 1625–26 to get Thomas elected to a county seat, Hugh had looked to him and had received from him many favours.[102]

Little local evidence of military preparation for the first Bishops' War has survived, but it indicates that Sir Hugh, who was commissioned colonel of a regiment of the trained band, drawing its four companies from Whitby Strand, Scarborough town,

[96] Memoirs MS, f.18r. (see below, p.86).
[97] PRO, SP16/220/3, 31.
[98] CSPD, 1635, pp.273, 294, 322–3, 326–7, 336, 339, 549; Memoirs MS, ff.23r.–v. (see below, pp.96–8).
[99] Memoirs MS, f.24v. (see below, p.100).
[100] J.T. Cliffe, The Yorkshire Gentry from the Reformation to the Civil War (1969), pp.310–11.
[101] Sheffield Archives, WWM, SP10(214).
[102] Memoirs MS, ff.9r., 24v. (see below, pp.74, 100).

Ryedale and Pickering Lythe, carried out his duties with exemplary zeal and success. In the past Scarborough's militia had consisted of no more than 36 poorly armed men; in 1638–39 Cholmley raised 24 from each of the four Quarters of the town.[103] Whereas Hoby had tried and failed to bring Scarborough's men even the nine miles inland to Hutton Buscel, Sir Hugh succeeded in reviewing his entire regiment on the moors above Pickering and Thornton Dale, twice that distance from the coast.[104]

It was at one of these general musters on the moor that Sir Hugh claimed he had 'caught cold and a dangerous sickness' which prevented him from continuing his duties and persuaded him to winter with his family in London.[105] Though the point was not made by Cholmley or anyone else, it must have been at this time, during the winter of 1639–40, that the rift opened between him and Strafford. One indication of Sir Hugh's loss of favour is that he was not recommended by the Lord Deputy for one of Scarborough's parliamentary seats as early as December 1639, even though it was already known by then that Cholmley had offered himself to the borough to serve as one of their Members in what became the Short Parliament.[106]

Why such an abrupt and decisive reversal took place at this moment is far from clear. Cholmley's assertion that Strafford broke their friendship because his refusal to pay Ship Money had 'carried the whole liberty of Whitby Strand' is probably only part of the truth.[107] What Sir Hugh failed to explain in his Memoirs – and indeed tried to conceal – was that on three occasions during the Short Parliament – 18, 20 April and 4 May 1640 – he had openly and impertinently challenged the legality of Ship Money. On the second occasion he was rebuked by Mr Solicitor for his 'boldness', and on the third he argued that if Charles wanted subsidies to fight the Scots he would have to reimburse all the militia costs of the past two years as well as concede Ship Money.[108] It was for these grossly insolent words that Sir Hugh was put out of all his commissions and summoned to answer for them before the Privy Council. Whereas Cholmley would have his reader think that he was falsely accused and unjustly treated, in particular by 'my lord' Strafford, in truth he was lucky not to join Sir John Hotham and Henry Bellasis in the Fleet prison.[109]

Why Cholmley had gone over to the 'opposition' so completely remains something of a mystery, but it is manifest that from then on there could be no reconciliation between him and his erstwhile patron, the earl of Strafford: the two were now enemies to the death. When Sir Hugh went back to Whitby in June 1640 to settle the major part of his estate on trustees he was anticipating not civil war but his own possible destruction or ruin in a conflict with the King's chief minister.[110]

By omitting from his Memoirs all reference to his parliamentary record because later he came to regard it as embarrassing or even shameful, Sir Hugh did himself a serious injustice. Between April 1640, when the Short Parliament opened, and September 1642, when he left London finally to take up Parliament's commission at Scarborough, Cholmley's name appears nearly one hundred times even in the bald summaries of the House of Commons *Journal*. In the more informative and detailed

[103] SRL, J. Chapman (ed.), *Scarborough Corporation Records*, 3 vols (1909), i, p.148; iii, p.112.
[104] M.Y. Ashcroft (ed.), *Scarborough Records 1600–1640*, NYCRO, 47 (Northallerton, 1991), pp.232–3; Memoirs MS, f.24r. (see below, p.99).
[105] Memoirs MS, f.24r. (see below, p.99).
[106] Ashcroft, *Records*, p.340.
[107] Cliffe, *Yorkshire Gentry*, p.318; Memoirs MS, f.24v. (see below, p.100 and n.329).
[108] E.S. Cope and W.H. Coates (eds.), *Proceedings of the Short Parliament of 1640*, Camden, 4th series, xix (1977), pp.161, 162, 194.
[109] Memoirs MS, f.24v. (see below, p.100); *Privy Council Registers*, x, 8, 15 May 1640, pp.476, 492.
[110] Memoirs MS, f.28v. (see below, p.109).

private diaries of House of Commons proceedings, such as the D'Ewes *Journal*, Sir Hugh's prominence in debate and committee is even more fully revealed.

In the Long Parliament Cholmley sat on more than 30 committees. They ranged in importance from the trivial, that determined the length of the Michaelmas term, to the crucial, that drew up charges against Strafford and Archbishop Laud, or examined complaints against Ship Money, monopolies and the King's army garrisoned in Yorkshire. Though never a chairman of any vital committee, and therefore not of the parliamentary rank of Hampden or Hotham, for nearly two years he was among the 20 or 30 most active and influential Members of the House of Commons.

During the first few months of the Long Parliament Sir Hugh was relentless and unscrupulous in his pursuit of fellow Yorkshiremen he regarded as enemies. Beginning with lesser victims, Sir William Pennyman, Francis Nevile and Sir William Savile, he finally reached the greatest of all, the earl of Strafford himself. Pennyman's worst fault in Cholmley's eyes was that he had been Strafford's constant friend.[111] Nevile and Savile had made themselves his enemies by revealing to the Privy Council what he, Hotham and Bellasis had rashly said in the Short Parliament.[112] Sir Hugh's contribution to the charges against Strafford at his trial was small but significant, and when he came to write his Memoirs fifteen years later he remembered it well enough to repeat, even though it was almost entirely untrue.[113] After their failure to find him guilty of a capital crime by judicial rules of evidence, Strafford's persecutors resorted to a Bill of Attainder. Needless to say, Sir Hugh along with his brother Sir Henry and the two Hothams all voted for it.[114]

On most issues that came before the Long Parliament in 1640–41 Cholmley was at one with Pym and the radical reformers. He welcomed the abolition of Star Chamber and the Council in the North; his opposition to monopolies, forced loans and free billeting was well grounded in his belief in what he called 'the liberty of the subject'. For Sir Hugh, however, these were matters of principle, not political manoeuvre: when Pym moved that the City of London should be compelled to lend money, Cholmley objected strongly that this was 'contrary to the fundamental liberty of the subject', and 'that every poore man and every riche man had equall power and right in the Lawes of the Lande . . .'.[115]

However, when Cholmley expressed concern for the well-being of the royal family, he found himself amongst a decreasing minority of Members. In February 1641, for instance, under pressure from the House, the Queen agreed to dismiss a papal representative from her household, but Sir Hugh was alone when he moved that the Commons might thank her for doing so. Given Cholmley's strong antipathy towards Catholics, his defence of Henrietta Maria on this occasion was to be recalled two years later when he changed sides after a private audience with her at York.[116]

In January 1642, after the King's attempt to arrest the five Members had undermined what little support he still had in London, Cholmley again made himself conspicuous by another conciliatory gesture. Whereas most of his fellow Members

[111] W. Notestein (ed.), *The Journal of Sir Simonds D'Ewes* (Yale, 1923), pp.104–5, 151–2, C.V. Wedgwood, *Thomas Wentworth, First Earl of Strafford 1593–1641. A Revaluation* (pbk edn, 1964), pp.341–2.
[112] Notestein, *Journal*, pp.322–3.
[113] Memoirs MS, f.25v. (see below, p.102 and n.344).
[114] Cliffe, *Yorkshire Gentry*, p.328.
[115] Notestein, *Journal*, p.382.
[116] *Ibid.*, p.324; J. Rushworth, *Historical Collections*, iv, pp.169–70; E.B.G. Warburton, *Memoirs of Prince Rupert and the Cavaliers*, 3 vols, (1849), ii, p.129.

were outraged by the King's conduct and demanded his apology for violating Commons privilege, Sir Hugh said that he regretted that the royal family had retreated to Windsor and moved that the House might 'think of some speedy way of removing these jealousies between the King and Parliament'.[117]

As for Cholmley's religious views at this time, they are hard to discover and define and even harder to relate to his political thoughts. To say that he was anti-Catholic to the point of paranoia is to say nothing distinctive about any contemporary Protestant, but perhaps Sir Hugh's prejudice was especially extreme because of his own family's association with Catholics and their continued strength in his locality. In 1641 there were said to be 138 recusants at Egton, 59 in Whitby and 38 at Brandsby, where his Cholmley cousins remained steadfastly loyal to the old faith.[118] Even before the Irish rebellion, Cholmley was worried about English papists taking up arms.[119] After the rebellion, like many English Protestants, he suffered from nightmares of Catholic invasion, rapine and slaughter.[120] In his irredeemably biased mind, he equated 'papist' with 'Straffordian'.[121]

Between future Royalists, like Hyde and Falkland, and future Roundhead leaders, such as Pym and Hampden, there were no fundamental differences during the first few months of the Long Parliament. By the autumn recess of 1641, however, when the future of the Church of England was debated, a great and growing divide opened up between Anglicans and Calvinists. On this crucial issue Cholmley can be identified with what D'Ewes called the 'episcopall partie'. Though Sir Hugh ultimately voted for the Grand Remonstrance, during the final stages of heated debate on Clause 189, which alleged that Anglican bishops had commanded the introduction of 'idolatrous and Popish ceremonies', he spoke strongly against it and was teller for the defeated Noes.[122]

Thomas Fuller identified two kinds of Puritans at this time: 'some mild and moderate, contented only to enjoy their own conscience; others fierce and fiery, to the disturbance of church and state'.[123] Clearly, Cholmley belonged to the first category. His Puritan leanings were pronounced but temperate: he wanted to keep bishops with reduced powers; to keep the Prayer Book in a revised form; to impose more severe penalties against recusants; and to insist that the ministry gave more emphasis to preaching. When the Commons discussed the controversial question of the proper location of the altar or communion table, Sir Hugh said that he did not care where it stood; the offence was to bow to it.[124]

As revealed in the Memoirs, Sir Hugh's personal and family life illustrates the same balanced position. He deplored the sexual licence of his forebears not simply or even mainly for moral reasons: in his view fathering too many bastard as well as legitimate children was a drain on a gentleman's estate. He disliked swearing, drinking, loss of temper and idleness; he condemned outdoor sports such as hawking, horse-racing and hunting, as well as indoor gambling, dicing and bowling. On the other hand, unlike

---

[117] W.H. Coates, A.S. Young and V.F. Snow (eds.), *The Private Journals of the Long Parliament, 3 January–5 March 1642* (New Haven, USA, 1982), pp.54, 63.
[118] Aveling, *Northern Catholics*, pp.412, 423, 426.
[119] Notestein, *Journal*, p.461.
[120] Coates, Young and Snow, *Journals*, pp.38, 193, 240.
[121] Memoirs MS, f.25v. (see below, p.102 and n.344); V.F. Snow and A.S. Young (eds.), *The Private Journals of the Long Parliament, 7 March–1 June 1642* (New Haven, USA, 1987), pp.217–18.
[122] W.H. Coates (ed.), *The Journal of Sir Simonds D'Ewes* (Yale, 1942), p.152; *CJ*, ii, 317.
[123] T. Fuller, *Church History of Britain* (Oxford, 1845), iv, p.327.
[124] J.D. Maltby (ed.), *The Short Parliament (1640) Diary of Sir Thomas Aston*, Camden, 4th series, xxxv (1988), p.91.

most Puritans, he expressed no hostility to the theatre or the pleasures of the dining table.[125]

The only direct contemporary reference to Cholmley's Puritanism is that he was 'kind and friendly to the Puritans or Professors of Religion'.[126] Here the author might have had in mind one such Puritan minister, Robert Remmington, vicar of Whitby from 1624 until 1638, who was a close friend of Sir Hugh and his family. Mr Remmington was mentioned several times, and always favourably, in both Cholmley's Memoirs and his 'Memorialls tuching Scarbrough'.[127] However, even by the time he wrote the Memorials during his post-war exile in France, Cholmley's view of Puritan radicals in general had probably hardened. What he wrote then of his old friend and former comrade, Sir John Hotham – that he did not approve of the ways of 'the Presiser cleargie' and came to 'disrellish there humours and wayes as anie man livinge' – reads like an autobiographical judgement.[128]

Finally, amongst the many virtues of his wife Elizabeth, Sir Hugh included her faithful attachment to the Church of England. He also noted pointedly that on her death bed she rejected a Presbyterian minister and asked instead for Archbishop James Ussher of Armagh. With these revelations in mind, it seems reasonable to accept the verdict of the historian of the Long Parliament that Cholmley was 'loyal to the Anglican church, with no leaning towards Presbyterianism', but to reject Gardiner's conclusion that 'he had nothing of the Puritan in him'.[129]

In Yorkshire, as elsewhere in the country, religious commitment was often the principal, though far from the only, factor determining Civil War allegiance. According to Dr Cliffe's findings, of 132 Puritan families in the county, 64 were actively Parliamentarian and only 24 Royalist; and of 157 Catholic families, 86 were Royalist and no more than ten supported Parliament. Not one Catholic gentleman in the North Riding fought for Parliament, while intensely Puritan knights, such as Matthew Boynton, Philip Stapleton, William Strickland, John Bourchier, Edward Rhodes, William Constable and Richard Darley, seem to have entertained few doubts about which side they would take.[130] Dr Newman found that one third of the officers in Newcastle's Royalist northern army were Catholics, a figure out of all proportion to their number in the region.[131]

If, therefore, Cholmley was neither Catholic nor Calvinist, neither Laudian nor Presbyterian, this would help to explain his predicament in 1642 when civil war broke out. He could not go north and joint the King at York since he believed him to be surrounded and supported there by papists and warmongers.[132] On the other hand, he was increasingly alarmed by the bellicosity of the Parliamentarian leadership in London. He opposed the Militia Ordinance of March 1642 because he thought it

[125] Memoirs MS, ff.4r., 5r., 6v., 7r., 7v., 10v., 15r., 15v., 24r. (see below, pp.66, 68, 70, 71, 72, 76, 82, 83, 99.
[126] Cliffe, *Yorkshire Gentry*, p.261; Dr Williams's Library, London, Maurice MSS, 'A Chronological Account of Eminent Persons . . .', vol.iii.
[127] Memoirs MS, ff.21v., 28r. (see below pp.94, 108 and n.393); Memorials (Scarborough) MS, f.13v. (see below, p.152).
[128] Memorials (Hothams) MS, f.239r. (see below, pp.128–9).
[129] Memoirs MS, f.35r. (see below, p.120); M.F. Keeler, *The Long Parliament, 1640–1, A Biographical Study of its Members* (Philadelphia, 1954), p.135; S.R. Gardiner, *History of the Great Civil War 1642–49*, 3 vols. (1886–91), i, p.122.
[130] Cliffe, *Yorkshire Gentry*, pp.344–8.
[131] P.R. Newman, 'The Royalist Army in Northern England 1642–45', 2 vols. (unpub. D.Phil. thesis, York Univ. 1978), i, pp.10, 27, 29, 49, 589.
[132] Memoirs MS, f.26v. (see below, pp.103–4).

was an act of war against the King; and he was appalled by the extremism of the Nineteen Propositions.[133]

If Sir Hugh had reason to disapprove of both sides and his overwhelming preference was for a peaceful settlement, why did he take up arms for Parliament in the autumn of 1642? After all, in the North Riding, as in many others parts of England, the neutrals far outnumbered either the active Royalists or the active Parliamentarians.[134] Identifying and weighing motives are the most elusive of historical quests and Cholmley's own explanation of his conduct at this crucial moment is far from convincing,[135] but with these reservations in mind some attempt has to be made.

Firstly, though he might have lacked enthusiasm for Parliament's cause, Cholmley had a pressing duty to defend his property, his tenants and his friends. Reports of Cavalier outrages against the homes and families of absent Yorkshiremen such as George Marwood of Nun Monkton, reported to the House of Commons on 18 August 1642, must have given Sir Hugh a powerful incentive to accept Essex's commission.[136]

Secondly, by September 1642, most of Cholmley's closest relatives and friends were committed to Parliament. His brother Henry, now commissioned colonel of the trained bands of Pickering Lythe and Ryedale, was already on the march with them to the battlefield of Edgehill.[137] His political ally and neighbour, Sir John Hotham and his son, were already fatally engaged. In April, King Charles had declared Sir John a traitor for denying him entrance to Hull. In July, Sir John requested the return of the Cholmley brothers from London to Yorkshire to counter Royalist recruitment there. Sir Hugh was deeply indebted to Hotham who had twice rescued him – once from bankruptcy and then from menacing Dutchmen.[138]

Most of Cholmley's other east Yorkshire kinsmen were on Parliament's side, or soon would be. Sir William Strickland of Boynton, a Member for Hedon, was Sir Hugh's brother-in-law. As a convinced Calvinist he knew where his allegiance ought to be, and, like Cholmley, could not be bought by the crown with a last-minute baronetcy.[139] Of his Legard relatives, 'uncle John' at Ganton was too old to be active, but Christopher at Anlaby had already suffered from Cavalier vandalism.[140] As for Sir Hugh's two intimate friends and relatives by marriage, Sir Christopher Yelverton of Easton Mauduit in Northamptonshire and Sir Roger Twysden of Roydon Hall, East Peckham, Kent, both were drawn towards Parliament, though not equally. Yelverton's bias was predictable: he was a 'third-generation Puritan' who had been mulcted by forest fines and had led local resistance to Ship Money.[141] He too could not be won over by a belated baronetcy. Sir Roger shared his brother-in-law's dread of civil war and his fear of parliamentary as well as royal tyranny. Like Sir Hugh he was an Anglican who deplored attacks on the doctrine and clergy of the established church.

---

[133] Memoirs MS, f.26v. (see below, p.104).
[134] Cliffe, *Yorkshire Gentry*, pp.336, 338.
[135] Memoirs MS, f.27r. (see below, p.105); Memorials (Scarborough) MS, f.8r. (see below, p.140).
[136] Memoirs MS, f.26v. (see below, pp.104–5); *CJ*, ii, 763; *LJ*, v, 302.
[137] *CSPD*, 1642, pp.366, 379, 387.
[138] HMC, *Thirteenth Report*, Appendix 1, p.41; *Ibid.*, *Portland*, i, p.42.
[139] Cliffe, *Yorkshire Gentry*, p.268; P. Roebuck, *Yorkshire Baronets 1640–1760* (Oxford, 1980), p.18. In none of his surviving writing did Sir Hugh refer to his baronetcy which was conferred by King Charles as late as 10 August 1642. Perhaps Cholmley was ashamed that it was offered as a belated bribe and accepted days before he took a commission in Parliament's army.
[140] Cliffe, *Yorkshire Gentry*, p.335.
[141] Keeler, *Long Parliament*, pp.403–4.

As a distinguished constitutional and legal historian who was convinced of the illegality of Ship Money he probably exercised some influence over Cholmley.[142]

On the other side, most of Cholmley's local enemies had already declared for King Charles. Sir William Pennyman of Marske and Sir William Savile of Thornhill, 'Strafford's creatures', as Sir Hugh called them, were both to die fighting for the Royalist cause. The Eures of Malton, the Wyvills of Osgodby and the Conyers of Whitby were all Catholics and in arms for the King. They could be expected to take advantage of Cholmley's absence. No doubt Sir Hugh was aware that as early as 7 July Captain William Wyvill had mustered Scarborough's trained band in the name of the King. As for Sir Robert Strickland of Thornton Bridge, another notorious Catholic, in June 1642 his trained band had attacked the house in York where Sir Hugh and the other Parliamentary commissioners were lodged.[143]

In conclusion, it seems that Cholmley was pushed reluctantly into Parliament's armed camp first by his violent rift with Strafford, by his acute hostility to Catholics and finally by his natural instinct to defend his estate and local authority, his kinsmen and his friends. But he had no previous experience of war and not the slightest relish for it. His attachment to Parliament's cause was conditional not convinced, and certainly not blind or desperate. Like many lukewarm Parliamentarians, he hoped that a negotiated agreement could be reached before it came to the disaster of outright civil war. Not all his relatives were on the same side, and he was appalled by the prospect of fighting his Cholmley cousins from Brandsby and his Bellasis cousin Henry of Newburgh Priory, who as Catholics had taken the King's side.[144]

IV CIVIL WAR

If Cholmley's Memoirs reveal little of his important and busy role as a leading member of the Long Parliament, his 'Memorialls tuching Scarbrough' are predictably brief on his record as a Parliamentarian colonel during the first six months of the Civil War. However, Sir Hugh's account of his military service to Parliament is not merely economical with words: it is also tendentious and unconvincing. Clearly, in retrospect, the Royalist Cholmley was anxious to convey the message that he was never a committed Parliamentarian officer; that he never really rebelled against the crown; and that during these six months he acted honourably and independently. In other words, the 'Memorials' were intended to vindicate their author in the eyes of fellow Royalists.[145]

Less partisan, contemporary evidence conveys a different story, however. Cholmley's commission derived from Parliament's Militia Ordinance and he accepted it after King Charles had declared it fraudulent and raised his battle standard at Nottingham. Moreover, Sir Hugh's argument that his commanding general was the Earl of Essex, who was Lord Lieutenant 'with the kings consent and approbation', conveniently concealed the fact that Essex had already been condemned as a traitor by Charles.[146] In short, Cholmley's belief that he was serving both King and Parliament was at best a self-delusion, and at worst dishonest.

[142] F.W. Jessup, *Sir Roger Twysden 1597–1672* (1965), pp.30–2, 42–3, 45–60.
[143] Cliffe, *Yorkshire Gentry*, pp.185–6, 333, 342–3; NYCRO, DC/SCB, B1 7 July 1642; Sir G. Duckett, 'Civil War Proceedings in Yorkshire', *YAJ*, vii (1882), pp.75–6.
[144] HMC, *Portland*, i, pp.90–1; *CJ*, ii, 938.
[145] Memorials (Scarborough) MS, ff.8r.–v. (see below, pp.140–3).
[146] *Ibid.*, f.8r. (see below, p.140); S.R. Gardiner (ed.), *The Constitutional Documents of the Puritan Revolution 1625–60* (Oxford, 34rd edn. rev., 1906), pp.248–9.

Cholmley's orders were to raise his old trained band and with it secure the town and harbour of Scarborough. He was also instructed to take control of Scarborough castle which overlooked both. There were two main reasons why Parliament chose to send Sir Hugh to Scarborough. First, the port there had become of great strategic value to the King; and second, Cholmley was thought to be the only trustworthy officer who had the local authority to win over the town's oligarchy without resort to force.

The King's failure to secure Hull either by persuasion in April or by siege in July 1642 was a most serious setback. Without the magazine there, which was said to contain weapons for 20,000 men, 7,000 barrels of gunpowder and 120 artillery pieces, the Royal army could not be adequately equipped.[147] This meant that Charles was now dependent on his wife's success in Holland where she had gone to raise money and buy arms for her husband's cause. However, even if she raised the money, bought the munitions and hired the transports for them, a safe harbour on the English coast had to be found where they could be brought ashore. Unfortunately for the King, Parliament soon controlled every seaport from Portsmouth to Hull and nearly every ship's crew in the fleet had deserted him. Consequently, if Charles was denied the use of Hull, then Scarborough was his next best choice. Newcastle was too far away from his northern headquarters at York, too close to the Scots, and too easily blockaded by Parliament's warships at the mouth of the Tyne. Bridlington Quay had no land or sea defences and might be surprised by a sortie from Hull. Whitby had a safe river anchorage yet it was too remote and inaccessible by land. In contrast, Scarborough had a protected haven, a defensible town and a massive castle; by a sound, level road it was less than a day's ride from York; and open to the North Sea it would take more ships than Parliament could spare to blockade it in all weathers.[148]

Cholmley did what was asked of him, and much more. Even though many of Scarborough's ruling body, particularly the five Thompsons, were Royalist by inclination, he won them over without coercion. The town was fortified, its trained band put at Sir Hugh's disposal, and a troop of dragoons raised at his request and the corporation's expense. The Thompsons meekly handed over the castle and with the professional help of his cousin, Browne Bushell, Cholmley converted it into a formidable fortress. Within three weeks he had recruited another 400 soldiers from Whitby Strand and Pickering Lythe. By the beginning of November, accompanied by reinforcements from the Hull garrison, he had brought 500 men to Stamford Bridge, nearly 40 miles inland from Scarborough and only six miles from the outskirts of Royalist York.[149] For a 'reluctant' Roundhead, Sir Hugh seems to have been surprisingly determined to make an unnecessary and dangerous demonstration for which he had no authorisation from his superiors.[150]

The first indication that Cholmley's loyalty to Parliament might be brittle came at the beginning of December 1642. The Earl of Newcastle had brought an over-whelming army of 8,000 men, a quarter of them cavalry, across the Tees and down to York, on the way brushing aside all opposition. As a result, Lord Fairfax, Parliament's

[147] I.E. Ryder, 'The Seizure of Hull and its Magazine, January 1642', *YAJ*, lxi (1989), p.139; *CSPV*, 1640–2, p.283.
[148] BL, *TT*, E85(17): *Two Letters from Sir Hugh Cholmley*, 18 Jan. 1743.
[149] HMC, *Bouverie*, (1887), pp.90–1.
[150] Cholmley's conduct at this time contrasts markedly with that of the Fairfaxes who had made a truce with the Yorkshire Royalists in late September at Rothwell, near Leeds. (BL, *TT*, E119(24): *Special Passages* 27 Sept.–4 Oct. 1642). The truce was immediately repudiated by the Hothams and overruled by Parliament. No one has ever accused the Fairfaxes of being disloyal to Parliament.

general in Yorkshire, summoned Sir Hugh to lead his force westwards to join him at Tadcaster, thereby barring Newcastle's route into the West Riding. Though the invitation was endorsed by the House of Commons, Cholmley flatly rejected it and instead retreated in the opposite direction all the way back to Scarborough.[151]

However, whatever sinister interpretation might have been given subsequently to Cholmley's action, at the time it was neither fainthearted nor rebellious: in the circumstances, he had no choice. Even if he had been able to cross the swollen Ouse south of York this would have meant putting the enemy as well as the river between himself and his home base. Cholmley's commission was to secure Scarborough and thereby deny it to the King, not to abandon it to the mercy of Newcastle's cavalry. Moreover, he could never have persuaded his captains and their men to stray so far away from their homes from which they had been absent for more than a month.[152]

Soon after his return to Scarborough, Cholmley received a letter from John Pym which greatly upset him. He was reprimanded for disobeying the order of his general, for abandoning the Fairfaxes to their defeat at Tadcaster, and for giving too much importance to Scarborough, 'a place conceived not to be very usefull'. Sir Hugh could not tolerate criticism of his honour or competence and therefore wrote a lengthy reply explaining and justifying his conduct to Speaker Lenthall. At the end of the letter, he emphasized that his wish was 'to contribute . . . to the settling the truth of the Gospel, liberty of the subject, and peace of the Kingdom . . . with as much honour as possibly may be to his Majesty'. Finally, he gave a warning that if there was not soon a 'good understanding' between Parliament and the King' the country was 'in danger to be ruined'.[153]

Nevertheless, whatever his reservations might have been, Sir Hugh enjoyed only a brief respite in Scarborough during Christmas: before the New Year he was again on the road westwards in search of the enemy. In January 1643, while he was still at Malton, news reached him that a Royalist force, commanded by Colonels Robert Strickland and Guilford Slingsby, had advanced as far as Guisborough. From here they were recruiting and threatening to move towards the coast at Whitby. Without waiting for orders or assistance, Cholmley immediately marched north over the moors and engaged the Royalists. The battle of Guisborough turned quickly into a rout: Sir Hugh's men took over a hundred prisoners, including Colonel Slingsby, and chased the Royalists out of the area. Not one of Cholmley's men was killed and only two suffered wounds.[154]

Cholmley's first experience of battle might have hardened his attachment to Parliament, but it only sickened and depressed him. In his report to London, he confessed: 'it grieves my heart to see . . . how I am forced to draw my sword not onely against my countrymen but many near friends and allies some of which I know both to be well affected in religion and lovers of their liberties'. Having looked bloody civil war in the face, he was more than ever convinced that Parliament must reach an accord with the King, even if this meant giving way to him on all outstanding issues except religion.[155]

But there was to be no last-minute peace treaty: what Cholmley dreaded most, an all-out war, was now inescapable. Nevertheless, there was still no breach yet between Sir Hugh and Parliament. After his victory at Guisborough, the House of Commons

---

[151] *CJ*, ii, 891, 893; BL, *TT*, E85(17).
[152] BL, *TT*, E85(17).
[153] *Ibid.*
[154] HMC, *Portland*, i, pp.90–1; Rushworth, *Collections*, v, p.125.
[155] HMC, *Portland*, i, pp.90–1.

was even more appreciative of his valuable contribution. The Queen's arrival from Holland was now imminent. If Sir Hugh held on to Scarborough and Whitby, she would have to bring her precious transports as far north as Newcastle or Sunderland, where Parliament's warships were waiting to intercept them. Cholmley was thanked for his past services and sent more money to pay for his future expenses.[156]

Most commentators, contemporary and recent, have assumed that Cholmley's defection to the Royalist side at the end of March 1643 was a direct result of his secret meeting with the Queen at York immediately before his declaration. Naturally, Parliamentarians were outraged by his desertion; the Commons resolved to impeach him for high treason; the London press called him 'Judas', 'cowardly' and 'apostate', and alleged that he was infatuated with and duped by Henrietta Maria.[157] At least two modern authors have even invented additional assignations in Scarborough and Whitby, which the Queen never visited, to perpetuate this sentimental silliness.[158]

A more serious interpretation of Sir Hugh's action is that he had plotted his defection in collusion with the Hothams, and that in secret they had agreed to surrender both Scarborough and Hull to the King. However, this explanation is also defeated by the facts. No correspondence between Cholmley and the Hothams has come to light: they were as much surprised and annoyed by Sir Hugh's announcement as anyone; and afterwards Sir John did everything in his power to recover Scarborough for Parliament. After Browne Bushell had broken his promise to Sir John and handed over the town and castle to his cousin, the Hothams mounted an unsuccessful and costly combined attack by land and sea on Royalist Scarborough.[159]

Unlike the Hothams, who had corresponded secretly with the Royalists from as early as December 1642, Cholmley did not disguise his true intentions or hide his real thoughts until days before his defection. Twice he had written to Speaker Lenthall expressing his growing misgivings about Parliament's failure to come to a negotiated settlement with the King.[160] Since the contents of these two letters were contemporary confessions and not retrospective glosses like his Memorials and Memoirs, they deserve to be valued as honest reflections of Sir Hugh's mind at this time. Certainly, Gardiner accepted this view when he concluded that, compared with the Hothams, Sir Hugh had a 'nobler nature' and was 'actuated by the purer motives'.[161]

On the other hand, Cholmley's motives were not unmixed with material calculation. The Queen's safe arrival at Bridlington and her triumphant progress to York must have had a profound effect on him: they demonstrated the overwhelming military power of the Royalists in Yorkshire and the feebleness of opposition to it. Sir Hugh must have felt demoralised, isolated and acutely endangered. The Hothams had done nothing to obstruct the Queen; on the contrary, it seemed that they had colluded in her success. Ominously, instead of moving southwards into Hotham territory in the East Riding, Royalist cavalry drove eastwards towards Scarborough. Sir Hugh sent out parties to destroy the bridges over the Derwent at Yedingham and the Rye at Howe and to occupy Pickering castle, but they were too late: Mackworth's men had already seized Pickering. Soon they had taken up quarters

---

[156] CJ, ii, 938.
[157] BL, TT, 669, f.7(2): Votes of the House of Commons relating to Hugh Cholmley; CJ, iii, 28; BL, TT, E270(33): Scottish Dove; Ibid., E294(20): Mercurius Britanicus; M. Bence-Jones, The Cavaliers (1976), p.159.
[158] C. Oman, Henrietta Maria (1976 edn.), pp.145, 148; Roebuck, Yorkshire Baronets, p.18.
[159] BL, TT, E95(9): A Letter from Sir John Hotham to Speaker Lenthall, 4 Apr. 1643; Ibid., E292(27): Letter from the Queen at York to King Charles, 30 Mar. 1643.
[160] BL, TT, E85(17); HMC, Portland, i, p.90.
[161] Gardiner, Civil War, i, pp.121–2.

in Sir Hugh's ancestral home and birthplace, Roxby castle, at Thornton. Even more alarming, a troop of Cavalier horsemen had raided deeply into Whitby Strand, plundered Fyling Old Hall, and stolen all Hotham's horses in the park there.[162] Within a matter of days, Abbey House would be ransacked and Scarborough overrun. It was only at this moment, in the middle of March, that Cholmley made his first secret overtures, in the guise of exchanging prisoners, to Mackworth at Thornton and General Goring in York. By the time he saw the Queen a week later an arrangement had already been reached. Their meeting was a diplomatic formality, not a decisive, dramatic occasion.[163]

Needless to say, none of this is to be found in Sir Hugh's subsequent account in 'Memorialls tuching Scarbrough': events at Bridlington, Pickering, Thornton and Fyling Old Hall are not mentioned. No doubt Sir Hugh wanted the world to believe that his motives for changing sides were just as disinterested and principled as they had been for taking Parliament's commission six months earlier. However, if Cholmley had merely resigned that commission and retired into neutrality, his estate and his reputation would still have been ruined: only by actively taking the King's side could he hope to save both. Also, his judgement of the situation at Scarborough and his delicate handling of it were justified by the outcome. As he intended, his coup cost not a single drop of blood on either side. Wisely, he allowed every officer, soldier and burgess to decide whether they wished to remain in Scarborough under a Royalist regime or depart. In his own description of these events Cholmley exaggerated his hold over the soldiers in the garrison but not his success with the town leaders, who with few exceptions accepted his and their change of allegiance.[164] He had refused the offer of 1,500 Royalist troops to intimidate the town into surrender because he wanted its inhabitants to think of him as their guardian not as their conqueror, and in fact most of them did seem grateful for his protection.[165]

Whatever Cholmley's reasons for changing sides might have been originally in March 1643, increasingly it became for him a matter of pride and honour that he endured the consequences of a decision that determined the rest of his life. What had been mainly an act of self-defence eventually brought him to the brink of self-destruction.

At first it appeared that Sir Hugh had gone over to the winning side just in time. The Fairfaxes were defeated at Seacroft at the end of March and routed on Adwalton Moor at the end of June. Parliament's resistance in the West Riding collapsed, leaving Hull as its only outpost in Yorkshire. In striking contrast to Cholmley's skilful play, the Hothams bungled their defection and were shipped off to London in chains; but Hull no longer posed a threat to Royalist hegemony in the North, or so it seemed. Newcastle was so confident of the security of the county that he took the bulk of his army southwards into Lincolnshire.

However, the Royalist successes of 1643 proved indecisive and short-lived: before the end of that year the tide had begun to turn in Parliament's favour. The second siege of Hull from 2 September to 11 October ended in humiliating defeat and final withdrawal. Before it finished Parliament made an alliance with the Scots which soon altered the military balance in the North. When the Scottish army crossed the border

---

[162] BL, *TT*, E95(9); HMC, *Portland*, i, pp.102, 104.
[163] BL, *TT*, E95(9); Rushworth, *Collections*, v, p.264.
[164] BL, *TT*, E95(9); Memorials (Scarborough) MS, ff.9r.–v. (see below, pp.143–4).
[165] Memorials (Scarborough) MS, ff.9r.–10r. (see below, pp.144–6); BL, *TT*, E97(8): *Certain Informations*, 10 Mar.–1 Apr. 1643.

at the beginning of 1644, Newcastle was compelled to march northwards to meet it. From that time onwards Royalist strength in Yorkshire rapidly ebbed away. When Sir John Bellasis was outmanoeuvred and forced to surrender at Selby, the Marquess had no choice but to retreat to York, thereby allowing the three armies of the Scots, the Eastern Association and the Fairfaxes to encircle the city. Any hope of a Royalist recovery was dashed by the débâcle on Marston Moor, 2 July 1644.

Nevertheless, instead of undermining Cholmley's resolve, these disasters seem to have stiffened it. He rejected Newcastle's invitation to go with him and his staff into exile. In reply he told the Marquess that he would not abandon or surrender his post at Scarborough until instructed by the King or forced to it.[166] When word from Charles in faraway Cornwall did reach Sir Hugh in August 1644 the message was to stand fast to 'the last extremity'. Cholmley was flattered into believing that a prolonged defence of the town and castle at Scarborough would misdirect Parliament's troops and thereby give Prince Rupert time and opportunity to 'make head again'.[167] The King's personal appeal to Sir Hugh's honour, allegiance and courage was well judged: from now on desertion was unthinkable.

Even so, Sir Hugh's conviction that his bogus offer of surrender terms 'meerley to gaine time and accomodations' really deceived Fairfax, diverted Manchester's army into Lincolnshire and Lord Leven's north to besiege Newcastle, was no better than wishful.[168] These major decisions of deployment after Parliament's forces had taken York on 16 July were made weeks before Cholmley made his terms known. The deliverance of the ports of Sunderland and Newcastle was considered to be of far greater priority than the capture of Scarborough, not least because of the vast stocks of coal on the banks of the Wear and Tyne which Londoners had been denied for the past two winters. Also, the Fairfaxes showed more interest in the Royalist castles at Pontefract, Knaresborough and Helmsley, not because they assumed that Cholmley was about to surrender Scarborough, but because it was now isolated, peripheral and too strong for forces under their command. Sir Hugh's repeated claim subsequently that Sir Thomas Fairfax had a thousand horse and three thousand foot only six miles from Scarborough conflicts with the facts that at this time he was besieging the weakest castle at Helmsley with only 300 cavalry and 700 infantry, who were ill-equipped and unpaid. It took three months to reduce Helmsley castle and almost cost Fairfax his life.[169]

By the end of 1644 Scarborough had ceased to be a port of entry for Royalist arms from the continent. There were now only four other strong-holds – Pontefract, Sandal, Bolton and Skipton – left to the King in the whole of Yorkshire; and with Parliament's troops quartered in neighbouring villages, Cholmley's 'Scarbrough horse' were restricted to making only the occasional surprise foray.[170] In these circumstances Parliament's committee in London preferred to wait until the early summer of 1645 before mounting an attack on Scarborough.

However, a new and dangerous threat from Scarborough now made the capture of its town, harbour and castle an urgent necessity. The fall of Newcastle to the Scots in October 1644 came just in time to release Tyneside coal to Londoners who had been

[166] Memoirs MS, f.27v. (see below, p.106).
[167] BL, Egerton MSS, 2884, f.41.
[168] Memorials (Scarborough) MS, ff.12r.–v. (see below, p.149).
[169] CSPD, 1644, p.447; R. Bell (ed.), Memorials of the Civil War, 2 vols. (1849), ii, pp.121–2; Memoirs MS, f.27v. (see below, p.106); Memorials (Scarborough) MS, f.12r. (see below, p.148).
[170] Memorials (Scarborough) MS, f.14v. (see below, p.153).

facing a possible third successive winter without sufficient fuel. Yet there was still one final impediment to the free flow of vital sea-coal traffic down the east coast: hardly a week passed without complaints from the London news-sheets of the loss of cargoes and colliers to Scarborough 'pyrates';[171] and the Royalist *Mercurius Aulicus* gloated over the many successes of the frigates of 'the gallant knight', Sir Hugh Cholmley.[172]

It was in response to this alarming assault on the capital's coal supply, and to pressure from the merchants of the east coast ports such as King's Lynn, Ipswich and Yarmouth, that Parliament's committee wrote to Lord Fairfax asking him to eliminate the threat from Scarborough.[173] Since Parliament's navy seemed incapable of maintaining a close blockade, particularly during winter weather, there was no alternative but to storm the town and seize its harbour. Cholmley might attribute his miraculous supply of 'coales, salt, and corne' to 'Devine power and providence', rather than to the boldness and skill of pirate captains such as Browne Bushell, but Parliament could not accept this explanation of their embarrassing and hurtful losses.[174]

Cholmley's own version of the fall of Scarborough town and harbour on Shrove Tuesday, 18 February 1645, to General Sir John Meldrum makes more sense than the triumphant, one-sided accounts of it in the London press. *Mercurius Britanicus* declared that Parliament's victory proved that 'God was visible at Scarborough', and it regretted only that the governor, that malignant traitor, had not been taken prisoner so that he could suffer the same fate as the Hothams who had been executed the previous month.[175] There was no truth in the Roundhead slur that Cholmley had planned to escape by sea but was forced back to the castle by the surprising speed of Meldrum's advance, or that he had terrorized the townspeople with his soldiers.[176] Surviving fragments of the corporation records indicate that Sir Hugh continued to enjoy the support of a majority of the depleted Common Hall as late as 25 November. Two days earlier, at an extraordinary gathering of the whole township in the parish church, he had promised that they would not be put to the fire and slaughter of a lengthy siege; that he would fall back to the castle if the town was attacked; and that only those who wished need follow him in there.[177]

Parliament was delighted by the news from Scarborough: the messenger who brought it was given £20, Meldrum was awarded £1,000, and, when thanks were given to God for their latest victories, Scarborough was placed at the head of the list.[178] But joy soon turned to disappointment when it was realised that Meldrum could not take the castle and that Cholmley's stubborn resistance could be broken only by a prolonged siege. In fact, the siege lasted 22 weeks and made huge demands on Parliament's resources. Meldrum had to call up the heaviest cannon, but the collapse of the keep which it caused blocked the only entrance and provided the defenders with lethal stone ammunition. To pay and supply his men Meldrum had to make appeals to the merchants of the east coast ports, who were anxious that

[171] BL, *TT*, E269(8): *The London Post*, 3 Feb. 1645; *Ibid.*, E269(14); *A Diary or An Exact Journal*, 7 Feb. 1645.
[172] *Mercurius Aulicus*, 11 Oct. 1644, *ORN*, I, iii, p.293.
[173] *CSPD*, 1644–45, p.94.
[174] Memorials (Scarborough) MS, f.14v. (see below, p.153).
[175] BL, *TT*, E270(15): *Mercurius Britanicus*, 17–24 Feb. 1645; *Ibid.*, E271(5): *Mercurius Britanicus*, 24 Feb.–3 Mar. 1645.
[176] B. Whitelocke, *Memorials of English Affairs*, 4 vols. (1732), i, p.133; J. Vicars, *England's Parliamentary Chronicle 1640–46*, 4 vols. (1646), iv, p.110.
[177] NYCRO, DC/SCB, A20, Common Hall Memoranda 1499–1737, 23, 25 Nov. 1644.
[178] *CJ*, iv, 59, 97.

Scarborough should again become a port of refuge for their ships, not for the King's privateers.[179]

Whether Parliament's commitment to the reduction of Scarborough castle was well judged in the military circumstances of the spring and early summer of 1645 is debatable, but undoubtedly it reinforced Cholmley's resolve to hold out to 'the last extremity'.[180] In the end, Sir Hugh was compelled to accept the most generous terms offered by Sir Matthew Boynton because his garrison were dying of scurvy, the castle well was running dry, and there was insufficient gunpowder to sustain a defence. Cholmley's own vivid account of the last days of the siege is largely confirmed by the balder London press reports.[181]

Cholmley was indeed very fortunate to get such terms of surrender.[182] After what he had done in March 1643, and considering the enormous losses and costs he had inflicted on Parliament since then, he might have expected to die on the scaffold like the Hothams. If Meldrum had lived he would have dictated harsher conditions than those offered by Yorkshiremen. Yet, when Sir Hugh, last of the defenders, emerged from the ruins of Scarborough castle at noon on 25 July, three days after his 45th birthday, his public career came to an end. The remaining 12 years of his life would be spent in foreign exile and private retirement. He died nearly a year before Cromwell and nearly three before the Restoration.

As Clarendon later acknowledged, Cholmley had served the King 'with courage and singular fidelity'.[183] His tenacious stand at Scarborough was a tonic to Royalist morale and infuriating to Parliament.[184] With never more than 700 men under his command, he could not have served the King's cause to greater effect: certainly not at Marston Moor or Naseby. However expedient Cholmley's initial conversion in March 1643, subsequently and increasingly he became thoroughly devoted to the 'old service'. The greater the sacrifices this service demanded, the greater his loyalty to it.

Nevertheless, there were limits to Cholmley's royalism. King Charles had offered him an English barony or any 'honour, command or benefit';[185] but he would accept no material reward for his service, partly out of pride and also because he hoped to return home, reunite his scattered family and restore his estate as soon as possible, even if this meant living under a republic. Unlike his cousin Browne Bushell or his successor as Royalist governor of Scarborough in the second Civil War, Matthew Boynton, who both died for the 'old service', even in defeat Sir Hugh had still much to live for. The war had hardened but not corrupted him: he could never have become a ruthless professional soldier like Meldrum, or a cruel one, like James King, Lord Eythin.

Sir Hugh had many virtues which the Civil War revealed at their best. He had a strong sense of public responsibility; he respected the liberties and rights of others; he always preferred compromise to conflict; and his judgement of men and situations was invariably astute. Though in the end he owed his bloodless and brilliant coup at Scarborough to the personal loyalty of Bushell, the episode demonstrated his

---

[179] HMC, *Eleventh Report*, Appendix iii, p.182; Suffolk CRO, Ipswich, HD36: 2672/25, 69, 77.

[180] *CSPD*, 1644–45, pp.446, 447.

[181] BL, *TT*, E294(11): *The Parliament's Post*, 23–29 July 1645; *Ibid.*, E294(15): *An Exact Relation*, 26 July 1645; *Ibid.*, E284(8): *A Diary or An Exact Journal*, 14 May 1645.

[182] The terms of surrender are to be found in Rushworth, *Collections*, v, pp.118–19 and BL, *TT*, E294(17): *Coppie of a Letter from Generall Poines*, 25 July 1645 (see below, pp.161–2).

[183] Earl of Clarendon, *History of the Rebellion and Civil Wars in England*, 6 vols. (Oxford, 1888), ii, p.468.

[184] *Mercurius Aulicus*, 11 Oct. 1644, ORN, I, iii, p.293; BL, *TT*, E285(7): *The Moderate Intelligencer*, 16 May 1645.

[185] Cholmley, *Memoirs* (1787), pp.iv–v.

diplomatic skill. The attempts of the Hothams to follow his lead in changing sides were by comparison sordid, inept and ill-timed. Coercion was always a last resort for Sir Hugh: he carried his officers and his soldiers with him, as he carried most of the burgesses of Scarborough, by his compassion and their consent. Again, in contrast, when in 1648 Colonel Boynton tried to bully Scarborough's Common Hall into obedience, it rebelled against him and he had to lock its doors. After 25 July 1645 there is no record of Cholmley returning to Scarborough, but the story that on that day the women of the town could scarcely be restrained from stoning him as he came out of the castle was probably yet another invention of the London propaganda machine.[186] Where his motives were concerned, Sir Hugh was capable of self-deception, but essentially he was an honest and honourable man.

---

[186] BL, *TT*, E294(15): *An Exact Relation*, 26 July 1645.

GENEALOGIES

Sir Hugh Cholmley's ancestry and family

John Cholmondeley of Chorley (Cheshire)

SIR RICHARD (I)
knt 1498, L.L. of Tower of London,
Constable of Pickering castle,
Steward of Pickering forest,
Roxby estate from 1519,
d.1521 *s.p.*

1512
Katherine, = **SIR ROGER**
dau. Sir Robert Constable   knt Flodden 1513,
of Flamborough,   inherited Roxby from his brother,
d.1585   d.1538

Margaret = (1) Sir Henry Gascoigne of Sedbury = (2) 5th E. of Westmorland
of Sedbury

Jane/Anne = 5th E. of Westmorland

SIR RICHARD (II) = (1) Margaret, dau. William,
1515–83   Lord Conyers of Hornby
'the great, black
knight of the North'
knt 1544, bought
Whitby estate,
constable
Scarborough castle,
HS Yorks. 1547–8.
1556–7,
MP Yorks. 1558

= (2) Catherine Clifford, dau. E. of Cumberland,
widow of John, Lord Scrope of Bolton
d. at Whitby 1598

FRANCIS = Joan Boulmer
d.1586 *s.p.*

Roger = Jane de la Rivers
of Brandsby

(Cholmleys of Brandsby)

Richard = Thomasin de la Rivers
of Brandsby

Margaret = James Strangways
of Sneaton

Jane = Ralph Salvin
of Newbiggin,
lord of Egton

Elizabeth = Roger Beckwith
of Selby

SIR HENRY = Margaret Babthorpe
c.1556–1616   of Osgodby d.1628
knt 1603
first
Protestant

John

Katherine = Richard Dutton
of Whitby

Richard Dutton

The Hothams of Scorborough

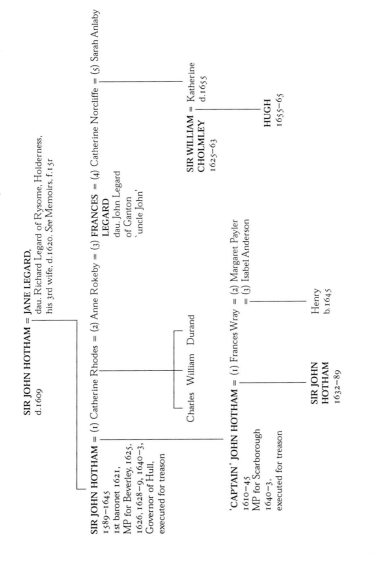

SIR JOHN HOTHAM = **JANE LEGARD,**
d.1609   dau. Richard Legard of Rysome, Holderness,
his 3rd wife, d.1620. *See Memoirs,* f.15r

SIR JOHN HOTHAM = (1) Catherine Rhodes = (2) Anne Rokeby = (3) **FRANCES** = (4) Catherine Norcliffe = (5) Sarah Anlaby
1589–1645   **LEGARD**
1st baronet 1621,   dau. John Legard
MP for Beverley, 1625,   of Ganton
1626, 1628–9, 1640–3,   'uncle John'
Governor of Hull,
executed for treason

Charles   William   Durand

'CAPTAIN' JOHN HOTHAM = (1) Frances Wray = (2) Margaret Payler
1610–45   = (3) Isabel Anderson
MP for Scarborough
1640–3,
executed for treason

Henry
b.1645

**SIR JOHN
HOTHAM**
1632–89

SIR WILLIAM = Katherine
CHOLMLEY   d.1655
1625–63

HUGH
1655–65

Descendants of Sir Hugh Cholmley

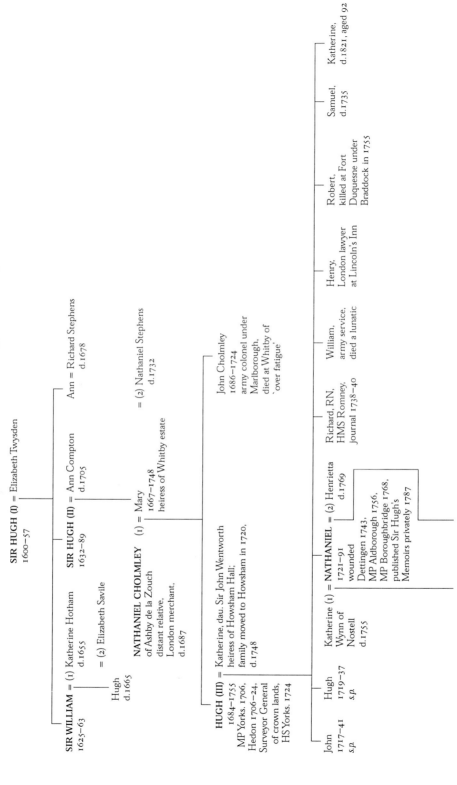

SIR HUGH (I) = Elizabeth Twysden
1600–57

SIR WILLIAM = (1) Katherine Hotham
1625–63   d.1655

= (2) Elizabeth Savile

Hugh
d.1665

SIR HUGH (II) = Ann Compton
1632–89   d.1705

Ann = Richard Stephens
d.1678

NATHANIEL CHOLMLEY (1) = Mary
of Ashby de la Zouch   1667–1748
distant relative,   heiress of Whitby estate
London merchant,
d.1687

= (2) Nathaniel Stephens
d.1732

John Cholmley
1686–1724
army colonel under
Marlborough,
died at Whitby of
'over fatigue'

HUGH (III) = Katherine, dau. Sir John Wentworth
1684–1755   heiress of Howsham Hall;
MP Yorks. 1706,   family moved to Howsham in 1720,
Hedon 1706–24,   d.1748
Surveyor General
of crown lands,
HS Yorks. 1724

John   Hugh   Katherine (1) = **NATHANIEL** = (2) Henrietta   Richard, RN,   William,   Henry,   Robert,   Samuel,   Katherine,
1717–41   1719–37   Wynn of   1721–91   d.1769   HMS Romney;   army service,   London lawyer   killed at Fort   d.1735   d.1821, aged 92
s.p.   s.p.   Nostell   wounded   journal 1738–40   died a lunatic   at Lincoln's Inn   Duquesne under
          d.1755   Dettingen 1743,   Braddock in 1755
                    MP Aldborough 1756,
                    MP Boroughbridge 1768,
                    published Sir Hugh's
                    Memoirs privately 1787

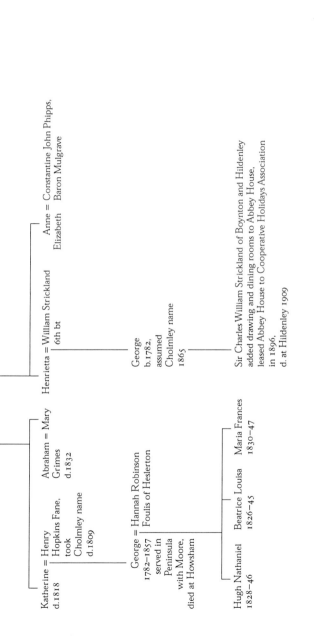

Katherine = Henry   Abraham = Mary   Henrietta = William Strickland   Anne = Constantine John Phipps,
d.1818   Hopkins Fane,   Grimes   6th bt   Elizabeth   Baron Mulgrave
took   d.1832
Cholmley name
d.1809

George = Hannah Robinson   George
1782–1857 Foulis of Heslerton   b.1782,
served in   assumed
Peninsula   Cholmley name
with Moore,   1865
died at Howsham

Hugh Nathaniel   Beatrice Louisa   Maria Frances
1828–46   1826–45   1830–47

Sir Charles William Strickland of Boynton and Hildenley
added drawing and dining rooms to Abbey House,
leased Abbey House to Cooperative Holidays Association
in 1896,
d. at Hildenley 1909

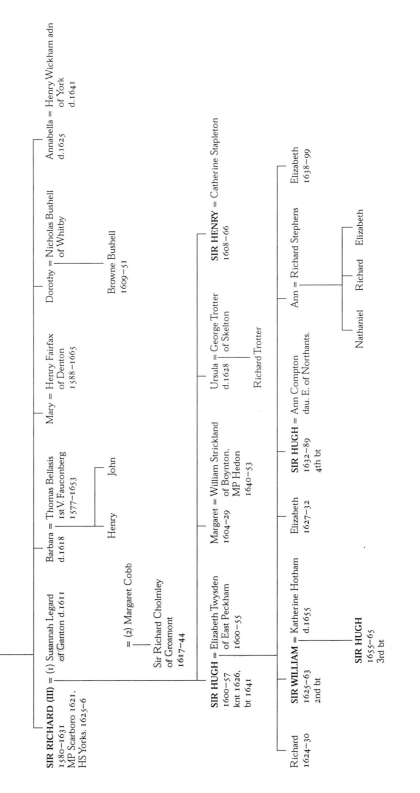

SIR RICHARD (III) = (1) Susannah Legard
1580–1631　　　　 of Ganton d.1611
MP Scarboro 1621,
HS Yorks. 1625–6

= (2) Margaret Cobb
Sir Richard Cholmley
of Grosmont
1617–44

Barbara = Thomas Bellasis
d.1618　　 1st V. Fauconberg
　　　　　 1577–1653

Henry　　　John

Mary = Henry Fairfax
　　　 of Denton
　　　 1588–1665

Dorothy = Nicholas Bushell
　　　　 of Whitby

Browne Bushell
1609–51

Annabella = Henry Wickham adn
d.1625　　　 of York
　　　　　　 d.1641

SIR HUGH = Elizabeth Twysden
1600–57　　 of East Peckham
knt 1626,　　1600–55
bt 1641

Margaret = William Strickland
1604–29　　 of Boynton,
　　　　　　 MP Hedon
　　　　　　 1640–53

Ursula = George Trotter
d.1628　　 of Skelton

Richard Trotter

SIR HENRY = Catherine Stapleton
1608–66

Richard
1624–30

SIR WILLIAM = Katherine Hotham
1625–63　　　　 d.1655
2nd bt

Elizabeth
1627–32

SIR HUGH = Ann Compton
1632–89　　 dau. E. of Northants.
4th bt

Ann = Richard Stephens

Nathaniel　 Richard　　Elizabeth

Elizabeth
1638–99

SIR HUGH
1655–65
3rd bt

Sources: Foster's *Pedigrees of Yorks. Families*, ii (1874); PB, MSS773, 4328, 4375; East Riding Portraits, *TERAS*, x (1903)

The Twysdens of Roydon Hall, East Peckham, Kent

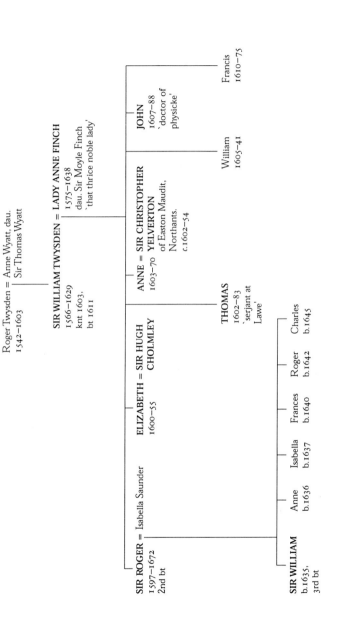

Roger Twysden = Anne Wyatt, dau.
1542–1603 | Sir Thomas Wyatt

SIR WILLIAM TWYSDEN = **LADY ANNE FINCH**
1566–1629 | 1575–1638
knt 1603, | dau. Sir Moyle Finch
bt 1611 | 'that thrice noble lady'

SIR ROGER = Isabella Saunder
1597–1672
2nd bt

ELIZABETH = **SIR HUGH**
1600–55 **CHOLMLEY**

ANNE = **SIR CHRISTOPHER**
1603–70 **YELVERTON**
of Easton Maudit,
Northants.
c.1602–54

JOHN
1607–88
'doctor of
physicke'

THOMAS
1602–83
'serjant at
Lawe'

William
1605–41

Francis
1610–75

SIR WILLIAM
b.1635,
3rd bt

Anne
b.1636

Isabella
b.1637

Frances
b.1640

Roger
b.1642

Charles
b.1645

Legards, Hothams, Cholmleys and Bushells

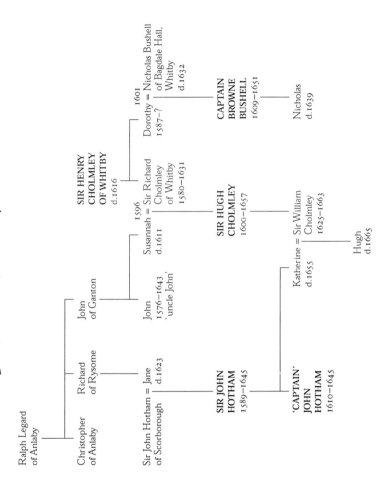

Ralph Legard
of Anlaby

Christopher   Richard   John
of Anlaby   of Rysome   of Ganton

Sir John Hotham = Jane   John   1596   1601
of Scorborough   d.1623   1576–1643   Susannah = Sir Richard   Dorothy = Nicholas Bushell
                             'uncle John'   d.1611   Cholmley   1587–?   of Bagdale Hall,
                                                      of Whitby   Whitby
                                                      1580–1631   d.1632

**SIR JOHN   **SIR HENRY   **CAPTAIN
HOTHAM**   CHOLMLEY   BROWNE
1589–1645   OF WHITBY**   BUSHELL**
                                            d.1616   1609–1651

'**CAPTAIN'   **SIR HUGH   Nicholas
JOHN   CHOLMLEY**   d.1639
HOTHAM**   1600–1657
1610–1645

                    Katherine = Sir William
                    d.1655   Cholmley
                               1625–1663

                               Hugh
                               d.1665

THE MEMOIRS

Introduction

I PURPOSE

After the sudden and shattering death of his wife in April 1655, Sir Hugh Cholmley's thoughts turned increasingly towards his own death and to posterity. By the end of the following year, the first rough draft of his Memoirs was almost complete.

At first, Cholmley's intention had been simply to praise his wife, or, as he explained in the preface, 'to imbalme her great virtues & perfections to future ages'.[1] As he gave more thought to the work, however, its scope widened. To single out only his 'deare wife' for commendation would mean excluding all those other women in his family who also merited praise: he could hardly describe the 'prime flower' without reference to 'the Garland'. Moreover, though twentieth-century feminist historians might be content to write only about members of their own sex, in the seventeenth century, as Sir Hugh explained, men had the 'greatest honour & reverence ascribed to them' and were 'commonly . . . the princypall Actors in the seane'. Therefore, his male ancestors and relatives could not be excluded either. So, what had once been intended as a dirge, written out of grief and gratitude, soon developed into a family history of the Yorkshire Cholmleys.[2]

'History' was a word that flowed naturally and frequently from Sir Hugh's pen, but not a word that he chose to describe his Memoirs. When he began the final section which dealt with his own life he first wrote, 'Beeing to write the History of my selfe . . .'; then he had second thoughts, crossed out 'History' and substituted 'Story'.[3] For Sir Hugh, history was an important subject for serious study, and it was about the more remote past and not recent events. Though he said nothing of his own reading, he was obviously proud to record of his wife that 'her cheife delight was in her booke being addicted to reade & well versed in history'.[4] Sir Hugh's father might not have been a scholar, but at least he was 'well red in History'.[5]

Cholmley's lively consciousness of the past was probably a consequence of the prime importance then given by the gentry to genealogy and family kinship. Between 1530 and 1666, the years approximately covered by his Memoirs, there were no fewer than four major heraldic visitations of Yorkshire. It was an age when rank and precedence were clearly established and society strictly stratified. One of the unsurprising purposes of Sir Hugh's Memoirs was, therefore, to confirm his distinguished ancestry and describe his kinship. As the author himself explained, without benefit of punctuation, the record of 'births matches fortunes and tymes of their deaths' of his 'Ancestors since there planting in Yorkesheire' would be 'usefull for pedigrees and evidenceing of titles'.[6] Even the most tenuous of blood and marriage ties were regarded as significant by Sir Hugh: kinship, to him, was an

---

[1] Memoirs MS (YML, Add.MS 343), f.1r. (see below, p.61)
[2] Ibid.
[3] Ibid., f.14r. (see below, p.79).
[4] Ibid., f.34r. (see below, p.119).
[5] Ibid., f.10r. (see below, p.76).
[6] Ibid., f.1r. (see below, p.61).

honourable bond which conferred both advantage and obligation. Without exaggeration, the historian of the Yorkshire gentry of this time wrote of the 'concept of clan solidarity', and Sir Hugh's Memoirs were a tribute to that concept.[7]

Sir Hugh's sharp sense of biological inheritance is evident throughout his Memoirs. He was proud that his forefathers were tall, strong men. His great-grandfather, Sir Richard (II), had been 'big & strong made haveing in his youth a very active able body, bold & stout'.[8] At considerable length he listed his father's exceptional physical qualities – his smooth, white skin, his chestnut-brown hair, curly but not frizzled, his handsome Roman nose, and his sweet, naturally-perfumed breath.[9] As for the women in his family, nearly all of them has been beautiful.[10] Though Hugh lamented that in his case poor nutrition had prevented him from developing the outstanding stature of his male ancestors, perhaps he meant the reader to conclude that he had inherited some of the more feminine characteristics of his father. Unfortunately, he refrained from describing his own appearance.

For Sir Hugh, however, genealogy was not merely a matter of physical inheritance: he believed that moral traits also were passed down from one generation to the next. At several points in the Memoirs he implied that the male Cholmleys all had a strong natural tendency towards wildness and irresponsibility; that they had bad, sometimes violent, tempers; that they were prone to idleness, gullibility and frivolity; and that they were far too amorous. In his own case, Sir Hugh readily confessed that he had totally misspent his youth, wasted his education, and sometimes given way to acts of violent temper, even in maturer years. Of other unspecified 'exstraviganses', however, he was 'temperate'; and clearly as soon as he was burdened with the heavy responsibilities of his inheritance, like Prince Hal, he was utterly transformed.[11]

If, then, the Memoirs began as a farewell tribute to Elizabeth Twysden and broadened into a family saga of the Yorkshire Cholmleys ending with the reformed hero, Sir Hugh himself, ultimately they were intended as a moral tract aimed at his descendants who were bound to inherit some or all of the family weaknesses. Cholmley's 'discourse', as he called it, was therefore dedicated to his two 'dearely bloved sonnes William and Hugh' and their unborn progeny.[12] It was to be read as a guide, a warning and an inspiration. Though he might be accused of casting dust in the faces of his ancestors, or, changing the metaphor, of defiling his own family nest, the truth had to be told; otherwise his work would lack moral value. It was not merely a question of holding up good examples to be followed; evil also had to be recognised if it was to be avoided. Besides, since Sir Hugh had no wish to broadcast his family's failings more widely than was necessary, his story was not to be published. Confident that the privacy of his revelations would be respected, he was therefore able to 'performe the duty [of] a Historian, which is to expresse all things with as much truth & clearenesse as may bee'.[13] In short, since no one outside the Cholmley family would ever see his Memoirs, he could write frankly and critically without fear of being disloyal to his ancestors.

[7] Cliffe, Yorkshire Gentry, p.11.
[8] Memoirs MS, f.4r. (see below, pp.65–6).
[9] Ibid., f.6v. (see below, p.70).
[10] Ibid., ff.4r., 6r., 11v. (see below, pp.66, 70, 78).
[11] Ibid., ff.4r., 5r., 10r., 10v., 16r. (see below, pp.66, 68, 75, 76, 83).
[12] Ibid., f.1r. (see below, p.61).
[13] Ibid.

II HISTORY

In accordance with his declared wishes, Sir Hugh Cholmley was buried next to his wife inside St Michael's church, at East Peckham in Kent. As his gravestone there records:

> Heer also lyes The Body of Sir Hugh Cholmeley her husband who for the great love he bore the virtue & worth he found in the said Elizabeth declined the being interred in his own country among his ancestors, and chose to be laid heer beside her.

This was Sir Hugh's final tribute to Lady Elizabeth. Also buried in the now-redundant church near Roydon Hall were Hugh's heir, William, who died in 1663, and his unmarried daughter, Elizabeth, who lived on until 1699. Sir Hugh's other son, named after him, and his descendants, returned to Whitby where they were buried in their own 'country'.

Like his father, the younger Sir Hugh Cholmley (1632–89) led an eventful, public life and later wrote about it at some length. Unlike his brothers and sisters, Hugh was the only child of Sir Hugh and Lady Elizabeth to be born at Fyling Old Hall. At the age of ten, when the Civil War began, he was sent to St Paul's school in London. Then, when his father changed sides the following spring, and his mother and two sisters went north to join him at Scarborough, young Hugh was left behind under the care of his school tutor. While his father stubbornly defied Parliament, and the London press railed against him, his son seems to have suffered no ill-treatment in the capital.[14]

In October 1645, young Hugh was permitted to cross the Channel and join his family. The Cholmleys were now in exile, but after many years of separation reunited in Paris. At the Stuart court at St Germain, the Prince of Wales promised to make young Hugh a Groom of the Bedchamber. This was the only reward for his service to the crown Sir Hugh would accept: from King Charles he had refused the offer of a barony for himself.[15]

In 1649 young Hugh came back to England with his parents. During the next two years he was tutored by a Fellow of Trinity Hall, first briefly at Cambridge – though he was never a member of any College there – before he returned to London. According to his own excuse, 'a violent flux' kept him in bed when in 1651 he would have preferred to fight with the royal army at the battle of Worcester. By this time, though still only a teenager, Hugh was engaged in business transactions arising from his father's new alum works at Saltwick, near Whitby. However, he appears to have suffered from at least one of the weaknesses of the male Cholmleys against which his father was to warn him: he was more interested in making love than making money. When Oliver Cromwell was setting up his Protectorate, young Hugh Cholmley was busy writing long love poems to a rich widow. Finally, in December 1653, at the age of twenty-one, his suit having failed, though not for want of trying, he again left England for Paris.[16]

Such, in brief outline, is the curious scrap of unfinished autobiography written by the younger Sir Hugh and printed as a makeshift, largely irrelevant, preface to his

---

[14] Cholmley, *Memoirs* (1787), pp.iv–v. This preface was omitted from the second edition of 1870.
[15] *Ibid.*, pp.iv–v.
[16] *Ibid.*, pp.v–ix, xxi.

father's *Memoirs* when they were first published in 1787. Cholmley's *Memoirs* occupied only 90 printed pages. They were followed by more episodes in his son's experiences – A Discourse of Tangier, A Journey Through France and Spain to Tangier in 1669–70 and, finally, a description of his construction of the harbour mole at Tangier when he was Surveyor-General of the works there. Altogether the reminiscences of the younger Sir Hugh amounted to more than three hundred printed pages, far out-weighing in bulk his father's *Memoirs*. Yet, because of their much greater historical interest and wider significance, the latter are much better known and valued than the former. Though he did not live long enough to see it happen, the greater causes of Sir Hugh the elder eventually triumphed: both the monarchy and the Church of England were restored. In contrast, his son survived to witness all his patient, costly and expert efforts come to nothing. The mole at Tangier, modelled on the great west pier at Whitby, was deliberately demolished by those who had painstakingly built it. Tangier itself, part of Catherine of Braganza's dowry, and the new settlement of Whitby put up next to it, were abandoned for ever by the English.[17]

The lives and works of the two Sir Hugh Cholmleys had little in common. Their *Memoirs*, the one short but more or less finished, the other, long, rambling and fragmentary, were published together in the same volume because a distant descendant decided to put some of his family's papers into print. Like the two Hughs, Nathaniel Cholmley (1721–91) of Whitby and Howsham, was an outstanding local benefactor and celebrity. He was also proud of his name and keenly aware of his distinguished ancestry. Probably the original manuscripts were already in poor condition and Nathaniel was concerned to preserve their contents in print. Besides, by 1787, the issues that wholly changed and almost destroyed the life and fortunes of Sir Hugh Cholmley senior were no longer so bitterly controversial: they were already history. Finally, more than a century later, no one cared much about the personal and moral matters that had been so important to Sir Hugh and so often in his thoughts at the end of his life.

Nevertheless, Nathaniel Cholmley respected the confidentiality of the elder Sir Hugh's Memoirs: he had them printed in a handsome, very restricted edition. At his expense one hundred copies only were made. In the words of the *Gentleman's Magazine*, which reviewed them in 1788, the Cholmley *Memoirs* had been printed 'for private use'.[18] Most copies therefore remained in the possession of the numerous members of the Cholmley-Strickland family and two centuries later the 1787 edition is extremely rare, and usually quoted, or misquoted, at second-hand.[19]

When Lionel Charlton was writing the first history of Whitby, Nathaniel Cholmley allowed him access to the Cholmley family papers, which included the original manuscript of Sir Hugh's Memoirs. Indeed, it seems more than likely that Charlton was the editor employed by Nathaniel Cholmley to prepare the Memoirs for later publication. Charlton's *History of Whitby* appeared in print in 1779, eight years before the *Memoirs*, yet it contains a summary of Sir Hugh's private work. Moreover, a significant number of errors in the printed edition of the *Memoirs*, caused by careless or

[17] The standard work on the short history of British Tangier is still E.M.G. Routh, *Tangier: England's Lost Atlantic Outpost, 1661–1684* (1912). For the younger Sir Hugh's involvement in the construction of the great mole, see NYCRO, ZCG, 'The Letter Book of Sir Hugh Cholmley, 1664–66'.
[18] *Gentleman's Magazine*, LVIII (1788), p.618.
[19] For example, B. Coward, *The Stuart Age* (1980), p.58 quoted Cholmley's printed *Memoirs* indirectly from Cliffe, *Yorkshire Gentry*, p.114, yet gives the author's name as 'Cholmondley'; J.A. Sharpe, *Early Modern England, A Social History 1550–1760* (1987), pp.171, 353, quoted the same passage from the *Memoirs* twice, but attributed it to 'Sir Richard Cholmley'!

THE MEMOIRS: INTRODUCTION

inexpert reading of the manuscript, first appeared in print in Charlton's *History*. For instance, when relating Sir Hugh's confrontation with armed Dutchmen in Whitby harbour, Charlton began by accepting the inaccurate date of 'about June 1637' and then, almost word for word from the manuscript, repeated Cholmley's own account of it. However, where Sir Hugh had actually written that he had 'advised' the Hollanders not to attack the Dunkirkers, Charlton read the verb as 'ordered', which was repeated in the printed *Memoirs*. Where Cholmley had written 'I gave him charge', Charlton added 'strict' between 'him' and 'charge'. Again, the word 'strict' reappeared eight years later. In the same paragraph, Cholmley's word 'drink' became Charlton's 'dine' and, excusably, 'colegarth' was converted into 'coal-yard'.[20] All these discrepancies could hardly have been coincidental: they must have been the responsibility of Lionel Charlton, or some other unknown editor from whom he made his own copy. More than a century later, another historian of Whitby wrote of Charlton that, whatever his other merits, he could 'only read the old writing imperfectly'.[21]

The earliest *Guide to Scarborough* was produced by the town's leading bookseller and antiquarian and published at York in the same year that Nathaniel Cholmley had Sir Hugh's *Memoirs* printed. Whether James Schofield really saw Sir Hugh's manuscript, as he claimed, is most doubtful. Schofield described the manuscript as a 'curious and valuable remain', and expressed his debt 'to the most obliging condescension of Nathaniel Cholmley esq., by whose favour we are enabled to present it to the public'.[22] There was no hint from Schofield of a printed version of the *Memoirs*, but it is clear that he drew his information from the published and not the manuscript work. For example, Sir Hugh had strongly condemned Members of both Houses of Parliament who, in the summer of 1642, left London to join the Cavalier court at York. Such men, he wrote, had 'ruined booth the King and Nation'. In the printed version the harshness of the verb 'ruined' was softened to 'misled'.[23] Unlike some of the misreadings of the manuscript already noted, this one at least was surely the result of deliberate falsification, not ignorance of seventeenth-century handwriting. Presumably, Sir Hugh had to be presented as a convinced Royalist, only temporarily diverted from his true allegiance by genuine misunderstanding: he could never have been a committed Parliamentarian who changed his mind. As Charlton himself put it: '. . . being deluded with the specious pretence of the Protestant religion's being in danger, and that the King's design was to subvert the rights and liberties of the nation, he (Sir Hugh) opposed the measures of the court for some time, but was at length fully convinced that the parliament was resolved not to act honourably with his Majesty . . .'.[24] So Charlton preferred 'misled' to 'ruined' and Schofield followed suit.[25]

Scarborough's first published local historian, Thomas Hinderwell, was heavily indebted, though without explicit acknowledgement, to both Charlton and Schofield. All three editions of his *History of Scarborough* referred, as Schofield's *Guide* had done, to the survival of a Cholmley manuscript which contained 'a detached account' of the town's experience of the First Civil War.[26] Yet this so-called 'manuscript' was not Sir High's 'Memorialls tuching Scarbrough', as might have been expected, but

[20] Charlton, *History of Whitby*, pp.315–16; Memoirs MS, ff.23r., 23v. (see below, pp.96–7); Cholmley, *Memoirs* (1787), pp.56–7.
[21] J.C. Atkinson, *Memorials of Old Whitby* (1890), p.viii.
[22] J. Schofield, *Historical and Descriptive Guide to Scarborough and its Environs* (York, 1787), p.92.
[23] Cholmley, *Memoirs* (1787), p.66; Memoirs MS, f.26v. (see below, p.104).
[24] Charlton, *History of Whitby*, p.316.
[25] Schofield, *Guide*, p.96.
[26] T. Hinderwell, *History of Scarborough*, 1st edn. (1798), pp.53–4; 2nd edn. (1811), p.64; 3rd edn. (1832), p.54.

again, as with Schofield, the printed *Memoirs* of 1787. Without so much as a reference to their publication, whole passages were quoted word for word from the printed *Memoirs* in all three editions of Hinderwell's *History*.[27]

One tell-tale error in Hinderwell's *History*, which appeared even in the shorter version of the third edition of 1832, came straight from Schofield, and not from the printed *Memoirs*. Sir Hugh was proud to recall that in the autumn of 1643 the Marquess of Newcastle had given him command of a whole brigade of cavalry in the Royalist army besieging Hull. This cavalry he described in a marginal additional note as 'a terse of the Army', meaning a third of it. The word 'terse' was correctly printed, though not explained, in the *Memoirs*, but in Schofield's *Guide* somehow the word had become 'curse'. Until revised to 'flower' in the longer version of the 1832 edition, the word remained 'curse' in Hinderwell's *History*.[28]

George Young followed Charlton with a second *History of Whitby*, published in 1817. Evidence survives that his preparation of it was extraordinarily painstaking. Amongst the manuscript collection of the Whitby Literary and Philosophical Society there is a bound note-book into which Young had carefully transcribed the first 242 pages of the 1787 edition of Cholmley's *Memoirs*. The pages of the note-book are water-marked 'C WILMOTT 1815' or 'C WILMOTT 1816'. Where Young believed the text to be inaccurate he added corrections in brackets. With historical facts he was invariably right. He knew, for example, that Sir Richard Cholmley (II) had bought the Whitby estate from Sir John, not Sir Edward Yorke, and that the Hothams lived at Scorborough, not Scarborough. Where there were blanks in the text, sometimes Young had supplied the missing information. For instance, he knew that the church in Micklegate, York, where many Cholmleys were buried, was dedicated to St John.[29]

Nevertheless, like Schofield and Hinderwell, Young did not have the advantage of seeing Sir Hugh's original manuscript. In his *History of Whitby* there is no evidence that he used anything other than the printed edition from which he had taken his own private transcription. That he went to so much trouble to write a copy suggests that he did not even have a printed version of his own. Young's handicap was the same as Hinderwell's: Sir Hugh's manuscript was still a jealously guarded family property and even the printed *Memoirs* were only 'for private use'.

Cholmley's *Memoirs* were printed again in 1870. This time the work of the father only, and not that of his son, was published. In outward appearance the slender volume looks like a cheap reprint. This is what T. H. Brooke thought in 1937. Though the Bodleian Library has a copy, correctly identified in its catalogue, surprisingly Brooke gave its date of publication as 1890. Only one hundred copies of this edition were produced, plus another three superior versions printed on Whatman's fine hand-made drawing paper. The edition of 1870 is now as rare as that of 1787.[30]

---

[27] T. Hinderwell, *History of Scarborough*, 1st edn., pp.54–9; 2nd edn., pp.64–9; 3rd edn., pp.54–9.

[28] Memoirs MS, f.27v. (see below, p.106); Cholmley, *Memoirs* (1787), p.69; Hinderwell, *History*, 1st edn., p.54; 2nd edn., p.67; 3rd edn., shorter, p.57; 3rd edn., longer, p.76.

[29] Whitby LPS, MS 929.2. For a long time this manuscript was thought to be the original holograph of Sir Hugh, but clearly it was copied by Young from the printed text of 1787.

[30] T.H. Brooke, 'The Memoirs of Sir Hugh Cholmeley', (unpub. B.Litt. thesis, Oxford Univ., 1937), p.1. Whitby LPS has three copies of the 1870 edition in its library, but none, surprisingly, of that of 1787. Scarborough Central Library has a fine copy of the 1787 print, though not one of 1870. Cambridge University Library has two copies, one of them annotated, of 1787, but none of 1870. The Bodleian Library at Oxford now appears to have only one edition of the *Memoirs*, that of 1870. A very fine, annotated copy of the original 1787 edition was recently auctioned in Whitby for £330.

The anonymous editor of the *Memoirs* of 1870 claimed that they were 'taken from an Original Manuscript, in his own Hand-writing, now in the possession of Nathaniel Cholmley, of Whitby and Howsham', even though by 1870 Nathaniel Cholmley had been dead for nearly 80 years. On its title page it also carried the date MDCCLXXVII, which should have been MDCCLXXXVII, the correct year of the first edition; but there was no other indication of the existence of an earlier print. Such a careless claim to authenticity puts a strain on the reader's credulity; and only when the book is examined in detail does it become obvious that the claim was genuine. Whoever was responsible for the 1870 edition must have seen Sir Hugh's own manuscript: at many places he read it differently from and more accurately than Charlton had done nearly a century earlier. Only a few examples of these discrepancies can be quoted here but enough, it is hoped, to establish that they were deliberate and significant, not accidental and not all trivial.

The clearest proof that the editor of the 1870 edition was using the original Cholmley manuscript is first to be found at the end of the section on Sir Hugh's grandfather. The first edition of 1787 reads:

> This Sir Henry . . . got a fall from his horse at the leap of a hedge, about the fifty-sixth year of his age (1616), and being a tall and corpulent man, was so bruised that Sir Richard Cholmley, eldest son to Sir Henry, succeeded to the estate . . .[31]

Apparently, some words after 'bruised that' are missing, and a footnote in the 1870 edition at this point confirms it: 'A few words', it says, 'are here illegible in the manuscript, but they probably were that "it caused his death", "Sir Richard Cholmley" beginning the next paragraph.' When the manuscript was examined by the present author it became clear what had happened. The bottom line of one sheet reads, '& beeing a tall & corpulent man was soe bruised yt', and the top line of the next sheet, 'Sr Rich Chom eldest sonne to Sr Henry succeeded to ye esstate as appears . . .' A line that was ignored in 1787, was 'illegible' by 1870, and has now disappeared altogether, either by wear or trimming.[32]

Usually the editor of 1787 included Cholmley's marginal afterthoughts in the body of the text. There was one exception, however, which in 1870 was not only noticed but also put right. After Sir Hugh had explained that his father and mother had spent seven years with the Legards at Ganton and then, in 1608, gone to live at Whitby, down the left-hand margin of the manuscript, he added the following details about his father's estate:

> haveing all the demeynes of Whitby Hausker Stanesker & Southward Howses for present maintnance w[hic]h were alsoe his wifes ioynture, And though of good vallew gave then but small rent/.[33]

Not a word of Sir Hugh's additional note was printed in 1787, whereas a footnote in the 1870 edition reads:

> Having the domagne of Whitby, Hausker Stanesacre, and Southward House, near Fyling Hall for support and maintainance, which were also his wife's jointure, and though of good value, gave them but small rent.[34]

---

[31] Cholmey, *Memoirs* (1787), p.16.
[32] Cholmley, *Memoirs* (1870), p.11; Memoirs MS, ff.5v., 6r. (see below, p.69).
[33] Memoirs MS, f.7v. (see below, p.72).
[34] Cholmley, *Memoirs* (1870), p.13.

The extra information about the location of 'Southward House' (in the singular) was the editor's, but otherwise the remainder was a rough transcription of Sir Hugh's original afterthought. By transcribing 'then' and 'them', the editor of 1870 missed a key point.

Some of the corrections made in 1870 could have been guessed without benefit of the manuscript. The first printed edition had contained many obvious errors. Where Sir Hugh had named 'Hilday' as one of the daughters of his grandfather, she first appeared in print as 'Kilday'. In 1870 'Kilday' was altered to 'Hilda'.[35] Sir Hugh had admitted that, unlike his grandfather, his father was not able 'to indite severall letters at one tyme'. By 'indite' presumably he meant 'dictate', but in 1787 'indite' became 'write' and was not correctly transcribed until 1870. The editor of 1870 never made the mistake of confusing 'Scorborough' with 'Scarborough'. Cholmley had explained that Hugh, his third son, was baptised in 'the great chamber' of Fyling Old Hall by Mr Remmington, the minister of Whitby. The first editor substituted 'church' for 'chamber'; the second restored Sir Hugh's original word.[36]

Other errors in the first edition could have been detected only by way of a careful examination of Cholmley's manuscript. For example, Sir Hugh had described how his wife was so weak after the birth of her eldest son that 'she could not move frō[m] her bed to the pallett but as I carried her in my armes'. In 1787, unaccountably, 'pallett' was transformed into 'toilet'; but in 1870 correctly rendered as 'pallet'.[37] Again, when Sir Hugh complained that ill-fortune had robbed his family of their supporters, he wrote of 'this tyme of collaption of friends'. The editor of 1787 preferred 'defection' to 'collaption', whereas in 1870 the original word was restored.[38]

It has been pointed out already that the first printed edition of the *Memoirs* made many minor, but cumulatively significant, changes to Cholmley's account of his dramatic encounter with Hollander seamen at Whitby in 1635. The overall effect of these changes was to make Sir Hugh even more heroic than he made himself, and the Dutchmen more aggressive and culpable than he said they were. The 1870 version restored some, if not total, accuracy to Cholmley's story. He had, in fact, 'advised', not 'ordered' the Dutchmen to behave themselves; he had given the Dunkirkers 'charge against', not 'strict charge against', offering injury to the Hollanders. However, what had first been written as 'drink' and printed as 'dine' again appeared as 'dine', thereby failing to convey Cholmley's sense that Dunkirkers and Hollanders had fallen out in a drunken brawl.[39]

Having said so much in defence of the 'cheap reprint' of 1870, its many, often surprising, imperfections have to be admitted. Some glaring inaccuracies of spelling in the 1787 edition were not corrected. 'Pexton Moore' in the manuscript became 'Paston Moor' or 'Paxton moor' in the first print and again in the second.[40] 'Skelton Castle', as written by Sir Hugh, really existed, but not the 'Skilton castle' which appeared in this form in both printed editions.[41] Though we might now spell his surname differently, 'Sr Will Sayvell' in the manuscript is readily identifiable, unlike

---

[35] Memoirs MS, f.5v. (see below, p.69); Cholmley, *Memoirs* (1787), p.16; (1870), p.11.

[36] Memoirs MS, ff.10r., 21v. (see below, pp.76, 94); Cholmley, *Memoirs* (1787), pp.27, 52; (1870), pp.17, 32.

[37] Memoirs MS, f.16v. (see below, p.85); Cholmley, *Memoirs* (1787), p.40; (1870), p.25.

[38] Memoirs MS, f.19v. (see below, p.89); Cholmley, *Memoirs* (1787), p.47; (1870), p.29.

[39] Memoirs MS, f.23r. (see below, p.97); Cholmley, *Memoirs* (1787), p.57; (1870), p.34.

[40] Memoirs MS, ff.14v., 24r. (see below, pp.81, 99); Cholmley, *Memoirs* (1787), pp.35, 59; (1870), pp.22, 36.

[41] Memoirs MS, f.19v. (see below, p.89); Cholmley, *Memoirs* (1787), p.48; (1870), p.29.

THE MEMOIRS: INTRODUCTION

'Sir William Cayvell' who materialised in 1870 and 1787.[42] Sir Hugh's uncle, 'Mr Jo. Legard', was still misread as 'Mr George Legard', who did not exist.[43] Sir Hugh's memory was fallible; but it was not so frequently careless as the printed *Memoirs* might suggest.

There were more serious mistakes than misspellings. When Sir Hugh had written, for instance, of events in 1649 'tuching bet erecting an allome woorke', in the first edition this became 'touching the better erecting my allum works'. Unfortunately, the second editor followed the first, not Cholmley.[44] If Sir Hugh had intended to write 'better' he had stopped at the 't' and then crossed out all three letters. He did not write 'my' or 'works'. The effect of this careless transcription was to imply that on his return from exile in France Cholmley set about improving an alum mine that already existed. In fact, sufficient evidence from other sources confirms that until 1649 no mining or manufacture of alum took place at Saltwick, the place Cholmley meant, but did not name.[45]

Though Sir Hugh never concealed the help he received from his brother after the fall of Scarborough Castle, the generosity of Sir Henry Cholmley appeared far greater in the printed than in the hand-written Memoirs. What had been originally written by Sir Hugh as 'Sr Henry Cholm who had lent mee 200l' was printed in 1787 and again in 1870 as 'Sir Henry Cholmley had sent me 200£'.[46] Was 'lent' innocently misread as 'sent', or was the change made knowingly?

Some of the eighteenth-century editing of Cholmley's manuscript, which might have been the result of unconscious or deliberate bias rather than mere carelessness, was also copied in the reprint of 1870. For instance, whatever his own anti-Catholic prejudice, Sir Hugh was honest enough to admit than in his grandfather Henry's time Abbey House at Whitby was a chief refuge for seminary priests, who came illegally into the country from the continent. However, where he wrote that his great-grandmother had asked, on her death-bed, for the 'Preists' to be put out of the house, the editors of 1787 and 1870 preferred 'priest' in the singular. Similarly, whereas Sir Hugh confessed that his grandfather, as well as his grandmother Margaret Babthorpe, clothed and fed Catholic priests in their home at Whitby, in both printed versions the phrase 'at Sir Henryes charge' was omitted and only 'at his ladys charge' included.[47] Whatever the editorial intention might have been, the effect was to put the blame for harbouring Papists more heavily on to a Babthorpe than a Cholmley.

If the printed *Memoirs* are a little less frank than the manuscript about the Catholic connections of the Cholmleys, they are also less 'Puritan' in language. Sir Hugh's phrase 'the Lo[r]d Jesus had not bene with mee' became 'the Lord had not been with me'.[48] 'Let my heart never forget to prayse the Lo[r]d' was twice printed wrongly as 'Let my heart never forget to pray to the Lord'.[49] Since Sir Hugh's religious outlook is a matter of some interest such apparently trivial alterations to his words are not entirely without importance.

No published historian has written at greater length about Sir Hugh Cholmley and

[42] Memoirs MS, f.25v. (see below, p.102); Cholmley, *Memoirs* (1787), p.64; (1870), p.38.

[43] Memoirs MS, 7v. (see below, p.72); Cholmley, *Memoirs* (1787), p.20; (1870), p.13.

[44] Memoirs MS, f.29v. (see below, p.111); Whitby LPS, PB, MS 4328, p.69; Cholmley, *Memoirs* (1787), p.74; (1870), p.45.

[45] See above, pp.12, 14.

[46] Memoirs MS, f.28r. (see below, p.108); Cholmley, *Memoirs* (1787), p.72; (1870), p.43.

[47] Memoirs MS, ff.4r., 5r. (see below, pp.66, 67); Cholmley, *Memoirs* (1787), pp.12, 14; (1870), pp.9, 10.

[48] Memoirs MS, f.18r. (see below, p.87); Cholmley, *Memoirs* (1787), p.44; (1870), p.27.

[49] Memoirs MS, f.30v. (see below, p.113); Cholmley, *Memoirs* (1787), p.78; (1870), p.47.

his family than Robert Tate Gaskin. Lionel Charlton's quarto volume gave inordinate space to the medieval history of Whitby and its Abbey, and disappointingly little to events after the Dissolution. Dr Young's two-volume history was also much concerned with the local Benedictines: the Cholmleys he confined mainly to a twelve-page biographical appendix at the end of the second volume. Even Canon Atkinson, whose knowledge of the area and understanding of the available documentary sources of its history were then unrivalled, restricted his published work to essays and anecdotes on selected subjects. He never wrote a continuous, comprehensive history of Whitby. Gaskin himself did not claim to have written a full, narrative history of the town: the sub-title, 'Chapters from the Life of its bygone People', to his *Old Seaport of Whitby* reveals the biographical bias of the work. Consequently, in a book of 450 pages Gaskin devoted as many as 87 entirely to the Cholmley family and more to matters that concerned it indirectly.[50]

It would be reassuring to discover that Gaskin had consulted Cholmley's manuscript, but his book contains no evidence that he ever saw it. Though he did not accept it uncritically, all Gaskin's explicit references were to the printed edition of 1787. At no point did he quote, or even acknowledge the existence of, either an original manuscript source or a second edition in print. Nevertheless, there are enough clues in his direct quotation from the *Memoirs* to indicate that he had indeed used a copy of the 1870 edition. He knew that Hugh Cholmley junior was baptised at Fyling Old Hall, not in Whitby church; that his father had 'advised', not 'ordered', Dutchmen to keep the peace; and that he had written 'ruined', not 'misled', when describing the ill-effects of Members of both Houses joining the King at York in the summer of 1642. These details Gaskin could have known only by reference to the second edition of Sir Hugh's *Memoirs*.[51]

There was one occasion where Gaskin noticed a discrepancy between the two printed versions and offered both interpretations to the reader. After listing his father's many physical charms, Sir Hugh had concluded with the meaningful comment: 'all w[hic]h rendered him favoured amongst the femall sex'. In 1787, 'favoured' was altered to 'famous', but in 1870 correctly restored.[52] In Gaskin's version, 'famous' is immediately followed by 'favoured' in brackets with a question mark inside them – (favoured?).[53] Unlike the editors of 1787 and 1870, Gaskin's familiarity with the locality and its history saved him from misspelling family and place-names in almost every case. Consequently, even without direct access to Sir Hugh's manuscript, Gaskin succeeded in producing the most accurate rendering of it in print.

When he wrote his thesis on 'The Memoirs of Sir Hugh Cholmeley' in the late 1930s, T.H. Brooke seems to have been totally at the mercy of the 1787 edition. He was aware of the existence of a second printed version, but dismissed it, unfortunately, as a 'cheap reprint'. Also, mistakenly, he assumed that the original manuscript in Sir Hugh's own hand could not be found, and he was prepared to accept that it was either lost or destroyed. On the other hand, to be fair to Brooke, there was a note of cautious scepticism in his final comment on Cholmley's manuscript: '. . . all attempts to trace the original manuscript have proved vain. According to the possessors of such family records as exist, the Memoirs have been "lost", a rather remarkable fate for such a bulky document.'[54] Whether Brooke really made exhaustive efforts to trace the

[50] Gaskin, *Old Seaport*, pp.103–89.
[51] *Ibid.*, pp.141, 145, 156.
[52] Memoirs MS, f.6v. (see below, p.70); Cholmley, *Memoirs* (1787), p.18; (1870), p.12.
[53] Gaskin, *Old Seaport*, p.120.
[54] Brooke, thesis, pp.1, 9.

manuscript cannot be said, but it seems that, like the present writer, he received no help from the surviving members of the Yorkshire Cholmleys.

Brooke was conscious, of course, that the 1787 edition must have departed at many points from Sir Hugh's manuscript: he noted that spelling and punctuation had been modernised, and that there were some obvious cases of slipshod transcription. However, Brooke was reassured by the style of the printed *Memoirs*, which he took to be mid-seventeenth, not late eighteenth-century, and he felt that the editor of 1787 had not taken the extreme liberties that the editor of Sir John Reresby's Memoirs had done. Accordingly, Brooke simply reproduced the printed version of 1787 with only minimal corrections as an appendix to his thesis.[55]

Without the manuscript, however, Brooke could not determine which errors in the text were printer's, which were the result of careless or inexpert reading of the original, or how many could be traced back to Sir Hugh himself: he had to resort to guesswork. Correctly, he surmised that Cholmley must have known that the name of his aunt was 'Hilda' and not 'Kilday': here was an obvious case of the editor being unable to distinguish between Sir Hugh's capital letters. On the other hand, Brooke also assumed, this time wrongly, that Cholmley was not responsible for misdating the opening of the Long Parliament. In fact, surprisingly, on this rare occasion, the mistake was Sir Hugh's: he had written in the manuscript that 'a Parlamt was agreed on & sumoned in Nov. following being *Anno Domini* 1641'.[56]

Brooke was able to convince himself that the only major inaccuracies in the printed *Memoirs* concerned sums of money, such as debts, incomes, land values, portions and fines. His 'irresistible conclusion' was that Cholmley had consistently exaggerated the figures or that the editor of 1787 had brought them up to match contemporary values.[57] Again, Brooke was mistaken: all but one of Sir Hugh's figures had been read and printed as he had written them. What Brooke failed to appreciate was that Cholmley had often translated values from past into contemporary terms which appeared to exaggerate them. Otherwise, Brooke comforted himself with a thought that was mainly wishful: he concluded that the possession of 'the manuscript would probably add nothing to Sir Hugh's account of his own career'.[58]

In his bibliography Brook cited the histories of Charlton and Young, though he gave the date of publication of the latter as 1810, instead of 1817. Schofield was not one of his secondary sources; and neither was Gaskin. The three editions of Hinderwell's *History of Scarborough* differ substantially from each other, and the third of 1832 is undoubtedly the most accurate and informative on the life of Sir Hugh Cholmley. Brooke referred only to the second edition of 1811. In conclusion, not only was Brooke ignorant of Sir Hugh's manuscript, he did not have even the best access to it through secondary sources.

Sometime during the 1950s, the Whitby antiquarian, Percy Burnett, made a manuscript copy of Sir Hugh's original Memoirs. He felt certain that it was indeed the manuscript of 1656. How he acquired it, and how afterwards he disposed of it, remain mysteries. Unhappily, Burnett did not have a copy of the first edition of the printed *Memoirs* to compare it with the manuscript: he had to rely entirely on the 1870 edition. He also had access to Dr Young's manuscript, but he did not know that it was a perfect copy of the 1787 print. Burnett soon realised that the old manuscript before

[55] *Ibid.*, pp.9–10, 162–309.
[56] Brooke, thesis, p.9; Memoirs MS, f.26r. (see below, p.103); Cholmley, *Memoirs* (1787), p.64; (1870), p.39.
[57] Brooke, thesis, p.10.
[58] *Ibid.*, p.12.

him and the later one in Young's handwriting were far from identical. He also noticed that there were many discrepancies between Cholmley's manuscript and quotations from his *Memoirs* in the histories of Young and Gaskin. Apparently, Burnett was unaware of Brooke's unpublished thesis, though it is doubtful whether he would have learned much from it: he probably knew more about the Cholmleys than its author. It also seems probable that Burnett did not appreciate that no historian had seen Cholmley's manuscript since Charlton in the 1770s.[59]

The document copied so carefully by Percy Burnett was almost intact: its pages had been bound together in red-leather covers. Perhaps because they had become worn and ragged, or they were too large for the covers, some of Cholmley's folios had been trimmed at the edges and had lost their bottom lines. On the last sheets many words down the right-hand margins were also lost, but the printed edition of 1870 indicated to Burnett what these words must have been. Only in a few places were there insertions or alterations in another, later hand. Most of Sir Hugh's gaps were still blank. No pages were missing; all of them were legible. The ink had not faded away or spread. Since whole pages and several paragraphs had been originally crossed out and re-written, it was clearly a first draft, not a finished, polished work.[60]

Percy Burnett spent the better part of a life-time copying out primary documents. He was an untrained expert, qualified only by high intelligence, tireless enthusiasm and unremitting practice. All his work, which runs to more than 70 volumes, was thorough, painstaking and accurate. His attention to the smallest detail was astonishing and admirable; his stamina was colossal. Burnett's copy of Cholmley's manuscript was word for word and letter for letter. He never knowingly changed a pen mark and only very rarely made a mistake: he copied everything just as it was written. The absolute reliability of No. 4328 in Volume 41 of Burnett's huge collection of transcripts is therefore guaranteed.[61]

Fortunately, about 20 years after Burnett made his transcript, and some time after his death, Sir Hugh's Memoirs were rediscovered. In September 1976, Professor G. E. Aylmer, then of York University, and Mr C. B. L. Barr, the Chief Librarian, examined a manuscript which had lately come into the possession of York Minster Library. To their experienced eyes, the document appeared to be 'the original holograph copy by Sir Hugh . . . showing signs of revision', but written on paper and in script of 'the mid-seventeenth century'. The manuscript, they decided, had been badly misused in early life, rather crudely repaired, and bound in red leather covers, probably at the time of the first print in 1787. Gold letters on the outside of the spine misleadingly described the volume as 'Memoirs of Sr Hugh Cholmley 1600'. Inside the covers were 32 sheets of foolscap size written on both sides in a mixture of secretary-hand and italics. As conclusive proof that this was indeed the same work as that transcribed by Percy Burnett, inside the front cover in his unmistakable hand were written the figures '4328', his reference number for the Cholmley manuscript.[62]

In the event, Burnett's transcript was a timely and providential undertaking. About

---

[59] Whitby LPS, PB, MS 4328, i.

[60] Whitby LPS, PB, MS 4328. Burnett's transcript has now been paginated.

[61] At this point, I must record my great debt to the officers of the Library of the Whitby Literary and Philosophical Society, in particular the late Mr G.N. Benson and Mr H. Brown, who amongst many other generous services provided me with their personal recollections of Percy Burnett, who died in 1972.

[62] There is another manuscript of Cholmley's Memoirs in the Cholmley (Howsham) papers in the Archives Department of Hull University Library: DCY 17/4; but it is very incomplete and no more than a nineteenth-century copy of the printed edition of 1787. Half a dozen pages are missing from the middle of the Memoirs, and the manuscript peters out before they end.

40 years later, in 1995, the manuscript is now in very poor condition. Some of Cholmley's sheets are so badly worn and the ink so blurred or faded that it would be extremely difficult to match, let alone improve on his version, even with the aid of ultra-violet light enhancement. Nevertheless, with the original, albeit decayed, manuscript and Burnett's excellent copy of it, it is now possible to produce a faithful and full facsimile of what Sir Hugh Cholmley wrote down in 1656.

III THE MANUSCRIPT

Naturally, there are many gaps and inaccuracies in Sir Hugh's manuscript. He could not have been expected to remember unaided every name and date, and often he did not try. Where he could not recall a detail he left a space in the manuscript which he probably intended to fill at a future opportunity. That opportunity never came: he did not return to Whitby to consult his family and estate records and to check his references. The blanks and the errors were still there when he died.

Only in a few instances did the editors of 1787 and 1870 resist the temptation to fill the gaps left by Cholmley. Usually, though not always, their insertions were correct: where they were not, a succession of commentators have pointed out their editorial errors. More than a century ago, the editor of *Flower's Visitation* wrote that the printed *Memoirs* were 'full of mistakes as to names, and dates, and facts'.[63] Young, Gaskin and Brooke all cited many examples of such errors.[64] However, since none of these men saw Sir Hugh's own work, none was able to distinguish between original and subsequent editing mistakes. In fact, as the manuscript reveals, Cholmley was usually more careful than his editors. One date that he could not forget was that of his wife's death. He was so deeply upset by it that he recorded the event of 17 April 1655 no fewer than three times. Unaccountably, both printed works substituted 'the 18th of April' in the last of these three entries.[65] Even Brooke did not notice this odd discrepancy.

Sir Hugh's manuscript was no more than a rough, first draft. It therefore contained many alterations, especially of numbers, and numerous deletions and additions, both above the lines and down the margins. Several lengthy passages were crossed out and entirely re-written. The longest of these revised passages ran to one and a third pages. In the main it described the events of 1632 and 1633 – the death of Sir Hugh's eldest daughter, the first Elizabeth, the birth of his son Hugh, the failure to deceive his mother by trying to pass off the nurse's baby as hers, the visit of Lady Anne to Fyling Old Hall, and, finally, Sir Hugh's initial failure to purchase Daletown and Aislaby. He crossed out all of it and then wrote a new paragraph on his efforts to repair Whitby harbour piers. On second thoughts he had recalled that this had taken place in the spring of 1632 before any of the family events already recorded. Cholmley wanted to maintain a strict chronology. As for the re-written passage, which was the one eventually printed, it is interesting to compare it with the original, deleted version. Sir Hugh softened the earlier formality of 'my daughter Elisabeth' to 'my little girle Bette', who in print appeared as 'Betty'. On his second attempt he also added that she was only four and a half years old when she died. Finally, he also remembered when

[63] C.B. Norcliffe (ed.), *Flower's Visitation of Yorkshire*, Harleian Society (1881), p.54, n.11.
[64] Young, *History of Whitby*, ii, pp.829, 832; Gaskin, *Old Seaport*, pp.105, 109, 119, 128; Brooke, thesis, pp.167, 168, 176, 185, 208, 252, 256.
[65] Memoirs MS, ff.31v., 34v., 35v. (see below, pp.115, 120, 121); Cholmley, *Memoirs* (1787), p.91; (1870), p.54.

he came to re-write the account of Hugh's birth that just prior to it his mother had suffered a heavy fall from her horse. The accident might have been fatal for both of them but resulted only in the baby having 'a wristled nale' in one of his little fingers 'as if it had bene crushed'.[66]

Another deleted then re-written section in the manuscript concerned Sir Hugh's father. Again, the author's afterthoughts make interesting comparison with his first. Originally, Sir Thomas Hoby was 'a troblesome neighbour'; six pages later he had become 'yt perverse troblesome neighbour'. In the deleted passage Sir Hugh argued that his father might have become as eminent as some of his highly successful contemporaries such as 'Sr Thom.Wentworth & Sr Jo Savell who by their owne active sperrets raised their persons & ffamuly to Honr. & greatness, beeing infearior to nether of them in understanding or vollubillety of speech'. The rewritten and subsequently printed version made the same claim for Sir Richard's potential ability and unfulfilled promise, but without naming Wentworth and Savile. In both accounts Sir Hugh wrote that his father could speak both 'elequently & rationally', which appeared in print in 1787 as 'eloquently and orationally'![67]

There are other instances where the re-written and printed version is less informative than Cholmley's erased first draft. When explaining how and why he became a North Riding Justice, Sir Hugh's first reference to Hoby was as 'a troblesome neighbour . . . who had cost my father many a 100 in sutes'. Later this description was changed to 'my fathers old enemy Sr Thom Hoby'.[68] Sometimes, even the slightest correction is revealing. 'I put my selfe in to ye Comission' [of peace] was Cholmley's first attempt. Later, he altered this to 'I condiscended to bee put in to the Comission'.[69] Perhaps he wanted to be thought of as public-spirited, and not ambitious.

There was just one heavily deleted paragraph in the manuscript that was not re-written and has never been printed. This paragraph occurs immediately before Sir Hugh's announcement of his marriage to Elizabeth Twysden. It reads:

> A little before my leaveing Grayes In, one Mr Lovesesse a Kentis gentleman brought mee acquainted in a journey with my deare wife by an accydentall meeting in Hide parcke wth some other friends of his, I liked her well as theire was good cause yet noe Motion set on foote but ye suppreame wisdome who orders all things & disposeth all things haveing determined it should be [a ma]tch betweene produced.[70]

At no other place in the Memoirs, except in this passage, did Sir Hugh even hint that he had ever seen, let alone met, his bride before they were married. So why did he cross it out? There seems no reason why he should wish to suppress reference to an accidental and respectable meeting in Hyde Park with his future wife. Suspicion soon gathers that Sir Hugh himself did not act as censor, and that the paragraph was erased by the editor of 1787. It is the only deleted part of the Memoirs not subsequently rewritten by the author. It is also the only passage in the manuscript so strongly crossed out by horizontal wavy lines that it has become very difficult to decipher: all

---

[66] Memoirs MS, ff.20v., 21r., 21v. (see below, pp.91–3); Cholmley, *Memoirs* (1787), pp.51–2; (1870), pp.31–2.

[67] Memoirs MS, ff.7r., 7v., 10r. (see below, pp.71, 72, 76); Cholmley, *Memoirs* (1787), p.27.

[68] Memoirs MS, f.22v. (see below, p.95), Cholmley, *Memoirs* (1787), p.55; (1870), p.33.

[69] *Ibid.*

[70] Memoirs MS, f.16r./Whitby LPS, PB, MS 4328, p.35 (see below, p.84).

other deletions are indicated by two or three parallel diagonals and remain perfectly legible. Not that the content of this paragraph is very significant. As Cholmley readily admitted, his marriage was pre-arranged. However, it might be of interest that he should believe the 'match' was determined by the 'suppreame wisdome', whereas we would be inclined to attribute responsibility for it to the two earthly fathers, Sir William Twysden and Sir Richard Cholmley.

Cholmley's abbreviations were sometimes peculiar and idiosyncratic, but his punctuation and spelling followed mid-seventeenth century fashions. 'Cholmley' was reduced to 'Cholm', 'Cho', or even 'Ch'; 'King' was invariably written as 'K', and 'Earl' as 'E.'. 'Peckham', 'Hotham' and 'William' lost their last letter and gained the abbreviation sign over the 'ā'. Similarly, 'from' became 'frō'. Sir Hugh used standard contractions of 'the', 'that', 'which', 'and', 'with' and 'your', but not of words beginning with 'por' or 'per'. Burnett was puzzled by Cholmley's habit of adding an extra 'e', as in 'soe', 'bee', 'doe', and 'mee' at the end of a word, or in the middle of one ending in 'ing', as in 'morneing', 'dyeing' and 'Fyleing'. 'Yorkeshiere' always got two extra 'es'. Yet this practice was again not uncommon in Sir Hugh's time. Cholmley also observed the custom of preferring 'y' where we would expect 'i', as in 'tyme', 'princypall' and 'affayre', and 'i' where we would use 'j', as in 'iniury', 'iust', 'iorney' and 'subiect'. Cholmley's spelling was consistently inconsistent. 'Cousin' also appeared as 'coosen' and 'cosen'; german as 'Jerman' and 'Jermyn'; and 'colonel' as 'corronall' and 'corronell'. In this matter, perhaps some allowance should be made for a north countryman's pronunciation of vowels. The word 'good' was nearly always written as 'gud', 'woman' as 'woeman', 'called' as 'cauled', 'both' as 'booth' or even 'bwth', and 'enough' as 'anuffe'. Sir Hugh's punctuation was conspicuously sparse. Full-stops are rare finds: the semi-colon served most of his purposes. Quotations benefited from neither spacing nor inverted commas.

If Brooke had found the original manuscript of the Memoirs he would have been surprised how 'unpolished' it was compared with what he thought were Cholmley's other extant writings, particularly his Memorials.[71] The Memoirs came nearly ten years after the Memorials so that the time difference might account for some changes in style and spelling. The Memorials, however, were commissioned by Clarendon for his use and Sir Hugh would have taken some pains with them, whereas the Memoirs were hastily put together and not meant to go outside the Cholmley family. All three Memorials were finished essays; but illness and then death prevented him from making a fairer copy of his Memoirs. Indeed, as the manuscript, but not the printed versions, shows, Cholmley changed his mind about the last part of his Memoirs. Eighteen months after Lady Elizabeth's death, by about October 1656, Sir Hugh had reached the end of his narrative. Then he decided to add a postscript in the form of a final tribute to his wife. At first, this eulogy was written in the third person until the point where he had just penned: 'After her husbands returne out of France they'. He was then seized with doubt, ran his pen through this last line, and then resumed in the first person with: 'After my returne out of France we . . .'. Subsequently, he went back over the postscript making the same conversion from third to first person.[72]

Cholmley's postscript, his last known work on paper, contained an exceptional number of mistakes, corrections, insertions, revisions and repetitions. As noted above, he recorded the date of his wife's death no fewer than three times: clearly, he was still profoundly distressed by his loss. Perhaps also, in this final year of his life, his own

---

[71] Brooke, thesis, p.10.
[72] Memoirs MS, ff.33r.–35v. (see below, pp.116–22).

mental and physical powers were rapidly deteriorating. We do not know the cause of his death.

IV HISTORICAL VALUE

Sir Hugh Cholmley wrote the Memoirs, in his own hand, during the last two years of his life. When his wife died in April 1655, he had been at Whitby, too far away for him even to attend her funeral in Kent. Soon afterwards, however, he left Yorkshire for the last time to live finally with his Twysden in-laws at Roydon Hall. His Memoirs were written there.

Because Cholmley wrote his family history and autobiography 350 miles from home, with few documents at hand and no one to help him, he had to rely almost entirely on his own memory. In these unpromising circumstances it is therefore astonishing that he was able to recall so much and so accurately. Where his memory failed he left blanks: he never knowingly invented. Occasionally, he thought he knew a date or a name that was wrong. Yet these omissions and errors matter little to a historian: the dates and names of his forebears can be readily retrieved from published heraldic visitations, parish registers and family pedigrees. What Sir Hugh recalled and chose to record, often in vivid language, remains of great value, particularly to the social historian of his times.

Professor's Stone's models of upper-class families in the sixteenth and seventeenth centuries have been subjected to many attacks from different directions.[73] For what they are worth, Cholmley's Memoirs lend support to Stone's critics, but none to his theses. According to Sir Hugh, the Cholmleys did not conform to either the 'open lineage family', which Stone believed existed between 1450 and 1630, or the 'patriarchal nuclear family', which allegedly flourished between 1550 and 1700.[74]

In fact, Cholmley's Memoirs reveal a richly varied pattern of marital relationships over several generations within the same family. Sir Hugh's great-grandfather, Richard (II), was so 'exstraordnarely given to the love of woemen' that his second wife, the formidable Lady Katherine, eventually refused to 'connive at [his] amorous courses' and denied him her bed 'for divers yeares'. The two were reconciled only by accident when 'comeing to a gentlemans house where there was strate of lodgeing' they were obliged to share the same chamber. The result was 'the lady that night conceyved with child which proved a sonne and was named Henry', Sir Hugh's grandfather. After this, the couple 'lived kindly together'.[75] That Katherine was the daughter of the Earl of Cumberland and widow of Lord Scrope before she married Sir Richard and that, according to Sir Hugh, she was of 'very great sperrit', might help to explain why she dared to deny the great black knight his conjugal rights.

However 'great', the great black knight, he was also unable to prevent Francis, his eldest son and heir, from marrying a woman whom he thought Francis should have kept only as his mistress. Tall and 'very valliant' as he was, this Francis was 'soe exceedingly over topped & guided by his wife' that 'it was thought she did [it] by witch craft or some exstrardnary meanes'. If there was a general rule that Elizabethan

[73] L. Stone, *The Family, Sex and Marriage in England 1500–1800* (1977) was originally reviewed critically by E.P. Thompson in *New Society* (Sept. 1977), and by K. Thomas in *The Times Literary Supplement* (21 Oct. 1977).

[74] Stone, *Family, Sex and Marriage*, Parts Two and Three. More recent investigations of family life during this period have also questioned the validity of Stone's hypotheses: see K. Wrightson, *English Society 1580–1680* (1982), pp.89-113; R.A. Houlbrooke, *The English Family 1450–1700* (1984), *passim*.

[75] Memoirs MS, ff.3r., 4r (see below, pp.64, 66).

wives were submissive and obedient to their husbands, then Joan Cholmley was an extreme exception to it. She was of such a 'haughty sperret' that over the porch to their new house at Whitby she had the first letter of her name precede that of her husband's, 'for where it should have bene F J she had made it J F'.[76]

In the next Cholmley generation, Sir Hugh's grandmother, Lady Margaret, exercised at least as much influence in the Whitby household as Lady Katherine had done previously at Roxby. Indeed, the regime at Abbey House in the 1590s resembled more of a matriarchy than Professor Stone's male-dominated models. Significantly, it was Lady Margaret, not her husband, who went to prison for persistent and unrepentant recusancy, and it was at her expense financially that 'symenary preists' were fed, clothed and sheltered at Abbey House. Sir Hugh was careful to distinguish between his grandfather's confirmation in 'the Protestant Relegion' and his grandmother's absolute conversion to it.[77]

Sir Hugh's father was heavily dependent on his wife, Susannah Legard. She was 'a very prudent discrett woeman', so that her sudden, early death had the effect of putting all Sir Richard's 'domesticke affayres in to disorder & occationed his breakeing up house'. In a marginal afterthought, Hugh even went so far as to claim that had his mother lived she would have 'prevented the saile of all those lands w[hic]h came to passe after her'. His conclusion was that 'wee may see a virtuous wise woeman is a great support to a famuly'.[78] Perhaps Sir Hugh's judgement on his mother's influence was derived from filial devotion more than reliable memory, but the high value he placed on the loyal support and guidance of a wife was real enough.

As for Sir Hugh's own marriage, whatever contemporary public convention or appearances, his Memoirs reveal that privately it was a partnership of loving equals. Though the match was arranged by their fathers, the couple were soon devoted to each other. If, like his male ancestors, Hugh had 'amorous courses', we are given no hint of them. Even without Cholmley's Memoirs, written explicity to praise 'her great virtues & perfections', it is clear that Lady Elizabeth was a woman of physical courage, determination and loyalty. Deservedly, she figured prominently in a recently-published work on seventeenth-century heroines. Of his wife's many outstanding qualities, Sir Hugh was most proud to recall her bravery during the siege of Scarborough Castle:

> . . . my deare wife indured much hardshippe & yet with little shew of troble, & though by nature according to her sex tymerous, yet in greatest danger would not bee da[u]nted but shewd a courridge even about her sex.[79]

If Cholmley's forebears usually had loving marriages, they also loved their children. Early in his Memoirs, Sir Hugh recounted how his great-grandfather had arranged to marry his daughter Katherine to Lord Lumley. Sir Richard had already paid part of the dowry, a thousand pounds, and the date of the wedding was fixed; but Katherine told her father that she would rather be dead than wed to Lord Lumley. She had fallen in love with her music and dancing teacher, a penniless, younger son called Richard Dutton. Though the Lumley match was obviously Sir Richard's strong preference, and by breaking it he lost face and forfeited the thousand pounds, Katherine was allowed to marry Dutton. Moreover, when he died, Sir Richard left his favourite

[76] *Ibid.*, f.4v. (see below, p.67).

[77] *Ibid.*, ff.5r., 5v. (see below, pp.67, 68); *APC*, 1592–93, pp.317–18.

[78] Memoirs MS, ff.7v., 11v. (see below, pp.72, 78).

[79] *Ibid.*, f.28r. (see below, p.108); A. Fraser, *The Weaker Vessel* (1984), pp.163, 164, 201–2, 209–10.

daughter, who had defied and disgraced him, land and leases to the value of five or six hundred pounds at Pickering. The Duttons seem to have lived long and happily on their Cholmley inheritance.[80]

Sir Hugh's own characteristic conclusion on this episode was that fathers should not permit their daughters to spend time alone with their young male tutors. On the other hand, the historian of mid–Tudor England might gather from it that the iron law of arranged marriages was sometimes more malleable than might be assumed; and that, in this case at least, paternal affection proved stronger than material self-interest. Whatever other families of the time might have been like, the Cholmleys were never a mere convenient group thrown together only by the need to procreate and to preserve inheritance.

The great black knight's indulgence of his daughter was typical, not exceptional, in the Cholmley family. Children frequently overrode their parents' wishes. At the age of 16, Hugh's father, Richard, refused to leave his new wife behind and return to his studies at Cambridge, as 'Sir Henry thought fitt'.[81] When Hugh himself was about the same age, his father gave him 30 pounds in gold, which he could not afford, and trusted him to take care of his own affairs at Cambridge.[82] There is no suggestion in the Memoirs that Hugh was ever chastised by Sir Richard for wasting his money and his youth in drinking, gambling and neglect of learning. On the other hand, though aware of his father's many faults, Hugh was strongly attached to him.[83]

Hugh and Elizabeth had six children altogether, born between 1624 and 1638. Two of them died young: the eldest boy, Richard, at the age of five, and the eldest girl, the first Elizabeth, when she was only four and a half. A quarter of a century later, Hugh was still moved to grief by his memory of them. Richard, he recalled, 'was much fairer & more beautifull then other my brood for his haire was amber couller his eies gray & his complection as fayre white & red as ever I saw'. With pride, Hugh remembered how even as a child he had 'the courridge & resolution of a man for beeing to have an incission on a lumpe which aroase in his arme he would say, father would you have it done & I answeard yes sweetheart for your Doctor thinks it necessary then would he say doe it & held his arme with out ether shrinkeing or whimpering, though blood and corruption rann out'.[84]

Richard was soon replaced by William, but when 'little girle Bette' died at Fyling Old Hall her parents' grief was greater still. 'Wee were exceeding fond of her,' wrote Sir Hugh, 'booth in respect she was like her Mother, & as witty a child I thinke as was in the world of her age . . .'. The couple were so upset that they could not bear to be reminded of their daughter. 'To put the death of our girle out of our myndes I with my wife & famuly removed to a place cauled Lankton neare to Malton.' They stayed at Langton on the Wolds all that winter and did not return to Fyling until Easter 1633.[85]

Putting newly-born babies out to wet-nurses would be today considered unnatural and cruel, but clearly it had no such implication for Hugh and Elizabeth. While they wintered at Langton, their latest offspring, the two-month-old Hugh, was left in the care of a nurse at Southward houses. Southward or Southwell (now known as South

---

[80] Memoirs MS, f.3r. (see below, p.64); Aveling, *North Catholics*, p.184.

[81] Memoirs MS, f.6r. (see below, p.69).

[82] *Ibid.*, f.15v. (see below, p.82).

[83] *Ibid.*, ff.10r.–10v. (see below, pp.75–6).

[84] *Ibid.*, f.20v. (see below, p.91); Cholmley, *Memoirs* (1787), p.50; (1870), pp.30–1. Both printed versions have 'whining' instead of 'whimpering'.

[85] Memoirs MS, f.21v. (see below, pp.93–4).

House Farm) was then a collection of four adjacent farms at the southern extremity of the Cholmley estate. At that time the main house there was occupied by George Conyers, a close family friend and long-standing tenant of the Cholmleys. When Hugh and Elizabeth came back to Fyling at Easter 1633 the infant Hugh, now about eight months old, was immediately recognised by his mother as hers even though he had been dressed in rough clothes and Sir Hugh had told the nurse to pretend that he was her own child. Hugh's comment was that 'it was pretty & admirable to see how by the instinct of nature she had found out her owne child'.[86]

The Cholmleys invariably put their children first. When Sir Hugh declared for the King in the spring of 1643, and Lady Elizabeth obtained a pass in London to sail to Whitby, she brought their two daughters with her. Ann was then eight and the second Elizabeth only four years old. The two girls stayed with their parents until the siege of Scarborough town began in February 1645. Elizabeth would not 'forsake' her husband 'for any danger'; but, 'not without great troble', they decided to send the girls to the safety of Holland. When Sir Hugh himself went into exile six months later, his first thought was to find his two daughters and send them back to their mother in Yorkshire. His second thought was to travel on to France, to find his eldest son William, and to rescue him from the fate of a mercenary soldier. The reunification of the whole Cholmley family – his wife, their two sons and two daughters – at Rouen in May 1647 was an event that brought the greatest relief and joy to Sir Hugh.[87]

Such personal details of Sir Hugh's family might well be unrepresentative, but other evidence in his Memoirs has probably wider and greater significance. On the subject of Sir Hugh's great-grandfather, for instance, the Memoirs provide several vivid glimpses of obsolescent feudalism. In his heyday, like a medieval tenant-in-chief, Sir Richard raised his own fighting men when called upon by the King to fight the Scots. At his fortified manor house at Roxby he kept 'a very great famuly at least 50 or 60 men servants'. These included 'iddle serveing men' who helped themselves to their master's meat, so that even when 'there had bene 24 peices of beefe put in a morneing in to the pot some tymes not one of them would bee left for his owne dinner'.[88]

Sir Hugh's image of the great black knight's retainers going into the kitchen and striking their daggers into the beef pot without the 'Cookes leave or prevety' is a memorable one for us as it was for him.[89] Plainly, he was sharply aware of the enormous changes that had occurred in the previous century. In the space of two or three generations there had been a revolution in the north of England. This revolution was illustrated by the contrast between Sir Hugh's own household at Abbey House in Whitby in the 1630s and that of his great-grandfather's at Roxby castle. Significantly, as Hugh noted, by the time he wrote his Memoirs, what had once been his family's 'cheife place of Recydence' was 'now most demollished'.[90] Though Sir Hugh himself had lived in a time of appalling violence, it would have been inconceivable for him or any of his contemporaries to employ a permanent retinue of professional bodyguards, as Sir Richard (II) had done, not unusually, in the 1550s. Sir Hugh was proud that before the Civil War he had between 30 and 40 in his 'ordnarely famuly', but these were relations and domestic servants, not armed, liveried retainers.[91]

[86] *Ibid.*, f.22r./Whitby LPS, PB 4328, p.50 (see below, p.94).
[87] Memoirs MS, ff.27r., 28r., 28v., 29r. (see below, pp.105, 107–8, 110–11).
[88] *Ibid.*, f.2v./Whitby LPS, PB 4328, pp.4–5 (see below, p.63).
[89] *Ibid.*
[90] *Ibid.*
[91] *Ibid.*, f.23r./Whitby LPS, PB 4328, p.53 (see below, p.96). Even when he rented a house in London in 1641, Sir Hugh has 'neare 30 in [his] famuly'. *Ibid.*, f.26r. (see below, p.103).

Of his great-grandfather at the time of the Scottish campaign of 1544, Sir Hugh wrote:

> . . . he . . . was a Coll. commaunding the men he had raised in his owne Country & meerely by his owne power & interest, for then pressing of men to the warres was not (as since) used, but the King wrote to persons of power & quallety in the severall Countyes to know how many men he would undertake to raise for him upon such an expedetion. And according to the agreemt an Indenture was drawne betweene the King & the party which raised the men when he undertooke to carry the men to the place of Randevoze and the King to enterteine them . . .[92]

When Cholmley penned these words doubtless he had in mind that in his own time, particularly during the Bishops' Wars, the impressment of troops, their leadership and maintenance had become matters of bitter dispute and grievance between subject and crown. In fact, like many of his fellow Parliamentarians, Sir Hugh had been mistaken to assume that impressment had not been used by the monarchy in former days, and that somehow it had been invented by the Stuarts and their evil counsellors.[93] Nevertheless, even if overdrawn, Cholmley's contrast between the vestigial feudal custom of his great-grandfather's age and his own society was still of some validity.

Quarrels between rival neighbouring families were just as intense, and perhaps more deadly, during Sir Hugh's lifetime than they had been during Sir Richard's, but they were usually fought out in the courts. Litigation succeeded private warfare, which by Tudor times had become ritualistic rather than real. As Cholmley recalled, when his great-grandfather's armed men brawled with those of his brother-in-law, the Earl of Westmorland, 'whether in London streets or elsewhere', they were careful not to kill each other: 'they fought only with Buckler & short sword & it [was] accoumpted unmanly to make a thrust'.[94] Half a century later, when Hoby and the Cholmleys went to war with each other their battles were conducted in Star Chamber and the Exchequer. Again, Sir Hugh's family history offers a vivid and concrete example of a well-known general historical trend.

Still on the subject of liveried retainers, perhaps it comes as a surprise to learn that, as late as 1619, Sir Hugh's own father had ridden at the head of '20 of his owne servants' to greet his cousin Lord Scrope when he returned to Yorkshire from London as newly-appointed President of the Council of the North. According to Hugh's enviable memory, Sir Richard's dependents were 'all well mounted & in handsome liveryes of gray cloath trimed with silver lace'.[95] Plainly, however, these well-dressed men were not like the warrior retainers of Sir Richard's grandfather: their purpose was to demonstrate respect and support, not private military and political power. Richard rode 60 miles to Doncaster to express his friendship and kinship, and by this gesture he probably hoped to win preference from his cousin. Not long afterwards, he was made a Deputy-Lieutenant of the county, a member of the Council at York, and a Justice of the Peace.[96] Significantly, all the statutes, dating from as far back as Richard II, forbidding subjects to retain private, liveried armies,

---

[92] Memoirs MS, ff.2r.–2v. (see below, pp.62–3).
[93] J.F. Cooper, *Land, Men and Beliefs* (1983), p.80.
[94] Memoirs MS, ff.2v.–3r. (see below, p.63).
[95] *Ibid.*, f.8r. (see below, p.73).
[96] *Ibid.*, ff.8r.–8v. (see below, p.73).

were finally repealed in 1628; presumably, by then, they were no longer necessary. A decade later, when Sir Hugh himself brought eight of his servants to Northampton to attend Sir Christopher Yelverton at his first Sheriff's Assizes there, they were dressed in Yelverton's livery, not Cholmley's: 'scarlet cloths with [silver] lace, & two of them had satten dubletts & scarlet britches'.[97] Wearing the livery had become almost entirely a matter of ceremonial display.

Here it has been possible to offer only a few glimpses of the historical potential of Cholmley's Memoirs: they contain much more unexplored and unexploited raw material. Social historians investigating sixteenth- and seventeenth-century medicine, hospitality, duelling, theatre or transport, for instance, would find something of interest in what Sir Hugh wrote; but no one, so far, has looked closely at his Memoirs. As long ago as 1859, the editor of Sir Roger Twysden's Journal noted that Sir Hugh Cholmley's 'history' was 'too well known to need further remark'; yet today his comment is no more accurate than it was then.[98]

Finally, what Cholmley remembered and chose to relate about himself and his family might be untypical, or even misleading, if given undue and uncritical authority; but the dearth of such qualitative evidence endows his Memoirs with special value. Without decrying the worth of the quantitative returns of demographers, they can reveal only abstract averages and impersonal generalities: they tell us nothing about the thoughts and feelings of individual people. Sir Hugh Cholmley's Memoirs are precious simply because they were a unique personal and private statement.

---

[97] *Ibid.*, f.24r. (see below, p.98).
[98] L.B. Locking (ed.), *Sir Roger Twysden's Journal*, Archaeologica Cantiana, II (1859), p.189.

[Letter from Sir Hugh Cholmley to Scarborough bailiffs, 1 February 1626 (see Appendix J, p.188). [NYCRO, DC/SCB, B1 General Letters; MIC 1320/520.] See also M.Y. Ashcroft (ed.), *Scarborough Records, 1600–1640* (NYCRO, 47, 1991), pp.161–2.] Reproduced by kind permission of the Dean and Chapter of York.

To my dearely bloved sonnes William and Hugh Cholmeley[1]

I dedicate this ensueing discourse to you two, first in respect you may by nature clayme an interest in and title to it, 2 in that I was first and cheifely moved to this warke by the love I boare to your indulgent Mother my deare wife; for beeing desirous to imbalme her great virtues and perfections to future ages, I considered it would not be soe proper nor soe much for her honour to speake of her single, as to bring her in her proper range and place, with those precedeing deserveing woemen Mothers of our famuly (amongst which she will be found a prime flower in the Garland) which as I conceyved could not bee soe exactly done with out mentioning their husbands, who in respect of their sex may not only clyme to have the greatest honour and reverence ascribed to them, but commonly are the princypall Actors in the seane. And theirfore I resolved to make them the cheife subiects of my discourse, and to beginne with our Ancestors since there planting in Yorkesheire, not only mentioning their births matches fortunes and tymes of their deaths which may bee usefull for pedegrees and evidenceing of titles, but alsoe discribeing and deportrateing their persons conditions and humours, though perhaps this [may] bee thought a warke more proper for another then myselfe in respect what tends to their prayse may be coniectured to be spoken out of vane glory, and in doeing the contrary I may bee likened to the birds which defile their owne nests, and to cast dust in the faces of my Ancestors; yet in regard noe other can say soe much of this subiect as my selfe, I can take the confidence to proceed[2] in this warke and the rather because it is not to bee published, Intending it only to you my children and such as it shall please god may discend [to] you. And I would have you understand that in doeing of this I desire to forget my relation, and to performe the duty [of] a Historian, which is to expresse all things with as much truth and clearenesse as may bee; if I bee playne in discribing ether virtues or imperfections, it is that you and succeeding posterety may immetate the good and avoide the ill, which that you may all ever doe shall bee the hearty and earnest[3] prayer of

your indulgent father |

Sir Roger Cholm.[4] sonne to John Cholm. was [blank] in discent after their comeing out of the famuly of chestheire, borne a younger brother his elder Sir Richard Leiutennt[5] of Tower in the tyme of King Henry the 8 dyeing without issue the lands and Inheritance discended to him lyeing part in Kent part in Yorkesheire. Sir Richard had married[6] one of the daughters of [blank] Nevell of Thornton bridge, which perhaps was the occation of his byeing some land there but this Roger was the first of

---

[1] Sir Hugh always used this spelling of his family name, but in the printed version of 1787 'Cholmeley' here became 'Cholmleys' and in that of 1870 it became 'Cholmley'. Cholmley is now the usual spelling.

[2] In both printed texts 'proceed' was read as 'prove'.

[3] The word 'earnest' was transformed into 'utmost' in both printed versions.

[4] Perhaps Sir Hugh wrote 'Cholm.' here because he was unsure of the exact spelling of his ancestral family name. The Yorkshire Cholmleys were descended form a junior branch of the Cheshire Cholmondeleys. John Cholmondeley of Golston was the father of Sir Roger and Sir Richard. Sir Roger was probably the first of Sir Hugh's forebears to adopt the shorter name (Flower, *Visitation*, p.53).

[5] In both printed versions 'governor' was inserted after 'Lieutenant'. As a trustworthy servant of the Tudors, this first Sir Richard was made steward of the northern castles that had once belonged to Richard III – Richmond, Middleham, Sheriff Hutton, Barnard, Wakefield, Sandal, Conisborough and several others (Brooke, thesis, pp.17–20). Eventually, Henry VIII made Sir Richard constable of the kingdom's most important fortress, the tower of London.

[6] In both printed texts, 'Elizabeth' was inserted here, but according to another authority her name was Anne (Foster, *Pedigrees*, II).

the famuly that planted and setled him selfe in that Country having married Katherine the daughter of Sir Marmaduke[7] Costable of Flambrough a very antient famuly and he one of the most eminent and potent persons at that tyme in the Country, this Sir Roger was knighted in expedetion in to Scotland in [blank][8] yeare of Henry the [blank][9] when the English had a great victory against the Scotts, he being come up to London about some affayres he fell sicke and dyed there the [blank] of [blank][10] his lady with these fower children survived him: Richard the eldest to whome discended the lands and inheritance, John a gallant stout young man slaine (and as I have heard not fairely) in the flower of his youth, by a wound in his heart of which he lived 2 howers, Ann married to the early of Westmerland[11] with whome he had but six hunderd markes in portion, which then was accoumpted a great some, and [blank][12] married to [blank][13] Gascoine of Sedberry neare to Richmond a great famuly in those dayes.

He was a blacke a proper stout man and improved his esstate having bought Roxby which after became the princypall seate to his son[ne][14] which is all can be said of him in respect of the great distance betwe[en] his death and the writeing of this.

Katherine his wife, daughter[15] to Sir Marmaduke Constable[16] of Flambrough after his death never married but lived most of her tyme in the citty of Yorke in a house which was her ioynture scytuate next to [on that – *interlineated*] street cauld [blank] which was since purchased by the Bellasses and she was a very pious and virtous woeman and lived to a very great age[17]

Sir Richard Cholmeley eldest sonne to Sir Roger after his fathe[r's] death succeeded to the inheritance and esstate which layed parte in yorkesheire part in Kent that beeing as hath bene before said, left to him by his brother. Sir Richard he was knighted in the [blank][18] yeare of Edward the 6th at the battle of Musleberry feild in Scotland where the English had a great victory over the Scotts and where he him selfe was a Coll. commaunding the men he had raised in his owne Country and meerely by his owne power and interest, for then presseing of men to the warres was

[7] In fact, Katherine was daughter of Sir Robert Constable and granddaughter of Sir Marmaduke. This error was corrected in the 1870 printed text but not in that of 1787 or in Foster (see Glover, *Visitation*, p.219).

[8] In both printed texts 'the fifth' was inserted in the manuscript blank. The year of the battle of Flodden was 1513, the fifth of the reign of Henry VIII.

[9] That Sir Hugh could not or did not check which Henry was king at the time of Flodden is a reminder that his manuscript was meant to be only a preliminary first draft and that he intended to fill the gaps in memory at a later time.

[10] Both printed versions here inserted '28 April 1538', a date accepted later by Foster.

[11] According to Glover's *Visitation*, p.221, the Cholmley lady who married Henry, earl of Westmorland, was called Jane not Ann.

[12] According to both printed versions, Margaret was the Cholmley lady married to Gascoigne of Sedbury. This is confirmed in Glover's *Visitation* p.221.

[13] 'Henry' was inserted here in both printed texts.

[14] Unaccountably, Sir Hugh's word 'sonne' was altered to 'family' in both printed versions.

[15] The editor of the 1787 text accepted Sir Hugh's 'daughter', but in 1870 the word was corrected to 'granddaughter'.

[16] The editor of 1787 retained 'Marmaduke', but in 1870 it was corrected to 'Robert'.

[17] Sir Hugh's 'very' was omitted in the 1787 text and restored in that of 1870. In fact, Katherine must have been exceptionally old when she died in York in 1585 after 47 years of widowhood (Glover, *Visitation* p.219).

[18] In both printed versions the editors inserted '5th' in Sir Hugh's blank and the battle of Musselburgh was indeed fought in 1551. However, Sir Hugh was mistaken: this Sir Richard (II) was knighted in 1544 by the earl of Hertford after he had taken part in the sack of Edinburgh and Leith (BL, Harleian MS 6063, f.15).

not (as since) used, but the King wrote to persons of power and quallety in the severall Countyes to know how many men he would undertake to raise for him upon such an expedetion. | And according to the agreement an Indenture [blank] was drawne (f.2v.) betweene the King and the party which raised the men,[19] when he undertooke to carry the men to the place of Randevoze and the King to enterteine them and to this purpose I have seene severall[20] Indentures betweene the King and some Yorkshire gentlemen amongst which the Cholmeleyes.

He[21] married to his first wife [blank][22] daughter to the[23] Lord Conyers by whome he had issue Francis Roger Richard and severall daughters. He was a great improver of his esstate and purchased lands of great vallew within the County of Yorke amongst other the Manners of Whitby Whitby laythes and Staxby[24] with the demeyne lands belonging to them, being parcell of the Monestary of Whitby. This purchased of one Sir Edward[25] Yorke by Indenture beareing date the [blank][26] who had bought the same of the Earle of Warwicke by Indenture beareing date [blank][27] which said Earle of Warwicke had the said Manners and lands granted him by King Edward the 6th by letters patents beareing date the 20th[28] day of May in the 4th yeare of the said King; yet he sold his lands in Kent beeing of very gud vallew, his cheife place of Recydence was at Roxby lyeing betweene Pickering and Thornton (now most demollished) where he lived in great Port haveing a very great famuly at least 50 or 60 men servants about his house. And I have bene told by some who knew the truth that when there had bene 24 peices of beefe put in a morneing in to the pot some tymes not one of them would bee left for his owne dinner; for in those tymes of iddle serveing men were accustomed to have their breakefast and with such liberty as they would go in to the kitching and strikeing their daggers in to the pot take out the beefe with out the Cookes leave or preverty, yet would he laugh at this rather than be displeased, sayeing would not the knaves leave mee one peece for my owne dinner. He never tooke iorney to London that he was attended with lesse then 30 some tymes 40 men servants though he went with out his lady. There was great differences betweene him and his brother in law the Earl of Westmerland and as I have heard upon this cause that after the death of his sister the lady Ann the Earle married the second sister Gascoines widdow, which occasioned continuall fighting and scuffles betweene the Earles men and Sir Richards when they mett whether in London streets or elsewhere, which might bee done with lesse danger of life or blood shed then in these sucedeing ages | because then they fought only with Buckler and short sword and it [was] accoumpted (f.3r.) unmanly[29] to make a thrust.

His first wife dyeing he married to his second the lady Katherine daughter to Henry first Earl of Cumberland and widdow to John Lord Scroope of Bolton. He had

[19] 'raised the men' was omitted from both printed versions.

[20] 'many' in the 1787 text.

[21] Cholmley means Sir Richard, his great-grandfather.

[22] Sir Hugh could not remember her name, but 'Margaret' was inserted here by the editors of 1787 and 1870.

[23] Here 'William' was added by the editors of both 1787 and 1870.

[24] Changed to 'Stakesby', the modern spelling, in the printed versions.

[25] Sir Hugh's memory was faulty here: it was Sir *John* Yorke, Treasurer of the Mint, who sold his Whitby estate of about 22,000 acres to Sir Richard for £5000 (Whitby LPS, PB 2018).

[26] The correct date of 2 July 1555 was inserted by the editors in 1787 and 1870 (CPR 1554–5, pp.257–8).

[27] Again, the correct date was inserted into Cholmley's blank – 18 April 1551 (CPR, 1550–3, p.34).

[28] Cholmley's memory was not at fault in this case: the crown had granted the lands to the earl for his 'fidelity, magnanimity and incredible good fortune' in suppressing the Norfolk rebellion (CPR 1549–51, pp.372–3).

[29] Only in the text of the 1870 edition is this word correctly printed; elsewhere it became 'unmannerly'.

first by her a daughter cauled Katherine and then some differences ariseing betweene them they parted bedds and did not cohabit as man and wife for divers yeares till comeing to a gentlemans house where there was strate of lodgeing or did not takeing notice of the difference they were fitted but one chamber for them booth where lodgeing together it pleased god the lady that night conceyved with child which proved a sonne and was named Henry and after this they lived kindly together. Upon an expedetion in to Scotland this Sir Richard did[30] by his will in caise his owne issue should faile bequeathed his land to his cosen Cholmeley of Cheshire out of whose famuly he was discended.

Francis Cholm. his eldest sonne married Mrs Joane Boulmer. Roger and Richard married two of the [daughters of Dall – *crossed out*] bastard daughters of Dallarivers to whom he gave his lands (being of gud vallew) [they he disinherited – *crossed out*] from his legitimate sonne. [blank][31] was married to Strangewayes [Esq – *crossed out*] then lord of Sneton and other lands of great vallew. [blank][32] marryed to Ralph Salven of Newbiggen esq, then owner of all Egton Lordshippe and much other land. [blank][33] married to [blank] Sir [blank][34] Beckwith knight. Henry the only sonne by his second wife married Margaret the daughter of Sir William Babthorpe knight. Katherine should have bene married to the Lord Lumley the treaty beeing soe farre advanced that Sir Richard Cholm. paid to him £1000 part of the portion, and the day prefixed for marrige she fell downe on her knees and beseached her father that she might rather bee carried to her grave then married to that Lord whome she could never love, to which he answeared rather than marry thee against thy likeing I will loose my money, and there upon the match was broken the true cause of which was that she then was in love with one Dutton a gentleman but younger brother who at the tyme was a servant to Sir Richard and taught his daughter to play and sing which may bee a goud monetion to posterety to be cautious how they enterteyne persons of that profession and quallety, or if they doe not to suffer their daughters to have much familiarety or to bee at any tyme alone with them, for [in] my owne tyme I have heard of divers young woemen of quallety have suffered in their reputation and had such or worse mischa[nce][35] by those who tought to sing and dance. This Katherine afterward[s] married this Dutton which Sir Richard in some sort connived at when it was too late to prevent. This daughter was his Dareling; of which he gave gud testimony of at his (f.3v.) death when he left her in [land and lease – *crossed out*] | to the vallew of five or £600 a yeare in land and leases.[36] This Sir Richard was possessed of a very great esstate worth at this day to the vallew of above[37] 10 thousand pound a yeare, out of which he gave 7 or 800 per annum apiece to his two younger sonns Richard and Henry, the rest he setled upon his eldest sonne Francis with power to dispose only of £500 per annum in caise (as he exspected) that he should be taken pressioner for he was a proper man and bred a souldiour, and for want of issue male in Francis to Henry the 4

---

[30] The editors of both printed versions misread this word as 'died' and thereby made nonsense of what Sir Hugh had written.

[31] 'Margaret' was inserted here in both printed versions. Margaret married Sir James Strangways, lord of Sneaton, near Whitby.

[32] 'Jane' was inserted in this blank in both printed texts. Her husband was Sir Ralph Salvin of Newbiggin.

[33] 'Elizabeth' was inserted here in both 1787 and 1870.

[34] 'Roger' was inserted into this blank in the manuscript in both printed texts. According to Glover's *Visitation*, Elizabeth was married to Roger Beckwith of Selby, eldest son of Sir Leonard Beckwith, from whom she was later divorced.

[35] Here the manuscript has a torn edge.

[36] In both texts 'leases' was printed as 'cash'.

[37] Wrongly transcribed as 'about' in both printed versions.

sonne and for want of issue male in Henry to Richard the 3 sonne and for want of issue male in him to Roger the second sonne. The Cholmeleyes of Bransby are discended of this Roger who would say the lady Scroopes great power with her husband Sir Richard was the cause this Roger was put by the inheritance, but that is not probable for [though she might endever to bring her owne sonne he – *crossed out*] if her power [had – *crossed out*] meerely had produced the puting her sonne in the intaile before Roger she might have applyed it alsoe against Francis who had the esstate after Sir Richards death and whose children if had any should alsoe have enioyed it againe though her power might prevaile to have her sonne put in the intaile next to Francis it is not probable but their was some other reason why Roger should be put behinde his owne younger brother Richard. And the very true reason why Roger came to be put last in the intaile was because Sir Richard doubted whether he was his owne sonne [or not – *crossed out*] hath bene told mee and theirfore did not only put him last in the intaile, but left him with out any younger brothers portion not leaveing him any land or other provision for a younger brother;[38] And truly Sir Richard loved his sonne Francis soe intyrely as if he married with his approbation and likeing he had let the whole esstate freely to him with out an intaile, and would often tell him he would doe soe if he would marry any but Mrs Jone[39] Boulmer, who though of a gwd famuly had noe gud fame and was of an humour he liked better for a Mrs[40] then wife for his sonne, soe that when he saw his sonne could not bee disswayded from marring her, he made this intaile which if he had not (he would say) that after he was dead his Ant traut[41] (for soe he allwayes cauled her) would make her husband soe dispose the land as not a fut should come to any of his blood; in which he was propheticall, for as soone as Sir Richard was dead the said Joane wrought soe with her husband Francis that he setled on her the £500 per annum he had to dispose, and presently after his death | she married a young husband [of mean (f.4r.) quality][42] to whome she gave of all land. The Indenture by which Sir Richard did make this intaile beares date the [blank][43] day of [blank][44] in the [blank][45] yeare of [blank][46] being betweene the said Sir Richard Cholmeley on the first part, Sir William Babthorpe knight on the other parte. He dyed in 63 yeare of his age at Roxby in the County of Yorke and lyes buried in the chancell of Thornton Church of which he was Patron.[47] He was tall of Stature, [and very browne – *crossed out*] and with all big

[38] Sir Richard's disinheritance of Roger caused much ill feeling between his descendants, the Brandsby Cholmleys, and Sir Hugh's ancestors, the Whitby Cholmleys. Even in Sir Hugh's lifetime, the Brandsby Cholmleys still claimed prior right to the Whitby estate. See *The Memorandum Book of Sir Richard Cholmeley of Brandsby, 1602–1623* (NYCRO, 44, Northallerton, 1988). The original manuscript is NYCRO, ZQC, MIC. 1456.

[39] The second letter in her name is probably meant to be an 'o', not an 'a', as the editors of 1787 and 1870 assumed.

[40] This was printed as 'mistress' in both printed texts.

[41] Though the last letter is certainly not a 'b', in 1787 and in 1870 the word was printed as 'Traub'. Cholmley might have meant 'traut' or 'trout', but its significance has been lost. Whatever its meaning Sir Richard did not intend it to be complimentary.

[42] When the manuscript was mounted this insertion in the original was cut away, but it appears in both printed texts.

[43] '31st' was inserted here in 1787 and 1870.

[44] 'October' was inserted in 1787 and 1870.

[45] '21st' was inserted here in 1787 and 1870.

[46] 'Eliz 1579' was inserted here in 1787 and 1870.

[47] In both printed texts, after the word 'patron', a date, '17 May 1579', was added. Though this date is plainly wrong if Sir Richard made an indenture in October 1579, it has often been repeated in later works (e.g. G. Young, *A History of Whitby* (1817), ii, p.829). In fact, as the parish register of Thornton shows, Sir Richard was buried there 17 May 1583.

and strong made haveing in his youth a very active able body, bold and stout, his haire and eies blacke and his complection very[48] browne in soe much as he was cauled the great blacke knight of the North though the wurd great [appropriated – *crossed out*; attributed – *interlineated*] to him not soe much for his stature as power and [esstate – *crossed out*; fortune[49] *interlineated*]; he was a wise man, and a great improver of his esstate, which might have prosperd better with his posterety had he not bene exstraordnarely given to the love of woemen. The lady Katherine Clifford daughter to Henry 1[50] Earl of Comberland by his wife the lady Margaret[51] daughter to Henry Earl of Northumberland being a widdow to John Lord Scroope of Bolton was second wife to Sir Richard Cholmeley. A lady of very great wisdome and piety [and beauty – *crossed out*[52]]; whilst she was wife to the Lord Scroope King Henry the 8 being informed of her beauty required her Lord who then followed the Court to bring his wife to London, [of which the said Lord – *crossed out*] but she knowing the houmer of that amorous Prince, her lord would by noe meanes bring her out of the Country, at which the King was soe[53] displeased as he forbad the said Lord to come ever after to the Court. And after she was married to Sir Richard Cholmeley though she had a very great sperrit she did with a singuler prudence and temper beare and connive at Sir Richards amorous courses. After that her sonne Henry came to be possessed of the esstate she lived for neare 20 yeares with him at Whitby and stirred not from thence. Of her humour and disposetion you may gesse much by the motto on her picture[54] which was this *Qui desidirium suum clausit cum Jove de Felicitate contendet.*[55] She was tall and a very beutifull person, of fayre and ruddy [cleare – *interlineated*] complection her haire [a kinde of flaction yellowish flaxon – *crossed out*; light[56] flaxon with a little inclynation to yellow – *interlineated*] which she tooke not of the Cliffords whu were blacke but of her Mother being a Percy, and was the first as I conceyve[57] gave a change to blackness of our famuly; she was in the profession of her Relegion a Roman Catholicke, and yet wee[58] may conclude in her harte dyed a Protestant for one of the last words she spoke [to] her sonnes wife [that the – *crossed out*'; daughter let the – *interlineated*] Preists[59] might bee put out of the house. She dyed the [blank] day of [blank] Ann Dom [blank][60] in [blank] yeare of her age, and lyes buried in the chancell of Whitby church under the great blew stone. |

(f.4v.)   Francis Cholmeley after the death of his father Sir Richard succeded to the esstate, and being their of possessed was not contended[61] but at the instigation of his wife Joane fell to suite with his two younger brothers Henry and Richard to recover from

---

[48] Perhaps the editors of 1787 and 1870 did not want the Cholmley ancestry to have been so dark and therefore they omitted Sir Hugh's 'very'.

[49] The word estate was printed as well as fortune in both texts.

[50] In both printed versions the figure one is transcribed as 'first'.

[51] 'Margaret' was added in the manuscript by a later hand.

[52] The editors of 1787 and 1870 preferred to keep the word 'beauty'.

[53] The editors of 1787 and 1870 added their own word 'much' after Cholmley's word 'soe'.

[54] This portrait of Lady Katherine Clifford was hanging in the dining room of Howsham Hall as late as 1903 ('East Riding Portraits' in *The Transactions of the East Riding Antiquarian Society*, X (1903), p.49).

[55] Cholmley abbreviated some of the Latin words, but they were all extended in print just as they appeared on the picture of Lady Katherine.

[56] The editor of 1787 misread this word 'light' as 'bright'. In 1870 this error was not repeated.

[57] The word 'conceive' was changed to 'imagine' in both printed versions.

[58] The word 'wee' was misread as 'one' in both printed versions.

[59] Perhaps significantly, the plural word 'Preists' became 'priest' in 1787 and 1870. Did the editors think that one Catholic priest harboured illegally at Abbey House was too many?

[60] The year '1598' was inserted here in both printed texts. All the other blanks on this line were left empty.

[61] This word became 'contented' in both printed versions.

them that fortunes left to the[m] for their portions, [but with in a yeare or two or 3 he dyed – *crossed out*] which came to noe issue by reason of his death. He recyded most at Whitby and built that house most fro[m] the Hall downeward much according to the proportion it now stands, and though the Country affoards plenty of stone yet his wife would needs[62] have the sides even to the ground all of wood, sayeing that would serve well anuffe for their tymes knowing she should not bring a child, and theirby doeing greater distruction to the woods; she was of that haughty sperret and had got such a hand over her husband ([as was thought by some witchcraft for – *crossed out*[63]] though[64] he was a very valliant man) that upon the porch at the enterance of the Hall doore she had set the first letter of her name before his for where it should have bene F J she made it J F. And though he dyed at Whitby would not permitt him to bee buried in his owne parish church with in his owne Manner but caused his body to bee carried to Beverley a place the Cholmeleys had noe relation to and buried there in a private church cauled Saint Maryes, sayeing he should bee buried in a place where never Cholmeley should sett his foot on him,[65] in which you shall here after heare she was mistaken and her purpose crossed as it were by divine providence.[66]

This Francis was a tall blacke man much after the make and proportion of his father [many understand – *crossed out*] a valliant and [unde – *crossed out*] compleate gentleman in all points sayving that he was soe exceedingly over topped and guided by his wife which it was[67] thought she did [it] by witch craft or some exstrardnary meanes. |

Sir Henry Cholmeley after the death of his brother Francis, by virtue of the Intaile (f.5r.) enterd upon the esstate. Roger Cholmeley then beeing dead one Marmaduke his eldest sonne possessed of a gud esstate by his Mother bastard daughter to Dallarivers, beganne to lay claime to the land as [next – *interlineated*] heire at Common law to Francis and commenced a suite against his unckle Henry in the Court of Wards for recovery of the land which proved very long and chargeable, but in conclusion A decree passed for Henry beareing date the [blank][68] where in is perticulerly exspressed the date of that Intaile and settlement and the testemonyes of the witnesses which prooved bwth that Intaile and the revocation of a former settlement made by Sir Richard; yet in respect that Roger never had any portion and preferrment out of his fathers esstate Sir Henry was content to give his nephew Marmaduke £50 a yeare Annuety for 3 lives, and a statute of a thousand Marks for performance which was a great incumberance to his land; [he married Margarett[69] to W. Babthorpe of Bapthorpe knight][70] his[71] wife at this tyme was a [Recusant and – *crossed out*] Roman catholicke and he lieving then at Whitby [being a port – *crossed out*] it was a receptackle to the symenary preists comeing from beyond seaes and landing frequently at that port, in soe much as I have bene told there hath bene in his house 3 or 4 of them together at a time and most comeing booth baire in cloathes or money have at Sir Henryes [his ladyes – *interlineated*][72] charge bene sent away with a

[62] The word 'needs' was omitted in 1787 and 1870.
[63] These words crossed through in the manuscript were deleted in 1787 and 1870.
[64] The word 'though' is an editorial insertion in the left margin.
[65] The word 'him' occurs on the extreme right-hand edge and was omitted in both printed texts.
[66] Both printed works at this point add 'She died April 28, 1586', but these were not written by Sir Hugh.
[67] Sir Hugh's past tense verb was altered to the present 'is' in both 1787 and 1870.
[68] Both printed versions have the date 4 May 28 Elizabeth 1586 inserted in Cholmley's blank space.
[69] Here Sir Hugh omitted the word 'daughter', which was added by the editors of 1787 and 1870.
[70] These words in square brackets were a marginal insertion in the manuscript.
[71] In the 1787 version the word was wrongly printed as 'this', but correctly rendered in the 1870 text.
[72] Both printed texts have only 'at his lady's charge', but it is not clear that Sir Hugh intended to cross through the words 'Sir Henryes'.

very[73] great supply of bwth, some in scarlet and satten with their men and horses the better to disguise their professions; all which Sir Henry connived at being a little then in his heart inclyneing that way though he went to church. And as the prossecution of papists was then seveare soe was he put to much troble and charge for his lady not only in respect of composetions but that she was often carried to and kept long prision as was most of the eminent Papists in those tymes;[74] Beeing allyed full coosen Jerman to George 3rd Earl of Cumberland who loved him dearely he frequented much his company which drew him to live in a higher Port and to a greater exspence and beeing much addicted to fleet hounds and horses which are vaine chargeable sports did much increase his exspences and which was worse then all the rest cairelesse in the management of his esstate and trusting too much to his servants soe that beeing by these severall wayes brought in to debt. First he beganne to sell that land which was given him as a younger brothers portion and had noe intaile upon it but when that would not satisfie and his sonne comeing to age he cast about for cuting of the intaile [which was by the lawyers helpe he soone did – crossed out] cauled a perpetuety beeing soe strongly settled as his father Sir Richard did thinke it not possible to cut it of for by a clause in it if he that was in possession went to alter the intale he was to forfitt that which was to bee alterd and cut of to him that was next to succeed[75] him in caise he was dead, yet by the lawyers inventions a way and meanes was found to cut of this perpetuity, which was manefested by that caise cyted in the Lord Cook[76] re[ports] |

(f.5v.) betweene Cholmeley and Humble which a man [may] make[77] this use of that it is not good to bee too sollistertous in setling an esstate or thinkeing to perpetuate a mans name and famuly [by too much limmit – crossed out] but leave it to a succeding providence esspetially if a mans sonne bee not apparently a waster for why should not he that I allredy see the proofe of bee trusted with my esstate rather than the child unborne who I know not [how he may prove – crossed out] (as [the wise man sayth – crossed out; Solloman sayth – interlineated]) whether he may prove a wise man or foole, a saver or a waster. After the death of his Mother the lady Scroope hee changed his residence from Whitby to Roxby where he lived most of the middle part of his age. He was knighted at Yorke by King James at his first comeing in to England. About this tyme it pleased god that he came to bee confirmed in the Protestant Relegion and his wife absolutely converted to it, and ever after both of them lived and dyed very zealous Protestants. After much land sold and debts still increaseing and haveing a numerous issue he confined him selfe to a [small – crossed out] proportion and turned the rest of[78] his land in to the hand of his eldest sonne (then married) for payement of debt and raiseing[79] his childrens portion, and about the 58[80] yeare of his age retyred with his famuly[81] into the citty of Yorke, where he continued till his death [which was about Anno Domini 1616 beeing in 63 yeare of age – crossed out]. He had by his said

[73] The word 'very' was omitted in 1787 and restored in 1870.
[74] The Catholic sympathies and activities of Lady Catherine Scrope, her son Sir Henry Cholmley, and her daughter-in-law, Margaret, during the last years of the reign of Queen Elizabeth are well documented in the Salisbury papers, in particular, HMC, Salisbury, ix, p.68; x, pp.9, 11; xi, pp.214, 456, and records of the Star Chamber, PRO, StaC 5/H50/4. For comments on Cholmley recusancy at this time see H. Aveling, Northern Catholics (1966), pp.181–3.
[75] This is a difficult abbreviation to decipher; the editors of 1787 and 1870 both read it as 'succeed'.
[76] In both printed versions the more familiar spelling of 'Coke' was preferred to Sir Hugh's.
[77] Part of this top line has been cut away and is now less than entirely legible.
[78] The phrase 'rest of' was omitted in 1787 but not in 1870.
[79] For the word 'raiseing' the editors of 1787 and 1870 substituted 'increase'.
[80] Cholmley first wrote 57 and then changed the 7 to 8.
[81] The editors of 1787 and 1870 added 'wife' to produce 'his wife and family'.

wife a numerous issue of which these sirvived him: Richard his eldest sonne married to Susanna daughter of John Legard of Ganton Esq.; Henry and John, all very tall handsome proper men; Barberey marryed to Thomas Lord Falconbridge,[82] who had lands given her[83] for portion at this day worth 8 or 10 thousand pound; Dorothy married to Nicholas Bushesell[84] Esq; Hilday[85] married to Toby Wright; Margaret to Tymothy Comyn[86] Esq.; Mary to Henry Fairfax second[87] sonne to the Lord Fairfax of Denton whose sonne is now in apairance to bee Lord; Susanna to Richard Theackston Esq.; Annabella to Henry Wickham [sonne to Bishopp Wickham person of Beedell one of the Kings Chaplinns and a learned worthy man – *crossed out*], chaplinne to King Charles the first a learned and eminent man in his tyme. This Sir Henry beeing much given to the pleasure of hunting and esspetially with fleet hounds which though I have seldome seene men prosper in their esstates that did soe got afall from his horse at the leape of a hedge about the 56 yeare[88] of his age[89] and beeing a tall and corpulent man was soe bruised that[90] | Sir Richard Cholmeley eldest (f.6r.) sonne to Sir Henry succeeded to the esstate as appears by his office after the death of his father beareing date [blank][91] He was borne in the month of October in the yeare 1580[92] his father being charged with debts and then not understanding his power to cut of the Intaile of his land, sent for his sonne Richard from Cambridge being but sixteene yeares of age and married him to Mrs Susanna Legard daughter to John Legard Esq. of Ganton in the County of Yorke with whome he had £2000 in redy mony a faire portion at that tyme. The father and Mother of this Susanna dyeing young she was bred and educated with her cosen Jermyn Mrs Jane Hotham wife to John Hotham of Scorbrough[93] in the County of Yorke Esq. and Mother to that unfortunate (yet truly noble and honest gentleman) Sir John Hotham who was beheaded by the Parlaments [authority – *crossed out*; power – *interlineated*] *Anno Domini* 1645. She was alsoe married at the said Mr Hothams house at Scorbrough. The said Susanna was two yeares elder then her husband, who in respect he was soe young after he had bene married 6 weekes his father Sir Henry thought fitt to send him againe to Cambridge but when he was halfe the way he could not bee perswaded to goe any further but turned backe and went to his wife and soe ever after cohabited with her. It was near [near – *interlineated*] fower yeare after or they had a child and then was borne there eldest sonne Hugh, who was but 19 yeare and nine monthes younger than his father. This Sir Richard was of an active stirring sperret and [at his first – *interlineated*] chanced to fall in to he was drawne in to one or two businesses proved [costly – *crossed*

---

82 The 1787 text reads 'Falconberg', but that of 1870 retained Cholmley's own spelling.
83 Both printed versions substituted 'him' for Cholmley's 'her'.
84 Both editors preferred the usual spelling of 'Bushell'.
85 In 1787, 'Hilday' was printed as 'Kilday'. This error was not repeated in 1870.
86 In 1787, 'Comyn' was printed as 'Conyers'. This error was not repeated in 1870.
87 The word 'second' was omitted in both printed versions.
88 Clearly, Sir Hugh's memory of his grandfather's age was confused.
89 At this place, both printed texts have inserted '(1616)'.
90 When the manuscript was cut to be mounted a few words at the bottom of this folio were lost. The missing words were probably something like 'it caused his death'. The editor of 1787 seems to have been unaware of the missing words and went straight onto the next line at the top of 6r. which begins 'Sir Richard Cholmeley . . .'. Though the editor of 1870 understood that the last line of 5v. had been lost, he still made nonsense of Sir Hugh's meaning by repeating the error made by his predecessor.
91 Here, in both printed texts, were inserted the words 'Sept.2, 1617, 15 Jac. I'.
92 Sir Hugh was not certain of the year of his father's birth. He wrote 1580 or 1583, the last digit could be 3 or 0. In fact, his father was born in 1580, married in 1596 and first became a father in 1600.
93 Sir Hugh wrote 'Scorbrough' and not 'Scarborough' as it appears in print in 1787. In 1870, the editor preferred 'Scorborough, near Beverley' to ensure that the reader did not think there had been a misprint.

out; chargeable – *interlineated*] to his father,[94] as first [being 21 yeare of age – *interlineated*] he was in the Earl of Essex his riseing in [blank][95] yeare of Queen Elisabeth which cost £3000. And a few yeares after [his give strikeing – *crossed out*] strucke[96] a gentleman in the Starre chamber the Court sitting, for which he should have lost his hand but that good friends and mony brought him of. He was knighted by King James at his first comeing out of Scotland and in his way to London at a place cauled Grafton in Northamptonsheire when Sir Thomas Bellassis (after created Lord Falconberge) and divers o[ther] young Yorkesheire gentlemen of quallety to the number of 23 were knig[hted][97] at the same tyme [together – *crossed out*] of which this Sir Richard was the first they beeing all presented together by the Lord George Clifford Earle of Comberland who entertayned the King at that place. He was of the tallest stature of men about the height of his father but slender and well shaped. His Mother [was] a very beautyfull woeman contributeing as did his Grand Mother to the whitening of those blacke shadowes formerly incydent to the famuly; for when he was very young his haire was of a light couller and his complection fayre, and acting the part of a woeman in a commodedy at Trenety collidge in Cambridge he did it with great applause and was esteemed beautifull; yet beeing growne to bee a man his complection grew browne and something inclynable to swarthy which yet may bee ascribed rather to his [much – *crossed out*] rydeing in the sonne and much useing of

(f.6v.) field sports in his youth | [rather – *crossed out*; then – *interlineated*] to nature; for the skinne of his body was [of a – *crossed out*][98] passeing white and of a very smouth graine and he had a most incomparable sweet breath, in soe much at many tymes one would have thought it had carried a perfume or sweet odarifferus smell with it, the haire of his head was chestnut browne and the end of his locks curled and turned up very gracefully, with out that frisling which his father Sir Henrys was inclyned to, his beard a yellowish light[99] browne and thinne before[100] upon the chinne as was his fathers, his eies graye his face and visage long with a handsome Roman nose, of a very wining aspect a most manly and gracefull presence; he had alsoe a rare voice beeing booth sweet and strong nature affording him those graces in singing which others endever to by art and practise, all which rendered him favoured[101] amongst the femall sex. He was very valliant as appeared upon divers occations but more perticulerly his beeing severall tymes in the field upon duells and not with out provocation for he was as farre from giveing offence as takeing it upon sleight causes. When he was about the age of 23 yeares comeing to London he went to see a play at Blacke Friers and comeing late was forced to take a stoole to sitt on the stage as divers others did, and as the Custome was betweene every sceene stood up to refresh him selfe, and whilst he was in that posture a young Gallant very brave clapped him selfe upon Sir Richards stoole, which he conceyveing[102] was only to ease the gentleman for a while, did not demaund his seate, which this Gallant perceyveing he beganne to laugh and jeare[103] sayeing here is a young gentleman I have not only put by his seat but beares it very patiently, and soe continued ieasting and making sport, in soe much as the company tooke notice

[94] Curiously, Sir Hugh first wrote 'favoret' then superimposed 'the' on the middle of the word.
[95] In both texts '43rd year' (1601) was inserted at this place.
[96] Sir Hugh first wrote 'strikeing' and then altered it to 'strucke'.
[97] Here the right-hand edge is worn and ragged: some letters have been lost.
[98] Again, the top line has almost disappeared and is now difficult to read.
[99] The word 'light' was omitted in 1787 but was printed in 1870.
[100] The word 'before' was omitted in 1787 but was printed in 1870.
[101] The word 'favoured' appeared as 'famous' in 1787 but was correctly transcribed in 1870.
[102] This word was printed as 'conjecturing' in both published texts.
[103] The editors of 1787 and 1870 both changed Sir Hugh's word to 'sneer'.

thereof, where upon Sir Richard said Sir is it not suffetient to doe mee an injury but
you must boast of it, and wispering him in the eare said if you bee a gentleman follow
mee and presently Richard went out and the gallant followed, and comeing in to an
open place close by, the gentleman said what doe you meane, sayth Sir Richard that
you will give mee immediately satisfaction with your sword for the affront you have
done mee, Sir, replyed the Gallant I have noe sword, then bye one sayth Sir Richard,
but I have noe mony about mee quoath the Gallant, I will furnish you sayth Sir
Richard and carring him to a Cutlers shoppe close by the Gallant turned over many
but could finde none to please him, in soe much as Sir Richard offerd his owne and
would take any other but nether did that please my Gallant who whilst he thus tryfled
away the tyme, his man came and brought with him a Constable, and suddenly
claspeing | his armes about Sir Richards middle, said Mr Constable lay hold on him (f.7r.)
this is he will kill my ladyes eldest sonne. And the Constable presently comaunding
him to keepe the kings[104] peace Sir Richard seeing him selfe sirprised said he ment the
gentleman noe harme though he hath done him iniury of which said Sir Richard I
will make the Mr Constable the iudge, and soe drawing the Gallant out of the shoppe
upon pretence to relate the matter to the Constable as soone as they were in the street
Sir Richard gave the Gallant two or 3 gud blowes and with all strucke up his heeles
and then turned to the Constable and said I now[105] Mr Constable promise you not to
meddle further with my ladyes eldest sonne who was willing to bee gon with his
beateing. And though a great Gallant and Gamster about the towne and one that
much frequented the ordnaryes and places where there was[106] most resort of company
he never appeared amongst them after

[[107] This Sir Richard was noe great schollar yet understood lattin, and wel red in
History had most singular naturall partes as a quike witt and apprehention a sollid
Judgement a contriveing head fitt for a statesman a fluent tongue soe that he would
speake booth elequently and rationally. He had not the guift of his father to indite
severall letters at one tyme, yet could use his pen as well as most men, and in earnest
had such singular partes and indowment of nature, as if he had not bene kept under
hatches by his fathers debts and the many uniust suits of a troblesome neighbour one
Sir Thomas Hoby, in all probabillety he might have proved a very eminent person
and as serviceable to the King and Country as his two Country men and
cotemperaries Sir Thomas Wentworth and Sir John Savell who by their owne
active sperrets raised their persons and ffamuly to Honour and greatness, beeing
infearior to nether of them in understanding or volubillety of speech. Yet notwithstanding these great virtues he was not with out his infirmetyes as a haughty sperret
and chollericke, though he could well bridle that when any might take advantage
thereby, a little imperious esspetially in his owne house and over his tenants and apt to
give harsh langewidge to them as also to the ordnary country people who came upon
Justice business which made him not popular in the Country all which may bee
imputed to a custome and a habbit taken by the example of some he lived or
conversed with rather then to his disposetion naturally inclyned to | a winony (f.7v.)
carridge and to affabillety and haveing [ever – *interlineated*] generally[108] a plauseable

---

[104] The word 'kings' was omitted from both printed versions.
[105] The word 'now' is missing from both printed texts.
[106] In both 1787 and 1870 the editors chose to add 'then the' in this place.
[107] At this point Sir Hugh began a long passage about his father which he subsequently crossed through and
rewrote in a slightly but significantly different form later in the Memoirs. The editors of 1787 and 1870
ignored this long deleted passage about Sir Richard and included only the later, rewritten version.
[108] Again, the top line has now almost disappeared and is made even more unreadable by Sir Hugh's
horizontal stroke through it.

deportment to strangers and persons of quallety; he had alsoe got an ill custome to sweare espetially when he was angry or in his sports if they went crosse to him, and two much like his Grand father in his love to woemen. And truly this is the worst and all can bee spoke against him by his greatest enemies, for extenuations of which this may be sayd in his behalfe that he was not hardned in his infirmetyes but would frequently condemne him selfe for them and though he could not fully suppresse, yet did much reforme and repent of them before his death. He was a well natured man charritable to the poore and compassionate to those in distresse of a very generous and noble disposetion and iust in his dealeing and as he had contracted a great debt was soliscitous and not quiet in his minde till he had taken a course to satisfie every man][109] Whilst he was under age he and his wife lived for the most part in the house with his father Sir Henry but after he came to age of 21 yeares, they went and boarded with her[110] brother [in-law – *crossed-out*] Mr John[111] Legard of Ganton, where they aboad for the space of seaven yeare and then went to keepe house at Whitby Anno Domini 1608[112] (haveing all the demeynes of Whitby Hausker Staneseker and Southward Howses for present[113] maintnance which were alsoe his wifes oiynture, And though of good vallew gave then[114] but small rent)[115] where he soe well managed the publicke and his owne private affaires he gained the reputation of a wise man a good Justice of peace and great husband soe that the world beganne to looke upon him as a persson likely not only to support but even to agrandour[116] his house and famuly which doubtlesse he had done but that he incounterd with variety of crosse accydents, [and chiefly one Sir Thomas Hoby – *crossed out*] amongst which a cheife one was a troblesome vexatious neighbour one Sir Thomas Hoby who haveing married a widow the inheritor of all Hackness lordship haveing a full purse noe children, and as it was thought not able to get one, delighted to spend his mony and tyme in sutes. This Sir Thomas exhibited 4 severall bills in the Starre chamber against Sir Richard had him alsoe in sute in the Exchequer, where he endeverd to over through all the Royalties and lybertyes belonging to the Manner of Whitby, which sutes were not only chargeable in them selfes but drew Sir Richard from his affayres to London and their occationed many exspences and increase of debt. The next crosse accydent was the death of his wife [lady – *interlineated*] Susanna[117] beeing a very prudent discrett woeman which put all his domesticke affayres in to disorder and occationed his
(f.8r.) breakeing up house. | This was in the yeare 1611 he being then 31 yeares of age. She had borne him six children Hugh Richard Margaret Ursuley John and Henry; Richard and John dyed young before her. About a yeare and a halfe after he married his second wife Margaret daughter to [blank][118] Cob Esq. and sister to Sir William Cob now of Adderbury in the County of Oxford knight. And soone after he had married he carried her to his house at Whitby. As I told you before Sir Hoby had

---

[109] This is the point where the deleted passage ends.

[110] The editions of 1787 and 1870 both have 'him' instead of 'her'.

[111] In both printed editions the Christian name is given wrongly as 'George' instead of 'John'.

[112] At this point Sir Hugh wrote a small x to refer the reader to a marginal addition down the left-hand side of the folio. The marginal addition here shown between brackets was entirely omitted in 1787 and badly transcribed as a footnote in the 1870 edition.

[113] The word 'present' was misread as 'support' in the 1870 footnote.

[114] The word 'then' was misread as 'them' in the 1870 footnote. Sir Hugh was trying to explain that the lands were worth more than the rents charged for them at that time.

[115] Here Sir Hugh's marginal addition ends.

[116] This word appeared as 'aggrandize' in 1787 and 1870.

[117] In both printed versions only the word 'Lady' appeared here, and not the name 'Susanna'.

[118] This space was left blank in both printed texts.

commenced against Sir Richard severall sutes and though he had a good purse and
great friends yet Sir Richard was soe ingenious and dilegent in the sollisceting his
business [as I had foiled now foiled Hoby in at them all – *crossed out*] he had now with
much honour and applause foiled him in them all, and brought Hoby to reason and an
outward shew of friend shippe, but to a voide future troble of suites which orrigonally
were occatoined in that Sir Richard would not suffer this Hoby to carry matters upon
the bench according to his humour which he loved to have satisfied whether right or
wrong, made meanes to get him selfe put out of the Commission of peace intending
to live quietly at home and pay his debts which were more increased because he had
purchased the lease of the Rectory of Whitby which cost him £1500. And that he
had alsoe undertaken the payement of some new debts of his fathers Sir Henryes and
the payement of his brothers and sisters portions, for which Sir Henry had put in to
his hand Growmond[119] and some lands in Fyleing, all which I verily beleived he had
over come by his frugalety and private liveing if that the Lord Scroope had not with in
3 yeare after come to bee Lord President of his Majestys Councell in the North and
Lord Leiutenant of Yorkesheire, which happened in the yeare 1619. And Sir Richard
beeing cosen Jermyn to him [once – *crossed out*; half – *interlineated*][120] removed, held
him selfe oblidged not only to wate upon him but to appeare in such a posture as was
suteable to their relation[ship][121] and the quallety of Sir Richards person, who was
now looked up[on] as the head of his famuly, his father beeing dead. The said Lord
Scroope comeing from London to enter upon his Command, Sir Richard mett him
beyond Doncaster at his entering in to the County of Yorkesheire about 60 miles
from his owne house attended with 20 of his owne servants all well mounted and in
handsome liveryes of gray cloath trimed with silver lace. After the Lord Scroope was
setled in his place he made Sir Richard a Deputy Leiutenant and one of the Councell
for though | there were but 4 of those cauled the learned Councell beeing all lawyers (f.8v.)
yet some others of the prime gentlemen of the Country were admitted in to that
Society and sat booth in Councell and upon the Bench upon causes, and soone after
Sir Richard condiscended to bee put into the Commission of Peace the Country[122]
findeing a very great want of him, and now friendshippe and kindness increaseing
betweene the said Lord Scroope and Sir Richard it drew him much to Yorke and
their by not only put him out of his retyerd way of liveing and neglect of his privat
affayres but occationed great exspence; soone after King James cauled a Parlament
beeing the 18 yeare of his Reigne and Sir Richard beeing chosen Burgesse for
Scarbrough went with all his famuly to London beeing then in ill disposition of health
which soe continued as he scarce went six dayes to the Parlament house dureing the
sitting of the Parlament he continued with his famuly at London till January 1622
when suddenly removed them all and went to his house at Whitby upon a
Proclamation of the Kings commaunding every man to repaire with their famulyes
to their ordnary habitations in their owne Countryes. He had the yeare before
married his eldest daughter Margaret a very personable and beautifull woeman to the
eldest sonne of Mr Walter Strickeland of Boynton, then cauled Mr William since Sir
William Strickland[123] with whome he gave £2000 and the December before this

---

[119] The editors of 1787 and 1870 retained Sir Hugh's spelling of the more familiar 'Grosmont'.

[120] It is not clear whether Sir Hugh himself, or someone later, scored out 'once' and wrote 'half' over it.

[121] Here the right-hand edge of the folio is worn away. The editor of 1787 accepted 'relation', but in the text of 1870 'ship' was added on to it.

[122] Both printed editions have 'that county' instead of 'the Country'. Sir Hugh meant the neighbourhood of Whitby, not the North Riding of Yorkshire.

[123] After the word 'Strickland' the words 'Knt. and Bart.' were printed in 1870 but not in 1787.

departeing from London he had married his eldest sonne Hugh to Elisabeth eldest daughter to Sir William Twisden of Peckham in the County of Kent knight and Baronet with whome he had £3000 portion £2500 of which in redy mony paid upon that marridge and the other £500 at end of six Monthes; and for which he setled upon his said sonne 500 per annum present maintnance and as much more after his death as made it £2700 per annum though the present rent was not above £1600 per annum many of his neare friends wise men did thinke he much over vallewed his esstate but in truth and reallety he did not, for those lands which he setled are at this day worth above three thousand pound a yeare, and much of it then beeing in lease and at a low vallew (as for example Nobles farme now cauled [Franke – *crossed out*; Mr – *interlineated*] Comins[124] paid but 20 ma[r]kes a yeare rent) it was very diffecoult for a stranger to understand the trew vallewes and improvements of the lands, but as he was very understanding in most affayres and matters of business soe perticulerly in this of the vallewation of his lands he had a great insight and iudgement.|

(f.9r.)   In the yeare 1624[125] he was made High Sheriffe of the County of Yorke, haveing the fortune to bee Sheriffe in last yeare of King James and the first of King Charles. King James dyeing new writts issueing out in King Charles name for a new Parlament Sir Thomas Wentworth after Lord Strafford and Sir John Savell after Lord Savell formerly competitors stood to bee knights of the sheare for the County of Yorke, and with such earnessness and opposition as they would not ioyne but each man endever to bring in his partner; Sir Thomas haveing married a daughter of the Earl of Comberlands Sir Richard Cholmeleys cosen Jermyn once removed, he had formerly in the like contests declayred him selfe for Sir Thomas and ever carried voices for him, now it was probable he would doe him all the right and favour he could, and after a long contest Sir Richard declared Sir Thomas and his partner (who was Sir Thomas Fairfax of Denton after Lord Fairfax) to have the plurallety of voices and retorned them both knights for the County. Savell haveing bene an antient Parlament man and soe had many friends and acquaintance in the house, made complaynt against the election and the sheriffe who beeing sent for up and convented before the Parlament did soe well plead and answeare for him selfe and his deportment as though the Election was made voide and the Country to goe to a new choice. Yet Sir Richard was quit, which is very[126] raire in the like caise. And comeing to a new Election, the contest was as great as before, but Wentworth and Fairfax carried it, Sir Richard haveing given all parties satisfaction by a teedious and trobolesome poleing.[127] This Shervalty cost Sir Richard a £1000 which increased his debts which were now growne to a great some and insupportable beeing above £12000;[128] which was misterious and incredable considering that 5[?][129] yeares before Sir Richard being sicke recommended the payement of his debts to his sonne Hugh, and averred them not much above £3000 and as for many yeares together he had given the world great testemony of his frugallety and prudence in manageing his affayres there did not now appeare any visable cause to taxe

(f.9v.) | him with the contrary. All that can bee said or immagined is that his carring famuly

---

124   This name was printed as 'Mr. Cumin's' in 1787 and 1870. For the rental values of the Cholmley estate in 1626 see the Writ of Extent (NYCRO, ZPK 11) below (pp. 167–73).

125   Sir Hugh was not sure of the year and first wrote '1623' before changing the figure 3 to 4.

126   The word 'very' was omitted from both printed versions.

127   Sir Hugh's account of his father's conduct is extremely partisan and should be balanced against that given in J.J. Cartwright, *Chapters in the History of Yorkshire* (Wakefield, 1872), pp.220–6.

128   From this point Sir Hugh wrote seven and a half lines which he then crossed through and then re-wrote without any significant change in meaning.

129   The figure is not clear. It seems that he first wrote the figure 4 and then a 5 on top of it. In both printed versions the figure is given as 'five'.

to London did not only put him out of his ordnary way of liveing but drew him to an exstraordnary charge, and though he had [lands of a faire vallew yet – *crossed out*] a gud esstate in land yet at present they were not in rent to let above £1600 per annum of which he had at least 8 or £900 in his owne hand; and partly by his liveing at London and exstraordnary Cheapenes of all guds about that tyme he made nothing or very little of those in his hand and the Lord Scroope affecting running horses had put him in to an Humour of breeding (which by exsperience I have found to bee vane and unprofitable) which runne over most of his demeynes; and occationed him alsoe to keepe two or three horses in trayneing at Kiplincoates and other places the yeare throughout; his Shrevalty as I told you had cost him £1000 and 2000 he had given with his daughter, but that which was one of the greatest canker wormes was use mony beeing then at 10 in the hundred, and he borroweing most at scriveners and as the custome then was gave to them 20s. for every hunder,[130] which amounted that mony to 11[131] in the hunderd, and which was worst he was runne much in areare for the very interest, soe that I conceyve for 3 or 4 yeares past he had borrowed even most[132] for his ordnary exspences. Another thing which contrebuted to be an increase of this debt was that, at his comeing to London a cosen of his one Mr Gascoine who made the pewter came to live in the house with him, and being addicted to studdy the phylossopher stone Sir Richard fell to be alsoe in love with it, soe that Gascoine him selfe did not onlly coyne mony out of him, but others of the same profession, for I once found a cancelled bond where in Sir Richard was to pay one of that profession £200 for a secret, and though he would never[133] acknowledge that studdy cost him much, certainely it was one great increase of this debt, and it is strange and remerqueable that he who haveing passed the greatest part of his life with the reputation of one of the ablest and wisest gentlemen of his Country should now at the age of 47[134] yeares when commonly men iudgements are ripest and growne more saige by exsperience should not only bee iugled in to such a fopery and delusion but even desire to intricate his eldest sonne there in too, for he would often perswade him to the studdy of it which when he declyned would tell him he | was soe incredulous he   (f.10r.) should never be better for his studdyes, to which his sonne would answeare Sir let me be no worse and I will never desire to be better; but certainely that which ingaidged him first was the crosseness of his affayres and [disabillety to mainteyne the port he was falne in to – *crossed out*] difficullety he found to support him selfe and pay his debts by his ordnary means and fortune and theirfore fell to this out of a confidence he had to make gold; though commonly those who have the conceyte in conclusion (according to the poverb) catch copper; [and] indeede this one thing may [according to my observation – *interlineated but crossed out*] deterre every wise man from that studdy, which is that I seldome saw any addicted that way but ether they were poore and necessetous, or in a declyneing fortune when they sett[135] to it;[136] one other cause of this debt as some would coniecture was his amerous humeur which was conceyved might bee costly but I have heard him protest it was not, however wee may beleive that it diverted god Allmightys blessings and that his labours and endevers did not prosper soe

---

[130] Sir Hugh omitted the final letter 'd'.

[131] Cholmley first wrote the figure twelve then altered it to eleven. Both printed versions gave '11£'.

[132] By altering Sir Hugh's order of words the editors of 1787 and 1870 changed his meaning here: they preferred: 'he had borrowed even for most of his ordinary expences'.

[133] Both editors read Cholmley's word 'never' as a weaker 'not'.

[134] Sir Hugh first wrote '45' then altered the '5' to a '7'. Both printed texts read 'forty-seven'.

[135] Both printed editions have 'fell' instead of 'sett'.

[136] At this point Sir Hugh placed a cross for the inclusion of an addition which he wrote down the left-hand margin beginning 'one other cause . . .'.

well as might have bene exspected from a man of his parts and inienuety.[137] His debts
thus increasing upon him and not beeing able to borrow with out his sonnes ioyneing
with him who was soe obsequeous as that he was ingaiged in most of them, yet now
haveing a child desired his father to take in to consederation some course for payement
of his debts for that the way he tooke would ruine them all, where upon Sir Richard
made over to his said sonne the whole esstate for 10 yeares for payement of the said
debts reserveing only £400 per annum for him selfe for that tyme, And then lived
retyredly at Whitby but it was not the Lords pleasure he should live to see these 10
yeare exspired for he dyed with in six.

[138]This Sir Richard was noe great scoller yet understood latin and well red in
History, had most singular naturall partes as a quike witt and apprehention, a sollid
Judgement a contriveing head fitt for a statesmen, a fluent tongue soe that he could
speak both elequently and rationally[139], he had not the guift of his father to indite[140]
severall letters at one tyme, yet could use his pen as well as most men, and in earnest
had such singular partes and indwments of nature, as if he had not bene kept under
hatches by his fathers debts and the many uniust sutes of that perverse troblesome
neighbour Sir Thomas Hoby and some other crosse accydents formerly related, in all
probabillety he might had appeared a very eminent person to the world and might
have agrandord[141] his famuly as well as some other [of] his contrymen and
cotempararies;[142] beeing in understanding and naturall partes not inferior to any of
them; yet not withstanding these his great perfections he was not with out his
infirmetyes as of a hauty sperret naturally cholericke though he could well bridle it
(f.10v.) when any might take advantage theirby; | a little too imperious over his servants and
tennants and apt to give harsh langwidge to them as alsoe to the ordnary country
people who came to him upon Justice businesse which made him not popular in the
Country; which was imputed to a habitt and ill custome taken by the example of some
person he lived and conversed with, rather than to his disposetion beeing naturally
inclyned to affabillety and haveing ever a plauseable deportment to all stranger[s] and
persons of quallety; he had alsoe got an ill custome to sweareing esspetially in his anger
or sportts when they went crosse to his mynde; and too much like his Grandfather in
his love to woemen. And truly this is worst and all can bee spoke against him by his
greatest enemies, for extenuation of which this may bee sayd, that he was not hardned
in his infirmetyes, but would frequently condemne him selfe for them, and though he
could not fully suppress did much reforme and repent of them before his death. He
was a well natured man charritable to the poore liberall and compassionate to those in
distresse, of a very generous and Noble dispossetion, iust in his dealeing and as he had
contracted a great debt was soliscitous and not quiet in his minde till he had taken a
course to satisfie every man.[143] Haveing taken a surfett of oysters which put him in to a
great looseness and continued violently upon him for [blank][144] weekes together

---

[137] The marginal insertion ends with the word 'inienuety' which was transformed into 'eminency' by the
      editors of 1787 and 1870.

[138] At this point St Hugh began a new paragraph and started to rewrite the long passage on his father which
      he had deleted from 7r. and 7v. above (see pp.71–2).

[139] The printed edition of 1787 has 'orationally' but that of 1870 transcribes the word correctly as
      'rationally'.

[140] Mistakenly, in 1787, this word was printed as 'write' whereas in 1870 Sir Hugh's 'indite' was restored.

[141] In both printed texts this word appeared as 'aggrandised'.

[142] Whereas previously in the deleted passage Sir Hugh had named two of his father's contemporaries,
      Wentworth and Savile, here he neglected to repeat them.

[143] At this point Sir Hugh had rewritten the passage he had previously crossed through on 7r. and 7v.

[144] Both printed editions retained Cholmley's blank.

turned in to the bluddy flix, which though troblesome and painefull he endured with great patience and courridge and as he had great knowledge in religion, gave great testemony of it to all about him booth in the tyme of sickness and at the hower of his death haveing his sences and understanding till with in an hower before he dyed which was about 2 aclocke in a fryday morneing in the Month he was borne October about which tyme he was 52 yeares and in the yeare of our Lord 1632, he dyed at Whitby house in the chamber over the seller and as he desired was buried in the chancell of Whitby Church under a great blew stone there where his Grand Mother had bene buried about 30 yeares before. |

He had by his first wife six children Hugh Richard Margaret and Ursulay, very tall (f.11r.) personable woemen, John and Henry. Richard and John dyed young before their Mother. Hugh was married to Elisabeth daughter to Sir William Twisden of Peckham [knight – *crossed out*] in the County of Kent knight and barronet, and before Sir Richards death had borne three children Richard William and Elisabeth of all which he was very fond. Richard dyed before him but William, then 5 yeares old, at the tyme left[145] in Kent with his Grand mother the lady Twisden. He would often speake of him to his sayd daughter in law with much exspression of love and fondness wishing him with him and beseaching the Lord to blesse him. Margaret married to Sir William Strickland knight and Ursulay married to George Trotter of Skelton Castle esq. were booth dead before him and lyes interred beside him, the one on his right the other on his left hand. Henry his youngest sonne then at the Inns of Court, though a proper man he left him but £50 per anuety, but it pleased god to blesse him that he married Katherine daughter to Robert Stapleton of Weighill Esq., and relect and widdow to Sir George Twisleton[146] of Burley in the County of Yorke knight and Barronet.[147] A proper man as tall as his father slender and well shaped and like his father in the face as well as stature but that his noase was not soe much Roman, a kind well natured man and loving trew friend valliant and ingenious and a good sollisicitor in law businesses[148] and diligent in all his affayres, he was knighted by Charles the 1st anno Domini 1641.[149]

By his second wife he had 4 sonnes of which the two last were twins and borne after their Mother had bene 10 yeare with out a child but dyed presently after they were come in to the world, the two which survived him were Richard and William, the one beeing 13 the other [blank][150] yeares of age. William dyed with in 2 yeare, Richard had left to him Growmond[and]married Margaret daughter to John[151] Lord Paulet relect and widdow to Dennis Roules[152] of Brixton in the County of Devonshire Esq. This Richard was a handsome proper gallant gentleman and being a Cornnett[153] for King Charles the 1st in these unhappy cyvell warrs which happend betweene him and his Parlament, he was knighted for his gud service at the takeing of the Citty of

---

145 Sir Hugh wrote 'left' but in print the word appeared as 'lived'.

146 Though Cholmley wrote 'Twisleton', the editor of 1787 carelessly converted it into 'Twisden'. In the printed version of 1870 the name appears in the same form as in the manuscript.

147 At this point Sir Hugh decided to add a postscript on his younger brother Henry and referred the reader to an additional passage in the left-hand margin.

148 The editor of 1787 omitted the word 'law' which was restored in 1870. However, both texts have 'business', not Cholmley's plural word.

149 At this place Cholmley concluded his marginal afterthought and resumed the narrative in the next paragraph.

150 Into this blank in the manuscript the editors of 1787 and 1870 had the word 'fourteen' printed.

151 The name John is missing from both printed editions.

152 This name is given as 'Rowles' in 1787 and 1870.

153 Though Cholmley certainly wrote 'cornet' it became 'colonel' in the text of 1787. In 1870 Cholmley's word was correctly printed.

Excestor, and after was made commaunder in cheife of all the forces which beseaged Lyme where he recyved a wound upon a sally by his shewing more vallour then became a person haveing the commaund (of which he dyed with in [blank][154] howers).[155] He was exceeding beloved and lamented by his soldiers, and after by the King him selfe not with out good cause for by his death not only the seage was broken up but the Kings affyres ever after in those quarters declyned. He left two daughters and his lady with child of a sonne borne and named Richard but dyed before he was a yeare old, [after he was slaine dead – *crossed out*][156] his lady carryed his body to bee interred at Brikton in Devonsheire. |

(f.11v.)   Susanna daughter to John Legard of Ganton in the County of Yorke Esq. was to Sir Richard Cholmeley first wife her parents dyeing whilst she was young she was educated with her cosen iermy[n] Mrs Jane Hotham wife to John Hotham Esq. of Scorbrough[157] some tyme with the Lady Dawny wife to Sir Thomas Dawny of Cowicke another of her cosen Jermyns, but the great love and friendshippe was betweene her and Mrs Hotham at whose house she was married at the age of 18 yeares beeing two yeares older then her husband. She was tall something above the middle stature of woemen, slender and well shaped, her haire a light chestnut her eies gray a slender well shaped face and though she passed under the notion of a browne woeman she had a very cleare complection booth for white and red, soe that she was by every one accounted very beautifull. She was a very vertus relegious woeman a loving wife and wise[158] and understanding in the mannageing of her husbands affayres booth domesticke and with out doores in his absence, and by her goodness and wisdome had got a great influence upon her husband, soe that the death of her was esteemed a very great blow and losse to Sir Richards esstate and famuly. (for if she had lived I doe conceyve she had prevented the saile of all those lands which came to pass after her, soe that wee may see a virtuous wise woeman is a great support to a famuly).[159] She boare to him six children Hugh Richard Margaret Ursuley John and Henry. Richard and John dyed before her the other sirvived her. Hugh the eldest being but XI yeares of age and Henry the youngest but 3 yeares old. Hugh beeing a scholler at Beverley Schoule and falling sicke Mrs Hotham then a widdow[160] sent for him to her house at Scorbrough, and this lady his Mother comeing thether purposely to see him, it pleased god she tooke the sickness which was a fever much stirring in those partes and there dyed in the 33 yeare of her age *Anno Domini* 1611 to the great regrert booth of her owne and husbands friends and lyes buried in the chancell of Scorbrough Church where her sonne Richard had bene buried before her. |

f.12r.   Margaret second wife to Sir Richard Cholmeley[161]

Margaret daughter to [blank][162] Cob Esq. was second wife to Sir Richard Cholmeley. He came acquainted with her at London and there married her, her Mother a

---

[154] Neither editor was prepared to guess how many hours this Richard Cholmley had taken to die when Sir Hugh had not been able to remember.

[155] This phrase shown inside round brackets was inserted after the word 'commaund', but would have been better placed to follow the word 'wound'.

[156] Sir Hugh struck through this phrase though his sense would have been clearer had he left it in.

[157] The edition of 1787 always has 'Scarborough' when Sir Hugh clearly wrote and meant 'Scorbrough' near Beverley. The printed work of 1870 is free from this error.

[158] The 1787 edition omitted the word 'wise', but that of 1870 did not.

[159] The previous words in brackets were added as a marginal afterthought to be inserted at this point.

[160] The phrase 'then a widdow' was omitted from both printed works.

[161] Sir Hugh's title to this section was omitted from both printed editions.

[162] No attempt was made to fill this blank in either printed work.

widdow then liveing in London. Sir Richard was 33 yeares of age and she 23 when he married her which was in the yeare of our Lord 1613. He had 1500 portion with her and 500 more upon death of a sister, [after he had she was 4 yeares with out – *crossed out*] he settled the lordshippe of Growmond to her eldest sonne which is £300 a yeare and besides it made to her in ioynture Hausker Stansiker and Hagget how[163]; which at this day are worth neare £500 per annum although the debts of her husband Sir Richard swelled to that height after his marridge with her, noe falt or blame can bee imputed to her for she ever[164] shewed her selfe a loving dutifull complyeing wife, and lived a great while at Whitby with him very retyred yet contentedly, and when there was a necessety of selling land to the deminution of the esstate, was willing to yeald up a god part of her ioynture vidz. Hausker and Haggethow; and to doe her right from her first marridge was a very gud kinde Mother in law, for his daughters beeing young she did not only bring them up with tenderness and kindness but when they dyed greived for them as if they had bene her owne children, though her husband bee dead continues still that love and kindeness to his children and Grand children as if they were come out[165] of her owne loynes, which I may say is not lost or ill bestowed for I am confident they doe all love and honour her as[166] much as if she were there owne Mother. And alsoe her daughter in law Sir Hughs wife and they did exceedingly love one another [soe that through the goodness and mercy of god this kindn – *crossed out*] which argues them booth to bee good woemen and that this kindness was recyprocall on all hands.

After the death of Husband she went to live at London and put her two sonnes out too schole there where William dyed, after when Richard was fitt for Cambridge[167] and that he went thether she went and boarded her selfe with in a mile that she might bee neare to looke after him beeing a very indulgent carefull Mother. And when he came to the Inns of Court she retorned to | to London againe and tooke lodgeing   (f.12v.) neare to the Middle Temple of which house he was in; [She tooke – *crossed out*] and there gave him the best education the towne could affoard.|

[This concludes the first part of the Memoirs concerning Sir Hugh's ancestry. The next leaf was left blank and Sir Hugh resumed on 14r. with an account of his own life.]

Sir Hugh Cholmeley   (f.14r.)

Beeing to write the [History – *crossed out*; Story – *interlineated*] of my selfe and my owne life, it putts mee in mynde of that fancy of the Emperor Charles the 5th. when he would have the ceremonyes of his funeralls performed upon him selfe whilst he was liveing, which though not fully yet in some perticulers doe perrolel; as that booth are Acts posthuma and never or seldome performed by a mans selfe or in his life tyme. Nor am I incensible with what difficulty and preiudice I undertake the [this – *interlineated*][168] worke, considering when I am to mention my owne blemishes and

---

[163] These names of parts of the Cholmley estate were printed as 'Hawsker, Stansicar and Hagget-how' in 1787 and 'Hawsker, Stanscar and Hagget-how' in 1870. The modern spellings of these places are Hawsker, Stainsacre and Haggit Howe.

[164] Instead of 'she ever' both printed versions have 'the end'.

[165] The words 'come out' were omitted in 1787 and again in 1870.

[166] The word 'as' was printed as 'so' in both editions.

[167] This Richard Cholmley was baptised at Whitby 17 October 1617 (*Whitby Parish Register*, p.10), and was admitted to Sidney Sussex College as a Fellow-Commoner in May 1635 (*Alum. Cantab.*, i, p.335).

[168] The word 'this' was written in a later hand. Both printed versions have 'this' and not 'the'.

imperfections, the fralty of [mans – *crossed out*; humane – *interlineated*] nature is such I
shall scarsely discerne them, or rightly iudge of them, or if I doe, perhaps bee
unwilling to have the world take notice, much lesse my selfe to bee the divoulger of
them. And if I mention ought may bee to my commendations or advantage, it will
bee thought pride or vane glory; but for the first, I require my sonns or one of them
when this shall come in to their hands if they knew any remarqueable infirmety in mee
which I have not [given a hint of – *crossed out*; mentioned – *interlineated*], that they add
it by way of postscript to this discurse,[and]to the same end I have [done – *crossed out*;
disclosed – *interlineated*] chose of my Predecessors, which is, that succeeding posterety
may avoide and endever to suppresse if they finde any seede or inclynation of it in
them selfes. And in caise the Reader [finde – *crossed out*; meet with – *interlineated*] ought
to my commendations, whether it bee in discription of my selfe or qualletyes, I desire
him to beleive I doe it meerely that in caise any succeeding posterety doe participate
of it, they may know it is from such a parent, it beeing often pleaseing to children to
finde some thing in them selfes resembling their [Grand or great Grand fathers – *crossed
out*] predicessors; Intending [by gods – *crossed out*; in relateing – *interlineated*] to use as
much truth and cleareness [in relateing this story – *crossed out*] as my weake Iudgements
and the fralety of humane nature will permitt [in relateing this story – *interlineated*] by
which there will appeare a series of gods providence and protection [over – *crossed out*]
towerds mee in the preservaion of mee from severall great dangers even from my
cradle to this present hower. And though I wanted much of the partes and abilletyes of
my father and Ancestors, you shall finde mee destened to the undertakeing of much
more businesse and Action then most of them, which beganne to fall [upon mee –
interlineated] when I was but a young man.[169] My father beeing dead I his eldest sonne
succeeded to the esstate as appears by my office found after his death beareing date[170]
[blank]. I was the first child of my deare Mother borne upon the 22th of July beeing a
(f.14v.) tuesday and on the feast day commonly cauled Mary Magdalens day in | the yeare [1600
– *crossed out*] of our Lord god *1600* at a place cauled Roxby in the County of Yorke
with in the hunderd of Pickering leith[171] neare to Thornton, now much demolished
but hereto fore the cheife seate of my great Grandfather, and where my Grandfather, Sir Henry Cholmeley then lived, which place (since I was married) was sold
by my father and selfe towerds the payement of his debts. My Grand Mother
haveing a child halfe a yeare after I was borne sent the two nurses out of the house,
and gave mee and my Ant both sucke for one day from her owne breasts.[172] She
who was my nurse prooved suddenly with child, but not revealeing it, I was thereby
soe weakened as I have heard my father say, when I was a yeare old I had not strength
to beare up my head but which way soever my necke turned there it layed; but her
beeing with child beeing discovered, I was put to another nurse by which meanes and
gods blesseing my life was preserved, yet it gave mee abackecast as I was a weake
sickly child for many yeares, and if it had not bene for this (which surely[173] abated
booth my strength and height of my Ancestores) I verely beleive I should have bene as
able a man of body as most in the Nation. At 3 yeares old the mayde which attended
mee let mee [fall out at the dyneing roome – *crossed out*; tumble – *interlineated*][174] out

---

[169] At this point Sir Hugh referred the reader to an afterthought which he wrote down the left-hand
     margin. The editors of 1787 and 1870 inserted his additional sentence into the text at the correct place.
[170] The words 'beareing date' were omitted from both printed works.
[171] Both printed texts have the modern spelling of 'Lythe'.
[172] In both texts this word is printed as 'breast'.
[173] Both printed works have 'sorely' here, but in the manuscript the word is definitely 'surely'.
[174] Both printed texts preferred Cholmley's second attempt 'tumble out'.

of the great chamber window at Roxby which (by gods providence) a servant [attendeing – *crossed out*; wateing – *interlineated*] on my Grandfather at dinner esspieing, leaped to the window and caught hold of my coate after I was out of the casement. Soon after I was carried to my father and Mother who then lived with her brother Mr John Legard at his house at Ganton 9 miles from Roxby where I continued for the most parte till I was 7 yeares old, and then my Father and Mother goeing to keepe house at Whitby I went with them and beginneing to ride in a little way by my selfe as wee passed over a common cauled Pexton Moore[175] one of my fathers servants rideing beside mee I had a desire to put my horse in to a gallop but he running away I cried out, and the servant takeing hold on my arme with intention to lift mee from my horse, let mee fall between booth, soe that one of them in his gallop troade on my hat, yet by gods protection I caught noe harme, nor my Mother who though with child and neare halfe gon with my brother Harry[176], at the fright leapt from the horse where she roade[177] behinde one[178]; but the next yeare beeing *1608* upon my very birth day being the feast of Mary Magdalen and I iust 8 yeares old by gods great | providence I escaped as great if (f.15r.) not greater danger then this, which was thus,[179] at my fathers house at Whitby afoare sayd there was a great fearce sow haveing 3[180] pigs nere a quarter old, which were to bee reared, these[181] lyeing close together a sleepe neare to the kitching doore, I being aloane out of folly and waggery beganne to kick one of them, in the intrime another riseing up occationed mee to fall upon them all and made them cry which the sow heareing lyeing close by came and caught mee by the leg before I could get up, and dragged mee halfe a scoare yeards under the window of the roome now cauled the cole larder[182] and what in respect of age and the amazement I was in could not helpe myselfe from my leg she fell to bite mee in the growne with much fearceness; when the butler carring up a glasse of beere to my father (then in his chamber) heareing mee cry, set downe the beere on the Hall table and runing out found the sow passeing from my groine to my throate. Before I was 10 years old I had the measells and small pox thrise and very subiect to agues and sicknes occationed as was coniectured[183] from the bad nurrishment of my nurses milke whilst she was with child. At 11 yeares of age I was sent to the freeschole at Beverley ([to – *interlineated*][184] one Mr Petty beeing the Master)[185] where takeing a feaver then rife[186] in that Country my cosen Hotham [Mother to the unfortunate Sir – *interlineated*] John Hotham then a widdow sent for mee to her house at

---

[175] Surprisingly, both in 1787 and 1870, the editors chose a mythical place 'Paston' Moor instead of Cholmley's real location which is still called by his name, Pexton Moor.

[176] The name 'Harry' was written later in the manuscript, and in print changed to 'Henry'.

[177] Both printed texts made nonsense of this by transcribing 'roade' as 'stood'.

[178] Again, Sir Hugh wrote 'one', but in 1787 and 1870 the word was printed as 'me'.

[179] The word 'thus' was wrongly printed as 'that' in 1787 and 1870.

[180] Cholmley first wrote the figure 2 then changed it to 3. In both editions it was printed as 'two'.

[181] In both printed editions the comma after 'reared' was ignored and instead placed after the next word which was misread as 'there'.

[182] Though the word is now difficult to read, the editors of 1787 and 1870 ignored 'cole' and printed only 'larder'.

[183] In the 1787 edition the phrase 'as was coniectured' was omitted, but correctly restored in the 1870 text.

[184] The editors of 1787 and 1870 seem not to have noticed that the word 'to' had been added to go inside the opening bracket.

[185] Hugh's arrival at Beverley was fortunately timed: a new school building had just been finished, and William Petty, the headmaster, who took such a liking to him, was a distinguished classical scholar and teacher.

[186] In 1787 'rife' was printed as 'ripe'.

Scorbrough whether[187] my deare Mother comeing to see mee caught the feaver and
their dyed to my great greife for she was a very fond[188] and indulgent Mother and I
loved her dearely. But my Master beeing chosen fellow of Jesus collidge in cambridge
and to leave his schoule loveing mee very much and thinkeing mee apt to learne was
unwilling to leave mee behinde and soe perswaded my father to let mee goe with
him thether (indeed before I was well fitt ether for learneing or yeares) for I went at
Michelmas *1613* being but 13 yeares of age and 3 Monthes[189] where when I came I
was admitted in the ranke of those cauled fellow Commoners; and there being one
Thomson[190] who 3 yeares before had bene sent from Beverley Schole by my sayd
Tutor he recommended him to bee my companion. He was indeed a gud scholler
and witty man, but given to drinkeing and [soe – *crossed out*] debaushed us all, soe that
I had bene utterley undone but [that another accydent a matter – *crossed out*] for an
interveeaneing occation which though it proved preiudetiall to my schollershippe
and learneing, by gods great mercy conduced to reclaime mee from my deboshery
and drinking; which was this, my sayd Tutor Petty was cauled from the sayd
(f.15v.) collidge to London to bee Tutor and Master to | the Earle of Arrundells [children –
crossed out] sonns in there fathers house[191] and at his departeing from the collidge
turned over his peuples to one Mr Slater a fellow of the collidge,[192] but I beeing
about this tyme with my father at London and to returne to Cambridge[193] he gave
mee £30[194] in gold sayeing though I had a Tutor to reade to mee I was old anuffe to
take caire of my selfe and order my owne mony [affayres – *crossed out*] and exspences
and that he would hence forward looke for a good accoumpt from my selfe booth of
my mony and deportment. Which speaches I ponderd much in my thoughts upon
the way as I retorned to Cambridge, concludeing that my Tutor was to bee
responsable to my father for my past Actions, but myselfe for the future, which I
prayse god tooke such impression in mee as from that tyme I quitted my drinkeing
companions which[195] ever after grew antipothous to my nature; yet did I not spend
my tyme soe profitablety as I ought to have done for I was naturally given to all sports

[187] Sir Hugh wrote 'whether', but the editors of 1787 and 1870 assumed that he had intended to write 'whither'.
[188] In both printed editions 'fond' was replaced by 'kind'.
[189] Cholmley closed his bracket after the word 'yeares'; in print, however, this bracket is not closed until after the word 'monthes'.
[190] Though the name is still legible, in the manuscript 'Thomson' has been crossed through. Neither editor chose to print the name. It is not clear who this College corrupter was. Marmaduke Thompson was a Beverley boy who eventually became a Fellow of Jesus, but he matriculated only a year before Hugh. Less is known of Peter Tomson who was ordained deacon at York in 1614 and priest in 1617, yet this Jesus man fits Sir Hugh's account better since he matriculated in 1609. I am grateful to Mr E.F. Mills, Jesus College Archivist, for these details.
[191] Petty continued to hold his Fellowship at Jesus until 1624, but long before then he was travelling tutor to the eldest son of the earl of Arundel. In Greece, Turkey and Italy, Petty collected antiquities for the earl's private collection and later spent several years in Athens as professor of Greek letters there. Perhaps out of a sense of guilt when he died in 1639 he left £200 to his old College. However, because of the dishonesty of his executors, the money was never received. For Petty's eventful and fruitful career see D. Howarth, *Lord Arundel and his Circle* (1985), pp.127–30. Unfortunately, Mr Howarth completely misunderstood Cholmley's own account of his association with Petty, and confused the latter with first Thomson, the College debauchee, and then Hugh's father, Sir Richard.
[192] This was Thomas Slater, Fellow of Jesus College from 1613 until his death in 1628. He was also vicar of All Saints' at Cambridge and is buried in Jesus College chapel (*Alum. Cantab.*, iv, p.88).
[193] The phrase starting with 'but' and ending with 'Cambridge' was omitted from the 1787 edition.
[194] Cholmley first wrote the figure 4 then altered it to a 3. Both printed editions adopted the figure 3.
[195] Both printed versions have 'and' instead of 'which'. It is not clear whether Sir Hugh developed an antipathy towards drinking, his drinking companions, or both.

and recreations and inclynable to play, and wanting my old Tutor to hold mee to my [books – *crossed out*] studdy I did not follow it close. Here at Cambridge I had like to have dyed of a plurecy contracted by a surfett in takeing cold and drinkeing[196] when I was hott; [and allsoe drinkeing – *crossed out*] At 17 yeares I left Cambridge and stayed a yeare in the Country with my father where I was soe [innetiated – *crossed out*; enterd – *interlineated*] in Hunting hawkeing and horse rases that I could not esely put them out of my mynde, when by riper yeares I saw the vanety of them, and theirfore I advise not to let children have any taste of them or bee taught to game, but as the wise man directs to bee trained in their youth in such courses as is fitt them to practise when they comes to be a man.[198] At 18 yeares I went to the Inns of Court and was admitted of Grayes Inn [which being a Grand – *crossed out*] at the end of a Michelmas tearme and their succeeding a Grand Cristmas it proved an ill tyme for increaseing my love to play and gameing, and made mee neglect the studdy of the law, soe that I was 3 yeare there and totally misspent my tyme to my great regrett since I came to bee of riper iudgement, and saw what advantage the studdy thereof might have bene to mee in conducting and mannage of affayres in the Country as well conserneing my owne private as the publicke, where every man that hath but a smackering[199] of the law though of no fortune or quallety shall bee a leader or director to the greatest and best gentlemen on the bench, which hath often put in to my mynde a sayeing of my father in law Sir W. Twisden a very great scholler | that (f.16r.) there were but two [sortes of studdyes – *crossed out*] things worth spending a mans tyme and studdy in, the one the law of god to teach him the way to heaven, the other the law of the Nation to direct him how to deport him selfe in this life and to manage his cyvell affayres; whilst I was here at the Inns of Court by cold taken I had got a very soare throate which had like to cost mee my life for I kept my chamber 10 weekes and the defluction of rumes[200] from my head had corroded holes in the almonds of my throate, and the humour soe violent the [Sur – *crossed out*] Chiourgion[201] could find nothing to correct it but tuching with Mercury water (which (though by gods blessing)[202] succeeded well) some physetions told mee since, the remedy was as dangerous as the disease. After I had quit the Inns of Court, before I was married I had a lodgeing in fleet street and lived at large all the winter about the towne; when I misspent my tyme more then before frequenting bowleing [allyes – *crossed out*; grounds – *interlineated*][203] and gameing houses more than ever (though for other exstraviganses I was temperate). After I was 21 yeares of age I had a hint given mee by a very neare friend that my father had settled most of his esstate upon mee after my Mothers death, with advise to travell form some tyme, which he gave purposely that I should avoide beeing drawne in to bonds with my father. Though I well understood by this settlement I was lesse dependent on my father, yet truly I did soe much love and honour him as it made mee not lesse duty full and observant then

---

[196] The words 'and drinkeing' were added later, probably when 'and allsoe drinkeing' were crossed out.
[197] Cholmley's original word has been crossed out and the word 'enterd' written above it as shown. Both printed works have 'entered'.
[198] Cholmley changed his mind about this piece of 'wisdom'. At first he wrote it out in the singular, then changed it to the plural, so that 'his' became 'their', 'him' was turned into 'them', and 'he' into 'they'; but he neglected to alter the verb 'comes'. Both editors preferred to retain the singular form.
[199] Cholmley's peculiar word was printed in both texts as 'smattering'.
[200] This word was printed as 'rheum' in both texts.
[201] Both editors adopted the modern spelling of 'surgeon'.
[202] Sir Hugh neglected to close this interior bracket, and all his brackets were omitted in the printed texts.
[203] Both 'allyes' and 'grounds' are missing form the printed works. The former suggests a game played indoors, the latter, a game played on outdoor grass.

before but submitted to his will and pleasure in all things, and was afer drawne in to great ingaigements for him.[204]

A little before my leaveing Grayes In, one Mr Lovesesse a Kentis gentleman brought mee acquainted in a iourney with my deare wife by an accydentall meeting in Hide parcke with some other friends of his, I liked her well as theire was good cause yet noe Motion set on foote but the suppreame wisdome who orders all things and disposeth all things haveing determined it should bee [a ma]tch betweene produced.[205]

The 10th December *Anno Domini 1622* (being 22 yeares of age in July past) I was married at the Church in Milkestreet London to my deare wife Mrs. Elisabeth Twisden daughter to Sir William Twisden of East Peckham in the County of Kent knight and Barronet, there beeing few present at the marridge besides our parents and (f.16v.) their famulyes my father resideing with his | at a house he tooke in Moorefeilds. My father had with her in portion £2500 in redy mony paid in one day before marridge and security[206] for £500 more at the end of six Monthes, after; and there was made to her in ioynture lands vallewed to £500 per annum but worth above six, and an esstate setled on mee vallewed by my father but at £2700 per annum but worth more. The marridge was kept at Sir William Twisdens house in Redcrosse Street being the corner house over against the crosse, since much of it converted into severall tennements but then soe good a house as few gentlemen in the towne had the like, and bravely furnished. Till my wife had borne mee two sonns we lived in the house with her father who recyded most part of the winter in London and at Peckham his house in Kent in sommer. The 25th of June 1624 my deare wife at her fathers house in Redcrosse Street boare[207] her first child beeing a sonne cauled Richard, her Grand Mother the Countiss of Winchelcy[208] her father and myne, beeing the [Gossipps – *crossed out*] witnesses[209] or as we then said godfathers and god Mother; my wife would not bee perswaded but she went full 40 weeks and it was a faire fine child as ever was borne of a woeman and before it was well dressed looked broad with eies and peart as if it had bene a Month old; but it had a red head which seemed strange to my wife but not to me many of my Grandmothers kinred haveing the like and some of her children; but by that it was a yeare old the haire changed to a dellecate amber couller which continued soe whilst it lived, he was carried to be nursed at Watering bury in Kent where I thinke he did not happen of a gud nurse booth in respect her selfe was neare forty and her milk almost two yeares old booth which I dislike, my deare wife recoverd pretty well till towerds the end of the Month when I thinke she tooke some cold which produced soe great a sickness as I thought she would have dyed+ to relate what she saw in a transe[210] in the end it turned to a kind of[211] running goote and brought her soe weake as for neare 6 Monthes together

---

[204] This last phrase beginning with 'and' and added later by Sir Hugh with a sharper pen.

[205] The whole of this paragraph is nearly obliterated by wavy horizontal lines, almost certainly not made by Sir Hugh. The suspicion is that this is a case of editorial censorship, not the author having second thoughts. It is the only crossed-out passage in the manuscript which Cholmley did not subsequently rewrite; it is the only one to be erased in this way; and, most significantly, not a word of it appeared in either of the printed works. Why the editors should have thought fit to delete the whole paragraph is puzzling.

[206] The editors of 1787 and 1870 preferred their own word 'surety'.

[207] This word was mistakenly printed as 'brought' in both versions.

[208] The editors of both texts adopted 'Winchelsea' instead of Cholmley's spelling of the name.

[209] 'Witnesses' was printed in 1787 and 1870.

[210] The phrase 'to relate what she saw in a transe' was written down the left-hand margin to be inserted after the cross. In both texts it was printed at this point.

[211] Sir Hugh's 'kind of' was omitted in 1787 and 1870.

she could not move from her bed to the pallett[212] but as I carried her in my armes. In February [1624 – *interlineated*; 23 – *interlineated but crossed out*; before this – *crossed out*] King James had summoned a Parlament of which I was a member my father haveing procured mee to bee chosen a Burgess for Scarbrough, and the King dyeing the 24 of March followeing 1624 in the 22nd of his Reigne | his sonne Charles the 1st, (f.17r.) summoned another Parlament of which I was againe returned Burgesse for Scarbrough. And the plage increaseing at London it was adiurned to Oxford where the King not well pleased with the Parlaments proceeding dissolved it, from thence I went in to Yorkesheire to my father and told him I haveing now one sonne and my wife great with child I beganne to bee very sencyble of his debts and the great ingaidgements I was in for him, which I conceyved[213] would ruine us and[214] the esstate if some speedy course was not taken for the payment of them, which could not bee done with out saile of land to which I should bee willing, but that could not bee done suddenly, and theirfore said I was advised to with draw my selfe and goe for a while beyond sea, for that probably the Creditors when they saw I was out of their reach would bee willinger[215] to forbeare sewing their bond and to proceed to violent courses, which would but increase the debt, esspetially beeing assured of satisfaction as soone as land could bee sold; which my father seemed to approve of soe that I retorned back to my wife who was at her fathers house in Kent where I intended to stay till [my wife was brought to bed – *crossed out*] her delivery which was the [blank][216] of December following *Anno Domini* 1625 being a tuesday when was borne my second sonne named William and cristoned in the chappell at Peckham house [her Mother the lady Ann her brothers Thomas and John beeing witnesses – *interlineated*][217] by the minister of that Parish; my wife had with her 10 dayes together a midwife who sayeing she heard a neighbour of hers was in labour with whom she should have bene my deare wife abounded soe much in charrety as she ever preferred anothers caise and condition before her owne would needs have the midwife to goe to this sicke woeman and all though I infinitely opposed it, beleiving she should be brought to bed of 3 or 4 dayes, but that night she fell suddenly in to soe strong labour as wee were forced to send for a midwife but halfe a mile from us and could scarse get her in tyme. My deare wife beeing past danger I had gotten a passe to travell and was redy to take my iurney for France when I receyved a passionate letter from my father exspressing much love and greiffe desireing mee not to goe beyond sea but to [goe down to him to Whitby which – *crossed out*] come speake with him [and I being much tuched with his condetion and troble – *interlineated*][218] alterd my resolution and stayed my iurney to France where in I must acknowledge gods great providence, for with out mee my father could not have carried on any business, soe that I very[219] beleive my | goeing (f.17v.) beyond sea would have occationed great disorder if not ruine to the esstate *rebus sic stantibus*. As soone as my wife was [perfectly recovered – *crossed out*; past danger – *interlineated*] I went downe in to Yorkesheire to my father then at Whitby who

---

[212] In the edition of 1787 the word 'pallett' was printed as 'toilet'; in that of 1870, however, it was restored as 'pallett'.

[213] Printed in both versions as 'concluded'.

[214] The words 'us and' were omitted in 1787 but restored in 1870.

[215] In both printed texts this word is given as 'willing'.

[216] Sir Hugh's blank was not filled in either printed text.

[217] The clause ending 'witnesses' was a later manuscript addition as shown. In both printed versions it was placed after the word 'Parish'.

[218] Sir Hugh's additional and later comment was printed in the place he intended between 'him' and 'alterd'.

[219] In print this word became 'verily'.

propounded the setting over the whole esstate to mee for 10 yeares reserveing to him selfe only £400 per annum in the intrime, the accepting of which my father in law did not approve as conceyveing I should not bee able to Master the debts, nor did my owne nearest friends much incourridge mee, for my fathers debts were above £11000 and my owne 6 or £700[220] perhaps occationed by my owne exstravigances for as I was allwayes inclynable to play soe of late to a higher pitch, partly out of desparation to see my fathers condition soe bad, partly [out of covetousness and fear necessety for my father did not pay mee well what I was to have for my owne allowance – *crossed out*; in that my father did not pay mee allowance set over to mee at marridge for my owne allowance – *interlineated*][221], and mony beeing now at 10 in the hunderd the very interest and what my father was to have amounted to neare[222] as much as the revennue of all the land was at present; But as I held it iust and Honble[223] that my fathers debts should bee payed soe I saw an impossebillety for the effecting it with out my undertakeing, not only in respect the Inheritance of the land was setled on mee but that my father was not able to ride about and take the paines the mannage and prossecuteing of that business would requite[224], wherefore I accepted the motion and a lease was made to mee for 10 yeares of all the esstate (payeing him £400 per annum) yet as the Lord knowes not with out great troble and griefe to my heart, in that my father should bee reduced to soe small a proportion to live on, and I as it were possesse the esstate before he was dead, though it was but temporary and for his use too; but the searcher of all hearts knowes their was nothing I more desired then to see him reestablished in to his esstate and former power and esteeme in the Country, though it was not his gud pleasure it should bee soe for with in five[225] yeares my father dyed I haveing then £4000 debt to pay.

About May 1626 I undertooke this business of my fathers debts, and resolveing to live in the Gatehouse at Whitby which was then inhabitable soe that there[226] I beganne to bee first a builder or rather a repairer, for what I did was most with in doores the out sid fabricke beeing much as it is at this day. |

(f.18r.)   My wife beeing at London and to come downe to mee beeing informed of the conveniency of sendeing by sea but not of the present danger wee beeing then at warrs with Spaine sent downe not only our house hold stuffe and plate to the vallew of 4 or £500, but her owne weareing apperrell almost to what she had on her backe or in some small cloke bag, the shippe and guds were unfortunately taken by a man of warre belong[ing] to Dunkirke and carryed thether, by gud happe I had before got downe a sute of Hangeings and bed for our owne[227] chamber else wee had bene to provide that[228] againe when mony was but scarse with us. In August 1627 she comes to mee with one of her brothers cauled William who remaned there with us that winter, all of us in the Gatehouse, when though a tyme of troble I have heard my deare wife often say she never lived with more content any part of her life then this

---

[220] Cholmley first wrote '5 to 600' then altered the figures to '6 or 700', as they later appeared in print.
[221] Sir Hugh's 'allowance' became 'sum' in print.
[222] The word 'neare' was missed out in 1787 and 1870.
[223] 'Honble' was extended to 'honourable' in both printed versions.
[224] In both printed texts 'requite' was changed to 'require'.
[225] Sir Hugh first wrote 'six' and then altered it to 'five'. Both printed works adopted 'six', though in fact if Hugh took over the estate in May 1626 and his father died in September 1631 then the interval was nearer five than six years (*Whitby Parish Register*, p.103).
[226] Though it made less sense than what Cholmley actually wrote, this word was printed twice as 'then' instead of 'there'.
[227] Cholmley's 'our owne' was printed as 'one' in the 1787 edition, but correctly restored in that of 1870.
[228] The word 'that' was omitted in both printed versions.

winter, for our selfes young people loved much and ioyed in one another and at the next house she had the company of my Mother in law which was very agreeable to her, and my sister Trotter, a handsome sweet natured woeman who my wife loved dearely, My Ant Bushell and other gud neighbours in the towne and though my selfe had many [trob – *crossed out*][229] business to troble and perplex my head in the day, god gave mee abillety to lay all under my pillow at night soe that then they were no troble to mee.

Those which shall[230] heare my father had settled £2700 per annum on mee[231] or shall view the great extent of land, being all his from Stoope[232] brow to Whitby Abbey except 2 oxgangs that antiently belonging to Allatsons, and the higher Normanby before my marridge sold to Newton;[233] may thinke it no diffecoult matter to pay these debts, but on the other side considering the condetion and posture of our esstate and affayres at the present, it had bene impossible to have paid them with out ruine of the esstate if the Lord [Jesus – *interlineated*][234] had not bene with mee, had not assisted mee and brought all things to comply and fall out for my advantage in the very nicke of tyme as they did; for though the land was really worth £2700 per annum, noe friend I had but my father him selfe did beleive it of that vallew, for much of it was in lease for 14 or 15 yeares at low rents and nether the tennants nor my fathers officers for their owne interests would admitt of his vallewations, and my unckle Legard who was my best friend and who I much relyed on, haveing a notion of them according to the | tyme he viewed them at the marridge of my Mother would not admit of my fathers (f.18v.) rate and improvement, all at present did not appeare above £1500 per annum and of that seven or eight hunderd in my fathers owne hand which in respect of the bad yeares the fall of the prisces of all guds at the tyme it would nether let nor rase the rent, by keepeing in our hand; the lands lyeing most intyrely togerher under two Manners [Whitby and Fyleing – *interlineated*] they were not soe very vendable much of them charged with my Grand Mother Mother and wifes ioyntures, the Inhabitants of the Country[235] not soe able [nor tradeing soe great – *interlineated*] as at present, few was in condetion to bee purchassors. My father in law who many thought most concerned for preserving the esstate gave mee for ruined, and would not interest him selfe in any sorte to assist mee, which made other friends stand at gaste[236] till they saw which way I might probably winde out of this laborinth, soe at first I was put to rely meerely on gods providence and direction, and my owne witts.

[237]You may immagine soe vast a debt had many and severall creditors most about London and in severall scriver shopps and though I intended noe man should loose a penny only desireing their forbearance till such tyme as I could sell land or rase mony, yet it was difficult to make them beleive soe, or keepe them from sewing their bonds, and running violent courses against mee, which must needs have increased the debt

---

[229] Sir Hugh had begun to write 'troble', changed his mind and crossed out the first four letters. In both the 1787 and 1870 editions his incomplete, erased word was printed as 'hot'!

[230] The word 'shall' was omitted in 1787 but not in 1870.

[231] The words 'on mee' were omitted in 1787 but not in 1870.

[232] In both printed versions Cholmley's second letter o was omitted from this place-name which is now spelled 'Stoupe'.

[233] In August 1621 the Cholmleys had sold the capital messuage of Normanby Hall, then occupied by Richard Conyers, gentleman, with its three garths and twelve closes, for £560 to Isaac Newton 'scholler', son of Christopher Newton, merchant of Whitby (Whitby LPS, PB 878).

[234] The word 'Jesus' was inserted but omitted from both printed editions.

[235] In the 1787 edition 'Country' was printed as 'county'; in 1870, Cholmley's word was restored.

[236] In both printed versions 'at gaste' became 'aghast'.

[237] At this point Sir Hugh began a new paragraph which was not acknowledged in either printed edition.

and consequently ruined the esstate, and theirfore to bring them to reason the first thing I did was to bye in two statues[238] of £500 a peece the greatest in cumberance on the land, and put them in friends hands I could commaund, and then have them extended, by which meanes I secured the land, endevering alsoe to let as much as possiblely I could of that my father had in his hand, next I gave land to as many as would take, leting the rest of the Creditors understand my intention to satisfie every man soe soone as possiblely I could, which gave them soe good content as I thinke not above two or 3 sewed their bonds; and with in two yeares by gods blessing I had ether paid the debts or given securety to their contents soe that I could passe freely and sayfely about my affayres and to some who had bene bound with my father with out mee and forced to pay it I did not only repay the princypall and use but charge of sute to a penny which they had bene put to. And now these debts beeing soe stated and setled as it was visable they would bee payed and a competent esstate remaineing, my good unckle Mr John Legard of Ganton (who had taken much paines to assist mee and divers iorneyes to London at his owne charge), together with that unfortunate but
(f.19r.)   Noble gentleman Sir John Hotham | my cosen Jermyn once removed [and deare friend – *interlineated*] became bound with mee for the satisfieing of some of the most importunate debts to the vallew of £2500 which was all the friends I was ever beholden to in this great exigent[239] and troble, which that I should soe soone and soe well settle is most miraculous and indeed had bene impossible as the esstate then stood if the devine providence in a most special and signall manner had not bene directing and concurreing, for if all things had not falne out pat and opportunely in the very nicke of tyme as they did, that is to say a propensenes in the Creditors to forbeare sutes, a willingness in some others beyond exspectation to take land, others comeing enexspected to bye land when I was in greatest plounge for monyes and thereby inableing mee to satisfie the most importunate Creditors, the esstate had certainely bene ruined. And theirfore I desire that I may all the dayes of my life acknowledge gods gudness to mee in the Conduct of this busness, for which I prayse his holy name, and pray my children may alsoe have it in rememberance as beeing conserned. And truly it was alsoe gods mercy and gudnes that I was diverted from my Jorney into France for by my comeing to my father the Creditors had a better beleife of my reall intentions to satisfie them, and I being young and haveing an able body was much fitter then my father to ride and toyle about this business which in truth was great, yet I praysed god it nether preiudiced my health nor deiected my sperrett for I carried in mynde a speach my father told mee he had from his unckle Sir Raph Babthorpe my Grand Mothers brother a wise gentleman, which was not to bee deiected for any troble and crosse, for when a mans owne heart [forsakes – *crossed out*; failes – *interlineated*] him all the world forsakes him, as by exsperience I have found they are apt to doe in affliction, [for it is a most incredable – *crossed out*] not only strangers but even a mans friends, for when I was in distresse and in danger to bee ruined by these debts, every man (except some very few perticuler [friends – *crossed out*; persons – *interlineated*]) looked coldly and shily [at – *crossed out*][240] on mee, and as soone as ever I appeared againe in publicke and that it was evident I should preserve a gud fortune,

---

[238] In print Cholmley's word became 'statutes'. In fact, these two 'statutes' were debts of a thousand pounds each to two London scriveners, Robert Harrison and John Betts. However, Harrison accepted £564 for his bond and Betts £568 for his. The former was bought by Sir Hugh's uncle, Henry Wickham, archdeacon of York, who had married Annabella Cholmley, the youngest of Sir Richard's sisters; the latter was purchased by another of Sir Hugh's uncles, John Legard of Ganton (NYCRO, ZPK 12, 13).

[239] Printed as 'in these great exigencies' in both editions.

[240] These words were printed as 'shyly at' in both versions.

those who before[241] would not have stept to the doore to doe mee a sleight curtesie or scarse afford mee countnance was now redy to faune upon and imbrace mee and theirfore no one thing should make a man more a gud husband and cautious to preserve his esstate then that he need not bee beholden to another, for when [he hath need – *interlineated*] he shall not only finde freindshippe | but the proverb (f.19v.) verefied that the borrower is a servant to the lender, which tooke as great impression upon mee as any man whose nature was to doe curtesies raher then [be beholden – *crossed out*] receyve [for one – *crossed out*] though my fortune was otherwise; yet in this tyme of collaption[242] of friends there was some few I must confesse in whome I found noe change or alteration, and amongst those I should bee most ingrate[243] and unworthy not to commememorate the love and the memory of that thrise Noble lady my wifes Mother the lady Ann Twisden, who I could not finde did love or esteeme mee [one iot – *interlineated*] lesse for any diminution or change in my esstate but manefested soe great kindness to mee as if it had bene in her power I [am confident I – *interlineated*] should have needed noe other person to support mee then her selfe. She was as beautyfull a person as most [of – *crossed out*] in – *[interlineated]* the Nation in her tyme and had a most graceful deportment of singuler parties and wisdome sirpasseing her sex, pious and virtous and had a passeing sweet gud nature soe that I must professe I never did know any woeman her parell in all points. My unckle Legard and that famuly of Ganton Sir John Hotham and my kinsmen the Trotters of Skelton[244] Castle were alsoe very kinde and firme to mee in my adversety and theirfore are to bee rememberd and to reioyce with mee in prosperety which I desire succeding posterety may carry in memory with a particuler love to those famulyes for my sake. The great love I boare to my deare wife and her two little boyes Dicke and Will made mee very dyligent and industrious in my affaires, and I prayse god I never wanted mony for our nescessary ocations or was in such strates and necescetys as frequently men are who have such trobles upon them; which I can only attribute to the great providence of the Almighty who most miracculussly supplyed mee as I had need.

At Midsommer 1627[245] I sent for my two little boyes to bee brought to Whitby who wear then in Kent, Dicke was 3 yeares old and Will a yeare and halfe. The day wee exspected them my father and I roade out to meet them on the way which wee did on the Moores a little above Hausker Intacke, poore Dicke who was a weake tender child, dropped and seemed weary with the iorney but Will, as soone as ever wee came to the coach sid fell a whopeing and hollowing and staireing upon us as if he had bene well acquainted in soe much | as old Mr George Conyers[246] of Fyleing (f.20r.) Thorpe who was sent to bring them [in to the Country – *crossed out*] from the south said to my father Sir you must bee very indulgent and take caire of this elder[247] child for he is very tender but if you turne this other on the Moores he will like and thrive

---

[241] The word 'before' was omitted in the 1787 edition but not in that of 1870.

[242] This word became 'defection' in print in 1787 but was correctly rendered in the 1870 edition.

[243] Both printed editions have 'ungrateful' here.

[244] In print this name was incorrectly altered to 'Skilton'.

[245] Sir Hugh first wrote '1628' and later the date was changed to '1627' and so printed in 1787 and 1870. Since Richard was born in June 1624 and William in December 1625, then the event described must have occurred in the summer of 1627.

[246] Usually described as George Conyers, gentleman, he had been High Constable of Whitby Strand and was a wealthy, substantial landowner. In 1627 he paid the Cholmleys £337 for two farms in Fylingdales, and, in 1633, Sir Hugh sold to him Middlewood Hall in Fylingthorpe for £420. (*NRQSR*, iv, pp.11, 52; Whitby LPS, PB 1772, 1779).

[247] This word became 'eldest' in both printed editions.

there, which I beseach the Lord he may they beeing falne to his [patremony shaire – *crossed out*; lot – *interlineated*] and portion by the death of his elder brother.

In October 1628[248] in the Gatehouse at Whitby was borne my eldest daughter named Elisabeth, and my wife as after the other two children the Month beeing out grew ill and worse by my goeing to London, which did alsoe doble my troble in respect of my businese and her indisposetion, which went ever neare my heart for I loved her dearely and tenderly, but at my retorne she grew better for my absence alwayes increased if not caused her illness.

The yeare following produced great greife to us booth, for in August 1628 dyed my deare sister Trotter[249] in child bed, and in January following her father[250] Sir William Twisden and in the spring she went to London to see her Mother I went not up with her, we begining then to build at Fyleing Hall[251] whether wee intended [as soone as possible with conveniency we would – *crossed out*; to – *interlineated*] remove for haveing now 3 children the Gatehouse grew too strate, and the place displeaseing since the death of my sister. This Fyleing was parte of my wifes ioynture at marridge and by my father vallewed at £200 per annum, but Mr Conyers who was tennant took advantage[252] by our beeing incumberd with debts, and would give mee but £160 rent a yeare and rather then have more land in my hand I let it soe for 7 yeares, with Provisoe to have the lease crenderd[253] up to mee in caise I went to live at it my selfe, which now I intended, and to beestow two or £300 to an old house there standing but as it is with most builders I exceeded my accoumpt for I thinke it cost [neare a £1000 – *crossed out*; £800 – *interlineated*] At the end of this somer[254] I brought my wife from London first to Whitby againe, but soone after my sister Strickeland chanceing to dye there,[255] wee removed to Fyleing Hall after Michelmas, where wee lodged in [that old part – *crossed out*] of the old house, yet the new (as I beleive) had an ill influence upon us for a ffrench woeman who wated on my little girle Betty that winter dyed there and my eldest sonne Richard had such a defluction of Rume as it put him in to a weakness of which he alsoe dyed in June following, to the great greife of mee[256] and my deare wife, soe that I wish this may bee a good monetion to posterety not to inhabitt in a new built house till the walls and plastering worke bee well and thurrowly dryed which will not bee in lesse tyme then a winter and sommer,
(f.20v.) for nothing is | more unholesome then the smell of lyme and morter and divers which in my knowlidge hath receyved great preiudice in their health and some lost their lifes[257] by it alsoe. This sonne of myne cauled Richard by the defluction of rume had a great filme growne over one of his eies and being to carry him to Notingham to an Occulist, at Ferry-briggs he fell in to convoultions fitts and there dyed and from

---

[248] Sir Hugh's mistake was printed as he wrote it. In fact, Elisabeth was baptised in Whitby parish church 29 October 1626 (*Whitby Parish Register*, p.21).

[249] Mrs Ursula Trotter, wife of George Trotter, was buried at Whitby parish church 22 August 1628 (*Whitby Parish Register*, p.101).

[250] Sir Hugh meant his wife's father, not his sister's; this was made clear in the edition of 1870, but not in that of 1787.

[251] This was Fyling Old Hall, originally a hunting lodge next to the abbot of Whitby's deer park. Though much altered since Sir Hugh's time, it still survives (O.S. map ref. 943028).

[252] This word was printed in both editions as 'advantage'.

[253] This word was printed in both editions as 'surrendered'.

[254] After the word 'summer', the 1870 edition had the year 1629 in brackets, which Sir Hugh did not write and which had not been printed in 1787.

[255] Margaret, wife of William Strickland esquire, was buried at Whitby parish church 28 October 1629 (*Whitby Parish Register*, p.102).

[256] The words 'mee and' were omitted form the printed work of 1787, but restored in that of 1870.

[257] This word became 'sight' in the first printed edition but was correctly printed in 1870.

thence his body was borought to yorke and layed in the church at the lower end of
Micklegate cauled [blank]²⁵⁸ close to my Grad[sic] Mother where she my Grandfather
my unckle John and Ant Jane Cholmeley lye all in terred,²⁵⁹ [He] was much fairer and
more beautifull then other my brood for his haire was amber couller his eies gray and
his complection as fayre white and red as ever I saw. My Grandmother dyed about a
year before haveing often said their was nothing she desired soe much as to see this
child which she never did but was destined to bee buried close to her side. He dyed at
the age of five yeares yet had the courridge and resolution of a man for beeing to have
an incission on a lumpe which aroase in his arme he would say, father would you have
it done and I answeard yes sweetheart for your Doctor thinks it necessary then would
he say doe it and held his arme with out ether shrinkeing or whimpering,²⁶⁰ though
blood and corruption rann out, the same resolution would he [doe – crossed out; use –
interlineated] in takeing of phisike which [naturally – interlineated but crossed out] he
could not endure.

At Michelmas 1630²⁶¹ I carried my wife my two children William and Elisabeth to
London where wee lived that winter at London in the house with my brother and
sister Yelverton²⁶² who were newly married And Midsommer following leaveing my
boy Will with his Grand Mother the lady Ann Twisden I and my wife and our little
girle returned in to Yorkesheire to our house at Fyleing hall, when wee came in to
the Country wee found my father very weak of a looseness of which he dyed at
Michelmas following.²⁶³

²⁶⁴My deare wife soone afer conceyved with child with my sonne the end of June
after beeing 1632 dyed my daughter Elisabeth to the great greife of mee and her
Mother wee booth loveing her very tenderly it beeing very like my wife and as witty a
child as [ingenious – interlineated] ever was of her age; [but the Lord – crossed out] and
the troble I tooke for this child together with some indisposetion upon mee before had
like to cost mee my life for I [contracted – crossed out; had – interlineated] a very sharpe
fitt of sickness, but god soone after was pleased to recompence my losse and troble
with the birth of my sonne Hugh borne there at Fyleing upon a Satterday the 21st day
of July beeing the eave of the feast upon which I was borne my selfe cauled Mary
Magdelen; he was [christened – crossed out; Baptised – interlineated] the great chamber at
Fyleing hall my brother in law Sir Christopher Yelverton my unckle Legard and Ant
Bushell²⁶⁵ being Gossipps, or witnesses; and to take it one Mr Reming²⁶⁶ the Minister

²⁵⁸ Cholmley left no blank space here though this was indicated in both printed editions. The name of the
church that Sir Hugh could not remember was St John's.
²⁵⁹ Cholmley's grandfather, Sir Henry, and his grandmother, Margaret, were both buried in St John's in
1616 and 1628 respectively. His uncle John Cholmley, younger brother of Sir Richard, was also interred
there along with Jane Cholmley, his unmarried sister. At this point Sir Hugh added an extra sentence
about the appearance of his eldest son Richard in the left-hand margin.
²⁶⁰ This word was changed to 'whining' in both printed works.
²⁶¹ Cholmley first wrote '1629' then changed it to '1630', the correct date.
²⁶² Elisabeth Twysden's younger sister, Anne, was married to Sir Christopher Yelverton of Easton Mauduit
in Northamptonshire. Hugh and Christopher were to become close friends and political allies.
²⁶³ Sir Richard Cholmley was buried in the chancel of Whitby parish church 23 September 1631 (Whitby
Parish Register, p.103).
²⁶⁴ The remaining 13 lines on this side of the folio and the whole of 21r. which follows were subsequently
deleted and rewritten later in the manuscript. However, since this first draft appeared later in a slightly
different form and was ignored by the editors of 1787 and 1870, it has been retained here.
²⁶⁵ This was Dorothy Bushell, wife of Nicholas Bushell of Bagdale Hall, Whitby, and mother of Captain
Browne Bushell, Hugh's Civil War associate.
²⁶⁶ This was Robert Remmington, vicar of Whitby from 1624 until 1638. He was a close and trusted friend
of Sir Hugh.

then preacher at Whitby, and the boy was put to nurse to one guddy dickeson at Southward houses[267] close by, but to remove the death of our girl my wife and I removed from Fyeling and tooke a house for the winter at a place cauled Lanckton

(f.21r.) neare Malton; about Easter | wee returned to Fyeling beeing now earnest to see her little boy whom she had not since he was 2 monthes old; before wee came to the house I gave order the Nurse should dress her owne boy, about half a yeare elder than mine, in my boyes coat and to have him in her armes when my wife came to the [house][268] and though the nurses boy had gray eies and mine black I had told my deare wife [they were] gray like my Dicks who was dead, which she much desired, soe that when she saw the nurses boy she tooke him in her armes and seemed fond of him and as well contented with him as [her owne], but after a while carring him in to an inner parler where the nurse made had our boy Hugh in her armes as soon as ever my deare wife cast her eie upon him [she gave a start and – *interlineated*] all the blood in her body comeing in to her face she said sweetheart this is my boy and takeing him in armes fell a kissing him with more fondness and earnest then she did the other. I keepeing a sober countnance began to tell her that was the nurses boy, but she would not bee perswaded but answeared I am sure this is my boy and if I must owne the other I will have this two, and indeed it was pretty and admirable to see how by the very instinct of nature she found out her owne child.

At Michelmas 1633 the Lady Ann Twisdens my wifes Mother did mee the honour and favour to come to mee at Fyeling hall [where I then resided, it being before I sold it – *interlineated*] and with her my brother Sir Rogers wifes[269] though then not married, here they remayned till March following I enioyed little of their company in the tyme beeing drawne much to London about the purchase of Daletowne[270] and Asleby[271] the latter of which beeing in the Crowne only dureing the heires of Leonard Dacres and all faileing after my purchasse it fell to the Earl of Arrundell and Lord William Howerd who had married the heires genral of the Lord Dacres and soe I lost the Lordshippe for 20 yeare till I purchad *de novo*. I was not ignorant [it] was a little continget yet was content to runne the hassard in respect I knew Daletowne a gud pennyworth. And now as well, for inableing mee to goe through this purchasse as to pay my debts I sold Fyeling hall and the demeynes to Sir John Hotham. |

(f.21v.)   [272]In Easter tearme 1632 I went to London for obteyneing something for reed-

---

[267] These are now known as South House Farm (O.S. map ref. 953037).

[268] The right-hand side of this sheet is rubbed and the ink now very faint. The words in square brackets have been taken from Burnett's transcription.

[269] Sir Roger, the eldest son and heir of Sir William and Lady Ann Twysden, was married to Isabella Saunder.

[270] As Sir Hugh suggests, the lordship and manor of Daletown in Hawnby, then consisting of five tenanted farms about seven miles north-west of Helmsley, were a promising investment. In January 1658, only two months after his death, his heirs sold the property to Thomas Bellasis, Viscount Fauconberg, for £2950. (Whitby LPS, PB 1360).

[271] Presumably, Cholmley meant Aislaby in Eskdale, an extensive manor which changed hands in 1640 for a thousand pounds. There was some difference of view about whether Aislaby belonged to Langbaurgh wapentake or Whitby Strand and it appears not to have belonged to Whitby abbey or any Cholmley before Sir Hugh. No record of his purchase has been found. (Whitby LPS, PB 411; *VCH, YNR*, ii, p.502).

[272] Clearly, Sir Hugh had got ahead of himself. He now realised that before the death of his daughter Elisabeth and the birth of Hugh he had to relate the subject of Whitby's west pier. This is why he crossed through what he had previously written on 20v. and 21r., and returned to Easter 1632. The paragraph that follows is now very faint and in parts illegible. Again, Burnett's transcription was an essential aid here.

efieing the peers at Whitby haveing not with out troble and difeculty perswaded the townsmen to Petetion the Counsell table for that purpose whereby the Earl of Straffords favour I procured liberty for a generall contribution through out England and could not get a townsman to imploy them selfes in it every one soe intent of his perticuler profitts as it made them neglect the publicke . . .[273] soe that after the grant the business had not bene prossecuted but that I got two of my honest neighbours about mee in Fyleing Dales to undertake the collection vidz John Faireside[274] and Henry Dickeson[275] by which meanes I thinke neare £500 was gathered[276] and that part of the peere to the west of the Harbour erected which in the iudgement of all men hath preserved a great part of the towne from being ruined by the sea and kept the Harbour open yet will not the townsmen bestow caire and paines to lay up one stone or fill up a breach when the sea hath made one. I wish with all my hearte the next generation may have more publicke sperretts.[277]

[278]At Whitsontyd I retoorned from London to Fyleing with the lady Yelverton my wifes sister who came to my wifes labour being then with child, at my comeing home I found my little girle Bette exstreame sicke who dyed with in a forthnight to the great greife of my wife and selfe for wee were exceeding fond of her, booth in respect she was like her Mother, and as witty a child I thinke as was in the world of her age being but 4 yeares and a halfe; her body was carried to Whitby and buried in the chancell neare to the wall betweene the doore of chancell and my fathers monument.[279] This griefe comeing upon mee when I had before some indisposetion of health had like to have cost my life, nor may I forget gods great mercy and deliverance soone after when I and my wife behinde mee rideing to take the aire passeing up an ascent the horses hinder legs sliped in to a quicke spring up to his very body at which my wife tombled of the horse and I backeward upon her leting goe the reine least the horse came upon us booth. She was with in 3 weeks of her tyme yet blessed bee god tooke no harme, though I have a conceyte Hugh then in his Mothers belly caught some harme in one of his little fingers which came into the world with a wristled nale as if it had bene crushed and soe continues.

The lord who after the saddest and blackest stormes causeth the sunne beames to breake out and refresh all creatures was pleased in the midst of these trobles to cheare up our hearts with the birth of my sonne Hugh of whome my wife was deliverd at Fyleing hall the 21 of July being a Satterday and eive to the feast I was borne myselfe vidz Mary Magdellens day. Wee had then but one child my sonne William, which

---

[273] There are several illegible words here which were omitted from the printed versions.
[274] John Fairside, Farside or Farsyde, was one of the Cholmleys' leading tenants, who also held land in Hutton Buscel and Scarborough. He and his son William had bought Hewlett wood and intake at the southern extremity of the Cholmley estate. (Whitby LPS, PB 1782).
[275] Henry Dickinson was another well-to-do Cholmley tenant. He lived in the mansion house on Thorny Brow and also held the farm at Spring Hill. Later, he and his son William bought Flash (Flask) farm from Sir Hugh for £460 (Whitby LPS, PB 540, 870, 884).
[276] Sir Hugh's brief reference to the collection is misleading. Three years later to Strafford he reported that some English counties had still not paid a penny and some of the money coming in was 'in fartheings at the tyme not current'. Even in 1638, six years after the first writs had been authorised, some were still to be issued (Sheffield Archives, WWM, Strafford Papers, 15(76), 10(214); see below, pp.190–1).
[277] Sir Hugh's censorious and self-congratulatory remarks about Whitby's west pier have been misunderstood as often as they have been quoted. The new pier was intended to protect Sir Hugh's own commercial and property interests on the opposite side of the mouth of the river Esk. The western riverside, now crowded with storehouses, landing staithes and boat-building yards serving the alum industry at Mulgrave, was protected naturally by Burtree Crag and West Cliff.
[278] At the beginning of this new paragraph the manuscript becomes more legible.
[279] Whitby's parish register does not appear to record Elisabeth's burial.

made his welcomme. He was baptised in the great chamber[280] by Mr Remington Minister of Whitby, my brother in law Sir Christopher Yelverton my unckle Legard and Ant Bushell beeing the witnesses or gossips. To put the death of our girle out of our myndes I with my wife and famuly removed to a place cauled Lankton, neare to Malton, and retorned at Easter to Fyleing, and she longing to see her boy who left but

(f.22r.) 2 Months old | being nursed neare hand at a place cauled Southward houses I gave order the nurse should dresse her owne boy (but halfe a year elder then myne) in my boyes coate, and to have him in her armes when my wife came in to the house; and though the nurses boy had gray eies and mine blacke I had told my deare wife they were [gray][281] like my Dicks who was dead which she much desired soe that when she saw the nurses boy she tooke him[282] in her armes and kissed [him] and seemed very well contented with him; till goeing in to an inner par[ler] where the nurses mayde had our boy Hugh in her armes as soone [as] ever my deare wife cast her eie upon him she gave a start [and all] her blood comeing in to her face, she said, o lord sweet heart [this is] my boy and running to him caught him in her armes and kissed him with much more [fondness and – *interlineated*] earnestness then she did the other yet I keepeing a sober countnance told her that was the nurses boy, but she replyed if I must have the other, I will have this too for I am sure this is my owne boy, and in earnest it was prety and admirable to see how by the instinct of nature she had found out her owne child.

At Michelmas 1633 the lady Ann Twisden my wifes Mother did mee the favour and honour to come to my house at Fyleing hall where I then resided and with her Mrs Issabella Sanders [now – *crossed out*; after – *interlineated*] wife to my brother Sir Roger Twisden. They remained here till March though I missed much of their company by beeing most of Michelmas tearme at London tuching the purchase of Daletowne and Asleby, the latter of which was in the crowne only dureing the lifes of the heares males of the lord Dacres all which faileing[283] soone after my purchasse it devolved on the Earl of Arundell and Lord William Howard of Nauworth Castle who had married the heires genrall [of the Lord Dacres – *interlineated*][284] soe that with in halfe a yeare after I had purchased I was outed by them and soe continued 20 yeares till I bought it againe, I knew the title was contingent[285] yet adventured, knoweing Daletowne worth my mony; As well for in ableing mee to pay my debts and goe through this purchasse at this tyme I sold Fyleing hall, and the demeynes to Sir John Hotham, as I said before these were set over to my wife in ioynture at £200 per annum yet was I forced to let them to Conyers for £160 but comeing to them my selfe I had improved them to £240 per annum and according to the rent I sold them after 15 yeare purchasse and £800 over for my house, which haveing sold I removed the spring following in to the gate house at Whitby where I remayned till my house[286] was repaired and habitable which then was very ruinous and unhandsome the walls beeing only of tymber and plaster, and ill contrived with in; and besides the repaired

---

280 From Sir Hugh's earlier reference on folio 20v. above p.91, it is clear that 'the great chamber' was in Fyling Old Hall. The 1787 edition has 'church' printed instead of 'chamber', whereas the 1870 version has 'chamber'.

281 In several places the right-hand side of this sheet is illegible. What Sir Hugh wrote here can be deduced from the previous draft of this passage and the two printed editions.

282 Both printed versions have 'it' here instead of 'him'.

283 In the 1787 edition 'faileing' became 'falling', but in 1870 it was printed correctly.

284 This insertion above and at the end of the line was not written by Sir Hugh though it was printed in 1787 and 1870.

285 This word was wrongly printed in both editions as 'continued'.

286 By 'my house' Sir Hugh meant Abbey House, the principal home of the family in Whitby.

or rather reedefieing the barne and I heightened the out walls of the Court double to
what they were and made all the wall round | about the paddocke soe that the place   (f.22v.)
hath bene improved very much booth for buty and profitt by mee more then all my
Ancestors for there was not a tree about the house but set in my tyme and almost by
my owne hand the Court levels which layde upon hangeing ground [unhandsomely –
interlineated] very ill watered haveing only the low well with in Almas close[287] which I
covered and alsoe [erected – *crossed out*] and discovered [and erected – *interlineated*] the
other adioyneing cundet and the well[288] in the Court yeard from whence I conveyed
by leaden pipes water in to the house Brewhouse and washhouse.

In December 1635 [upon a tuesday – *interlineated*] was borne my daughter Ann at
the said gate house baptised in the church at Whitby by Mr Remington.[289] The
Country beeing destitute of a Justice of peace I put my selfe in to the Commission of
peace haveing at Hackness a troblesome neighbour one Sir Thomas Hoby who had
cost my father many a 100 in sutes and beeing the next Justice and haveing occation to
act much with him I carried my selfe as curteously as was possible and alsoe gave him
complyance with him as must I could.[290] The Country suffering much for want of a
Justice of peace there not beeing any with in 12 miles of Whitby [I put my selfe in to
the Commission – *crossed out*] I condiscended to bee put in to the Commission, the
more unwillingly inrespect I was to ioyne and act for the most part with my fathers
old enemy Sir Thomas Hoby, but I resolved to avoide all differences and give all the
compliance that might bee but he was of such a nature unlesse a man became his very
slave there was noe keepeing freindshippe for he loved to carry all things afer his owne
way and humour [whether right or wrong – *crossed out*] how uniust or iniurious
soever, and with in a yeare being at the Sessions and differing in oppinion with him he
thought to put an affront on mee by determining the matter after his owne mynde but
I puting it to the oppinion of the bench had them all on my side, in soe much as he
turning about said to the gentleman that satt next him, his Grand father once crossed
mee thus on the bench but I made him repent it and soe will I this man, and truly
soone after he began a sute against mee in the Starre chamber, and I one against him in
the Court at Yorke but findeing him selfe to have the worse end of the staffe procured
the Lord Coventry then the Lord Keeper to send for mee and to compose booth, but
after this checke [I gave him – *interlineated*] in the Sessions he never appeared there
more, nor was soe active and formidable to the Country as formerly;[291] The Sydnams
now possessed of Hackness may in [a great measure – *crossed out*] some sorte thanke
mee for it for I beleive[292] Sir Thomas Hoby to make the Lord Coventry his friend

[287] This name was printed as 'Almsers-close' in both editions. Sir Hugh was referring to Almshouse Close,
      the extensive pasture on the west side of Abbey House which separates it from the town of Whitby.
[288] Both editions misprinted this word as 'wall'. Sir Hugh clearly meant to explain that a new well had been
      dug in the courtyard, whereas previously there had been only one source of water, the old well in
      Almshouse Close.
[289] Ann was baptised in Whitby parish church 7 December 1634 (*Whitby Parish Register*, p.29). Again, Sir
      Hugh had the wrong year.
[290] Having reached this point, Sir Hugh then crossed out the previous six lines and started again with the
      words 'the country'.
[291] Sir Hugh first took his seat on the North Riding Bench at Helmsley early in 1632, but whether by
      design or accident he did not meet Sir Thomas at the Quarter Sessions until October that year.
      However, the confrontation here described by Cholmley probably took place much later, at Malton in
      July 1635, the only other occasion when the two sat together. Sir Thomas did not bring his action in Star
      Chamber until the end of 1636. By this time he was nearly 70 years old and, particularly since the death
      of his wife, Lady Margaret, in 1633, a spent force. Sir Hugh gives himself too much credit for Hoby's
      decline and absence from the North Riding Sessions after July 1635.
[292] 'I believe' was omitted from both printed works.

against mee in this difference propounded[293] his cosen Sydnum in marridge to my
Lords Granchild and soe setled Hackness on him which in right belonged to Mr
Dakins next kinsman[294] to Sir Thomas his lady whose land that was.[295]

In Springe 1636 I removed from the gate house in to my house at Whitby being
now finished and fitt to receyve mee and my deare wife (who was excellent at
dressing and making all handsome with in doores) had put it in to a fine posture and
(f.23r.) furnished with many gud things soe that I beleive there | were few gentlemen in the
Country of my ranke exceeded it.

[296]Soone after my deare wife miscarried of a child haveing bene soe not above 10
weeks. I was at this tyme made a Deputy Leiutent and Coronell over the trayned
bands with in the Hunderds of Whitby Strand, Rydale, Pickering Leyth and
Scarbrough towne, for that my father beeing dead the Country looked upon mee
as the cheif of my famuly and haveing masterd my debts I did not only appeare at all
publicke meetings in very handsome [gentilemanly – interlineated] equapage but lived
in as handsome and plentyfull a fashon at home as [any] gentleman of my ranke [in all
the Country – interlineated]; I had [neare – crossed out] betweene 30 and 40 in my
ordnarely famuly a chapline who said prayers every morneing at six, and againe before
dinner and supper; a Porter who meerely attended the gates which were ever shut up
[before dinner – interlineated] when the bell rung to prayers and not oppened till one
[aclocke – interlineated] except for some strangers who came to dinner which was ever
fitt to receyve 3 or 4 beside my famuly with out any troble: and what ever their fayre
was they were sure to have a hearty welcome.[297] Twice a weeke a certaine number of
old people widdowes or indigent persons were served at my gates with bread and gud
pottage mad of beefe which I mention that those who succede may follow the
example.[298]

About June 1637[299] two Holland men of warre, had chassed in to Whitby Harbour a
small pickroone or vessell belonging to the King of Spaine which had in her only 30 men
and two small gunns; one of the Hollanders had 400 men and other 200 and the captaines
leaveing their shipps at Ancker in the roade came with their long boates [on land –
interlineated] with 40 men every one haveing his pistolls. The Dunkirker for more
securety had put him selfe above the bridge, and placed his two gunns upon his decks
with all his men redy to defend. I haveing notice of this feareing they might doe here [the
like affront – interlineated] as they did at Scarbrough [when they – interlineated] landed a
100 men and took a shippe belonging to the King of Spaine out of the Harbour,[300] sent

[293] In print this word became 'proposed'.

[294] There is an ink blot over the word 'kinsman' which is missing from both printed editions.

[295] This marks the end of an afterthought in the form of a marginal insertion which began 'The Sydnams'.
Sir Hugh's account of why Hoby came to make John Sydenham his heir and why he advanced his
marriage to Lord Coventry's granddaughter is too tainted with spiteful malice to be accepted. For an
alternative view see J. Binns, 'Sir Hugh Cholmley of Whitby, 1600–57: His Life and Works' (unpub.
Ph.D. thesis, Leeds Univ. 1992), pp.275–8.

[296] The sentence that follows was an afterthought inserted in the margin.

[297] The next two lines have been heavily and effectively deleted by a method not usually employed by Sir
Hugh himself.

[298] Cholmley was conscious that he had inherited a tradition of dispensing alms and hospitality that had
originated with the Benedictine monks of St Mary's abbey.

[299] Sir Hugh first wrote '1636' then changed it to '1637'; both are wrong. The incident he describes took
place early in December 1635 since his report of it to the Council at York was dated the 10th of that
month (CSPD, 1635, p.549). Both of Cholmley's editors repeated his error.

[300] This 'affront' had taken place at Scarborough the previous July. It was the second 'insolency' of this kind
to occur at Scarborough during that month. Cholmley's version mixes elements from both incidents. In
the first one, after a gun battle inside Scarborough harbour, the Dutchman captured the Dunkirker and

for the Holland captaines and advised[301] them not to offer any act of Hostelety for that the Spanyerd was the Kings freind and to have protection in the Ports;[302] after some expostulations they promised not to meddle with the Dunkirker if he offerd noe iniury to them, which I gave him charge[303] against and to trust to the Kings protection; these Holland captaines leaveing mee and goeing in to the towne sent for the Dunke captaine to drinke[304] with them and after some cupps fell to blowes and difference, and presently one [of] the cheife captaines goeing out of the house musterd all his men together[305] and soone after tooke occation | to quarrell with (f.23v.) him, at the same tyme orders his men to fall on the Dunkirk shippe, which they soone surprised the captaine and most of the men beeing absent. I beeing in my Court Yeard heareing some pistolls discharged and beeing told that the Dunkirke and Hollanders were at odds made hast in to the towne haveing only a caine in my hand and one that followed mee with out any weapon thinkeing but my presence would pacefie all difference and when I came to the River side [neare above at the stay – crossed out] on the sand betweene the colegarth[306] and the bridge[307] I found the Holland captaine with his pistoll in his hand calling to his men then in the Dunkirke shippe to send aboate for him. I gave him gud words [and told him he had not – crossed out] held him in treaty till I got neare him and then giveing a leape on him caught hold on his pistoll, which I became master of, yet not with out some hasserd from the shippe for one from thence leveled a Musket at mee, but I espieing it, turned the captaine betweene mee and him which prevented his shooteing.[308] After I had taken the Captaine I caused aboate to bee manned with men for retakeing the shippe; which as soone as it approached the Hollanders fled out; and got to their owne shippes [which rideing soe neare and haveing soe few men I did – crossed out] In the after noone I intercepted a letter from shippebord to the captaine that he should bee of gud cheare for at night midnight[309] they would land 200 men and take him away, and in respect they had by force taken a Dunkirke shippe not long before out of Scarbrough Harbour I coniectured they might bee as bold here, and theirfore I gave notice to Sir John Hotham at Fyleing then high sheriffe of the County who came to mee and summoned in all the adiacyent trayned bands. Wee had I thincke

---

towed it away. Twelve days later, after a Spanish frigate had sought refuge in Scarborough harbour, its Dutch pursuer put 'three or fower score men ashore with musketts and pikes' to prevent the escape of their enemies. Scarborough's bailiffs persuaded the Dutch to return to their warship after the Spanish agreed to release some Dutch fisherman to their fellow countrymen. (*CSPD, 1634–35*, p.273; M.Y. Ashcroft (ed.), *Scarborough Records 1600–1640*, NYCRO, 47 (1991), pp.274–6).

[301] Cholmley's word 'advised' was strengthened to 'ordered' in the edition of 1787; however, in 1870, 'advised' was restored.

[302] Whether Cholmley believed this to be true is not clear. However, he probably did know that the Dutch actions at Scarborough had been strongly condemned by the Privy Council which had authorised the arrest of any future foreign invaders. (Ashcroft, *Scarborough Records*, 47, p.277).

[303] The word 'strict' was printed in the edition of 1787 between Cholmley's 'him' and 'charge', but not in the edition of 1870.

[304] Both printed works changed Cholmley's 'drink' to 'dine', even though the reference to 'cupps' in the next line clearly indicates his meaning.

[305] The two lines between 'with them' and 'and soone' were crossed through in the manuscript and entirely omitted from both printed versions. However, these lines have been restored because they clearly convey Cholmley's meaning that the quarrel broke out when both sides were the worse for alcohol.

[306] In both printed editions, 'colegarth' was altered to 'coal-yard'.

[307] The one coal garth on the east side of the Esk at this time was located at Alder Waste. The sands between it and the bridge down stream where this episode took place must therefore have been to the west of Grape Lane.

[308] At this point, unlike Cholmley's manuscript, the two printed versions start a new paragraph.

[309] The word 'midnight' was added later in another hand in the margin.

200 men on the garde that night, but then soe in exspert as not 310 amongst them except some few sea men knew how to handle their armes or discharge a Musket, and it had bene happy for this nation had they continued till now in ignorance; these shipps continued hovering before the Harbour for 2 or 3 dayes till I sent the Captain to Yorke who was after sent for to London by Order from the privie Counsell who well approved my layeing hold of him [and gave mee thanks for it – *interlineated*] I thinke he remayned prisoner neare 2 yeare till the Prince Pallatine came over and [begged – *crossed out*] he obteyned his release.[311]

[312]This sommer I carried my wife to London about Easter to viset her Mother and stayed in the South partes till towards Michelmas. |

(f.24r.)   [313]This sommer my brother and sister Yelverton with some other freinds did mee the favour to come to Whitby where they stayed 10 weeks [all which tyme I was betweene 50 and 60 in house hold – *interlineated*]; And he being made Sheriffe next Hollantide the spring after I carryed my wife and layed[314] with him at [his] house in Northamton sheire [cauled Easton – *interlineated*][315] and had 8 of my men to attend him at the Assizes with [?][316] his livery which was scarlet cloths with [silver][317] lace, and two of them had satten dubletts and scarlet britches [suitable] as some of the princypall of his owne had; from Easton [I] carryed my wife to see her brother at London and then returned to Whitby before Michelmas.

Anno Domini 1639[318] in preparation to the Kings march [in to Scotland against – *crossed out*] against the Scotts I had much business about Mustering and trayneing the Souldiours of the trayned bands and many iorneys to yorke to consult with the Vice President[319] and rest of the deputy leiutenants. And about June the King sent downe his Army in to Yorke sheire and himselfe came to it in August the Earl of Northumberland was Genrall from whome I had a commission divers of the Corronells of the trayned bands [with their regiments – *interlineated*], was caued to March with the King in to Northumberland[320] amongst which I had bene one but

---

[310] Both printed works have 'one' here, but it looks more like the figure 3 than anything else.

[311] No wonder the Privy Council was pleased with Cholmley. At Scarborough in July two Dutch captains, Browne and Cornelius Clauson, had violated the king's peace and outraged national honour but had returned safely to Holland. In contrast, if we are to believe Cholmley's story, he had taken Captain Alexander Adrianson van Croning single-handedly without loss or injury to anyone (*CSPD, 1635*, pp.322–3, 572). The first editor of Cholmley's memoirs, who was probably Whitby's first historian, Lionel Charlton, deliberately altered several words in the manuscript to suggest that Sir Hugh had taken a bolder line with the Dutch than he claimed himself. In fact, there was no need to exaggerate Cholmley's courage: it was sufficiently manifest in his manuscript.

[312] Both printed versions start this new paragraph with '*Ann.Dom.* 1637'. If these words and figures were written by Sir Hugh in the margin, they are no longer discernible.

[313] Both printed versions start this paragraph with '*Ann. Dom.* 1638', which was probably written in the left-hand margin but is no longer visible.

[314] Not surprisingly, both previous editors preferred their 'stayed' to Sir Hugh's 'layed'.

[315] Easton is one of the most common place-names in England. Sir Hugh meant Easton Maudit, about eight miles east of Northampton.

[316] There is an illegible word here in the manuscript which both editors ignored.

[317] The right side of this sheet is now rubbed and the ink almost invisible at the edge.

[318] Sir Hugh first wrote 1640 then altered it to 1639. Both editors accepted the correction as accurate.

[319] Sir Edward Osborne was then vice-president of the Council in the North, and during the absence of the president, Viscount Wentworth, in Ireland, Osborne was principally responsible for raising the local militia.

[320] Like many subsequent students, Sir Hugh confused the two Bishops' Wars of 1639 and 1640. At the time of the first war, King Charles came to York in March. The English forces were then commanded by the earl of Arundel. The farcical campaign ended in June that year with the pacification of Berwick. The earl of Northumberland was in command during the second war (August to October 1640). At that time the King arrived at York in August 1640 and from there went on to Northallerton.

that at that tyme I hade caught cold [and a dangerous sickness – *interlineated*] upon viewing[321] and trayneing my whole Regement together on Pexton[322] Moore [neare Thornton – *interlineated*]; where one Halldure [of Pickering – *interlineated but crossed out*], a stubborne fellow of Pickering[323] not obeyeing his captaine and giveing mee some unhadsome languidge I strucke him with my caine and felled him to the ground the caine was tipped with silver and hitting iust under the eare had greater operation than I intended; but ether the man was ill or else counterfeted soe to bee freed from servise, which I willingly granted and glad when he was well, but it was a gud monetion not to bee too hasty on the like or any other provocation, for passion doth not only blinde the iudgement but produceth ill effects.

This winter I carried my wife and famuly to London where wee stayed all winter and [when – *crossed out*] the spring following 1640 was drawne those two pictures of my selfe and my deare wife, resembling us booth yet both to our disadvantage esspetially hers.[324]

Anno Domini 1640 I was chosen Burgess for Scarbrough in the Parlament cauled the Short Parlament in breaking of with the King was ill advised for there was many wise gentlemen of it and well inclyned for his and the publicke good; at this tyme my Regement was commaunded to March to the borders Northward upon apprehention of the Scotts approach but I being to attend the Parlament my brother Sir[325] Henry Cholmley then my Leiutenant Corronell went with it but noe further then Durraham, where he receyved a Counter commaund, and was to retyre backe.[326] At the begining of this Parlament the Earl of Stafford,[327] then Deputy of Ireland, retorned to London, and I comeing to his lodgeings to [wate – *crossed out*] doe my service to him, was not only barred the freedome of goeing in to his chamber | I had (f.24v.) used but when he came out saluteing divers other gentlemen he passed by mee as if he knew mee not and with some scorne which my nature could ill disieast;[328] I had

---

[321] In the first edition 'viewing' was printed as 'raising'. but in the second edition the word was correctly read.

[322] Again, Sir Hugh's Pexton Moor north of Thornton still exists by that name, whereas the 'Paxton-Moor' printed in both editions never existed.

[323] The name of this 'stubborne fellow' was written as 'Halldure', but in print it was changed to 'Hallden'.

[324] Two portraits of Sir Hugh have survived. There is a three-quarters length picture, said to be by Sir Peter Lely, which shows him wearing breast-plate and sword and carrying helmet and baton [the notorious silver stick?]. This picture belongs to Major G.R.H. Cholmley of Place Newton and was reproduced as an illustration facing p.74 in P.S. Jeffrey, *Whitby Lore and Legend* (Whitby, 1952). Secondly, there is a better known half-length portrait, said to be by Janssen, which belonged to C.D. Cholmley Harrison and used to hang in Howsham Hall along with all the other family pictures. This picture has often been used as a book illustration, for example facing p.100 in J.T. Cliffe, *The Yorkshire Gentry* (1969), and was probably the one painted in 1640 since it closely resembles that of Lady Elizabeth, which also used to hang in Howsham Hall ('East Riding Portraits', *Transactions of the East Riding Antiquarian Society*, x (1903), pp.41, 45).

[325] Hugh's younger brother Henry was not knighted until the end of 1641, which might explain why the editor of the 1787 edition omitted the title 'Sir' before his name.

[326] Sir Hugh's explanation that his brother took command of his trained band regiment during the second Bishop's War because he was then attending the Short Parliament does not tally with the dates of these events. The Short Parliament opened on 13 April and was dissolved 5 May. The second Bishops' War did not begin until August by which time, as Sir Hugh is about to reveal (see below, f.24v.), he had been deprived of all his commissions, including his colonelcy.

[327] Sir Hugh meant 'Strafford'. In fact, Thomas Wentworth had been created earl of Strafford in January 1640 with the office of Lord Lieutenant of Ireland.

[328] The date of Strafford's public rebuff of Cholmley is not certain. Since the two were both in London throughout the winter of 1639–40, the incident might have happened at any time during this period. It is possible that Strafford did not believe that Sir Hugh's 'dangerous sickness' was anything other than a dishonest excuse for avoiding his duty of military service. In December 1639 Cholmley had failed to get the Lord President's endorsement for his seat at Scarborough which suggests that even by then he was already out of favour (Ashcroft, *Scarborough Records*, pp.340–3).

before professed much service and love to his person, and must confesse had receyved
divers favours and respect from him, and truly not with out cause and obligation [on
his side – *interlineated*] for his first ladye daughter to the Earl of Cumberland was my
fathers cosen-iermyn once removed and as my father had ever stood firme for him in
all contests with Sir John Sayvell for being knight of the sheare soe more perticulerly in
the last yeare of King James and first King Charles at which tyme my father was sheriffe
and consequently a great cause of the Lord Straffords (then Sir Thomas Wentworth)
his carring the place against Sir Joohn Savell, which was indeed a princypall cause of
the said Sir Thomas his comeing to the dignety and honours he had after, but now
being displeased at my refuseing to pay shippe mony which carried the whole liberty
of Whitby Strand after my example,[329] he did not only give mee this personall
discountnance formerly mentioned but put mee out of all Commissions *vid.* of the
peace [oyer and terminer – *interlineated*] Deputy Leiuetennancy and Corronell. And
the Parlament being broake caused mee to bee cauled beefore the Counsell and indeed
charged with wurds I nether spoke in the house nor could bee proved against mee, yet
for further vexation I was commaunded for 3 weeks or a Month to attend the Counsell
table *de die in diem*;[330] my lord had alsoe put Sir John Hotham out of all commissions for
refuseing shipmony, and him and my cosen Mr Henry Bellassis [eldest sonne to the
lord Faulconbridge – *interlineated*] for some wurds they had spoke in this Short
Parlament: all which I wish from my heart had not happened for it did not only
produce inconvenence and preiudice to my lord person but even to the Nation too I
feare as you may coniecture by the story. Beeing all of us at lyberty and returned in to
the Cuntry where the Kings Army was quarterd to the burthen of the Country and the
[stirreing up discontents – *crossed out*] much discontent of the greatest parte of the
gentry which inborne our owne sufferings[331] made us more apt to comply soe that at a
publicke meeting [of the gentry – *interlineated*] at the High Sheriffs [great chamber –
crossed out] in Assize weeke wee all agreed to make an addresse and complaynt to the
Lords of the Counsell table a remonstrance and the greivance lyeing on our Country,
for which purpose the Lord Wharton[332] my cosen Mr Henry Bellassis Sir John
(f.25r.) Hotham and my selfe | were chosen to draw a petion to that purpose and wee with
draweing together in to a private roome had quickly done it, Sir John Hotham and my
selfe haveing before betweene our selfes [contryved – *interleaved*] and penned it and
had it redy[333] in our pockets. This was s[igned] by above a 100 of the princypall
nobillety and gentry of the County at our owne[334] and a gentleman sent up purposely
to deliver it [which startled the Counsell this being the first act – *crossed out*] . . .[335] ever

---

[329] Cholmley's claim, though often quoted, should not be accepted at face value. Dr Cliffe has pointed out
       that Yorkshire paid the whole of the £12,000 Ship Money charged on the county in the writ of 1639
       (Cliffe, *Yorkshire Gentry*, p.318). On the other hand, Cholmley fails to record that in April and May 1640
       he vigorously opposed Ship Money in the Short Parliament (E.S. Cope and W.H. Coates (eds),
       Proceedings of the Short Parliament of 1640, Camden, 4th series, xix (1977), pp.161–2, 194).
[330] Cholmley protested his innocence of disloyal and impertinent speeches in the House of Commons, but
       the record indicates otherwise. He was most fortunate not to be imprisoned with the other Yorkshire-
       men (*CSPD, 1640*, pp.154–5; Cope and Coates, *Proceedings*, pp.161–2, 194).
[331] Both printed versions here read 'increase of our sufferings' though Sir Hugh did not write 'increase' and
       he did write 'owne'. The sense of his word 'inborne' might be conveyed best by 'in addition to'.
[332] Philip Lord Wharton of Healaugh (1613–93) was a Puritan and firm Parliamentarian who subsequently
       fought at Edgehill (J.W. Clay, 'The Gentry of Yorkshire at the time of the Civil War', *YAJ* xxiii (1915),
       p.392).
[333] This word 'redy' was omitted from both printed works.
[334] A word seems to be missing here, probably 'meeting'. Both printed versions also omit 'at our owne'.
[335] The manuscript is now too faded to be read in several places on the top third of this sheet. The editions
       of 1787 and 1870 simply omitted without explanation several illegible words and phrases.

that did . . . which was in a prety high style of in substance (though not in playne tearmes) it imported that the Country would not lye longer under these pressures, and beeing the first action that did with a baire face complaine of the kings prerogative which went high in those tymes did something startle the Counsell and [seemed a thing of – *crossed out*] in truth proved a thing of great consequence for it did not only animate the Scotts Army which then was on winge in their owne Country and that till now stood in feare of the trayned bands [of our Country – *interlineated*] (which was 13 thousand) to bee ioyned with the Kings Army, but gave incourridgement to the Earls of Bedford Hartford Essex Warricke Southampton Bristol Claire and divers other Lords to conveane together and petition the King for a Parlament.[336] Soone after the Kings comeing in to our Country, summoned all the [trayned bands and – *crossed out*][337] gentlemen to Yorke where he propounded to have all the trayned bands to March with his Army at their owne charges, which he found not the Country inclynable to, [though some he – *crossed out*] and their in the face of my Country would have restored to mee my Commission for my Regement taken from mee by the Lord Stafford [*sic*] the Lord Leiutenant of our County but I refused the accepting, sayeing, ether I did not deserve to have it taken from mee or not soe soone to be restored but after I went privately to the King to thanke him for his favour, and told him I did not refuse accepting the Regement [because – *crossed out*; that – *interlineated*] I declyned to doe his Majestie service but because [I would not serve under the – *interlineated*] the Earl of Stafford [*sic*] being now Genrall of the Army and lyeing under his displeasure; but that my brother [Sir Henry Cholmeley – *interlineated*] being my Leiutenant Corronell if he pleased might have the Regement and would be redy to doe his Majestie service, the King replyed they will not March with him and I answeareding they would he said I should bring them to the place of Randevouz which I did and they chanced to bee on the Kings guard at Northallerton when that night the Scotts passed tyne[338] and had foiled the Kings Army; upon this the King retreateing to yorke that hether he brought his Army. | And the trayned bands [sent home many – *crossed out*] dismissed many of them being   (f.25v.) of them selfes retorned home [by reason of my absence – *interlineated*][339] but the Earl of Strafford who by infirmeness[340] of health had stayed at London was now come to the King at Yorke that occationed againe the summoning of the gentry to attend the

---

[336] This was the petition dated 28 July 1640 which was presented to a meeting held at the house of Sir Marmaduke Langdale in York. Cholmley's claim that over a hundred gentlemen signed it is not corroborated: there were only 47 names on the official list sent to the Privy Council. The petitioners claimed that the county had spent £100,000 the previous year on military preparations, and they protested against forced billeting of soldiers in the strongest terms (PRO, SP16/461/38). Since the petition was addressed directly to the King and delivered to the Privy Council, presumably it was meant as an insult to Strafford, the king's representative in the county. Cholmley's further claims about the effects of the petition are not convincing. The Privy Council was not so much 'startled' as annoyed: it commanded its signatories to be more respectful, particularly to the Lord Lieutenant, the proper channel, and it dismissed their grievances as exaggerated and unfounded (*CSPD, 1640*, pp.595–7; Rushworth, *Collections*, III, pp.1214–15). Cholmley's suggestion that the Scots had been deterred by their fear of the Yorkshire trained bands until they heard of the petition over-stretches belief. As for the peers' petition, it was not presented to the King until a month later, after the Scots had invaded England. Cholmley got only five of their twelve names: Southampton and Clare were not signatories, whereas two Yorkshire ones, Howard of Escrick and Mulgrave, were (PRO, SP16/465/16).

[337] Though Cholmley crossed out 'trayned bands', the editors of 1787 and 1870 chose to include these words.

[338] On the night of 28 August 1640, when the Scots crossed the Tyne, Cholmley's Bluecoats stood guard over the King at Northallerton.

[339] The word 'home' was omitted from the 1787 edition but not from that of 1870.

[340] In both printed versions Cholmley's word became 'infirmities'.

King when he againe propounded[341] the haveing of the trayned bands to March at their owne charge and to meet the Earl of Stafford [sic] the next day at the towne Hall to consult of this but in the intrime the night before the gentlemen met at an In and there drew a petion in answeare to the Kings proposetions shewing they could not consent to the Marching of the trayned bands in respect of the great pressure upon them and desired his Majestie to call a Parlament. This was signed by the Nobillety and greatest part of the gentlemen to the number of 140, and the Lord Fairfax chosen to deliver it, which he could never[342] bee admitted to doe, but the next day when most of the gentry was gon out of towne[343] the Earl of Strafford intended to dash this peticon and when most of the signors were gon out of towne with some few gentlemen his creatures and deliverd to the King the sence of the Country quite contrary to what they intended and had expressed in the great petion,[344] where upon the Lord Wharton Mr Henry Bellassis Sir John Savell Sir John Hotham my selfe and some others to the number of 16 of the princypall and most active gentlemen being met together with intent to petetion his Majestie against the answear given by the Lord Stafford [sic] and to informe his Majestie of the great Petion, [one of the Number – interlineated] Sir William Sayvell[345] undir hand gave notice to the Court of our meeting and their upon the Lord Warton my cosen Bellasis Sir John Hotham and my selfe were sent for to the King who told us it was not lawfull for us to meet in that manner upon petions that he might question us in the Starr chamber for it, but would at this tyme passe it over because he loved us all well, but charged us never to meddle more in petetioning him in that kinde and after many gud words dismissed us, but the next morning my selfe and Sir John Hotham being redy to put foot in to stirrappe he sent one Stockdell[346] a Messanger to bring us to him, and when wee came reprehended us in very sharpe woords telling us wee had bene the cheife cause and promoters of all the petetions from the County (which in deed was truth) in plane tearmes that if ever wee meddled or had any hand in any more he would hang us, to which I answeared Sir wee are then in a very sadd condetion for then our Lord President[347] and those you set governors

(f.26r.)   over | us may iniure and oppresse us with out any hopes of redresse since wee being Country gentlemen and with out acquaintance in Court have no meanes but by

---

[341] Both editors preferred their own 'proposed' to Cholmley's 'propounded'.

[342] By substituting 'not' for Cholmley's 'never' the editors of 1787 and 1870 failed to convey the full sense of his meaning.

[343] In both printed editions Cholmley's comma after the word 'doe' was ignored, and his meaning destroyed by the insertion of a full stop after the word 'towne'.

[344] This 'great petition' was that of 12 September 1640. It came after the humiliating defeat at Newburn, the loss of Newcastle and the royal retreat back into Yorkshire. Cholmley's description of events is damaged by his uncontrolled bias against Strafford. He failed to record that at a public meeting on 13 September Strafford persuaded the majority of about two hundred Yorkshire gentry to finance their trained bands for a further month and to agree that the petition should not include their call for a Parliament. The King had already decided to have a new Parliament and Strafford wanted him to take the credit for it and not appear to have conceded to one reluctantly under duress. As for Strafford's 'creatures', at his subsequent trial, Cholmley alleged that they were known Papists, if not all convicted recusants – another gross calumny motivated by resentment and revenge. Now, even 15 years later, in the privacy of his memoirs, Sir Hugh could not bring himself to admit that his arch-enemy had won over the majority of the county's gentry, and that the militant 16 had been out-manoeuvred as an anti-Strafford faction. (Rushworth, Collections, III, pp.1264–5; CSPD, 1640, pp.624–5; D. Parsons (ed.), The Diary of Sir Henry Slingsby of Scriven (1836), pp.56–8; J. Rushworth, The Trial of Thomas, Earl of Strafford (1680), pp.603, 613–15.)

[345] Sir William Savile of Thornhill became 'Sir William Cayvell' in both printed versions.

[346] In the printed works the name of the king's messenger was given as 'Stockdall'.

[347] By 'our Lord President', and not 'the Lord President', as it appeared in print, Cholmley clearly meant Lord Strafford.

Petetion to make our greivances knowne to your Majestie, to which the King answeared when soever you have any cause of complaynt come to mee and I will heare it. I humbly thanked his Majestie and soe wee were dismissed and did not after meddle in that sorte nor was there cause for the King haveing summoned all the Nobillety to yorke a Parlament was agred on and summoned in November following being *Anno Domini* 1641.[348]

I was chosen Burges for Scarbrough for this Parlament and leaveing my wife children[349] and famuly at Whitby myselfe went to London but findeing business succed ill betweene [my – *crossed out*] the King and Parlament the Scots Army being possessed of Northumberland and the Bishoppricke I feared there advance in to Yorkesheire which did not a little disquiet my mynde and thoughts for my deare wife and children the snow being soe great I could not possible remove them [soe soon as I desired – *interlineated*] but at the end of February[350] as soone as the wayes were passeable I had her and all my famuly to London where they remayned some monthes and after removed to Thisselworth[351] the next years to Chiswicke to the Lord Paulets which he lent mee, in bwth these places I prayse god I lived in great plenty and in a handsome condetion haveing neare 30 in famuly 4 coachhorses and 1 saddle horse; I was most parte of the weeke in London to attend the Parlament [which sat close – *interlineated*] and returned home every Satterday.

Haveing as I formerly mentioned denyed shippe mony and shewed myselfe for the publicke libertyes I had a great esteeme and interest amongst them in the Parlament soe that when the King went in to Scotland *Anno Domini* 1641 I was nominated to goe one of the Commissioners from the Parlament in to Scotland but nether affecting the nation nor the imployment I got my selfe of.[352] May *Anno Domini* 1642 the king being retyred to yorke the Lord Howard of Escricke Ferdinando Lord Fairfax myselfe and Sir Phillop Stapleton were nominated Commissioners[353] from the Parlament [to goe to yorke to the King – *interlineated*] the pretence was to give the King and Country a right understanding of the sincerety of the Parlaments intentions, but when I came to receyve the Instructions from Pime[354] who had order to give them wee were plainely enioyned to draw the trayned bands to gether and to oppose the King in all things was for the Parlaments service, this I refused to accept sayeing it were to beginne the warre which I intended not, where upon Pim bid mee draw the instructions to my owne mynde, which I did but the Lord Fairfax and I departeing in a coach before they could bee finished they were brought to us by the Lord Howard and Stapleton and though not soe large as at first yet other wise then I did assent to or could approve of; when wee came to yorke there was few about the King | few[355] but   (f.26v.) souldiers of fortune and [or – *interlineated*][356] such as were noe friend to the publicke

---

[348] The year was in fact 1640; however, Sir Hugh's mistake was not corrected in either printed edition.
[349] The word 'children' was omitted in 1787 but not 1870. By this time Sir Hugh and Lady Elizabeth had four children, William, Hugh, Ann and Elizabeth.
[350] This would have been February 1641.
[351] Cholmley's name was printed as 'Isleworth' in both editions.
[352] The parliamentary commission to Scotland was appointed in August 1641. Cholmley makes no effort to conceal his dislike of the Scots but does not reveal his reasons for turning down the place of a commissioner. The members of the commission were the Earl of Bedford, Lord Howard of Escrick, Sir William Armyn, Nathaniel Fiennes, John Hampden and Sir Philip Stapleton (*LJ*, iv, p.366).
[353] Surprisingly, Sir Hugh omitted the name of the fifth member of the commission that went to York in May 1642 – his own brother, Sir Henry Cholmley.
[354] The name was printed in its more recognisable form as 'Pym'.
[355] Sir Hugh wrote a second 'few' here to present the king's position more favourably, but it was not printed in 1787 or 1870.
[356] Both editors preferred Cholmley's 'or' to his 'and'.

peace, and here I discovered there was a party about the king who held intelligence with another prevalent one in the Parlament booth which soe well concured in fomenting disstractions as when soe ever the King offerd ought was reaseable the party in Parlament caused it bee reiected and whenever the Parlament did seeme to comply to the King the [their – *interlineated*] party with him made it disliked soe that the Searcher of all hearts knowes I was infenitely trobled at the disstractions was like to succed [after some prayer to the Lord for – *interlineated*] directions and truly in the depth of my troble takeing a little psalme booke[357] in my hand I used to read in, I first cast my eie on the 6 and 7 verse in the 120 psalme which was

6   My soule hath dwelt with him that hateth peace

7   I am for peace but when I speake they are for warre

and then reading in the succedeing 121 psalme truly my heart was [in – *crossed out*] lightened[358] and cheared up beyond immagination, soe that ever after I went chearefully on in performance of that duty I was upon with out any troble or disturbance.[+359] Whilst wee were here at yorke the Lord Keeper Littleton and divers others of the Lords house as alsoe of the house of Commons stoale privately away and came to the King whose condition they thought prospering, but my oppinion was they had ruined[360] booth the King and Nation by quitting the Parlament as I told many of them, in which I proved too propheticall.[361] Here was sent to us the commission a paper of the 19 proposetions[362] from the Parlament to his Majestie, most uniust and unreasenable ones as ever I thinke was made to King. When wee were to have presented them it fell to my turne to have red them, but I would not in respect [I thought them uniust and unreasenable to be offerd to the King – *interlineated*] and soe put it to Sir P Stapleton[363] to read, I carried back the Kings answeare to these proposetions, and aboute a Month after when the Earl of Holland was sent to his Majestie then at Beverley,[364] I was nominated [to – *crossed out*] a commissioner with him, but dislikeing the imployment I got freed and Sir John Holland put in my place.

About the latter end of August[365] I was [importuned – *crossed out*; desired – *interlineated*] by the Earl of Essex[366] and some others to goe in to yorkeshire and to draw my Regement for the secureing Scarbrough, which at first I refused but after being much importuned conceyveing these preparations of warre would end in a treaty and that my selfe who desired nothing but that the King might enioy his iust rights as well as the subjects theirs and that I should in this matter be a more indifferent arbitrator then many I saw take armes and more considerable with my sword in my

---

[357] In both printed versions this became 'Psalter-book'.

[358] Though Cholmley crossed out 'in' and then wrote 'lightened', both editions have 'enlightened' printed.

[359] At this point a cross marks the place in the manuscript for the insertion of an afterthought which was written down the left-hand margin. The marginal addition ends with the word 'propheticall'.

[360] Sir Hugh's strong word 'ruined' was softened to 'misled' in the edition of 1787 but restored correctly in that of 1870.

[361] Again, in 1787, Cholmley's phrase was altered to 'to be prophetical', but correctly printed in 1870.

[362] The Nineteen Propositions were approved by the House of Lords 1 June 1642 (*LJ*, v, p.97) and despatched the following day to the King.

[363] Cholmley wrote only Stapleton's initial; in 1787 this was transformed into 'Richard'; and in 1870 correctly printed as 'Philip'.

[364] The King had moved from York to Beverley in the first week of July. The Earl of Holland there delivered to him Parliament's final invitation to return in peace to his capital.

[365] To mark the official start of hostilities, the King had raised his battle standard at Nottingham on 22 August 1642.

[366] The Earl of Essex had replaced Strafford as Lord Lieutenant of Yorkshire in May 1641 and soon after restored Cholmley to all his commissions. However, it was as General of Parliament's army that Essex instructed Sir Hugh to secure the town and harbour of Scarborough.

hand and in better capaserty to advance a treaty then by sitting in the house of Commons where I had but a bare vote I accepted this imployment. This imployment was something hassardous at this tyme in respect divers gentlemen in yorkesheire declayreing for the King were all redy in Armes, I had for my better securety a troope of horse from London and 200 promissed mee at Hull which when I came I could not have to serve with these horse. | How I deported my selfe in these imployments and (f.27r.) when how and for what causes I quit it and the Parlament I shall forbeare to speake now but referre the Reader to the Accoumpt I have given booth of that and the seage of Scarbrough together,[367] in which it will appeare I did not forsake them [sic] Parlament till they did faile in performeing those perticulers they made the grounds of the warre when I was first ingaidged *vidz.* the preservation of Relegion protection of the Kings person and lyberties of the subiect [nor did I quit them then – *interlineated*] for any perticuler ends of my owne, but meerely to performe the duty and alleagence I owed to my Soveraigne, and which I did in such away as was with out any deminution of my honour ether as a gentleman or souldier.

My wife was at London when at Scarbrough I declayred for the King, and they being netled that they had lost a person soe usefull to them as I had bene, did not only passe some sharpe votes in the house of Commons against my person,[368] but plunderd my wife of her coach horses and used coarsely, yet she procured a passe to come to mee and with her my two girles the elder then not above 8 yeares of age came to Whitby in a shippe haveing soe prosperous and quike a passage as she said she would never goe up and downe againe to London but by shippe. I had bene now neare a yeare from her and she being with in London and not yet understanding the causes why I quit the Parlament nor the trew State of the difference betweene the King and Parlament was very earnest and fearce[369] for their party, but after I had unmasked to her the Parlaments intents and clearly presented to her their proceedings and the state of affaires, she then was as much against them, and as earnest for the King and contynued soe to her death; afer she had bene 2 or 3 dayes at Whitby I brought her to Scarbrough where I was then Governor for his Majestie by a Commission from the Marques of Newcastle Genrall for the King in the North partes, and was governor booth of the towne and castle. I had likewise a Commission for being Corronell of Horse and another to bee Corronell of dragooners, and had Commission to order all marine affayres with in all the ports from Tease to Bridlington and to iudge of all marine matters that fell with in that extent. Here wee lived in a very handsome port and fashion but upon such an accoumpt as I thinke not any[370] in imployment for the King or Parlament did the like for I had nether pay nor allowance but maynteined | the port[371] of the Governors place upon my owne purse, not haveing the worth of a (f.27v.)

[367] During his exile at Rouen, in 1647 Cholmley had written a lengthy paper at the request of Sir Edward Hyde (later the earl of Clarendon), describing and attempting to justify his Civil War record at Scarborough from 1642 to 1645. He called this essay 'Memorialls tuching Scarbrough'. Sir Hugh's narrative was eventually edited by Sir Charles Firth, then Regius Professor at Oxford, and published in the *English Historical Review* in October 1917. A copy of the original manuscript which Firth used is among the Clarendon papers in the Bodleian Library, shelf marked 22, no.1669. Cholmley's holograph was almost certainly destroyed by a fire at Lincoln's Inn in 1751 or 1752. (Binns, thesis, pp.515–18.) For 'Memorialls tuching Scarbrough' see below pp.140–63.

[368] Cholmley was not only deprived of his Commons seat and permanently disabled, the House resolved that he should be impeached for high treason (*CJ*, iii, p.28). Even the Ventian ambassador commented on the severity of the punishment (*CSPV, 1643*, pp.263–4).

[369] The editors of 1787 and 1870 judged 'fearce' to be too strong, and toned it down to 'firm'.

[370] Again, Sir Hugh's word was too sweeping for his editors: his 'any' became their preferred 'many'.

[371] The word 'port' became 'post' in both printed editions.

chickeing out of the Country which I payed not for till the tyme wee came to bee beseaged.[372] At the seage of Hull the Marques of Newcastle required my presence and would needs impose on mee the Command of Brigade of horse which was a terse[373] of the Army, and whither I carried him my owne Regement of horse beeing the best in the Army consisting of 350 men raised at my owne charge and likewise I drew 400 foot out of my garrison.[374]

Anno Domini 1644 killing the bird[375]

After the battle of Hesse Moore[376] the Marques of Newcastle came to Scarbrough and layed at my house two dayes till I had furnished him with a shippe to goe beyond sea, at his departure he thanked mee for my interteynement told mee he had some feare I should have stayed him said the game[377] was all for lost on the Kings side and wished my departure with him which I supposed he conceyved would bee some countnance to his, my answeare was I could wish his stay, that if he had commited an error I knew my duty soe well I was not to call him to accoumpt but obey he being my Genrall; that for my owne part though the place was in noe defenceable posture I ment not to render till I heard from the King or was forced to it. And after [the battle of Hessay Moore – *crossed out*] the Marques his departure most of the Gentlemen of the Country which came thither with him dislikeing the strength of the place procured passes ether to remayne at home or to goe to Prince Rupert then in Westmerland; which gave such discurridgement to the foot souldiers as many of them ranne away, and indeed I was at present in a very sad condetion for as the towne by scytuation not tenable soe the castle ruanous with out habitation or provisions, or amunetions considerable.[378] Sir Thomas Fairfax was come with in 5 miles with a thousand horse,[379] and I had intelligence foot was designed to follow from yorke where the forces under the commaund of Manchester the Lord Fairfax and Scoth Army layde at guise[380] haveing not imployment nor any considerable impediment in that Country but Scarbrough;[381]

---

[372] This claim should not be accepted at face value: Cholmley was receiving military supplies from the Royalist arsenal at York, from overseas agents at Dunkirk, as well as the proceeds of North Sea privateering provided by captains such as Browne Bushell and John Denton (HMC, *Portland*, I, pp.113, 116–18, 121; Ashcroft, II, p.33; *CSPD, 1644*, pp.157–9; see below, p.153).

[373] This word meaning one third was correctly printed in both editions, but in T. Hinderwell, *The History and Antiquities of Scarborough* (York, 2nd edn., 1811), p.67 it became 'curse' and in the third edition of this book (Scarborough, 1832), p.76 it had become 'flower'.

[374] This sentence beginning 'At the seage of Hull' was written as an afterthought down the left margin of the folio but marked by Sir Hugh for insertion at this point.

[375] Whatever was meant by 'killing the bird' and whether Sir Hugh himself wrote these words cannot be determined.

[376] Hesse or Hessay Moor is better known as Marston Moor, the site of the decisive Royalist defeat of 2 July 1644.

[377] Cholmley's 'the game' were printed as 'he gave' in both versions.

[378] This assertion is not corroborated by the evidence in Scarborough's corporation records of heavy expenditure on strengthened gateways, walls, ditches, sentry houses and artillery batteries. By 1644 the castle's defences were greatly improved by the construction of cannon platforms, particularly South Steel and Bushell's batteries.

[379] Though Cholmley made a similar claim in his 'Memorialls tuching Scarbrough', it seems more likely that Sir Thomas never came nearer than Helmsley castle which he besieged with only 300 cavalry and 700 infantry, all badly clothed and unpaid (Bell, *Memorials*, ii, pp.121–2; see below, p.148).

[380] Instead of 'at guise' both editions printed 'all quiet'.

[381] Cholmley was again engaged here in wishful thinking. After the fall of York on 16 July 1644, there were still several strong Royalist garrisons in Yorkshire besides that at Scarborough. As Lord Fairfax informed his masters in London towards the end of August, Pontefract, Knaresborough and Helmsley were also in enemy hands and well supplied to defend themselves. He might also have mentioned others such as Skipton, Sandal, Sheffield and Bolton castles (*CSPD, 1644*, p.447).

I was not in a condetion to with stand this storme nor knew how to resist it but by propoundeing proposetions for rendering which I did by Mr Henry Darley a pressoner with mee who a Commissioner from the Parlament to the Scots I had fetched out of their Army dureing the seage of yorke;[382] he did not perfectly understand how matters passed betweene the Armyes and beeing desirous of liberty under tooke these proposetions, and a cessation for 20 dayes whilst they were sent to the Parlament [in the intrime I sent a messenger to the King put my – *crossed out*][383] the man being partly over ioyed with liberty partly overreached in his imployment gave them at yorke such assurance of my rendering, that Manchesters Army Marched to the South the Scotts to beseage Newcastle and the [Lord – *crossed out*][384] Fairfax his forces sat downe before Hemsley castle,[385] soe that before the 20 dayes was expired I had put the towne and castle in to much better posture of defence, had brought in 400 loades of corne from out of the feilds and was out of feare at the present to bee beseaged [with foot – *crossed out*]; Darley returneing from London with answeare to the proposetions[386] the Lord Fairfax sent them to mee requireing my answeare.[387] Indeed there was as much granted to my selfe as I could exspect yet not soe much as was propounded by the proposetions of which | some being of that nature I was (f.28r.) assured would not bee assented to, and their by I had occation to breake of the treaty; being out of feare to bee beseaged at present though it had bene impossable for mee to have held out [which I did – *interlineated*][388] for about 12 monthes after but that [all] my wants was supplyed most miraculously ([as I had occation – *crossed out*]) with all necessaryes as if they had bene dropped [downe – *interlineated*] from heaven as I had occation and need, and as doth appeare at learge in the relation of the seage of Scarbrough.[389] At the beginning of February following began the seage of Scarbrough towne[390] when my wife [who would not forsake mee for any danger – *interlineated*] desired mee to send in to Holland my two girles whome I parted with not with out

---

[382] Henry Darley had been taken at night-time from his home at Buttercrambe, ten miles north-east of York, by a raiding party sent out from Scarborough by Sir Hugh on 3 June 1644. The event was gleefully described by Cholmley in his 'Memorialls' (see below, p.147).

[383] These crossed out words were not printed. Cholmley was certainly in correspondence with the King in July and August 1644, but unfortunately only one letter, that from Charles to Sir Hugh, has survived from this time (BL, Egerton MSS 2884, f.41).

[384] Sir Hugh remembered that Sir Thomas, and not his father, had besieged Helmsley castle and crossed out the abbreviation for 'lord'. Nevertheless, the title was printed in both editions.

[385] Sir Hugh was deluding himself if he really believed that the promise of his surrender of Scarborough had diverted the Scots north to Newcastle and the army of the Eastern Association southwards. These major decisions of deployment were taken weeks before Cholmley broadcast his propositions; Newcastle was rightly considered of far greater importance than Scarborough; and once York had fallen and the King's northern army been beaten and dispersed, Scarborough had become too remote and isolated to be of use to him.

[386] Cholmley's word was printed as 'proposal' in 1787 and 1870.

[387] Sir Hugh kept a copy of the reply he received from the Committee of the Two Kingdoms dated 26 August to his nineteen propositions and wrote it down in his 'Memorialls' (see below, pp.152–3).

[388] Sir Hugh could have written either 'above' or 'about', but in print the word appeared as 'about'. In fact, since the truce or treaty expired on 4 September 1644 and Cholmley surrendered the castle on 25 July 1645, he held out for less than a year.

[389] This is Cholmley's peculiar way of describing the benefits to him and his garrison of the prizes brought into Scarborough by privateers such as Browne Bushell and John Denton. According to the 'Memorialls', there were more stolen cargoes carried into the harbour in the month before the close siege began in January 1645 than in all the previous time Cholmley had been governor of the town (see below, p.154).

[390] According to Sir Hugh's earlier and more accurate account in his 'Memorialls', General Sir John Meldrum began the close siege of the town at the end of January 1645 and stormed it three weeks later on 18 February (see below, p.154).

great [tro]³⁹¹ble for I was fond of them [and the elder but 7 years of age – *crossed out*];³⁹² with [them] I sente to wate on them a french gentle woeman a chamber mayde a man servant and a [grave – *interlineated*] Minister one Mr Remington³⁹³ and his wife to bee supper intendents over all. We were in the towne and castle beseaged above 12 monthes³⁹⁴ dureing which tyme my deare wife indured much hardshippe and yet with little shew of troble, and though by nature according to her sex tymerous, yet in greatest danger would not bee da[u]nted but shewed a courridge even above her sex.

By the Artickles of render³⁹⁵ wee had liberty to March to the King or passe beyond seas and heareing the King to bee then remoate³⁹⁶ in Wales at Ragland castle and in noe gwd condetion and my selfe nether in bodily health nor haveing forces to serve him, my eldest sonne in France who had noe supply from mee of a yeare before, and my two daughters in Holland I thought it requesite to take caire of my children and health which at the tyme was soe imperfect³⁹⁷ (as I had attempted to passe to the King I had in probabillety dyed by the way) and there upon tooke shippe at Bridlington leaveing my deare wife not a bove £10 in her purse nor myselfe about five more then defrayed my passage, for though my good brother Sir Henry Cholmeley had lent³⁹⁸ mee £200 at my comeing out of the Castle I had distributed it amongst the officers and souldiers to relieve their necessityes. At my comeing in to Holland I sent my daughters immediately to their Mother in England who were to have landed at Bridlington but meeting with a great and dangerous tempest were driven in at Lincolneshire at a place cauled Grimsby, and being thus left alone my wife and children thus [seperated – *crossed out*] dispersed from mee, I was in great troble and saddenes but the Lord was my comforter in whome I trusted and who in his gud tyme

---

³⁹¹ Here the letters have been covered by a repair patch on the folio.

³⁹² These crossed out words were not printed perhaps because Sir Hugh's memory was faulty. His elder daughter Ann was baptised 7 December 1634 and his younger, the second to be called Elizabeth, was baptised 5 August 1638, so at the beginning of 1645 they were ten and six years old respectively.

³⁹³ Though Robert Remmington had moved from Whitby in 1638 and become rector of Lockington, one of Hotham's parishes in the East Riding, he had taken refuge in Scarborough under Cholmley's protection. Nevertheless, Remmington seems to have been still well regarded in London. When, in his propositions of August 1644, Cholmley asked that all the clergymen then in the town should be reinstated and not lose their livings, the Committee for Both Kingdoms rejected this request, 'excepting Mr Remmington to whom the proposition is granted' (see below, pp.150, 152). Remmington was ejected from his living at Lockington in 1647, but given another at Guisborough in 1650. In 1661 Remmington was restored to Lockington (R.A. Marchant, *The Puritans and the Church Courts in the Diocese of York, 1560–1642* (1960), pp.271, 453).

³⁹⁴ This statement has deceived many historians: taking Cholmley's words literally, they assumed that the siege must have begun in February 1644. For example, see Hinderwell, *History of Scarborough* (3rd edn 1832), p.79; J.B. Baker, *The History of Scarbrough* (1882), pp.76, 81. In fact, the close siege of the town lasted only three weeks and that of the castle less than six months.

³⁹⁵ The articles of the surrender of Scarborough castle signed on 22 July, Cholmley's 45th birthday, and carried out on 25 July were printed and published in London at the end of the month in 'The Copie of a Letter from Major General Poines . . .', BL, *TT*, E.294(17). They are also to be found in Rushworth, *Collections*, v, p.118.

³⁹⁶ In both editions 'remoate' was printed as 'removed'.

³⁹⁷ Cholmley marked the following bracketed words, written down the left margin, for insertion at this place.

³⁹⁸ Sir Hugh wrote 'lent' and not 'sent' which was preferred by his editors. When he had gone over to the King his brother Sir Henry remained loyal to Parliament, yet there appears to have been no loss of fraternal friendship between them. As Sir Hugh noted below (f.28v.), in 1640 he had made his younger brother a principal trustee of the Whitby estate, and Sir Henry not only ensured that Lady Elizabeth, in her husband's absence abroad, received her entitlement but that his nephew William, who was in Paris, also received maintenance (J.W. Clay (ed.), *Yorkshire Royalist Composition Papers* in *YASRS*, xviii (1895), p.22; PRO, SP16, 502/40).

did bring us all againe to a happy meeting.[399] In Holland by gods providence I had £600 which was | my support till it pleased god to make the tymes more favorable (f.28v.) and that I could get some support out of my estates which now was all sequesterd by the Parlament. After I had bene [a fortnight – *interlineated*] or 3 weeks in Holland haveing seene the Hage Amsterdam and some other good townes I went to Flushing and there tooke shippe for France and landed at Calais and from thence by the Messenger went for Paris. At Minstrall[400] a place in the way wee had scarse enterd the towne when it was allaromed by 500 Spanish horse which followed us, to which I had bene a good booty for haveing £300 in English gould about mee which escape was a [very] good monetion to carry my mony for the future by bill of exchange rather than in specie. When I came to Paris I found letters to a marchant from my eldest sonne William then upon his retorne out of Italy that in case he had not spedy supply from mee he should bee forced to turne souldior and trale a picke in Catelonia for his subustance, which gave mee further ocation to prayse god for my quiting England, else my poore boy had beene put to great danger and hardshippe.

At my comeing to Paris, I wrote to my brother Sir Henry Cholmeley to send to mee my younger sonne Hugh Cholmeley who had bene left at Pauls Schoule in London, at my wifes comeing from thence till this tyme.[401] I had not bene 3 weeks in Paris when I fell very sicke in which tyme it pleased god to bring sayfe to mee my eldest sonne William from Italy (and my brother Trotters kind letter [to lay his per – *crossed out*] a tyme to try my friends and if I had need to Pay).[403] As soone as I recoverd health I with my 2 sonns went to winter in Rone[404] where was my wifes brother Dr John Twisden and her eldest brother Sir Roger Twisdens eldest sonne cauled William.[405]

In February 1646[406] I sent my eldest sonne William in to England to looke after my esstate, which proved very fortunate for haveing upon foresight of these trobles *Anno Domini* 1640 made the Manner of Whitby with a great part of my other lands over to use of my sonne William and settled another part of my lands for raiseing portions [to my younger children – *interlineated*] he with the helpe of my brother Sir Henry Cholmeley who proved a faythfull brother and trew friend to mee and with whome I had left these two deeds. At my comeing out of England he got these lands out of sequestration which was not only a meanes to support us but to make my

---

[399] Cholmley provided no punctuation here, but his editors placed a full stop after the word 'Holland'. There was, of course, no 'happy meeting' for the whole family in Holland, where Sir Hugh stayed only three weeks to raise some money before moving on to France. As Cholmley himself later explained (f.29r.), there was no complete family reunion until 1647 at Rouen. Cholmley did not explain how he acquired £600; perhaps, like the Queen before him, he raised the money in Amsterdam by pawning jewellery.

[400] This place-name was printed as 'Montreal' in both editions. Almost certainly, Cholmley meant Montreuil, which lies on the oldest and shortest road between Calais and Paris, now known as the N1.

[401] As Hugh subsequently explained in what became the preface to his father's printed memoirs and his own Account of Tangier, about the age of ten, in 1642, he had become a boarder at St Paul's school in London and remained there until called to Paris by his father in October 1645 (*Private Memoirs of the Cholmley Family* (1787), p.iv).

[402] It will be recalled that Sir Hugh's sister Ursula, who had died in 1628, was married to George Trotter of Skelton castle.

[403] These words in brackets were written down the left margin and marked for insertion at this point, but their meaning is far from clear. Presumably, Sir Hugh's 'if I had need to Pay' is a reference to his composition fine.

[404] Printed correctly as 'Rouen'.

[405] See Twysden family tree.

[406] Cholmley would have written '1645', as it was printed in 1787, but the figure 5 was altered to 6 on the manuscript and the date was printed in 1870 as '1645–6'.

Composetion the easier, though the freeing and holding them were chargeable to us by underhand gratuetyes nor could the trew benefitt be made of the esstate till my retorne in to England.[407]

Aprill 1646 my selfe sonne Hugh brother Dr Twisden and my nephew Twisden went to Towers[408] where I remayned till July following and then leaveing them there retorned to Paris where I resided till March 1647 and then went to Rouen wether in May following my wife came to me with my eldest sonne and hir two daughters and (f.29r.) soone after came alsoe my sonne Hugh | from Towers soe that here it pleased the Lord to give mee my deare wife and children a comfortable meeting who had not bene all together of 5 yeares before. I tooke a house here at Rouen and lived I praysed god handsomly and plentefully for the space of a yeare and a halfe,[409] but the plage increaseing at Rouen I tooke a house at Gallion[410] 16 miles from Rouen the Archbisshops [of Rouens – interlineated] seate where booth by him and divers gentlemen recydeing there, I was receyved with much respect and kindness, but upon a difference betweene the King of France and the Paretians[411] and warre growing hott, and souldiors stirring on every hand wee being in an open towne thought fitt to remove for Roauen. It chanced to bee soone after the Parlament had [cut of – crossed out] taken away the kings head, at which the french were soe incensed that the people were redy to stone us at our landing from the River[412] and truly but that wee had formerly lived there and knowne by many to have bene of our Kings party, I verely thinke they had done us some mischeife. My monyes falling short my deare wife with her two daughters resolved for England. She had brought some household stuffe in to France with her and what in respect of the Plage and warre thought it not sayfe to leave[413] it in France but shipped it in an English bottam for England which I thinke betrayed it in to the hand of an Ostend man of warre, [who pretended a Commission from the King of England – crossed out; soe that as by warre and plunder wee had before lost most of our stuffe soe now on the sea by – interlineated] piracy had the remainder taken.[414]

In February 1648[415] I carryed my deare wife to Deepe.[416] The next day the Governor sent a gentleman to invite us all to his house [to dinner – interlineated] but she being to take shippe could not pertake of his favour her two daughters my brother Dr Twisden [and] nephew William Twisden went with her for England and haveing

---

[407] According to the records of the Committee for Compounding with Delinquents Sir Hugh had placed the whole of his estate in the hands of his brother and other trustees except for the manor and lands of Fyling. Since this part of the Cholmley estate was valued at only £170 per annum, Sir Hugh was able to escape with a fine of only £850. In contrast, fellow Yorkshire Royalists such as Henry Bellasis, Thomas Danby, George Wentworth and Henry Hildyard had to pay out thousands of pounds to rescue their properties (YRCP, ii, YASRS, xviii, p.22).

[408] Printed correctly as 'Tours'.

[409] During this period Sir Hugh wrote his three Memorials for Hyde.

[410] Gaillon is about 20 miles south-east of Rouen in the direction of Paris.

[411] Cholmley meant Parisians which is how the word was printed in both editions.

[412] Clearly, the party had gone down the river Seine from Gaillon to Rouen.

[413] Instead of Sir Hugh's 'leave', both editors preferred 'have'.

[414] Ironically, and perhaps justly, the former governor of a privateers' refuge, Scarborough, whose ships had plundered English east coast shipping for more than two years, was now the victim of what might well have been Scarborough pirates. Captains Browne Bushell, Francis Fawether and William Cooper are known to have operated out of Ostend when they could no longer use Scarborough (J.R. Powell and E.K. Timings (eds), Documents Relating to the Civil War 1642–1648, Navy Records Society, 1963, pp.203–4).

[415] The date was printed as 1648 in the first edition and altered to 1648–9 in the second.

[416] The spelling was altered to 'Dieppe' in the printed works.

a very great storme at sea it pleased god by that he deliver[d] them from the danger of being taken by a Pirat. After my wifes departure I had a very noble interteinment and reception at the Governors. The breaches peeced[417] up betweene the King and Parisioners I retorned with my sonne Hugh Cholmeley to Rouen, and soone after to Paris where haveing notice that the Parlament had admitted the Kings party to a composetion (but some few excepted persons) I thought fitt to retorne for England, and soe takeing shippe at Calais landed at Dover[418] June *1649*, and from there went post to Gravesend and there by water to London where I found my wife in blacke and white Court in the Old Baley. She had before my comeing to London paid the first part of my composetion which was £450 my g[ood][11] Mother in law and sister Cholmeley wif[e to][419] | my brother Richard[420] with a great deale of forwardnes (f.29v.) beeing bound with my sonne William for it which at that tyme was a great kindness for friends are best discovered in adversety and this was a tyme when my wife found not soe many as she exspected; yet my deare brother Sir Henry Cholmeley being in yorkesheire [wrote to my wife – *interlineated*] he would bee bound to what some soever she had need of for my use.

In August 1649 I went in to yorkesheire and at Whitby I and my sonne enterd in to the Artickles with Sir Nicholas[421] Crispe tuching the [bet – *crossed out*] erecting an Allome woorke[422] and let him a 3^d for 21 yeares [for which he paid £200 – *interlineated*] rent per annum. We alsoe gave to my brother Sir Henry Cholmeley in retorne of all his kindnesses a sixt part in the said Allome works with out any rent for 26 yeares; which said sixt part he let after to Crispe for £150 per annum rent.

Whilst I was in france one Tayler an Alderman in yorke had sewed[423] mee to an outlarie upon pretence of some lead he had at Scarbrough, carried up and made use of in the Castle in tyme of the seage and for this had sent 6 souldiors now whilst I was a Whitby, and as I came [out] one Sunday in afternoone from the Church and entering in at the wicket of the great gate one of these souldiors layd his hand on my shoulder and said he arreasted mee, the rest being near him drew their swoords and my sonne William Cholmeley and my cosen Richard Trotter[424] and a french man of myne and another of my sonnes beeing with mee drew theirs and were tilting at one another. I had myne by my side but did not draw it till a souldior came running at my sonne behinde him then I drew and made him stepd backe and one of them discharged betweene mee and my sonne. I thinke wee might have drivem them out of the Court

---

[417] Cholmley's word was downgraded to 'made' in both printed editions.

[418] Both printed texts have four dots between 'Dover' and 'June' which were not on the manuscript.

[419] The lower part of this folio is now in poor condition: the bottom corner has been torn or eaten away and two mending strips have blanked out some words.

[420] Sir Hugh refers here to his step-mother, Margaret Cobb, his father's second wife, her daughter-in-law, also Margaret, daughter of Lord Paulet, and his half-brother, Richard Cholmley (1617–43). Both Margarets were now widows. Young Richard, who had been given Grosmont by his father, had died gallantly in the service of the King at the siege of Lyme in Dorset.

[421] Nicholas was rechristened 'Richard' in both printed versions.

[422] At this point both printed works mislead the reader by changing what Sir Hugh had written into 'touching the better erecting my allum works'. Cholmley had no alum works until 1649. His first direct engagement in the local alum industry on his own land was at Saltwick Bay, on the coast a few miles east of Abbey House. The death of the King the previous January meant that the royal monopoly on alum mining and manufacture no longer existed. Only after the Restoration in 1660 were Sir Hugh's heirs faced with a royal demand for annual rent.

[423] This word was printed in both texts as 'forced'.

[424] Richard Trotter was the eldest son of George Trotter, who had died in 1647, and Ursula Cholmley, Sir Hugh's sister. In 1650, when he sold part of Fyling Ness to William Cholmley, Richard Trotter was described as a gentleman of Gray's Inn (Whitby LPS, PB 1295).

yeard but I considerd how obnoxtion [*sic*] I lay to [the] indignation of the tyme, and
that souldiery beeing then powerfull and prevelent if any of them should miscarry noe
law would punish them but if any of them should bee killed our lifes and esstates
would bee prosecuted with all the rigour that might bee, soe that I thought it best not
to contest by force, and [geting being neare the Cundit in Court yeard call to them to
– *crossed out*][425] required them all desist and put up their swoords for that I ment to
stand and fall by the law and their upon renderd my selfe to them. I offerd them baile
but they would not accept any with out Taylers consent, to whome I sent my cosen
(f.30r.) Trotter to pray him to meet mee at Malton next day whether my | cosen Trotter was
come but noe Taylor for he would not see him nor parle of the business[426] till I was in
the castle of yorke. And I being assured I had nether given order for [melteing – *crossed
out*] disposeing his lead and that there was but a few pigs spent in the Garrison though
he layd his action to the vallew of £800[427] did not know but their might be divers
other false pretensions against me nor how farre it would tend to my preiudice being
in the Castle, and theirfore resolved if it were possible to escape out of there hands and
then to appear to his Action, and because I would not have my friends involved in my
escape I ordered my sonne and cosen Trotter to leave mee earely next morneing
haveing only a french man with mee, who knew the Country. I had furnished these
six souldiors with 5 ordnary Country horses soe that two roade duble, and my selfe
had a little galloway which gave noe suspetion and was as it were by providence
brought to bee my deliverier for a friend of Wills comeing to Whitby meerely to
see[428] him had hurt the horses backe and forced to leave him there. By the tyme I was
a quarter of a mile out of Malton I leapt over the ditch on my right hand and bid the
souldiors addew sayeing I did not love to goe to prision, and setting spurs to my horse
he road up towerds Hilldingley[429] and the prety beast carried mee cleare[430] from them,
in which I must ever acknowledge gods great mercy and gudness for at present the
tymes were unfavorable to the Kings party tho [they – *crossed out*][431] had compounded
I had bene ruined if they had once got mee in prision for that would have
incourridged others to have sued mee for trespasses upon action of warre, I went
immediately post to London[432] with intention to reverse the outlawry and answeare
his action but findeing he had omitted my title of Barronet my Councell told mee the
writ against mee did abate, and he finding his error durst not proceed me[433] further
upon that. And theirfore he commenceth an action against my sonne William upon
pretence he had promissed I should bee a trew prissoner, which in truth was false, yet
he sends these 6 souldiors againe to Whitby who upon the Sabboth day in the
morneing open the doore and goes up in to the chamber where my said sonne was,
there arrests refuseing ether to take bale to answeare the sute or to come on horse
backe but caused him to walke a foot to Yorke and in very wet unseasenable wether,

---

[425] These crossed-out words were never printed, but they convey precisely the location of the incident here
described (see plan of Abbey House and grounds c.1700 (Whitby LPS, PB 5939): p.8).
[426] Here both editions made nonsense of Cholmley's words by printing them as 'nor part with the earnest'.
[427] This figure was wrongly printed as '300£' in 1787 but correctly transcribed in the 1870 edition.
[428] The word 'see' has been inserted by another hand in the manuscript; but it was printed in both editions.
[429] Sir Hugh probably knew that the township of Hildenley, two miles west of Malton, had once belonged
to his ancestor Roger Cholmley of Roxby and was then part of the estate of his brother-in-law, William
Strickland of Boynton.
[430] The word 'cleare' became 'clean' in both printed texts.
[431] In print, these words became 'though they'. Presumably, Sir Hugh meant that though royalists like
himself had compounded for their estates they were still subject to persecution and prejudice.
[432] Cholmley's phrase was altered in both printed editions to 'I went immediately for London post'.
[433] Cholmley's 'me' was changed to 'any' in 1787 and in 1870.

useing him both uncyvelly and barberously. As soon as my sonne came to Yorke the Sheriff bailed him but the busines comeing to a tryall Tayler got these souldiors to sweare my sonnes promisse for my beeing a | a trew prissoner soe posetively and (f.30v.) others that I had taken away his lead which was as false as the other. My sonne was cast in £400 damage, but by good happe it being upon a specyall verdet that gave some dispute of it in Courts at London, and in the intrime[434] my sonne brings an action against Tayler for these souldiors Arresteing him and refuseing to take bale and carring him in soe barberous a manner to Yorke, a foot; and alsoe the warrant was not directed to these souldiors by name but to all Baliffes in genrall soe that they did it with out authorety. And there upon the Jury gave my sonne £600 damage, soe that in conclusion Tayler was glad to make his application to mee [and take it for a favour – *interlineated*] to pay £300 downe in redy mony and release all suites actions and demaunds booth against my selfe and sonne, and truly this was a business of great consequence and advantage to us not only in poynt of profit in this particuler, but poynt of reputation, for the gud successe we had in this, deterred others ever after from prossecuteing any action of warre against mee, and for which let my heart never forget to prayse the Lord[435] all the dayes of my life.

Anno Domini 1651 the Parlament made an order that none who had bene of the Kings party should for a certayne tyme come with in 10[436] miles of London. I conceyveing my being in Yorkesheire would draw a greater suspetion upon mee choase my brother in law Sir Roger Twisdens house at Peckham for the place of my confinement, yet haveing before intended and prepared for Whitby where my sonne William was necessarily to reside tuching the erecting the Allome works[437] my wife with my daughter Elisabeth and famuly went downe thether my daugher Ann remaineing with her unckle Sir [Roger] Twisden. My deare wife remained the winter in the Country but with little comfort for want of my company. The next Spring was the tyme of great Action in Scotland their King[438] being at head of them, and gave such allarums and suspetion as many gentlemen in divers Countyes were committed and here in Kent my selfe [and brother in law Sir R Twisden – *interlineated*] taken by a party of horse from my said brother Sir Roger Twisdens house early in the morneing upon the 26th of Aprill 1651 being a Satterday and were carried to Leids prison,[439] where were alsoe the Lord Ashton[440] who had bene Maior Genrall of the Kings Army Sir Thom. Culpepper[441] and others. Here I remained 8 weeks and then we were all set at lyberty by order from the Counsell of State | entering into good[442] bond to appeare (f.31r.) at the Counsell of State upon tenn dayes summons at any tyme with in a yeare when we should bee cauled upon. Now percyveing my deare wife sollitary, in the Country,

---

[434] In both texts Cholmley's 'intrime' was printed as 'time'.
[435] In both printed versions these words became 'pray to the Lord'.
[436] The figure could be 10 or 20: in print it became 'ten'.
[437] These were the newly-opened Cholmley works at Saltwick Bay.
[438] Interestingly, though still Royalist in sympathy, Sir Hugh referred to Charles II as 'their King', not his or England's. Presumably, his antagonism towards the Scots is some explanation of this, since there is no evidence elsewhere in the manuscript that he was afraid it might be read by his political enemies.
[439] Leeds Castle in Kent is about a dozen miles north-east of the Twysden home, Roydon Hall near East Peckham.
[440] Lord Astley (not 'Ashton'), formerly Sir Jacob Astley, was one of the most distinguished and one of the last of the field commanders of King Charles I; he surrendered in March 1646.
[441] Sir John (not 'Sir Thom.') Culpeper had been a close adviser of King Charles who had made him his Chancellor of the Exchequer in 1642. Along with Sir Edward Hyde, the future Lord Clarendon, he had acted as a moderate, civilian influence in the king's 'cabinet', often in opposition to the headstrong Prince Rupert.
[442] The edition of 1787 omitted the word 'good' and that of 1870 replaced it.

and findeing a great misse of her company I desired her retorne and propounded[443] the sending a coach from London for her, for at that tyme she had none of her owne, the tymes requireing our liveing as retyredly as might be and beside it was impossible to have kept any coach horses, for they would have bene taken for Armyes service. She remembering the gud passage formerly she had by sea from London to Whitby at the beginning of the warre, would now come up noe other way but by sea[444] where she was on shippe boord 10 or 12 dayes and in ruffe wether soe she resolved never[445] to passe that way againe. At last she arrived at Graves End whether I went to meet her and brought her to my brother Sir Roger Twisdens house at Peckham where we remayned neare a yeare and in July *Anno Domini* 1652 wee with my two sonns and two daughters retorned to Whitby, where wee had not bene all together of above 7 years before[446] and now the Lord had heard and answeard my prayers made to him when wee were soiourners in a strange land that he would in his gud tyme bring mee my wife and children to a comfortable meeting at our owne home at Whitby. The place as I told you had bene plunderd [of all – *crossed out*][447] but my wife being there before with her owne huswifery had made some beding and being most excellent at addorneing and fitting a house had now put in to a condetion to receyve our selfes and a friend. My intention was to live retyredly and with a small famuly yet were wee neare[448] 30 persons. Here wee remained till June 1654 when wee all retorned to London to consummate the marridge of my eldest daughter Ann which was concluded[449] with Mr Richard Stephens, eldest sonne to Mr Nathanniell Stephens of Glostersheire. They were married the beginning of July 1654 and with in a month after my occations drew mee in to Yorkesheire but my wife haveing noe mynde to remove from London tooke lodgeings at Westminster neare her daughter. In August following my sonne was married to the lady Hothams daughter;[450] and the lady Lepington now lady Saint Johns being in yorkesheire came purposely to his weding and was a weeke at my house at Whitby, [where she did not dislike the – *crossed out*][451] At Michelmas I retorned to London and brought my deare wife to lodgeings in Russell Street [where – *crossed out*] the next doore to the Raine deere[452] where wee remayned all winter till the end of February following when my occations requireing

(f.31v.) my presence in the North. After my departure | she went to my sister[453] Cholmeleyes house at Chiswicke, but findeing her selfe not very well she came to London about

---

[443] Instead of 'propounded', both editors preferred 'proposed'.

[444] Instead of 'sea', both editions printed 'ship'.

[445] Both editions omitted 'never' and instead had 'resolved to pass not'.

[446] In fact, the whole family had not been together in Whitby since 1640, twelve years earlier. About the same time that Sir Hugh had come north in September 1642 to take up his Parliamentary commission at Scarborough, his eldest son had been given leave to cross over to France (*CJ*, ii, p.763) and he had not returned to England until early in 1646. Young Hugh had been away from Yorkshire even longer. Since returning to England with his father in 1649 he had spent a year at Cambridge and two more in London and Kent. (Cholmley, *Memoirs* (1787), pp.v–vi.)

[447] Cholmley crossed out 'of all' but the words were printed in both editions.

[448] The word 'neare' was omitted in 1787 and restored in 1870.

[449] Instead of Cholmley's 'concluded', both editors substituted 'contracted'.

[450] William married Katherine Hotham of Fyling, the youngest daughter of Sarah Anlaby, fifth and final wife and now widow of Sir John Hotham (1589–1645). The marriage alliance with the Hothams must have been most pleasing to Sir Hugh.

[451] These deleted words were not printed.

[452] Curiously, Cholmley's Reindeer Inn became a 'Roe-deer' in the 1787 printed edition. However, the editor of the 1870 version had the name printed correctly.

[453] The 1787 edition reads 'her sister', whereas that of 1870 has the correct version of 'my sister'. Here Sir Hugh meant the widow of his dead half-brother, Sir Richard Cholmley; this becomes clear when later he elaborates on his wife's last days (see below, f.34v.).

the 6th of Aprill *1655* and lodged at the lodgeing of her cosen the lady Katheran Moore in Bedford Street in Common[454] Garden where after being a weeke sicke of a feaver she dyed[455] the 17th of [Aprill – *crossed out*] the said Month of Aprill making a most pious and christian end as more perticulerly appears by the perticuler relation and discription of her selfe. The sadd[456] newes of her death came to mee at Whitby, from whence I removed with 3 or 4 dayes being indeed not able to endure the sight of those roomes and places in which I used to enioy her company, and besides I desired to bee at London to comfort my daughter Stephens who was great with child and with in [2 month – *crossed out*; 10 weeks – *interlineated*] of her accoumpt. My daughter Elisabeth was at the tyme with my sister Yelverton[457] and [lodged – *crossed out*] bedfellow to her cosen Ann Yelverton since married to the Lord Mandevell. My sister offerd to my deare wife that my said daughter should still remayne with her but my deare wife desired she might after her death live with my brother Scriant Twisdens wife[458] and upon very prudent considerations as that [the liveing in a place amongst greate persons and in a high way might – *crossed out*][459] her cosen Yelverton was to be married to the Lord Mandevell, and they and my sister being to live all together my daughter Bette[460] would be bred amongst greater company and in a higher way then was fitt for her fortune. At the entrance in to the doore[461] at Whitby house there was a place left where we intended to have our Armes set up to gether which yet was crossed by one fate or other soe that she would often say if it were not done in her life it would never bee done and she should be forgotten, but since her death I have caused booth our Armes to bee erected in that place cut out in a stone I sent from London.[462] | I have alsoe written on the backe of her picture and her scutcheon that (f.32r.) the memory of her may bee preserved to posterety. [I have performed all she desired of mee and would have – *crossed out*][463] She desired Hugh Cholmley[464] might have a chamber bought in the temple[465] which I have done and that I would marry my

[454] Sir Hugh probably made a mistake here in writing 'Comon Garden'. Later, he referred to the same place as 'Covent Garden' (see below, f.35r.). Both editions printed 'Covent Garden', not Cholmley's error.
[455] From this point onwards for the next two sheets, as he describes the death of Lady Elizabeth, Sir Hugh's handwriting increases in size and there are more deletions than formerly.
[456] Instead of 'sadd', both editions have 'sudden'.
[457] Sir Hugh's younger daughter Elisabeth was staying with her aunt Anne Yelverton at Easton Mauduit in Northamptonshire.
[458] Serjeant Twysden, younger brother of Lady Elizabeth, was to become Sir Thomas Twysden, baronet and judge, and founder of the Twysden family of Bradbourne in East Malling, Kent. His wife was Jane Thomlinson. (F.W. Jessup, *Sir Roger Twysden* (1965), pp.14, 35, 105).
[459] These deleted words were not printed.
[460] The editors of both printed versions substituted 'Bess'.
[461] Both printed texts have 'the door *of* Whitby House'; but it is not clear whether Sir Hugh meant over the gateway entrance to the grounds or on the lintel of the house door.
[462] Unfortunately, this inscribed stone is no longer at Abbey House. However, surprisingly, Sir Hugh does not mention the inscription which has survived on a stone set in a brick wall enclosing the New Gardens at Whitby. The inscription explains that the wall was built by Sir Hugh and Lady Elizabeth in 1652 to protect the orchard they had planted on this bleak, exposed hillside. Then beneath a shield carrying the Cholmley and Twysden arms it reads:
'Our Handy worke like to the Frutefull tree
Blesse thou O Lord; let it not blasted bee.'
[463] All these words deleted by Cholmley were omitted from both printed works.
[464] This is not Sir Hugh's own son, as might be supposed: by 1656 he was 24 years old and probably considered too old for entrance to one of the Inns of Court.
[465] Hugh Cholmley, son of Sir Henry of West Newton Grange and nephew of Sir Hugh, after some years at Peterhouse, Cambridge, was admitted to the Inner Temple in November 1656, just at the time his uncle was writing this (*Alum. Cantab.*, i, p.334).

daughter Elisabeth as soone as conveniently I could, and as soone as a gud oppertunety is offerd god permiting I will promote it all I can.[466] I have performed all else she desired and should relegiously and willingly have done whatever it had bene more to the utmost of my power. I have erected [where she was buried – *interlineated*] a blacke Marble[467] to her Memory to which I beare so much love and honour as by gods permission I intend to declyne the being interred in my owne Country amongst my Ancestors that my body may bee layed by her, which I beseach the lord to grant if it bee his will. It is now a yeare and halfe since she departed this life most of which tyme I have recyded amongst her friends, whome I love very much and where I shall for the most parte I think continue except the lord change my condetion, to whose protection and providence I commit the remainder of my dayes, the number and nature of which he only knoweth.[468] I beseach they may bee for his glory and then I am pleased however he pleaseth to dispose of mee.[469] |

[Sir Hugh left 32v. blank and then resumed on a new sheet, in a much smaller and better controlled hand, with a final tribute to his wife.]

(f.33r.)   E[lisabeth] T[wisden] Wife to Sir Hugh Cholmley

Elisabeth eldest daughter to Sir William Twisden of great Peckham in the County of Kent knight and Barronet (by the lady Ann daughter to Sir Moile Finch of Eastwell in the County of Kent, by Elisabeth his wife who after his death was created Countesse of Wincheley)[470] was wife to Sir Hugh Cholmley. She was borne the 18th of August being a tuesday *Anno Domini 1600* and married the 10th of December being alsoe a tuesday *Anno Domini 1622*.

She was of the middle stature of woemen, and well shaped yet in that not soe singuler, as in the beauty of her face, which was but of a little Moddell and yet proportionable to her body, her eies blacke and full of loveliness and sweettnes, her eie browes small and even, as if drawne with a pensell, a very little pretty well shaped mouth, which some tymes (escptiyally when in a muse or studdy) she would draw up in to an incredible little compasse; her haire a sad chessnutt, her complection browne but cleare with fresh couller in her cheeks, a loveliness in her lookes inexspresseable and by her whole composure was soe beautifull sweet creature at her marridge, as not many did parrellel and few exceed in the Nation. Yet the inward indowments and perfection of her mynde did exceed those outward of her body, being a most pious virtus person of great inienuety, and a discerneing iudgement in most things; of a sweet good nature compassionate beyond immgenation in soe much there was

---

[466]   Elisabeth Cholmley never married. She died in 1699 and was buried near her parents.
[467]   The black marble stone was set in the floor near the south wall of the chancel of St Michael's church at East Peckham. Unhappily, the marble is now badly damaged and St Michael's is classified as a redundant church.
[468]   When he wrote these words in November 1656 Sir Hugh had almost exactly another year to live.
[469]   At this point, both printed texts read '[He died at East Peckham the 30th of November 1657, and was buried in the church at that place.]', which of course does not appear on the manuscript.
[470]   In 1591, William Twysden, eldest son and heir of Roger Twysden of Roydon Hall at East Peckham, married Anne, daughter of Sir Moyle Finch of Eastwell and Elizabeth, who eventually became Viscountess of Maidstone and Countess of Winchelsea. Anne had been brought up at the Court of Queen Elizabeth and the marriage gave the Twysdens access to the royal court from then on. (Jessup, p.11).

nothing she tooke more content in, or more agreeable to her disposetion, then to bee helpfull to every bodyes need of what quallety or condetion soever, and more tuched with another bodyes want then her owne, charritable to the pure a perfect Semarritan redy to poure oile into every bodyes wounds, of a most Noble and Generous mynde and would not doe an uniust or Dishonourable Act to gaine the world, apt to remitt trespasses and did not reteyne revenge longer then her anger which was son past in a moment. She was of a tymerous nature, though in great danger had a courridge above her sex, evidenced upon severall occasions whilst she was with mee[471] in the seage of Scarbrough, and more perticulerly upon the fall of the Castle when Meldram sent proposetions to mee with menaces that if they were not accepted, he would that night bee Master of all the world and the Castle (and in caise one drope of his mens blood was shed, not give quarter to man or woeman but put all to the sword, and she conceyveing I would more resent this in respect of her being there, came to mee with out any deiection or troble and prayed mee I would not for any consideration of her doe ought might bee preiudetiall to my owne honour or the Kings affayres. She was alsoe a most indulgent parent a chast and loveing wife, and would never disserte mee for any strate or danger, testified by leaveing her friends [who were loath to parte with mee[472] – *interlineated*] and goeing to live soe remote from them at Whitby with mee when I was soe much incumberd with my fathers debts. | Next, when I declared for the King, she being at London tooke shippe there (f.33v.) and came downe with her two daughters immediately to Scarbrough,[473] and would nether before nor in the seage be perswaded to leave mee, though dureing that tyme she endured much troble and inconvenience, for the Castle[474] being beaten downe she was forced to lye in a little Cabin on the ground,[475] sevrell monthes together, where she tooke a defluction of rume upon one of her eies which trobled her ever after, and got alsoe a tuch of the scurvie then riffe in the Castle and of which it was thought she was never well quit after.[476]

Whilst [we] were thus beseaged in the Castle she did not ommit to visit sicke persons, and take [an exstraordnary – *interlineated*] care of them, making such helps and provisions as the place would affoard, in soe much as her maydes were soe over wrought and tryled[477] with it as one of them in the night stoale away thinkeing to get in to the towne, but the enemies gardes takeing her for a spie caused her retorne, which was acceptable to her lady, there being not persons in health to attend the sicke. At the render of the Castle she procured an Artickle that the Garrison in my house at Whitby might bee removed and she have liberty to live in it, but the Captaine liked the place soe well he would not out, till one of his servants dyed of the plage, and before he durse returne againe she unexspectedly (leaveing her two daughters behinde her (at one Mr Pearchyhayes) [neare Malton –

---

[471] At first Sir Hugh had referred to himself in the third person; later he changed his mind about this form and altered all references to the first person. Only the altered version is given here as it was in print in both texts.

[472] Sir Hugh wrote 'mee', but probably meant 'her'. Both printed versions have 'her'.

[473] In the earlier account of this event (see above, f.27r.) he had written that Lady Cholmley had first gone to Whitby before coming down to Scarborough.

[474] By 'Castle' Cholmley meant the keep, which had provided lodging for the officers and families in the garrison until it was split in two by Meldrum's cannon-royal.

[475] In his 'Memorials tuching Scarbrough', Sir Hugh had previously described these makeshift shelters as 'poore Cabbins reared against the walls and banckes in the Castle yeard' (see below, p.157).

[476] Both printed versions failed to convey exactly Cholmley's meaning. The 1787 edition has 'she was not well after'; and that of 1870 reads 'she was not quite well after'.

[477] Both printed works have 'toiled' instead of Cholmley's word.

interlineated][478] adventured over the Moores [in a dangerous season they being – *interlineated*] then coverd with a thicke snow and soe got in to the house and kept possession though in a sad condetion for I and her two sons were beyond sea and her girles she durst not bring thether [in respect of the late sickness – *interlineated*][479] She had only one mayde and one man servant cauled Thom Knowles who [was] cooke and as she was solletary soe ill accommodated, for all things, in the house being plundered, she had nothing but what she borrowed and the bed soe hard she would complaine she could not bee warme, nor able to lye on it. Soe she would say this was the saddest and worst tyme of her life, yet her sperret would not submit to make complaint and application to the Parlaments Committee at Yorke, as most others did, who disposed all my esstate. The winter over and the house free from danger she got her two girles to her and my brother Sir Henry Cholmeley had procured a 5th parte of the esstate for her selfe and children with which she shifted neare two yeares, and then came with her two girles to mee to France, where she remained neare two yeares more until my occasions necessateted her retorne with her two daughters in which passage from Deipe she was by gods providence deliverd from two dangers a tempest and a Piratt. |

(f.34r.)   The people [and Country – *interlineated*] about Whitby owe a perpetuall obligation to her memory, they and the Country being much improved and refined by her comeing thether, for as divers (and of the best in the Country) desired to have their daughters in service with her, soe being dismissed with many good qualletyes they did communecate them to others and thus not only the younger sorte and some of low ranke had improvement, but even the elder and the best quallety of house keepers in the towne by her example and acquaintance did much improve and reforme booth in manner and handsome deportment of their persons and neatness in their houses and liveing; she being very courteous and affable to her neighbours of all ranks and often goeing amongst them to visit. She contributed much to the beautefeing of the house at Whitby being a good contriver with indoores and haveing a most singuler faculty to make and order furneture for houses, and dresse it after the best mode which many cannot doe though they have stuffe which guift she had from her Mother bred up in Quene Elisabeths Court; soe that it may be said with out flattery, in this perticuler, she exceeded all the woemen of that famuly who preceaded her and perhaps scarse shall bee perrolleled by those who succeed; of which posterety might have had better testemony by the stuffe which she had got in to that house if the cyvell discentions had not occationed the plunder and losse of it. What is now remaneing there was by her caire and industry provided after her retorne out of France but not of the same worth as the other was in it before, partly in respect my purse could not soe well furnish her as before, and partly in that it was not discretion to bestow much cost in furneture considering the unsetlednesse of the tymes; soe what was done now was for necessety and present use more then ornament, and truly the blankets and much beding was made or got in by her owne huswifery and industry[480] with out much exspence of mony. There is[481] a suite of

---

[478] "Mr Pearchyhayes" was Christopher Percehay of Ryton, two and a half miles north of Malton. Christopher has been described as a 'long-lapsed Catholic' and 'political neutral' who retained his place on the North Riding Bench after the Civil War (H. Aveling, *Northern Catholics: The Catholic Recusants of the North Riding of Yorkshire 1558–1790* (1966), pp.304, 307).

[479] Cholmley's 'sickness' (by which he meant the plague) became 'illness' in both printed texts.

[480] The first edition of 1787 contains many minor errors and omissions in this area. For instance, 'or got in' and 'and industry' are not printed. In the 1870 version, however, these words were included.

[481] Again, whereas Sir Hugh used the present tense here, in 1787 it was altered to the past tense 'was'. The editor of the second printed version did not repeat this error.

greene cloth hangeings with flowers of needle worke wrought by her selfe and mayds, which I much esteemes and prisse itt, and heartly wish may be soe by the posterety it shall please the Lord is to possesse them, and theirfore [I] desire for hers and my sake they be preserved with an exstraordnary caire. In her younger yeares when first a house keeper she imployed her selfe and mades much with their needles but her cheife delight was in her booke being addicted to reade and well versed in history. She was by constitution inclyned to mellancholly, yet genrally pleasant and gud company and loved mirth. She was a trew friend as was in the world and did not only love her owne kinred intyrely but alsoe all myne.[482] And to such as had need would have bene more helpefull then my [fortune – *crossed out*] esstate conveniently could permit. Yet after the enumeration of soe many virtues and gud qualletys it cannot bee immagined she was with out frailtyes and imperfections, as noe more then all other woemen, the greatest of which and all that can bee charged upon her was that she was passionate and soone provoked to anger and would some tymes say what she did not intend or thinke; but it was quikly over | and it never did any harme but to her selfe; she could not master her (f.34v.) passion yet would bee sencyble and sorry for it. If she had taken impression of any thing it was hard to remove it with reason or argument till she had considerd of it with her selfe; nether could she well endure adversety or crosses though it pleased the Lord to exercise her with them by my many trobles and the calamety of the tymes.[483] She would bee too much trobled at evells which could nether bee prevented nor remedied and some tyme discontented with out any great cause esspetially in her indisposetion [of health];[484] and being of a tender constitution and spunne of a fine thred, every disaster tooke impression on her body and mynde and would make her booth sicke and often inclynable to be[485] mellancolly esspetially in my absence; her mynde and inclynation was to the South though in love and complyance to mee she passed most of her tyme in the North, which perhaps might have bene with more content and a greater blessing if had she done it because the Lord had cast her lot there. And now haveing lade open all her imperfections which may bee reckoned rather frailtyes then faults, and considering how much her virtues and perfections doth over balance them, I hope posterety will have the memory of her in great honour and veneration as I am sure all have that knew her but esspetially my selfe who best knew her virtues and worth and have the greatest losse of her.

After my retorne out of France wee lived much in London and the South yet about 1652[486] wee went to keepe house at Whitby haveing not bene there together of 7 yeare before[487] where she remayned constantly till Midsommer[488] 54 when she retorned to London to the marridge of her eldest daughter Ann to Mr Richard Stephens of Glostersheire which in respect of the remotenes I was something averse to, but she[489]

---

[482] At this point in the manuscript a small cross indicates that a marginal addition ending with the word 'permit' is to be inserted here.

[483] Here Sir Hugh placed a cross to indicate the point for the insertion of a marginal afterthought which probably ended with the word 'health'.

[484] Here the margin has been cut away. Both printed texts have 'of health' as the last two words, but that of 1787 has 'disposition' instead of 'indisposetion'.

[485] The words 'to be' have been written in a different hand above a blot which has obscured Sir Hugh's original words.

[486] In the manuscript the last figure 3 was altered to 2. Both printed editions have 1652. Previously (see above, f.31r.), Cholmley had written that they had returned to Whitby in July 1652.

[487] See above, f.31r., note 446.

[488] Both 'constantly' and 'Midsommer' were omitted from the 1787 edition, but not in that of 1870.

[489] In 1870 this word was misread or misprinted as 'the', yet correctly printed as 'she' in 1787 – a rare case of the first edition being superior to the second.

marvelous earnest for it sayeing she found him to bee soe[490] gud a natured man she knew
her daughter would bee happy in him and caired not in to what Country he carried her.
In [February – *crossed out*; January – *interlineated*] 1654[491] I haveing occation to goe in to
Yorkesheire she went to Chiswicke to my sister in law my brother Sir Richard
Cholmleys lady where was alsoe my Moher in law[492] my fathers widdow, who my wife
loved in tyrely, purposeing to stay their till my retorne, but findeing her selfe not very
well and desirous to see my daughter Stephens then breeding child, she went to London
the 6th of Aprill intending to retorne with in a few dayes, but the Lord god had other
wise decreed, for she fell in to a feaver there of which [she] dyed, the 17 of Aprill 1655
being Easter tuesday about 12 of the clocke in morneing soe that her birth marridge and
death was all upon tuesday. |

(f.35r.)　　Before she fell sicke every one thought she looked exstreame well and reteyned soe
much beauty as one would have iudged her not above forty though she was to be 55
the 18th of August following. She kept her chamber not above 8 dayes and the
Phesetians thought her in noe great danger till the moreneing she dyed when her
sister Yelverton the lady Katherine Moore [daughter to the Earl of Wincheley her
cosen – *interlineated*][494] at whose lodgeing in Covent Garden she dyed, adviseing her
to send for a [divine][495] and propound only such as she knew to be presbeterians,[496]
answeared she needed them not. At last my sonne in law Mr[497] Stephens askeing her if
he should fetch to her the Bishoppe of Armath,[498] she sayd with all my heart I pray
doe, who comeing not above 2 or 3 howers before she dyed after he found her well
prepaired for death as indeed she had ever a great knowledge in Relegion and a strong
fayth [soe now in her sickness had given great testimony – *interlineated*] of it he told
her he was come to marry her to the Lord Jesus to which she replyed O blessed day
that I am to be married to my Saviour the Lord Jesus which wurds never went out of
her mynde[499] or scarse out of her mouth but was often be repeating them whilst she
lived. She had endured her sickness with great patience and blessed be god[500] And
though her eie sight failed had her senses and could speake almost even to the last
breath. And it pleased the great god which sp[ans the][501] heavens and disposeth of the
dayes of man for the rough passa[ge and] the many trobles and tossing she had in her
life, to give her a smouth and q[uite] agreeable departure out of the world, for never
any departed this life more [truly saint] like then she who I am sure is now a blessed

[490] The word 'soe' was omitted from the first printed edition, but not from the second.
[491] Sir Hugh originally wrote 'February 1653', then crossed out February and wrote 'January' above it. The figure 3 has been crudely altered to 4. The 1787 edition printed 'February 1654' and that of 1870 'February 1654-5'.
[492] Confusingly, both ladies were widows of Sir Richard Cholmley, the one Sir Hugh's father, the other, his half-brother.
[493] This sheet is now badly frayed at the right and bottom edges and crude repairs sometimes obscure the script.
[494] It will be recalled that Elizabeth's mother was the Countess of Winchelsea and her younger sister Anne (1603–70) was the widow of Sir Christopher Yelverton (c.1602–54) of Easton Mauduit, Sir Hugh's close friend and political ally.
[495] Where Cholmley's own words have now been lost, I have inserted those to be found in the printed versions.
[496] At this point, both printed texts added the word 'she'.
[497] The words 'in law Mr' have been added later in a different hand.
[498] Cholmley's spelling was altered in print to 'Armagh'. The archbishop of Armagh was James Ussher (1580–1656), the eminent theologian.
[599] Cholmley's phrase here was changed in both printed texts to 'words were never out of her mind'.
[500] Sir Hugh crossed out the next line of words and then re-wrote them.
[501] From this point downwards the folio is badly worn along the right edge.

one in Heaven. A trew daughter of the Church of England dyeing in profession of [that] fayth booth in doctrine and discipline here esstablsihed and practiced since the Reforma[tion] in the tyme of Edward the 6th till the beginning of these trobles.

She brought in to the world six children Richard William Elisabeth Hugh Ann and Elisabeth. I prayse god all baptised ac[cording] to the forme required by the Church of England; Richard and the elder Elis [abeth] dyed young the other fower survived her her eldest sonne William and daughter Ann were also married and Williams wife and Ann with child before she dyed which she much ioyed in, though it did not please the Lord she should live to see their issue, she was much averse to the marridge of William to the lady Hothams daughter as she would say meerely because that lady [the mother – *interlineated*] had an ill nature, which I pro[test] was more then I did thinke or immagine though I had known her as well as she, but she had a notable guift to iudge of peoples disposetions and did iustly here as since we have found by exsperience. My son [William] being married in Yorkesheire and my deare wife at London she [not seeing her] daughter in law after she was married but heareing [her sonne and she lived comfortably together at Whitby became]⁵⁰² | to love her very (f.35v.) much, and haveing a house in Whitby towne which she had bought with her owne mony she bequeathed it to her said daughter in law requireing that it might bee soe passed to her as she might dispose it at her pleasure with out her husbands consent, and alsoe gave to her her owne best Cabinet, and if she had lived intended as soon as her daughter Stephens was brought to bed to have taken a iirney purposely in to Yorkesheire to have bene assistant at the labour of her said daughter. It was not gods will that my selfe or sonnes should be with her at her death, I and William being in Yorkesheire and Hugh in Northamptonshire, she often wished mee but sayd she saw it could not be and theirfor submitted to gods pleasure. My sonne Stephens suplyed our places testefieing as much love and respect to her booth in her sickness and after death as if he had bene her owne child,⁵⁰³ She departed this life the 17th⁵⁰⁴ of Aprill 1655 being tuesday [upon which day of] the weeke she was borne married and dyed. Her desire was to have bene buried at Whitby conceyveing I [intended] to bee layed there alsoe, but thinkeing it would be too great a troble and a charge⁵⁰⁵ to carry her body thether, wished it might be interred at Peckham church in Kent by her father and Mother which accordingly was donne and where I have erected a black marble to her memory set on her grave⁵⁰⁶ and in respect of my absence the funerall was very private yet with such circomestances as was decent and requesite for her quallety, for on fryday morneing very earely by daybreake⁵⁰⁷ the body was carried out of towne in a hearse with 6 horses all in morneing, attended with another coach and some horsemen, that went next with the body in to Kent. My sonne Hugh came in tyme to wate on it which was met on the way by her 3 brothers Sir Roger, the Seriant and Francis Twisden, with their wifes and children and retennue, and interred at the feet of her father in the private quire belonging to that famuly, to whose memory I have erected a blacke Marble stone (manuscript ends here but printed texts continue with the following words) with mine and her coat of arms, engraven together in one escutcheon, and with this inscription upon the stone: 'Deposited the body of the Lady

---

⁵⁰² The bottom line of the manuscript is now completely missing.
⁵⁰³ The following sentence is a marginal entry marked x for insertion at this point.
⁵⁰⁴ Unaccountably, this figure appeared in both printed works as '18th'.
⁵⁰⁵ Both printed texts omitted 'and a charge', words which were added later and have become very faint.
⁵⁰⁶ The phrase beginning 'where' and ending 'grave' was omitted in both printed versions, perhaps because Cholmley repeats this information a little later.
⁵⁰⁷ Cholmley's word was altered to 'day-light' in print.

Elizabeth Cholmley, daughter to Sir William Twisden, of East Peckham, in the county of Kent, knight and baronet, wife to Sir Hugh Cholmley of Whitby, in the county of York, knight and baronet, by whom she had six children. She was very beautiful, of great ingenuity, and a discerning judgement; in great dangers had a courage above her sex; of a most noble and sweet nature, compassionate to all in distress; a virtuous chaste, loving wife, indulgent parent, and true friend; and, which was above all, a most pious and religious person; and in belief and assurance of salvation, and eternal life, by the death and merits of Christ Jesus, died the 17th[508] of April, *anno Domini* 1655, in the 54th year of her age, after she had been married 32 years.'[509]

---

[508] This time the date of Lady Elizabeth's death was printed correctly.

[509] The editors of the 1787 and 1870 texts took this inscription from Lady Elizabeth's tomb which is near the south wall of the chancel in St Michael's church at East Peckham. They modernised the spelling but otherwise printed it correctly.

THE MEMORIALS

Introduction

As early as 1646, Sir Edward Hyde, then a royalist exile in Jersey, was already gathering information for and writing what ultimately became his account of the course of the First Civil War in his *History of the Rebellion and Civil Wars in England*.[1] For events in the north of England, about which he admitted ignorance, he naturally applied to the Marquess of Newcastle, who had been overall commander of the king's army there in 1642–44 until his flight to Hamburg after the disaster at Marston Moor. However, Newcastle was still smarting from the humiliation of that catastrophic defeat, and refused to help. Since Hyde was anxious to draw upon the first-hand experience of royalist combatants he was therefore obliged to turn to more junior officers; he asked Sir Hugh Cholmley for his assistance.[2]

By the end of 1647 Sir Edward had reached the first battle of Newbury in his narrative of the war, and it was probably at this point that he wrote his request to Cholmley, who was also an exile living in Rouen. Lord Hopton seems to have acted as Hyde's messenger.[3] Keen to justify his extraordinary conduct in the late war and also to defend the honour and reputation of his dead cousin, Sir John Hotham, as well as his own, Sir Hugh was quick to comply with Hyde's wishes. At the end of April 1648 Sir Edward told Hopton that he had recently received 'a civil letter from Sir Hugh Chomely', and that he intended to learn as much as possible from their correspondence.[4]

Cholmley wrote at least three 'Memorialls', as he called them, for Hyde's *History*. He might have written more, but only three were noted by the editors of the *Clarendon State Papers* in 1773, and no other has been discovered since. All of Sir Hugh's own original manuscript copies were probably destroyed by fire in 1751 or 1752. A letter dated 7 July 1752 written to Hugh Cholmley (1684–1755), great-grandson of Sir Hugh, referred to a fire at Lincoln's Inn in London 'by which Mr Henry Cholmley lost everything'.[5] This misfortune was almost certainly the same as that mentioned by James Schofield in the first edition of his *Guide to Scarborough*, published in 1787. According to this source, the Cholmleys had intended 'to gratify the curious public' by publishing Sir Hugh's manuscripts which included 'an exact journal of the siege', but all his precious papers 'were entirely consumed'.[6] Presumably, the 'exact journal of the siege' was a reference to Cholmley's 'Memorialls tuching Scarbrough'. Schofield's sad story was subsequently accepted and repeated by a succession of Scarborough's historians, notably Hinderwell and Baker,[7] who seem to have been unaware, as Schofield had been, that one of Sir Hugh's papers, that on the

---

[1] Bod Lib, Clarendon MS 2354.
[2] C.H. Firth, 'Clarendon's History of the Rebellion', *English Historical Review*, XIX (1904), 46–8, 52.
[3] Bod. Lib., Clarendon MS 2673.
[4] *Ibid.*, MS 2770.
[5] Whitby LPS, PB MS 571.
[6] J. Schofield, *Guide to Scarborough* (York, 1787), pp.86–7.
[7] Hinderwell (3rd edn, 1832), p.70; Baker, p.74.

Hothams, had already been published in the second volume of the *Clarendon State Papers*.[8]

The editors of the *Clarendon State Papers* found copies of Cholmley's three Memorials amongst the earl's huge archive. All had been written in the same skilful, professional hand in a style similar to Sir Hugh's own but much superior in penmanship. Since the editors were unfamiliar with Sir Hugh's handwriting, however, they assumed that all three were original holographs. Only when the three are compared with Sir Hugh's own manuscript of his Memoirs does it become obvious that the surviving Memorials were written by a secretary or copyist and not by their author. Even if generous allowance is made for a marked deterioration in handwriting between 1648 and 1655–6, when Cholmley wrote his Memoirs, there are still too many discrepancies in calligraphic style and even spelling to be explained simply by failing eyesight or trembling fingers. For example, in his Memoirs, Yorkshire is invariably written as 'Yorkesheire', with two extra es, whereas in the Memorials it loses one e to become 'Yorkeshire'; and it seems highly unlikely that Sir Hugh would ever have written 'Skarbrough', which appears on the first line of 'Memorialls tuching Scarbrough'.[9]

'Some Observations & Memorialls touching the Hothams' was the only one of the three to be printed in the *Clarendon State Papers*. When making their selection the editors were aware that Cholmley had written two more Memorials at Rouen in 1648, but these were rejected on the grounds that they were 'too immaterial' for publication, whereas that on the Hothams was included because it contained 'some particulars . . . omitted in the *History of the Rebellion*.[10] In fact, the great earl had made little use of any of Sir Hugh's works mainly because by the time he received them in Jersey the Second Civil War had started and he was summoned to France to join the Prince of Wales. At the end of what became Book VII with the relief of Newark in March 1644, Hyde's narrative came to an abrupt stop. Moreover, when more than twenty years later a second exile provided him with the leisure to resume his unfinished *History*, he had neglected to put Cholmley's Memorials in his baggage.[11] As for the material value of Cholmley's account of the battle of Marston Moor and his own experiences of civil war during the years 1642 to 1645, judgement must be left to their readers. Suffice it to say here that Sir Charles Firth believed them to be worthy enough to be published in the *English Historical Review* in 1890 and 1917.[12]

[8] *CSP*, ii (1773), pp.181–6.
[9] See illustrations for a comparison of scripts and spellings.
[10] Bod. Lib. Clarendon MS 1809; *CSP*, ii, p.186.
[11] Firth, *EHR* XIX, 49, 52, 54; Edward, Earl of Clarendon, *The History of the Rebellion and Civil Wars in England*, ed. W.D. Macray, 6 vols. (Oxford, 1888), iii, p.327.
[12] *EHR*, V (1890), 345–51; *EHR*, XXXII (1917), 568–87.

That if Sir John Hotham could have beene assured of the King and Queens pardon for what hee had donn or said in Parliamt, and received into there grace and favour, hee might have beene made a faithfull and serviceable person to them; the denying of which (or att least answering itt coldly) was a great motive to his undertaking that imployment att Hull.[1]

After Sir John had undertaken that imployment for Hull hee had some occasion that deteined him att London; soe that upon notice of the Lord of Newcastles beeing gone thither, young Hotham was sent down to shew to the townsmen his fathers authoritie from the Parliament, and to draw forces into the towne.

As soone as young Hotham came into the Countrie he immediatelie drew into the towne of Hull three or 400 of the trayned bands, and the day he entered with them into the towne, there was the greatest tide[2] that ever had beene seen or heard of, the water flowing into the market place, soe that noe man could pass there; which was taken for a strainge omen, and proved not oneley fatall to the father and sonne, but even to the Kingdome.

That Sir John Hotham, when hee departed from London, gave assurance to some of his nearest friends, that hee would not deny the King entrance into Hull, and surely had nott donne itt, but that hee was informed by some person neare the King, in case hee permitted his Majesty entrance, hee would loose his head[3]; and itt is conceived the same person did most prompt the king to goe to Hull.

That when the newes was brought to London that the King had a designe to goe to Hull, some of Sir John Hothams friends moved in the house of Commons that they would declaire whether they intended by the order granted to Sir John, that hee should deny the King entrance, in caise hee came to Hull; but the motion was

---

[1] Sir John had already made himself into a leading opponent of King Charles, outside as well as inside the House of Commons. He had led resistance to Ship Money in the East Riding; he had put obstacles in the king's way when he was trying to raise the Yorkshire militias against the Scots during the Bishops' Wars; in the Short Parliament of April–May 1640 his criticism of the king's policy was so outspoken that after its dissolution the Privy Council put him in the Fleet prison; along with Cholmley he was joint author of three petitions in the summer of 1640 which provoked a personal threat from Charles if they had a hand in any more; and, like Sir Hugh, as a result of his behaviour, he had been deprived of all his royal commissions. (Cliffe, pp.313, 314, 316, 317–18, 321, 322, 326, 327; Cholmley's Memoirs, ff.24v., 25r., 25v.) In the Long Parliament, Sir John had become one of the senior opposition Members who were determined to abolish the Council in the North and Ship Money, and above all disgrace and kill his arch-enemy, the earl of Strafford. Given this background, it therefore seems improbable that by 1642 Charles could have brought himself to offer 'grace and favour' to Sir John Hotham. Furthermore, if Parliament had not had absolute trust in Hotham he would not have been given such a supremely vital commission. Just as Sir Hugh tried in his Memorials on Scarborough and his later Memoirs to conceal or understate his enthusiasm for Parliament's cause in 1642, so here he tried to do the same unconvincing service for Sir John.

[2] Cholmley's word 'tide' was printed as 'sight'. Young Hotham had been denied entry to Hull by its burgesses when he first appeared before its gates on the 16 or 17 January 1642, whereas Lord Newcastle was already in the town with a secret commission from Charles to secure the magazine there (I.E. Ryder, 'The Seizure of Hull and its Magazine, January 1642', YAJ, 61 (1989), 139–48). In fact, both were unwelcome to Hull's governors, and it was not until 23 January, after they had received warnings from London, that Captain Hotham was allowed in with his East Riding trained bands. Newcastle left the same day; but the mayor and aldermen were still most reluctant to provide accommodation for Hotham's men (A Perfect Diurnall, 1 Feb. 1642).

[3] Sir John had been appointed governor of Hull by both Houses on 11 January (CJ, ii, 371, 372). According to two different sources, Hotham had warning from two men of the king's intentions (CJ, ii, 551; Reckitt, p.27).

shuffled off, and the house made noe expression in the point, so that if the King had
entred by force, Sir John might have borne the denyall upon his owne shoulders.[4]

The Earl of Newcastle had not beene long with his forces in Yorksheire when
there beganne a treatie betweene him and young Hotham; whom together with his
father they sought to draw to the Kings partie. Sir Marmaduke Langdell, a great friend
of young Hothams, was the mover betweene him and the Earle[5]; and this was sooner
layd hold on, in that the Lord Fairfax was now made a generall for the Parliamt of the
forces of Yorkesheire, and some other adiacent Counties; which discontented old Ld
Hotham; and though the sonne had as much as in reason hee could exspect, (and
more then fell to his shaire) beeing made Lieutenant Generall to Fairefax, yet hee was
not well pleased, thinking himself not soe absolute as before for his father keeping
Hull, hee commanded in cheife in that feild, and rainged the Country with out
controwle.[6] But this treaty ripened but slowly, in respect the Hothams were cautious
(f.238v.) of beeing ingaidged too far, having an | eie at the inclination of the Scotts; whoe if
they appeared or Parliament they conceived would balance the business on that side;[7]
yet surelie this treaty much blunted young Hothams activeness and (is conceived)
retarded his march to Thornton Bridg; by which meanes Generall Gooring passed
saifelie with the great convoy, with out which the Lord Newecastles army, att the
present, could nott have subsisted for want of ammunition and arms.[8]

The Queenes comming to Bridlington[9] had brought such a Magazine of armes and
ammunition, my Lord of Newcastles armie begann to bee very formidable, and young
Hotham having retyred himself (and those forces which belonged to him and his
father) from the Lord Fairefax, and beeing then att Beverley, began to have fresh

[4] This is a case difficult to sustain. From the outset, when Hotham received his parliamentary commission, both Houses made it plain that he was not to deliver up Hull to anyone, least of all the king, without their prior consent (CJ, ii, 372). Nor could Hotham have been in any doubt about the critical value Parliament placed on Hull, its safe harbour and its magazine with arms for 16,000 men (CJ, ii, 493; Tickell, pp.342–3).

[5] The correspondence between the Hothams and Newcastle is to be found in HMC, Portland MSS, I (1891). It starts in December 1642, little more than a fortnight after the earl had brought his royalist army southwards into Yorkshire. Sir Marmaduke Langdale (1598–1661) was a close friend, neighbour and relative of the Hothams. From the forced loan of 1627 to Ship Money in 1639–40, he had a long record of resistance to royal taxation (Cliffe, pp.313, 315, 318, 320). Langdale did no go over to the king's party until midsummer 1642 (Cliffe, p.334). Later he became a Catholic (F.H. Sutherland, Marmaduke, Lord Langdale (1926)).

[6] Again, Sir Hugh's account of the Hothams sounds suspiciously autobiographical. Cholmley was also resentful of Fairfax's overall command in Yorkshire, even to the point of deliberately disobeying his orders on one occasion (Bell, Fairfax Memorials, I, p.26; BL, TT, E.85(17): Two Letters from Cholmley to the Speaker, 18 Jan. 1643).

[7] Cholmley's chronology seems faulty here. The Hothams were not likely to be influenced by the Scots as early as 1642: their treaty with Parliament was not made until as late as September 1643, long after the Hothams had defected to the king. Cholmley might have been misled by his knowledge of subsequent events.

[8] George Goring (1608–57) had landed at Newcastle with a cargo of arms and reinforcements from Holland at the end of January 1643. With him was General James King, later Lord Eythin, and several other professional veterans. Cholmley had sent out a regiment from Scarborough to prevent their crossing of the Tees at Yarm, but there, under Captain Medley, they were badly beaten and many taken prisoner. (HMC, Hastings MSS, II, 92; BL, TT, E.95(9): Letter from a worthy Captain . . ., 7 Apr. 1643). Cholmley was most perturbed by his defeat, especially when he heard that Medley and his men had been cruelly mistreated as prisoners in Durham castle. Perhaps this helps to explain why he so resented Hotham's failure to intercept Goring's progress south to York at Thornton Bridge, the crossing of the Swale. (Mercurius Aulicus, 8, 15 Feb. 1643, ORN, I, i, pp.95, 105).

[9] Queen Henrietta Maria landed at Bridlington Quay on 20 February 1643 with a huge convoy of arms, ammunition, mercenaries and money.

motions of treating; and there upon makes a iourney for one night to the Earl at Bridlington, upon couller and pretence of the exchainge of prisoners; there he demanded his father to bee made a viscount, and himself a barron, that they might have twenty thousand pounds in money, and a Patent to the father to be Governor of Hull during his life, all which as itt would have beene granted, soe probably accepted, but that in this nicke of time, Sir John received some assurance of the Scotts coming into England, and that young Hotham (by his allyance and friendshipp with the Wrays) was chosen Generall of Lincolnesheire; yet both parties made this advantage by the treatie, that as the Lord Newcastle forboare to come neare Hull and Beverly, where the Hothams esstaite laid and which was their prime quarters, soe young Hotham though hee had above a thousand horse and Dragooners did not interrupt the Lord Newcastles march from Bridlington which might easilie have beene donn, his army beeing over-chardged with baggaidge, and the season soe tempesstuous that his forces were very much dispersed.[10]

Immediatelie after this young Hotham goes to be Generall for the Parliament in Lincolnesheire; soe that the treatie was off the hinge, till such time as hee was laid hold on att Nottingam by Cromwell, which the father did soe much resent as hee did nott onelie write to the close committee in a menacing style for his sonnes inlardgement, but was otherwise so passionate in woords and deportment that it gave the Parliament a great suspition of him, besides, hee had with too much confidence beene tampering with the Captaine of a Parliament shipp that layd att Hull, whoe had given some private informacions against him;[11] soe that the Parliament beganne imedyatlie to contrive for his surprisall. In the interim young Hotham breakes loose from Cromwell, and comes to Hull where the father and sonne thincke itt verie opportune to renew the treatie with my Lord Newcastle; and thereupon Sir John writes that letter, which was after (att the battle of Yorke) taken in my Lords cabinett, and cost both the Hothams there heads, being the greatest evidence against them, esspetially the father.[12] And though this was applyed to there desstruction, there was noe possitive ingaidgement to quitt the Parliament, though with out doubt they had now not onely inclination but resolution to doe it, but

[10] For young Hotham's extravagant terms, we have only Cholmley's words here. Clarendon's only source for repeating them was Cholmley's 'Observations'. Also, even if Hotham had had 'above a thousand horse and Dragooners', which seems a grossly exaggerated figure, they would have been no match in numbers for the cavalry in Newcastle's army under Goring and Langdale. The only factual statement in this passage is that the queen's route from Bridlington to York took a road over the north Wolds via Boynton, Burton Fleming and Malton, giving the Hotham estate in the Beverley area the widest berth. Nevertheless, considering the season of the year and the steep gradients of the Wolds, it seems that there were probably other sound reasons why the queen preferred to take her 500 waggons on this northerly route. Moreover, even local royalists were not spared by the queen's troops: the Thompson house at Kilham was ransacked by them (*YRCP, YASRS* xv (1893), 15). Finally, Cholmley's explanation for Hotham's change of mind – that he was assured the Scots were about to join Parliament – also lacks credibility and support from other sources.

[11] Captain Moyer of Parliament's warship the *Hercules* played a key part in revealing and defeating Sir John's plans.

[12] Only two of the eleven charges against Sir John at his trial for treason referred to particular letters that he had written: the seventh, the letter to his son at Lincoln, and the eighth, his letter to Parliament concerning his son's ill-treatment and imprisonment at Nottingham. However, since neither of these letters was addressed to Lord Newcastle neither could have been 'taken in my Lords cabinett' after the battle of Marston Moor. In fact, none of the many letters written by both Hothams was especially incriminating, but collectively they amounted to a strong case against both father and son. Since Sir Hugh was besieged in Scarborough when the Hothams were brought to trial in London, and exiled in France when he wrote these words, he cannot be regarded as much of an authority on the evidence against the Hothams.

steared themselves with soe much cautiousness and selfe ends, as it could nott carry a blessing along with it, for if they had imideatlie declaired for the King, quesstionless
(f.239r.) they might have mastered Hull by there owne power; or att | least they might have had that from my Lord of Newcastle would have prevented their beeing surprized; but they thought to linger out the treatie not onely for the better accomplishing there owne demands, but that they might more clearely discern which way the business of Reading would inclyne, beeing then upon the Crisis.[13]

Young Hotham, whilst hee was restrained at Nottingam, sends his servant to the Queene then att Newarke,[14] (I know nott whether hee wrote or sent a a message) but hee makes great professions of his service to the King, and desires the Queene to apply her forces for his enlardgment. This servant whoe hee trusted and imployed to the Queene, was nott onely a sonne to one of his fathers tennants, but child to his nurse that gave him sucke; and yet this fellow afterwards came to be the principall witness against him.

The townsmen of Hull having received instructions from the close committy to seaze upon Sir John Hotham, first surprize the Castle and blocke houses, then go to take Sir John in his owne house; but hee having some intelligence esscaipes out of the towne, thincking to goe to his owne house 9 miles from Hull, which was fortefied.[15] In passing Beverley hee was stopped by the Boynetons,[16] beate off his horse, and after a barbarous usage hee was carried to Hull where his sonne was allreadie prisoner, beeing seized on by the townsmen. And it is most remarkeable that hee whoe had soe much interest in those parts, as none but himselfe could have put the towne of Hull into that possture against the King, found nott soe much as one man to lift a hand in his behalf.[17] For which to give some reasons so far I can coniecture: That some of his principall officers were corrupted and bribed against him, the hearts of his soldiors much allyanated by his being too streight handed, and yet knowne to be rich in purse.[18] The townsmen though att first well-affected to the Kings cause, yet soe affrighted with the disorders of the Lord of Newcastles army, they would not thincke of comming under that power. Pelham, a townsman and one of the Burgesses in Parliament, did much steare the inhabitants and did not love Sir John.[19] The seamen, whoe had a great influence in this as other maretine townes, found it stand with there interest and trade to sticke to the Parliament, and therefore could not endure to heare of anie chainge in there Governor.[20] And lastlie, there beeing many of the Presiser

[13] The siege of Reading began on 16 April 1643, immediately after negotiations between king and Parliament at Oxford finally broke down. The town fell to Essex on 27 April. No doubt Cholmley could not help himself from comparing his own successful defection in March 1643 with the prevarication and fatal failure of the Hothams to follow suit.

[14] Cholmley wrote 'Newarke' but it became 'Newcastle' in print.

[15] The Hothams had their principal house at Scorborough, about three miles north of Beverley.

[16] Sir John was arrested by a party of horsemen led by Colonel Matthew Boynton, second son of Sir Matthew Boynton of Barmston. When he tried to take flight Hotham was knocked off his horse by a blow from a musket butt.

[17] Again, Cholmley seems to be making an implicit comparison of the Hotham's failure with his own brilliant and bloodless coup at Scarborough.

[18] In 1643 Sir John was said to have had 'at least £4,800 in ready money' (Cliffe, p.382).

[19] Peregrine Pelham, MP for Hull from 1640 and mayor in 1649–50, was a rich merchant who lived in Hull and signed the death warrant of King Charles.

[20] There is some truth in this generalisation concerning the political inclinations of seafaring communities. Most of England's 'maretine townes' did indeed side with Parliament from the beginning of the Civil War, but the reason was self-interested commercial calculation rather than religious or ideological conviction. Again, Cholmley may have had in mind that Scarborough's only committed Parliamentarians, the Harrisons, the Nesfields, John Lawson, Thomas Gill and Peter Hodgson, were all seafaring men.

cleargie come thither for sanctuarie, they neither loved Sir John not hee them; of whome though hee made use out of politicke ends he did as much disrellish there humours and wayes as anie man livinge, and that they knew soe well, as they did not onelie give all the information they knew against him to the Parliament, but underhand fomented all sortes of people against him.[21]

The Boyntons having thus seized upon Sir John att Beverley, sent him imediatelie prisoner to Hill, conducted by his owne troope, of which manye had a perticuler relation to him, commanded by Ledgeard his neere kinsman whom he had raised and put into that imployment;[22] and yet there was not soe much as a motion for his inlardgment and esscaipe, or much resentment for his suffering. Soon after this hee and his sonne are sent in a shipp to London; and att there first commitment the sonne gives under his hand in writing to his father a paper which cleares the father from | beeing privie to those treaties he had with Lord Newcastle; but apprehending after (f.239v.) wardes that this might preiudice his owne cause, hee requires the sight of itt, which after hee got into his hand he tore it in peeces.[23]

It fell to the fathers lott to be first brought to tryall whoe answered in blunt and in ruffe tearmes, beeing not onelie inclynable that way by nature but more out of an apprehension his service to the Parliament did much exceed his transgressions; but the sonne understanding his fathers deportment had donne some preiudice (though hee was not of a smoother nature) did att his tryall demeane himself with that submissiveness and respect both to the Parliament and his Judges att the counsell of war, that surelie hee had thereby gained friends to save his life if his father had beene first executed, but as the business came to bee managed itt advanced him nothing.

The father had many powerfull friends, as Sir Philip Stapleton[24] and others of the Presbyterian partie, soe divers of the Independants his mortall enemies, hee having uttered some speaches against Cromwell and the independants in generall, which much exasperated the whole partie.[25] Yet his friends thought that if his sonne were first executed they should have power to save the father. Soe that they first obteined his reprieve for some dayes and then endeavored all they could to bring on his sonnes

---

[21] Here Cholmley meant the Puritan preachers and clergymen who came into Hull for sanctuary from all parts of Yorkshire and Lincolnshire when they were overrun by royalist forces. Most notable of these extremists was John Saltmarsh, a kinsman of Hotham, who feigned sympathy with Sir John's discontent with Parliament in order to betray him. Saltmarsh later became a chaplain in the New Model Army (DNB).

[22] Colonel John Legard of Anlaby was Sir Hugh's captain of Scarborough castle in 1642–43, but he had refused to change sides with him in March 1643 and came over to Hull to join Parliament's garrison there. The Hothams and Legards were closely interrelated. This John Legard was killed at Brigg soon afterwards.

[23] Cholmley appears to be the sole source for this incident, and it might well betray his prejudice against the young Hotham rather than privileged knowledge.

[24] Sir Philip Stapleton of Warter Priory married one of Sir John's daughters. He was MP for Boroughbridge and one of Yorkshire's Puritan gentry who led the opposition to Strafford.

[25] Cholmley's assertion that the Hothams were ultimately the victims of Cromwell and 'the Independants' in the Commons is supported by direct evidence. One of the chief charges against the son, which brought about his arrest at Nottingham, was that lodged by Cromwell in person; he alleged that Hotham's 'rude troops out of Yorkshire' had plundered friend as well as foe while their General carried on a secret, treasonable correspondence with the queen, then at Newark (J. Hutchinson (ed.), *Memoirs of the Life of Colonel Hutchinson* (1905), pp.151–2). Sir John was so incensed by the treatment of his son that he wrote to London demanding that Cromwell 'be delivered to justice' (Rushworth, *Collections*, v, p.274). Subsequently, at his trial, the younger Hotham was accused of having betrayed Cromwell during a skirmish in Lincolnshire (Rushworth, *Collections*, v, p.799). Finally, when it came to votes in the Commons, Cromwell twice led the party that refused to grant a reprieve to Sir John (*CJ*, iii, 734; *Ibid.*, iv, 4).

tryall, which was soe expedited that in few dayes the Counsel of war had passed sentence against him, an a time fixed for his execution. In the interim the repreive for the father being elapsed, hee was carryed to the scaffold, and his friends not being able to gett a second repreive from the house of Commons, obtained itt from the Lords, which gave Sir Johns enemies in the House of Commons more power to stopp all future repreives and to press his execution.

As the fathers friends expedited the sonnes tryall out of hopes to save the father, soe the sonne endeavored by all the meanes hee could to have his father executed, conceiving hee might then save his own life;[26] which it is probable hee had (nott that he had more friends) for when it came to quesstion in the house of Commons whether the Iudgement of the Counsell of warr should pass against them, it was carryed out by six voyces against the father, whereas there was not six persons spoake for the sonn, but that if the father had beene once executed those which had beene his friends would then have beene as earnest for saving the sonne; whereas the sonne beeing executed the fathers enemies were never content till they had his blood alsoe.

The second repreive for Sir John being obteined from the Lords, the day of the sonnes execution approaches, and hee was brought to the Scaffold, where beginning to speake sharply against the Counsell of Warre and the Parliament, beeing interrupted, he dyed like a Roman;[27] having beene often times heard to say (when hee was in his greatest prosperitie) that hee did no expect anie good from the Parliament; Staites and Commonwealthes never rewarding anie mans merritts but by death.

(f.240r.)   In the | intrime betweene Sir Johns first and second repreive hee dreamed his sonne and hee chainged wifes, which some interpreted to be accomplished in that the sonne was putt into the coffinn and buryed in the grave which were made for the father.[28]

The time of the second repreive expired for the father, his friends could not renew it; soe that hee was brought to the Scaffold and seemed to take his death with more patience than did the sonne, having (as it is thought) even till [h]is head struck off some hopes that his former services to the Parliament would in conclusion have produced his pardon.

They were both convicted meerely for treating with the ennemie and having an intention to deliver up the towne of Hull.[29]

Sir John manie yeares before his death, or these troubles beganne, would often say he would never come uppon a Scaffold to say good people take example by mee, but would dye with his pistoll in his hand; by which we see, Man purposeth, but it is God that disposeth.

---

[26] Cholmley's preference for the father over the son is again evident here. The younger Hotham's petition on his own behalf suggests that it was not delivered until the execution of his father had become unavoidable and imminent. On the other hand, it is true that both Houses were much more favourably inclined to the father than the son (Rushworth, *Collections*, v, 802, 803; Stirling, I, p.92).

[27] Captain Hotham was beheaded on Tower Hill on 1 January 1645. If, in his final speech from the scaffold, he tried to attack his enemies, we have only Cholmley's testimony here for it. Nevertheless, as reported officially, his speech was unrepentant: he refused to admit that either he or his father had committed treason (Rushworth, *Collections*, v, 803).

[28] Sir John had five wives and his son three. The son spent his last night with his wife Isabel, who conceived and bore a son nine months later (Stirling, I, pp.92–3).

[29] As so often in this account of Sir John's motives and actions, Cholmley must have been conscious of his own similar situation but very different fate. For the text of Sir John's unconvincing defence see Reckitt, pp.119–28. Sir Hugh's word 'meerely' emphasizes his incorrigible bias: making treaties in wartime with the enemy leaders and plotting with them to deliver up a place of such great strategic importance could hardly have been classed as minor indiscretions. In fact, of course, there were 11 charges against Sir John of which several alone constituted acts of treason.

Sir John was a man of good understanding and ingenuitie, yet of a rash and hasty nature, and soe much wedded to his own humour, as his passion often over ballanced his Iudgment, and yet hee was able to give good councell and advice where his owne interrest was not concerned. Hee was valyant and a verie good friend, and if his own perticuler interest had not beene concerned would not have forsaken his friend for any adverse fortune. He was a man that loved libertie, which was an occation to make him ioyne att first with the puritan partie, to whome after hee became neerer lincked meerely for his owne interest and security, for in more than concerned the civill libertie hee did not approve of their wayes. Some of his most intimate friends whoe often moved him to quit Parliament and come to the King found him very inclynable, making protestation that hee did not exspect a treatie, when if the King should but offer that which was reasonable and the Parliament not except, hee would desert them.

And how ever the sonne was more tampering and ingaiged in the treatie with the Lord Newcastle, surelie the father had more reall affection to the Kings cause and peace of the Kingdome, for it appeared the sonne blunted the fathers inclinations that way, and beeing a very politicke and cunning man lookt cheifly at that which stood most with his own perticuler interrest, and uppon that score diverted his father, whoe otherwise (as is beleived) would more frankly have declaired for the King. And yet I have heard his father made this ingenious | confession att his death, that it was ambition and covetousness had beene his ruine, and bought him to that end.[30]   (f.240v.)

To conclude, Sir John Hotham was the first man whoe moved in the house of Commons that the Archbisshopp of Canterberrie might be chardged with high Treason, and yet the person that suffered imediatelie before him upon the same staige.[31]

---

[30] Though Sir Hugh knew Sir John and his son better than most contemporaries, Clarendon did not accept all of his conclusions when he came to write his *History*. Indeed, Clarendon's ill-will towards the father in places reads more like Cholmley's hostility to the son. According to Clarendon, Sir John was 'without any bowels of compassion or the least touch of generosity' and he was untrustworthy and deceitful. However, some of Cholmley 's personal observations about the senior Hotham Clarendon did accept, in particular his natural conservatism, his attachment to the established church, his rough and crude manners, and the main reason for his ruin – his 'great covetousness . . . and great ambition' (Clarendon, *History*, ii, pp.259, 261–2, 263).

[31] Sir John was executed on 2 January 1645, Archbishop Laud on 10 January.

Memorialls touching the Battle of Yorke

INTRODUCTORY NOTE

Any student of the events of 1642 to 1646 would find it hard to resist the conclusion that the battle of Marston Moore was the most decisive, as well as the biggest and bloodiest, of the First Civil War. Royalist defeat ruined the marquess of Newcastle, destroyed his Northern army, effectively robbed King Charles of his most northerly counties and the city of York, and severely damaged Prince Rupert's reputation for invincibility. On Parliament's side, Marston Moor provided proof of the indispensable value of Scottish assistance and raised Cromwell to the status of leading commander. Nevertheless, despite their obvious importance and the deserved attention many historians have given to them, the events of 2 July 1644 on Marston Moor remain far from clear; and in this context of continuing interest and debate Sir Hugh Cholmley's contemporary 'Memorialls touching the Battle of Yorke' retains a small but significant place.[1]

In 1978 Dr Peter Newman published a paper on the battle which, though it was concerned mainly with primary sources, almost ignored Cholmley's 'Memorialls'; they were relegated to end-notes and dismissed briefly as of small importance.[2] However, only three years later, when Dr Newman's fuller treatment of the battle was published, he assigned far greater prominence than previously to Cholmley's literary contribution. Indeed, perhaps by way of atonement, Newman's second evaluation seemed to go too far in the opposite direction: not only had Sir Hugh no 'political or personal axe to grind', but the privilege he enjoyed of listening to the accounts of many leading Royalist participants only hours after the battle made his 'Memorialls' 'crucial'.[3]

Sir Hugh had been host to the Northern Royalist staff officers who had accompanied the marquess of Newcastle on his way, via Scarborough, into continental exile. As Cholmley later recorded in his Memoirs, the marquess 'layed' at his house in the town 'two dayes' before he was 'furnished . . . with a shippe to goe beyond sea'.[4] Most of the defeated Royalist officers arrived from York at Scarborough on 3 July and set sail on the 4 or 5 July, so that Sir Hugh would have heard several eye-witness versions of the battle very soon after it had happened.[5] Later, other high-ranking Royalist commanders, such as Henry Constable, Viscount Dunbar, who had fought at Marston Moor, took refuge with Cholmley in Scarborough castle.[6]

In a literal sense, therefore, Cholmley's 'Memorialls' were entirely one-sided: all his information, as well as his natural bias, came from the Royalist side. Indeed, his sources were even more selective than that, since he heard the personal accounts of only Newcastle and the senior officers of his Northern army. Though at one point Cholmley wrote, 'I have heard the Prince in his owne private opinion', there is no

[1] Most notably: C.H. Firth, 'Marston Moor', *TRHS* 2nd series, xii (1898), 17–79; A. Woolrych, *Battles of the English Civil War* (1961), pp.63–80; P. Young, *Marston Moor* (Kineton, 1970); P.R. Newman, *Marston Moor, 2 July 1644: The Sources and the Site* (Borthwick Papers, no.53, York, 1978); P.R. Newman, *The Battle of Marston Moor 1644* (Chichester, 1981).

[2] Newman, *Sources*, pp.44–5, n.22. 'He [Cholmley] adds little of interest to a revision of the sources . . .'.

[3] Newman, *Battle*, p.6.

[4] See above, Cholmley's Memoirs, f.27v. (p.106).

[5] Clarendon, *History*, iii, p.376, note; Margaret, Duchess of Newcastle, *The Life of the Duke of Newcastle* (1667), p.53.

[6] *DNB*.

evidence that he had ever met Rupert or any of his officers after Marston Moor and before he put pen to paper.[7]

Nevertheless, as Dr Newman has pointed out, whatever its deficiencies, Cholmley's version of the battle possesses a number of advantages over other contemporary accounts. Because he was not a participant who witnessed only one part of what all commentators agree was an extraordinarily confused and confusing battle, he was able to form an overall view. Because he heard the reports of only senior officers, he was able to eschew the trivial and irrelevant details. Because he was not himself a combatant, he had no personal reputation to advance or defend. Because he was not directly and personally involved, he made no attempt to describe the details of the day, but instead provided a perceptive, objective and convincing summary of the reasons for Parliament's victory.

As Firth noted nearly a century ago, Royalist accounts of the battle of Marston Moor are fewer and less informative than those available from the other side.[8] *Mercurius Aulicus* was eager to report Rupert's relief of York, but naturally reluctant even to admit that a crushing defeat had been suffered soon afterwards. At first it conceded that only 600 of the King's soldiers had died on Marston Moor, and later its description of the battle there owed more to the brief and misleading official dispatch of the allied generals than to any Royalist witness.[9] With Cholmley's assistance, Clarendon might have been expected to present a reasoned Royalist analysis of what proved to be the biggest battle of the Civil Wars, but in fact, in Firth's words, what he eventually put down in his *History* was 'worthless'.[10] First of all, Clarendon did not write it until about 1670 during his second exile; secondly, when he went abroad, he left Cholmley's 'Memorialls' behind in England; and thirdly, what he called 'that unfortunate battle' so upset him that he preferred to pass over it without a 'full relation'.[11]

Unless the so-called 'Rupert's Diary' is taken as the Prince's work (which no one now does), Rupert wrote nothing of note on the battle of Marston Moor. Newcastle refused Hyde's request for information and thereafter never broke his silence on the subject. Eythin was overwhelmed by a sense of guilt which he admitted only to Rupert in a private letter.[12] The version to be found in the *Life of Newcastle*, written more than 20 years after the event by his doting duchess, is little more than an exaggerated and at times ridiculous apology for her husband.[13] Indeed, all the first-hand Royalist accounts are seriously defective. Sir Henry Slingsby's Diary is usually considered the best of them, but it was written several years later, and it is far from clear where its author was on 2 July or even whether he was present on the battlefield. Though Slingsby's home was only a few miles distant and he knew the terrain better than any other commentator, his description of it and what took place over it is disappointingly brief and patchy.[14] The remaining Royalist eye-witnesses left even less of value: Ogden's short letter contains the astonishing conclusion: 'More of the Enemyes slayne then of ours . . . and soe few killed';[15] Sir Philip Monkton, who rode

[7] Memorialls, f.153v. (see below p.137).
[8] Firth, *TRHS*, 2nd ser. xii, 62.
[9] *Mercurius Aulicus*, 6, 13 July 1644, *Oxford Royalist Newsbooks*, I, iii, 162, 172–5; *CSPD*, 1644, p.311.
[10] Firth, *TRHS*, 2nd ser. xii, 62–3.
[11] Clarendon, *History*, iii, p.375.
[12] Newman, *Battle*, pp.128–9.
[13] *Life of Newcastle*, pp.49–50.
[14] D. Parsons (ed.), *The Diary of Sir Henry Slingsby* (1836), pp.110–16; G. Ridsdill Smith, *Without Touch of Dishonour* (Kineton, 1968), pp.76–8.
[15] Firth, *TRHS*, 2nd ser. xii, 71–2.

in the frontline of Goring's dashing cavalry charge, conveyed only the utter chaos of a battle fought out in smoke and darkness;[16] and Arthur Trevor's letter adds only some clarification to the disposition of the Royalist armies on the eve of the battle.[17]

In short, since this was a battle of exceptional size, complexity and contradiction, Cholmley's attempt to explain, clarify and interpret what happened on Marston Moor on the evening of 2 July 1644 is particularly valuable. In the absence of written testimony from the marquess himself, from Rupert, from Eythin, or from any of the other most senior officers on the Royalist side, Cholmley's version, based on his privileged conversations with several of them so soon after the battle, helps to fill vital gaps in the primary evidence. Finally, Dr Newman was surely right to argue the case for Sir Hugh's commendable objectivity.[18] Though he might have exaggerated Eythin's personal responsibility for Newcastle's disastrous decision to desert the Royalist cause, unlike Clarendon, Cholmley seems to have made an honest attempt to check his prejudice against the Scotsman.[19]

---

[16] Firth, *TRHS*, 2nd ser. xii, 52–3; Newman, *Sources*, pp.13–14.

[17] T. Carte (ed.), *Ormond Papers*, I (1739), pp.55–8; Newman, *Sources*, p.14.

[18] Newman, *Battle*, p.7.

[19] Dr Newman argued that 'Rupert had every cause in the world to blame Eythin for a large part of the defeat' (*Battle*, p.128). He drew the line, however, at Warburton's description of Eythin's behaviour as 'traitorous' (B.E.G. Warburton, *Memoirs of Prince Rupert and the Cavaliers*, ii, p.444). Clarendon's verdict, which was not derived from Cholmley, was that 'not withstanding the unavoidable prejudice of being a Scotchman', General King had 'ordered his foot with great wisdom and dexterity' (*History*, ii, p.466).

Upon Sunday the [blank][1] of June Prince Rupert had passed the river of Owse at a place called Burroebridge 16 miles from Yorke,[2] before the great Army that beseaged the Cyttie had intelligence of his beeing so neare, which caused them that night to raise their seage, and the next morning to draw nearer into a body a pretty distance from the Cyttie on the south side. The beseaged, when they saw the enemie had quit their trenches, did not understand the cause till about noon that day Captain Leg[3] brought news of the Princes approach, who Marched through the forrest of Gautrees[4] on the north side of the Cyttie, knowing that to lye most open. That evening the Prince sent Generall Goring[5] to the Marquess[6] to desire hee might the next morning by fower a clocke have all his forces drawne out of the Cyttie to ioyne with his, for which the Marquiss presentlie gave order, and accordinglie all the foote were at 2 a clock that night drawne in a body expecting to march out of the Cyttie, when there came an order from Generall King[7] that they should not march till they had their play, where upon they all quitt their Coullers and disperse. This I had from a gentleman of qualitie of that Countrie who was a collonell and had command there and present att the time. But in justification of King, some say that there was not halfe the foot, for manie of them beeing plundering in the enemies trenches where they found good bootie, they could not be drawne together soe soone. True itt is manie were wanting but doubtless there was a considerable number. Again King denies hee sent anie such messidge, but that itt beeing pay day the soldiers would not out of the Cittie without itt and raised this of themselves. Certainlie a report was divulged that King sent such an order, from whence soever itt came, and that dispersed the soldiors, which accydent may seeme preudiciall to the Princes affayres, whoe probable (if those forces att Yorke had ioyned with his at the time prefixed) might have acted something upon the enemie in their retreat or before they had put themselves into order or gained that plaice of advantage they had att the Battle.[8]

The Parliament Army had left a bridge of boates over the river Ouse at the west side of the Cittie unbroaken up over which the Prince passeth his army on Tuesday morning by fower a clocke,[9] and finding the enemie upon a quicke march pursues

---

[1] The date was Sunday, 30 June 1644.

[2] Boroughbridge is in fact on the river Ure. In a brilliant, rapid manoeuvre Rupert had surprised and outflanked Parliament's siege armies encircling York by taking an unexpected northerly route from Knaresborough, crossing the Ure at Boroughbridge, the river Swale at Thornton Bridge, and then approaching the city from the north, down the east bank of the Ouse.

[3] Captain William Legge was a professional Royalist officer who had displaced Sir John Hotham as governor of Hull in 1639 on the king's insistence and against Wentworth's advice. He served in the king's army throughout the Civil Wars with distinction and outstanding fortitude. In 1660 he refused a peerage but accepted the rank of Lieutenant-General.

[4] The forest of Galtres.

[5] George Goring (1608–57) was at this time Lieutenant-General of Horse.

[6] William Cavendish, earl, marquess and ultimately duke of Newcastle (1593–1676) had commanded the king's army in the north since the end of 1642. From 23 April 1644 he and his army had been besieged in York (*DNB*).

[7] James King, a professional Scottish soldier, veteran of the continental war, created Baron Eythin in 1643, served as General of the Foot in Newcastle's army.

[8] Clearly, Cholmley was aware of the crucial significance of the failure of King's infantry garrison to join Rupert on the battle field on the morning of 2 July. Sir Hugh was no friend of General King, but here he refrained from the temptation to blame him entirely for the fatal delay.

[9] Lord Manchester's army of the Eastern Association, which had occupied the Clifton area on the north-east side of the city, had crossed the Ouse at Poppleton, but in retreat had failed to destroy the bridge of boats there.

them; but they beeing to pass over a moore where there were ditches and slowghes of water, itt gives them advantage to march with less disorder, and though theire was continnuall skirmishes betweene the Horse which were in Reare and van of the two Armyes, yet the Prince was not earnest to ingaige in exspectance of the York forces.

But the Parliaments army, finding themselves still pursued comming to a place of advantage, make a stand and recall those forces which marched in theire van of [which] some were advanced nine miles and itt is thought many would never have
(f.153v.) returned | had they beene resspetted till the next morning.[10] The place where they made a stand was a rising ground (with some hedges and ditches and corne feilds on each side) from which they might clearly veew the Princes army below in the plaine, and yet themselves not so perfectlie to be discerned. As soone as the Parliaments army made a stand the Princes did the like drawing themselves into order for Battle, but acted nothing still in exspectance of the Yorke forces. About 9 a clocke the Marquess accompannied by all the gentlemen of qualitie which were in Yorke (whoe cast themselves into a troop commanded by Sir Thomas Mettam)[11] came to the Prince who said, 'My Lord, I wish you had come sooner with your forces, but I hope we shall yet have a glorious day.'[12] The Marquess informed [him] how that his foot had been a plundering in the enemyes trenches and that it was impossible to have got them together att the time prefixed, but that he had left Generall Kyng about the woorke, whoe would bring them up with all the expedition that might be. The Prince seeing the Marquisses foot were not come up, would with his owne forces[13] have beene falling upon the enemie, but that the Marquess deswaded telling him hee had 4000 good foote as were in the world. About 4 a clocke in the afternoone Generall King brings up the Marquesses foot, of which yet many were wanting, for heere was not above 3000.[14] The Prince demanded of King how hee liked the marshelling of his army, whoe replide hee did not approve of itt beeing drawne too near the enemy, and in a place of disadvantage. Then said the Prince, 'They may be drawne to a further disstance.' 'Noe sir', said King, 'it is too laite.' It is s[ai]d King dissuaded the Prince from fighting, saying, 'Sir, your forwardness lost us the day in Germany, where your selfe was taken prisoner',[15] upon the disswasions of the Marquess and King, and that it was so neare night. The Prince was resolved not to ioyne battle that day, and therefore gave order to have provisions for his armie

---

[10] The Scottish army, under the earl of Leven, was in the van of the allied retreat, and its leading column had almost reached Tadcaster (*CSPD*, 1644, p.311).

[11] Sir Thomas Metham commanded Newcastle's Lifeguard of gentlemen volunteers and was killed in the battle.

[12] Cholmley is our only authority for all of these words. Clarendon's shorter and much less revealing version of Rupert's greeting to Newcastle, 'My lord, I hope we shall have a glorious day' (Clarendon, *History*, iii, p.376, n.), which Gardiner accepted (*Civil War*, i, p.374), fails to convey the full weight of Rupert's disappointment that the marquess had not brought his infantry with him on to the battle field.

[13] Cholmley's word 'forces' was wrongly printed as 'foot'.

[14] The time of General King's arrival on Marston Moor is crucial. One of Rupert's officers, Mr Ogden, agreed with Cholmley that he did not reach the battlefield until 4 p.m. (*TRHS*, 2nd series, xii (1898), 71–2); whereas Colonel Sir Francis Cobbe, commander of Clifford's Tower during the siege, who supplied the information for the so-called Rupert's Diary, brought forward his arrival there to 2 p.m. (Young, *Marston Moor*, p.213). By 2 July the York garrison probably numbered only about 3,000 (Wenham, *Siege*, p.xi).

[15] Again, Cholmley's account here is the only source for what seems to have been an acrimonious exchange between the prince and General King. Rupert had probably rebuked the Scotsman for his late arrival and King retaliated by reminding the prince, with utter tactlessness, of an embarrassing event six years earlier in the Palatinate. Rupert and King had blamed each other ever since and their wounds had never healed; now they were re-opened.

brought from Yorke, and did not imagine the enemie durst make anie attempt; so that when the Alarum was given hee was set upon the earth att meat a pretty disstance from his troopes, and manie of the horsemen were dismounted and laid on the ground with there horses in their hands.

The reason why they fell thus suddenlie upon the Price (as manie coniecture) is that a Scottish officer amongst the Prince his horse, whilst the armyes faced one another, fled to the Parliaments armie and gave them intelligence; and itt was further observed that Hurry a Scotchman having the marshalling of the horse in the Princes right wing, his owne Troope were the first that turned there backes. Yet I have heard the Prince in his owne private opinion did not thinke Hurry culpable of Infidelitie.[16] |

Upon the Allarum the Prince mounted to Horse and galloping up to the right (f.154r.) wing mett his own Regiment turning their backes to the enemie, which was a thing soe strange and unusual, he said, 'Swounds, doe you runne, follow mee.' So they facing about, hee led them to a chardge, but fruitelesslie, the enemie having before broaken the force of that wing, and with out any great difficultie, for these Troopes which formerlie had beene thought unconquerable, now upon a Pannicke feare (or I know not by what faite) tooke scarr and fled, most of them with out striking a stroake, or having the enemie come neare them, made as fast as they could to Yorke. Those which gave his defeat were most of them Crumwells horse,[17] to whome before the Battle were ioyned David Leshley, and halfe the Scottish horse;[18] and whoe kept close together in firm bodyes, still falling upon that parte[19] of the Princes forces which seemed to make most resistance, which were the foote, who fought most gallantlie and mainetaened the feild 3 houres after the horse had left them, where most of the Marquesses foote were slaine beeing as good Men as were in the world.

But as the Princes right wing went to wracke, so his left was very prosperous, for Generall Gooring whoe commanded that did with the Northerne horse charge the enemyes right wing so fearcelie and home as that hee made the three Generalls viz. Manchester, the Lord Fairefax and Lesheley[20] quitt the feild and flye nere twenty miles several wayes beleeving the day was lost. In soe much that Goring was possest of many of there ordnance, and if his men had but kept close together as did Crumwells, and nott dispersed themselves in pursuite, in all probabilitie itt had come to a drawn battle att worse, and no great victorie to be boasted of on either side. But Gorings men were much scattered and dispersed in pursuite they knew ever[21] of the defeat of the Princes right wing. Yett at the dawning of the day there was rallyed together two thousand horse whoe had great inclination to have acted something upon the prevailing partie of the enemies other wing, but that they were prevented by an order to retyre to Yorke. The next morning the Prince had thoughts of a new supply of fresh foote out of Yorke to have attempted some thing upon the enemie, but that he was disswaded by Generall King, and though the enemie was much broaken and disperst (and not possessed of the Princes Cannon and Baggage till the next morning)

[16] Major-General Sir John Hurry or Urry was a professional Scottish soldier who changed sides three times during the Civil Wars (DNB), so that it seems rather odd that anyone should believe him not to be 'culpable of Infidelitie'. At the time when Sir Hugh wrote these words there is no record that he had ever met Prince Rupert.

[17] Oliver Cromwell was Lieutenant-General of Horse in Manchester's army of the Eastern Association.

[18] David Leslie was General of Horse in the Scottish Army.

[19] Cholmley wrote 'parte'; 'quarter' was the word printed.

[20] Alexander Leslie, the earl of Leven, fled as far as Leeds, and Lord Fairfax went all the way to Hull, both believing that the battle was lost.

[21] Here 'knew ever' became 'could know' in print.

yet att the present theire staite and condition was not soe perfectlie[22] known, and therefore Kings counsell not to be condemned.

The Prince had his broaken forces retyred to Yorke, and though the greatest part of the other army was scattered likewise, yet Crumwell and those victorious partie of the enemies left wing kept the feild that night, which did not onelley make them the next day maister of the Princes Cannon and baggadge, but gave the victorie holie to that side, and with such reputation as itt brought many of that party, which, giving the battle for lost, were fled into Lincolnesheire and other places fortie or 50 miles from the place of battle. |

(f.154v.)   Now to draw all these perticulers into a compendium, and give some probable coniectures for the miscarriage and losse of this business, many doe impute much to the Prince that hee would ingaige to fight that day, considering not onlie many of the Marquesses foote were wanting, but even of his own horse to the number of 15 hundred or 2000 which were gone rambling into Yorke; and that if hee had deferred the fight a few dayes, Collonel Clavering had been up with a thousand or 1200 fresh men.[23] Hee came into the countrie with such dread and reputation, he might not onelie have increased his owne army, but surelie the enemies would have diminished. In answeare to which in the Princes behalfe itt is said hee did neither know the Marquesses men would fall short, nor that soe many of his owne were absent; that all had orders to be in readiness on Tuesday morning by fower a Clocke; that he was obleidged not to lett the enemie march too farr out of his reach, having a command from the King to fight the Scottish army where soever hee met them; and though for that reason hee followed them so close, it is evident he had not that day ingaiged if the enemy had not forced [it] upon him. So those obiections beeing answeared, some other more probable reasons are to be looked for, which as farr as I can disserne into the business may be these:

1 The Princes army, or ever hee was awarre, was drawne too neare the enemie, and into some place of disadvantage, which may be impwted rather to his commanders that had the leading of his van and marshelling his forces then to himselfe.

2 It is conceived those which had relation to the Marquess his armie did not in there affections so harmoneouslie comply to this great worke as was requisite, in respect the Prince had a supreame commission above the Marquess, so that his forces came very untowardlie out of Yorke though they performed there part well in the battle, and though the Marquess, beeing of a great spirritt and having had an absolute power in those parts, could not but resent the being subordinate to another, and did it so farre (as I have heard) before the battle hee resolved, though the Prince should have the day, to quitt his imployment and the kingdome upon this point. Yet certainelie for his owne perticuler hee did as much as he could to advance the Kings affayres att the present, and even in the day of battle demeaned himself most gallantlie, beeing one of the last (of soe manie Generalls) that quitt the feild that day.

3 The enemies keeping close and firm together in a body after they had routed the Princes right wing; and though in that for the active parte it is most to be imputed to Crumwell and his horse, yet it is thought the ordering and advice to doe soe came from David Leshley, an experienced old soldier, and as this was an advantage to the enemie soe the breaking and scattering of Gorings men in pursuite in the other wing was as great a preiudice and loss to that party. |

---

[22] Cholmley's word 'perfectlie' was printed as 'generally'.

[23] Colonel Sir Robert Clavering was then at Newcastle. He did not link up with Rupert until after the battle of Marston Moor was lost. What numbers Clavering commanded is a matter of some doubt and dispute (see Newman, *Battle*, pp.26–7, 36).

4 Lastle, there was something above reason to be attrybuted onelie to the hand of (f.155r.)
   God, that soe manie curragious men (soe often victorious) as was in the Princes
   right wing should turne there backes with out scarce striking a stroake and taking
   so great a scarr as they could never be brought to make a stand; where as if they had
   stood to fight doubtless the victorie had gone on their side.

The Prince after two dayes rest having rallyed together about foure thousand horse
and some few foote marcheth towards Westmorland, hee and the Marquess having
once agreed that the Marquess should goe to Newcastle, whether the Prince should
return as soone as hee could recruite his foote; which if itt had accordingly beene
pursued had beene of great advantage to the Kings affaires, for had the Marquess
remayned in thos parts surely a great number of the broaken forces[24] would have
beene rallyed together, and it would have given incourraidgment to the Kings friends
and partie there. Where as upon his departure all most every one (esspetially such as
had perticuler relation or affeccion to his person) quitt the Kings service and went to
their own homes. But, as is said, Generall King, conceiving the Kings affairs
absolutelie destroyed by loss of this battle, perswaded the Marquess (against all the
power of his other friends) to quitt the kingdome. Soe that the Marquess, leaving Sir
Thomas Glemman[25] in Yorke to gaine as good tearmes for the Cyttie as hee could,
himselfe with King and other perticuler friends, goes to take shipping att Scarbrough,
whether he was at first a little shie to come, being informed the Governor Sir Hugh
Cholmeley would not permitt him passage, but keepe him prisoner. But the Marquess
soone found the contrary by the governors usage whoe knew his dutie was to obey his
generall and nott to quesstion his errors; and the governor was so farr from
interrupting his passidge, as that when hee found the Marquess resolved hee gave
him all the expedition, fearing his stay there might draw the forces at Yorke sooner
against Scarbrough. The second day after the Marquess his coming to Scarbrough, hee
tooke shipping for Hambrough, beeing accompanied with his two sonnes, the Lord
Faulconbridge, Lord Widderington, Sir William Widdrington and some other of his
spetiall friends. General King, the Lord Conwath, and persons that had relation to
them went in annother shipp.[26] There was divers other gentlemen of that Countrie
whoe desired to pass at the same time, but the governor would not permit them, itt
being as hee conceived preiudiciall to the Kings affaires.

---

[24] Again, 'forces' was printed wrongly as 'foot'.
[25] Sir Thomas Glemham was a professional officer and had been Royalist governor of York from October
     1642 until November 1643, then of Newcastle, and finally of York again. He surrendered the city to the
     allied commanders a fortnight after the battle of Marston Moor (*DNB*).
[26] Newcastle's party numbered about 70. His two sons were Colonels Viscount Mansfield and Lord
     Cavendish. His brother, Sir Charles Cavendish, was also with him. A fuller list is to be found in
     Rushworth, *Collections*, v, p.637.

Beeing to give you some Memorialls touching the affaires of Skarbrough, I shall beginn with remonstrating how the Governor,[1] Sir Hugh Cholmeley, came first to be imployed in the Parliament service, and upon what grounds hee quitt the same; nott onely for the vindication of the said Governor, my spetiall friend, whoe may suffer in some mens oppinions for want of a right knowledge of that perticuler, but that some things in the relation thereof may prove pertinent to the generall story of these times. Therefore you must know before there was a stroake strucke, whilst the Parliament made glorious and spetious pretences to take up armes meerely in there owne defence, for Religion [religious?] liberties, peace of the kingdom, and protection of the kings person, when men hoped the preparation on both sides might produce some happie treatie and accomodation, Sir Hugh Cholmeley, then a member of the house of commons, having a commission from the earl of Essex, Lord Leiutenant (with the kings consent and approbation) of the County of yorke, to be Collonell of a Regiment of foote of the trained bands of that County, and which had formerly beene under the command of the said Sir Hugh. That in the beginning of September 1642, the said earle required the said Sir Hugh to repaire into Yorkshire to raise the said regiment, and to draw the same to Scarbrough (whose forces were parte of that Regiment), and to remaine there onely for securing the Towne. The said Sir Hugh beeing to take his iourney for Yorkeshire (the Earle of Essex not then in London) the close committee[2] would have added to Sir Hughs Instructions, the taking into his custody the Castle of Scarbrough, to which Sir Hugh replyed that the Castle did not belong to the king, but to one Thompson, a Burgher of the Towne,[3] and the Parliament beeing att that time nise to take any mans inheritance from him by force, the committee desired him (serving then in Parliament as a burgess for that towne) to use his interest with Thompson to be content to put the same into his hands for service of king and Parliament. To which Sir Hugh condiscended, soe that with out any commission but meerely that from the Earle of Essex to raise the Regiment, hee tooke his iourney for Yorkeshire beeing (as I have heard him solemly protest) induced thereunto, not onely out of indulgencie to his country and desire to preserve the same, but out of a sence and apprehension that persons ill affected to the peace of the kingdome did intrude themselves into imployment; and that if there came a treatie hee thought himselfe a more indifferent person then many others whoe had taken armes, and with his swoord in his hand should be in better capacity to promote peace, having noe other end then to preserve the libertie of the subiect and to render the duties to his majestie.

After Sir Hugh was come into Yorkeshire hee had in few dayes drawne to

[1] Almost invariably throughout the manuscript Sir Hugh wrote of himself in the third person, which has misled some readers into thinking that he was not the author. For example, see P.J. Nash, 'Doncaster, Ripon and Scarborough, circa 1640 to 1750' (unpub. Ph.D. thesis, Leeds Univ. 1983), p.372, n.177.

[2] Cholmley meant here the Committee of Safety appointed jointly by the Commons and the Lords to direct Parliament's war effort.

[3] During the 1620s Scarborough castle had passed out of the hands of the crown into those of the Thompsons of Scarborough and Humbleton. According to the records of the Committee for Compounding, by 1642 Stephen Thompson, eldest son and heir of Francis, had already acquired possession of the castle from his father (Yorkshire Royalist Composition Papers, i, YASRS xv (1893), pp.3–9); whereas in a letter from Cholmley to Pym, dated 3 November 1642, he gives Francis Thompson as the owner's name (HMC, Bouverie MSS (1887), p.90).

'Memorialls tuching Scarbrough', Clarendon 22, f.8r. By kind permission of the Bodleian Library, University of Oxford.

Scarbrough the greatest part of his Regiment, and had alsoe the keyes of the Casstle (but nott with Thompsons good will, for hee was verie much affected to the kings cause and how be itt as formerly said).[4] Sir Hughs commission was meerely for securing [the] towne, yett receiving noe monyes from the Parliament in 5 mounthes spaice, hee was for his subsistence and security forced into many actions hee never intended or foresaw att his first undertaking the business;[5] and as itt pleased God hee
(f.8v.) sped verie | hapely in many of them, soe after his greatest successes[6] hee never ommitted to sollicitt his friends in the Parliament to imploy there indeavours for pece, and twise hee wrote to the Speaker of the house of Commons,[7] signifing hee had embarqued himselfe in imployment for preservation of the peace of the kingdome, that hee now found the taking up of armes nott to be the way to itt; and that hee saw nothing could produce peace but a good treaty with the king, and rendering him his iust rights; and therefore desired that might be thought upon; otherwise hee apprehended the kingdom in danger to bee ruined. But this letter was suppressed, beeing not thought fitt to be published in the House, and indeed itt did soe nettle those persons whoe had a designe to foment these troubles as by there power they obtained order from the house of Commons and the earle of Essex to require Sir Hugh to quitt Scarbrough as a place unusefull;[8] but hee having soe farre ingaged his friends and countrymen would not doe itt, rendring some reasons for itt to the close Committee, whoe partly in resspect they knew nott how to remove him, and partly that he was often acting things acceptable to Parliament, they seemed to connive without further pressing his removall, or giving libertie to stay.[9]

After the Queenes comming into that country Sir Hugh was earnestly sollicited by some friends and allyes (which were of the kings party) to quitt the Parliament, whoe

[4] Stephen Thompson's testimony to the Committee for Compounding indicates that Sir Hugh agreed to pay him rent for the castle at £50 per annum, and that he kept up the payments for at least the next two years (YRCP, i, YASRS xv, pp.3–9).

[5] This claim of Cholmley, repeated in his Memoirs (f.27r.–v.), that he received no money from either Parliament or later the king, is contradicted by evidence from other sources e.g. HMC, Bouverie, p.90; CSPD 1625–49, p.644; CJ, ii, 938.

[6] Significantly, Sir Hugh only hints here of his exceptionally bold initiatives on behalf of Parliament – his advance as far as Stamford Bridge in November 1642, the occupation of Malton in January 1643 and the decisive victory over Slingsby and Strickland at Guisborough soon afterwards. These were much more than mere foraging sorties forced by lack of funds.

[7] In December 1642, after his retreat back to Scarborough from Stamford Bridge had earned a rebuke from Pym, Cholmley wrote two letters to Speaker Lenthall explaining and justifying his conduct since his first arrival in Scarborough the previous September. The letters were endorsed by his officers who added a supporting statement (BL, TT, E85 (17)) and printed by order of the Commons 18 January 1643. By that time Sir Hugh had written a third letter to Lenthall from Guisborough describing his victory there 16 January. It was this letter which contained expression of the author's strong repugnance against the war and his plea for a negotiated settlement, even if this meant making concessions to the king (HMC, Portland MSS, i, p.90); and it was this letter that the Commons 'suppressed' (CJ, ii, 938).

[8] Sir Hugh is careful to omit the vitally relevant fact that he had disobeyed direct orders from London and his commanding officer, Lord Fairfax, to link up his forces with those of the latter at Tadcaster and instead retired all the way back to Scarborough in the first week of December 1642. It was his rank disobedience and the subsequent defeat of the outnumbered Fairfaxes at Tadcaster that nettled Pym and his colleagues at Westminster, and it was in a letter from Pym that Scarborough was called a 'place . . . not . . . very usefull' (BL, TT, E85(17)). Clearly, these words rankled with Cholmley.

[9] Again, either deliberately or as a result of poor memory, Sir Hugh misleads the reader. Both Parliament and Fairfax soon came round to accept that he had been wise not to venture any further westwards beyond Stamford Bridge, and that by denying it to the king Cholmley's hold on Scarborough was indeed of great value. After his victory at Guisborough, which had saved Whitby from Royalist occupation, the Commons thanked Sir Hugh for his loyal and outstanding service and authorised more money and reinforcements for his northern outpost at Scarborough (CJ, ii, 926, 938).

thought itt might nott onely conduce to the quiet of that County, but have some influence towards the generall peace of the kingdome. Whereupon Sir Hugh began to consider how ill the Parliament prosecuted those grounds and pretences they made when hee was first embarqued in there imployment, the kings faire and reasonable propositions and inclinations to treaty,[10] the oathes of alleagiance and protestacion, both obliging protection of the kings person, and that nothing less intended, as appeared by there severall encounters att Edge Hill and other places, all which with many other considerations, as I have heard Sir Hugh say, did not onely convince his iudgement but his conscience too, and induced his resolution to quitt Parliament and serve the King. But before hee gave assurance of itt, hee desired to speake to the Queene then att Yorke, which could not be without difficultie, considering a great part of the Lord Newcastles army was quartered betweene Scarbrough and Yorke, and therefore tooke this course to affect itt. Having the Queenes promiss and the Marquis of Newcasstles pass for his safe access to Yorke, and returne to Scarbrough, taking onely a French servant, and a gentleman well knowne to the Lord Newcastles army, hee goes out of Scarbrough earely in the morning,[11] and then putting a blacke patch upon one eye passed to Yorke without beeing discovered. As soone as itt began to be darke hee was conducted by the Lord Jermyn to the Queene, to whom Sir Hugh said hee was come with great affection and desire to serve the king and her majestie, but before hee fullie declaired his resolution hee must make two modest requests to her: 1. that shee would bee pleased to give him her royall assurance not to divert the king from performing those promisses hee had made to the kingdome. 2dly, that shee would endeavour the speedie settling the peace of the kingdome; these without anie selfe ends beeing the onely request hee made, to which, after her Majestie had given him a verie satisfactory answeare, hee promissed to quitt the Parliament and to serve the king to the uttmost of his power, but before | hee should (f.9r.) declaire his resolution publickly, hee desires 3 weekes time for returning the Commission hee had from the earl of Essex, and to bring his wife and children from London. It was conceived Sir Hugh might be prevented, or att least interrupted in this designe and intention, and therefore itt was propounded to him that att the time hee ment[12] to communicate his minde to the Garrison hee should draw some of the Lord Newcasstles fources into Scarbrough, which Sir Hugh refused, answearing hee did not meane to surprise any person under his command, or in the garrison, resolving to leave every Man to his liberty, ether to stay or departe. That hee was confident in a faire way to put the Castle with the owners consent into the Kings power; which was all hee would promiss more then his owne person, though hee conceived most of his souldiors and commanders would follow his example. After one nights stay verie privately in Yorke, Sir Hugh returnes to Scarbrough, and within 2 or 3 dayes dispatches a servant for London to returne the Commission to the earle of Essex, but Sir John Hotham, having had some intimation of Sir Hughs beeing att Yorke, stayes his servant, opens the letters, and writes to Sir Hugh to disswade him from quitting the Parliament, and withall adviseth Mr John Legard[13] (Captaine of the Castle) that in caise Sir Hugh persissted in that resolution to give itt all the

---

[10] This is a reference to the negotiations then taking place at Oxford. How much Cholmley could have known of these negotiations when at the time he was 250 miles away cannot be said.

[11] Cholmley sneaked out of Scarborough on 20 March 1643.

[12] This word was printed as 'went' (*EHR*, xxxii, 571).

[13] John Legard, eldest son and heir of Robert Legard of Anlaby, was the officer who wrote an astute assessment of the military value of the castle (BL, *TT*, E85(17)). After his refusal to change sides with Cholmley he was killed at Brigg fighting for Parliament.

impediment hee could. Upon this Letter from Sir John Hotham Sir Hugh resolved the next day to communicate his intention to the Garrison, and indeed itt was nott longer to be deferred, for Ledgard had not onely divulged that the Lord Newcastles army was to be brought into the Towne to cutt there throates, but the next morning with two Duch Leiutennants comes into Sir Hughs chamber with resolution (as hee after expressed in a Letter to the Parliament) to kill him. But itt pleased God Sir Hugh was ready to goe out of his chamber and having his Pistoll in his hand they durst attempt nothing. Butt comming to the porte of the Castle Sir Hugh tooke occasion to tell the soldiors hee heard of some distempers in the Towne raised meerely uppon misapprehensions, whereupon Ledgard beganne to speake high and insolent woords, conceiving hee had the greatest interest in the soldiors, as beeing there Captaine, but hee was much misstaken for Sir Hugh caused him [presently – *crossed out*] instantly to be committed and then calling together the soldiors and officers of the Garrison, communicated to them his resolution to quitt the Parliament, giving them reasons for it, but leaving every Man to his owne libertie either to stay here or to departe, and every person that had either horse or armes of his own to take and dispose them as hee pleased. After which time there was not twenty of the soldiors that left their Corronnell, nor of the officers more then Ledgard and the two Duch Leuitennants.[14]

Ledgard after his commitment grew very submissive, and earnestly importuned Sir Hugh for his departure to Hull, promising as soone as hee came there to procure Captaine Browne Bushells enlardgement (whoe [was] a Captaine of Scarbrough Garrison, and beeing att Hull Sir John Hotham had stayd and committed him prisoner upon the intelligence Sir Hugh ment[15] to quitt the Parliament).[16] To this Sir Hugh
(f.9v.) condiscendeth, and Ledgard | with his wife and family pass to Hull together with all such of the Towne as desired to quitt itt, which were not above 4 families, and to carry with them what goods soe ever belonged to them.[17] The foote were of the trained bands and there armes were there owne, and most of the horse raised by Sir Hugh and his friends, and armed att his owne chardge without ever having farthing allowance, soe that the Parliament could not pretend any interest in any of these.[18]

The Garrison att this time consisted of 600 foote, a 100 horse and a 100 dragooners, all which (except the few before mentioned) were very willing to goe Sir Hughs way, soe that the Garrison was imidiatly settled for the King without the least mutiny or dissturbance.

[14] For a rather different version of these events see Legard's own contemporary account (BL, *TT*, E95(9): *A Letter from a worthy captain . . .* 7 April 1643). As this valuable document reveals, the 'two Duch Leiutennants' were Captain Froom and Lieutenant Vanderhurst. Cholmley failed to record that there were other officers who deserted him and went to Hull, notably Sir Thomas Norcliffe of Nunnington Hall, captain of a troop of horse, and Lieutenant Thomas Strangeways of South House, Ugglebarnby (1620–69), who later became a major of horse under Fairfax and Cromwell.

[15] Here again, 'ment' was printed as 'went' (*EHR*, xxxii, 572).

[16] Captain Browne Bushell (1609–51), formerly of Bagdale Hall, Whitby, was Sir Hugh's first cousin. An account of his extraordinary career can be found in J. Binns, 'Captain Browne Bushell: North Sea Adventurer and Pirate', *NH* XXVII (1991), 90–105.

[17] One of these families was that of John Lawson, master mariner, who offered his merchant ship to Parliament for service in the North Sea. Other leading townsmen who refused to live under a Royalist regime were John Harrison, William Nesfield, Thomas Gill and Peter Hodgson – all religious radicals with shipping interests (J. Binns, *A Place of Great Importance: Scarborough in the Civil Wars, 1640–60* (Preston, 1996), pp.94–5).

[18] Again, Cholmley 'forgot' to mention that a majority of the 44 members of Scarborough's ruling body, the Common Hall, had voted and paid for a company of dragoons in November 1642 (NYCRO, DC/SCB, A20, Common Hall Memoranda, 21 Nov. 1642), and that the same townsmen had approved and collected a succession of heavy levies on the borough to cover the costs of its defence.

And now having declaired the authoritie Sir Hugh had from the Parliament and his deportment in the quitting of itt, I refer itt to all impartiall judgements whether hee had deservedly occasioned those scandalous votes, passed against him in the house of Commons, chardging him with perfidiousness and breach of faith, where as hee never had any authority from the Parliament touching the Castle, but on the contrary theire order to quit itt.[19] And touching the Commission from the Earle of Essex hee had donn as much as layde in his power to returne itt; which if hee had nott, though itt be a formality to be observed where a Man serves a forraine Prince, yett surely amongst conscientious and judicious men itt will not be conceived a circumstance of that necessitie betweene a King and his subjects, whoe through error and misstakes beeing misled from there duty and alleagiance may nott att any time returne to the same without any scandall or indecorum, and without asking permission from those persons whoe would not onely denie but by all meanes in there power oppose the same.[20]

With in a few dayes after Sir Hugh had settled the Garrison hee went to doe his service to her Majestie att Yorke, and whilst hee was there Captaine Bushell returnes from Hull to Scarbrough, whoe though hee was to be sett att libertie upon Ledgards ingaigement, yett, as hee avers, Sir John Hotham would nott doe itt till hee had made him sweare to use his endeavours for the regaining Scarbrough to the Parliament, which as soone as hee came thether hee presently puts in execution, and having his Brother Leiuetenant att aleven a clock in the night is lett into the Castle with 40 seamen, whoe seaze upon the Captaine, and turne all the soldiors out att the gaite, and then declaire for the Parliament.[21]

The Bailiff of the Towne beeing a person favouring that party,[22] and privie to the place, and the townes men over awed with the Castle they were likewise brought to conformity and complyance. Sir Hughs principall officers were seized upon, and the common soldiors threw downe there armes, and most of them went to there owne homes beeing of the country adioyninge. Upon notice of this business Sir Hugh makes all the haist hee could towards Scarbrough, taking some troopes of the Lord Newcastles army, and that night quartered att a little village called Falsgrave | a (f.10r.) quarter of a mile from Scarbrough towne; and from thence writes to Bushell to meet him the next morning att the gaite of Scarbrough towne, whither Sir Hugh (attended onely with three of his owne servants) was come before Bushell, soe that hee found the gaites shut and not to be opened, Bushell having the keyes in the Castle. There was onely townesmen upon the guarde, and those expressed great joy to see Sir Hugh and to have him amongst them. As soone as Bushell came hee goes out to Sir Hugh whoe puts him in minde of the relations betweene them, and the favours hee had donn him. Bushell of a rash but flexable and good nature, partlie out of the remembrance of the obligations received from Sir Hugh, partlie out of the apprehension of the difficulty to holde the place, having nothing but those few

---

[19] This is plainly untrue. Clearly, Cholmley had a bad conscience about his military service in Parliament's name and did everything here to minimise its value and seriousness. He wanted his readers to believe that his commitment to Parliament in 1642–3 had never been more than half-hearted (*CJ*, ii, 831, 926, 938).

[20] It seemed necessary to start a new paragraph here which did not occur in the manuscript.

[21] Bushell's recapture of castle and town for Parliament on 30 March 1643 was most fully reported in Legard's letter written at Hull the following day (BL, *TT*, E95(9)). Browne's younger brother was Henry Bushell, who had been made lieutenant of the castle guard during Cholmley's absence.

[22] Sir Hugh must have meant John Harrison, senior of the two bailiffs in October 1642 for the fourth time, and a close friend and ally of John Lawson. According to Harrison's later sworn testimony, he refused to cooperate with Cholmley when he changed sides and consequently suffered imprisonment first in Scarborough castle and later at York (M.Y. Ashcroft (ed.), *Scarborough Records 1641–1660* (1991), p.166).

men in to Castle to confide in, with some contrition acknowledges his errour, presentlie opens the gaite of the Towne to Sir Hugh, and gives him the keys of the Castle. And all things were put immediatlie into the same condition and quiett they were in before this business hapned. The soldiers [who had] departed in few dayes returned to there cullors. Soe that the regaining the Castle was as sudden as the surprisall, and may bee thought more strainge, considering that certainely Bushell had resolutions att first to hold itt for Parliament, having sent to Sir John Hotham to send (by sea) men and ammunition, which the next day after the rendor came in 2 *Pinaces* which appeared before the harbour; and though att first they were verie shie and cautelous, Sir Hugh soe handled the matter hee had gott the Captaines and soldiers all with in the Castle gaites before they knew that Bushell had renderd it.[23]

Soon after Major Rosse[24] a Scotch man brought from Yorke to Scarbrough 200 musketts, 20 barrells of powder and match proportionable, with a letter from the Lord Jermin, whoe writes to Sir Hugh Cholmeley that the Queene desires hee would accommodate the said Ross with a shipp to carry those armes and powder for Scotland, the one halfe being for the Earle of Antrim the other for the Lord Boyne. Heereupon Sir Hugh imidiatly writes to the Lord Jermin to intreat him to move the Queene that shee would be pleased to take itt into consideration whether the sending those armes and ammunition into Scotland att this time might not prouve prejudiciall to his Majesties affaires, for these reasons. The Scotts had not then declaired to ioyne with the Parliament (nor did not in above six mounthes after); they seemed now to stand att *gaise*, nott resolving which parte to take; that if they had anie inclination to ioyne with the Kinge, they might skarr at this, which might divert them; that if they intended to take parte with the Parliament this might give them better rise and ground then yett they had to raise an Army; hee thought the Parliament of England would make greater use of this to the Kings preiudice then soe small a quantitie of armes and ammunition could advantage his affaires. In answeare to this the Lord Jermin wrote to Sir Hugh [that] the Queene was diverted from sending those armes and ammunition into Scotland, and that hee might dispose them as hee would, soe that the armes were employed to the use of the Garrison and the powder for the army,

(f.10v.) and neither then or at any other time was there any armes or | ammunition sent from Scarbrough into Scottland. The Parliament after prints the Lord Jermyns letter sent by Maior Ross to Sir Hugh,[25] inferring some thing from thence to the preiudice of his Majesties affaires and the Queenes person. Now as well for clearing that point as that in the future this may not be brought amongst other reasons why the Scotts tooke up armes to ioyne with the Parliament, I thought fitt to mention this perticuler.

It would be too tedious to recite all actions and things relating to the Governor and garrison at Scarbrough.[26] I shall therefore onely mention two perticulers which may be pertinent to the generall hisstory of the times, and soe come to the story of the siedge.

[23] Bushell's defection from Parliament on 31 March 1643 ultimately cost him his life exactly eight years later on the scaffold on Tower Hill. Cholmley's account of the events of 30–31 March is mostly confirmed by the testimony of eye-witnesses presented at Bushell's trial for treason (Ashcroft, *Records*, pp.165–8).

[24] Sergeant-Major Rosse was an officer in the service of Lord Aboyne. The episode that follows is partly confirmed in other sources e.g. HMC, *Portland*, i, pp.113–14; HMC, *Various Collections*, viii, p.59. The Earl of Antrim confirmed that he had received arms via Scarborough (HMC, *Portland*, i, p.121).

[25] This letter was printed in *CJ*, iii, 86.

[26] Between April and September 1643, Cholmley's 'Scarbrough Horse' were actively successful against isolated Parliamentarian forces and outposts in east Yorkshire. They plundered Mulgrave castle to the north and threatened Wressle castle to the south (Binns, *Place of Importance*, pp.99–100). Between 2 September and 11 October 1643, Cholmley took part in the siege of Hull, which he mentioned briefly in his later Memoirs (f.27v., see above, p.106).

Att the beginning of the siedge of Hull there was a little leather bagg full of letters brought to Sir Hugh Cholmeley which was cast up by the sea with in his own land att Whitby, about 12 miles from Scarbrough. The letters were wett, and few of them ledgable, but one that was most was a letter from generall King[27] to his agent att Hambrough, which was to require him to send with him with speede all his horses, and in caise hee could not gett saife passage to England, hee should send them to Scottland, where Generall Leshley[28] would give them a saife conduct. And as itt seemed strainge that there should be soe great a confidence and correspondencie betweene King, Leiutenant Generall to one of his Majesties greatest armyes, and Leshley, whoe was declaired Generall of the army which was to come against the King, soe in the bringing these letters to veiw there seemed to be a kinde of providence, for upon examination these beeing to be carried into Holland by one Captaine Cocke, hee beeing taken by a Parliament shipp close to Tinmouth Haven, casts this bagg with letters over boord which are carryed in the sea above a hundred miles before they are cast upon the land. Sir Hugh impartes these perticulers to the Marquiss of Newcastle, but hee had soe great assurance of Generall Kings fidelity that hee interpreted the great acquaintance and friendshipp formerly betweene Leshley and King might give him confidence to write such letter; the discoverie of which produced nothing but Kings displeasure against Sir Hugh.

The next perticuler is this. Mr Henry Darly,[29] one of the Parliaments Commissioners imployed for bringing in the Scotts, and still resident with them, layed att his fathers house 4 miles shorte of Yorke att a place called Buttercram, and thought himselfe in great security in resspect the army which besiedged Yorke were quartered round about him, and that there was noe ennemy nearer than Scarbrough, which had noe considerable forces. Besides betweene him and that place close att his doore was an unfoordable river[30] | over which was a draw bridge, which (through confidence of (f.11r.) securitie) the Governor understood was often undrawne up in the night. Heere upon the Governor drawes out fiftie of his best horse and choicest men putting them under the command of Maior Crompton, communicating the designe onely to him, which was to march to Buttercram, and to endeavour the surprising of Darley. This was about 9 of the clocke in the night, and Crumpton soe well performed the service that hee had Darlie out of the enemies reach before they made anie pursuite, and brought him to Scarbrough the next day by 12 a Clocke.[31] |

[27] James King, afterwards Lord Eythin, was Lieutenant General of Foot in the Royalist northern army of the Marquess of Newcastle. Cholmley was already prejudiced against him by this time because he had maltreated some of the Scarborough men under Captain Richard Medley he had captured at the battle of Yarm in January 1643 (*Mercurius Aulicus* 8 Feb. 1643, *ORN*, i, p.74; HMC, *Hastings MSS*, ii, p.92). Since Sir Hugh does not give the date of King's letters it is impossible to judge whether his suspicion was well founded. Parliament concluded the alliance with the Scots on 25 September 1643, three weeks after the siege of Hull began. By the time Leven was appointed the siege was over. It is a curious thing that Sir Hugh should have regarded this 'perticuler' to have had a bearing on the general history of the times. One explanation might be that after the events of 1644 Cholmley came to regard King as a traitor to the royalist cause.
[28] Alexander Leslie, the earl of Leven, who commanded the Scottish army in alliance with Parliament.
[29] Henry Darley was eldest son and heir of Sir Richard Darley of Buttercrambe and a close friend of fellow Puritan, Sir Matthew Boynton (Cliffe, *Yorkshire Gentry*, pp.322–3).
[30] This daring raid took place on 3 June 1644 (BL, *TT*, E50(30): *Exact Relation*, 12 June 1644; *CSPD*, 1644, p.203). Buttercrambe is ten miles from York and stands on the river Derwent.
[31] There are only eight lines of writing on f.11r. and 11v. was left blank. Perhaps Cholmley originally intended to say something about the battle of Marston Moor and the flight of the marquess of Newcastle via Scarborough into continental exile and left space for these events, then later changed his mind and instead wrote a separate memorial on the battle and its aftermath. The passage of the marquess and his staff through Scarborough is also recorded in the later Memoirs (f.27v.; see above, p.106).

(f.12r.)   But to come to the siedg of Scarbrough, the Marquiss was noe sooner shipped but
the Governor beganne seriouslie to consider his condition, which indeed was verie sad
as the caise stood; for the Towne was nott att all fortifyed,[32] and (if itt had beene) no
tenable with less then fouretimes the number of Men then in the Garrison, and though
the Castle was strong by scituation, itt had not with in itt either habitation for soldiors
or places for Magazine, and as the provision for victualls were but small, soe for war
less, there beeing but 23 barrells of powder and 3 bundles of matche. And that the
governor may not be thought culpable for these defects, you must know hee had often
desired they might be taken into consideration, but could never obteine itt; beeing
ever answered the place was of sufficient strenght against surprise, and the Marquesses
army beeing maister of the field, there was no apprehension of a siedge.[33] But not with
standing all these wants and inconveniences the Governor sett a good countenance of
the business, and beganne to fortifie the Towne, having given advertisement to Prince
Rupert of his condition, whoe put the governor in some hopes hee might recruite
suddenly in Westmorland and Cumberland, and would then come and raise he siedg at
Yorke, which yett held out. How ever the Governor conceived during that hee
should be in noe great danger, but with in 3 weekes Yorke was rendered;[34] and the
gentlemen and straingers then with in Scarbrough, partlie in that the Articles of Yorke
were soe plausable, and partlie that they found the place soe ill provided, quitt it,
procuring passes either to goe to Prince Rupert or to live att there owne houses.[35] The
Generalls departure and the gentlemens thus quitting the towne strucke soe great a
terror into the common soldiors as that they ranne away dayly, soe that the Garrison
was reduced to 300 foote and 200 horse, and many of those wavering. Sir Thomas
Fairefax was advanced with in 6 miles of Scarbrough with a thousand horse, and 3
thousand foote ordered to follow.[36] Heereupon the Governor summons together his
principall officers and some two or three gentlemen of qualitie that remained in the
Towne and whoe hee knew [were] verie firme to the Kings cause,[37] acquaineting

[32] This is most misleading. As early as October 1642, soon after Sir Hugh's arrival in Scarborough, in
response to his proposals the Common Hall agreed to pay for substantial physical improvements to the
town's land defences: new gates were put up, the walls repaired, ditches dug, sentry houses built and
occupied, cannon placed at the entrances and a permanent night watch organised (NYCRO, DC/SCB,
A1, Common Hall Minutes and Orders, 1623–49, 16, 20, 31 Oct., 13, 21 Nov., 5, 19 Dec. 1643). The
truth is that Cholmley did not want to admit that the town had been fortified for Parliament in 1642–3
before he changed sides.

[33] On the contrary, all other evidence indicates that Cholmley had made considerable improvements to the
castle defences long before the battle of Marston Moor. As early as November 1642 he reported to Pym
that he had already spent £200 'in repairing the castle, mounting ordnance etc' (HMC, Bouverie, p.90).
The following month he wrote of the castle: 'I have fortified the place in much better manner than it
was' (BL, TT, E85(17)). Both Bushell's battery, an outwork commanding the only entrance to the castle,
and South Steel battery, which defended its sea cliff flank and enfiladed the dyke in front of the curtain
wall, were erected in 1643 (NYCRO, DC/SCB, A1, 12 Apr. 1643; J. Schofield, An Historical and
Descriptive Guide to Scarbrough (York, 1787), pp.88–9).

[34] After the battle of Marston Moor on 2 July 1644, the Royalist garrison at York held out for only a
fortnight until 16 July.

[35] At the end of his 'Memorialls touching the Battle of Yorke' Cholmley had written that he would not
allow some Royalist gentlemen to go into exile overseas (f.155r.; see above p.139).

[36] I have found no evidence to corroborate this claim that Sir Thomas came so close to Scarborough, and it
is even more doubtful that he had a thousand horse with him at the time. Indeed, his father could spare
very few troops for distant 'sieges' of Royalist garrisons still holding out in Yorkshire and his son
probably came no closer to Scarborough than Helmsley (CSPD, 1644, p.447; Bell, Memorials, ii, pp.121–
2). Nevertheless, in his Memoirs, Cholmley insisted on bringing Sir Thomas another mile nearer to
Scarborough (f.27v.; see above, p.106).

[37] The Royalist gentlemen included the Thompsons. Christopher, the youngest, accepted the post of senior
bailiff in October 1644, and Francis, Richard and Timothy Thompson all allowed themselves to be re-

them with the enemies designes and staite of the Garrison not able to indure a siedge, and therefore propounds the offering of artickles to the Committy for both King- domes; and requiring from the Lord Fairefax a cessation from acts of hostelitie for twenty dayes, whilst those should be sent to London and considered of; [and] that Mr Darley, then prisonner in the Castle, should be moved to carry the artickles, and have his libertie upon procuring the cessation. The motion was exceedinglie approved of [by] every man, and Darley, greedie of libertie, was readie to undertake the business, but desires the treaty might be with the Lord Fairefax, which the Governor refuseth under pretence the articles of Yorke were not iustlie observed, and that hee demanded something not in my Lords power to grant, but in truth because a treaty with the Lord Fairefax would bring a shorte issue, which did not sorte with the Governors ends beeing to gain time, and to have all the armyes att Yorke dispersed; and therefore holds him to his iorney to London, which rather than to continnue he accepts. And first hee procures a Cessation for 20 dayes, with bounds of quarter for the Governor to six miles distance from Scarbrough, soe that neither the Governors forces were | to goe out of (f.12v) these bounds nor the Lord Fairefaxes to come with in them. Then he departes from Scarbrough carrying with him the propositions, and when hee comes to Yorke gives such an assurance of reducing Scarbrough by treatie as the forces att Yorke disperse, the Lord Manchester[s] army to the south, the Scotts to Newcastle, and the Lord Fairefaxes forces drawne to besiedge Pontefract and Hemsley Castle, whether Sir Thomas Fairefax goes in person, leaving those horse in there quarters neere Scarbrough.[38]

This treatie tooke such impression that itt was generally reported and beleeved Scarbrough would be renderd, though to anie rationall and impartiall man, whoe seriouslie peruseth the propositions, there will little appeare to give an occasion of such construction. For it is evident not onelie certaine perticulers are required which either the Parliament could nott or assuredlie would nott grant; but to prevent the Governors beeing surprised by there complyance and concession, in the last artickle hee reserves 3 dayes time[39] after the returne of the Committyes answear to consider how farr hee would consent and accept, with out beeing concluded by ought had passed in the Propositions. And further to tesstefie the cleareness of the Governors intentions, hee dispatched messengers to the King and Prince Rupert with coppies of the articles, shewing the streight hee was in, and necessitie to sett on foote this treatie, but with assurance of his fidelitie to his Majesties service, and that this was meerely to gaine time and accomodations.[40] The Propositions sent from Sir Hugh Cholmeley to

---

elected to the First Twelve in the Common Hall at the same time. John Hickson, gentleman, who had served as junior bailiff in the previous year, accepted the office of coroner. Tristram Fysh, now head of another leading Scarborough family, identified himself as an active and committed Royalist when he became junior bailiff in October 1644 (NYCRO, DC/.SCB, A20, 23 Oct. 1644; *CJ*, iv, 523; Ashcroft, *Records*, p.258).

[38] It seems highly improbable that Cholmley's offer to surrender Scarborough had any effect on the deployment of Parliament's armed forces in the north. Sir Hugh was flattering himself if he really believed that Manchester's army of the Eastern Association would not have returned southwards, the Scots would not have gone north to take Sunderland and Newcastle, or the Fairfaxes given priority to Pontefract and Helmsley castles had they not thought the fall of Scarborough was imminent (see above, p.26 on Cholmley's Civil War career).

[39] Article 18 of the propositions asked for two days, not three (see below, p.151).

[40] Whether Cholmley's offer to surrender was genuine or bogus remains an unanswerable question (Newman, thesis, I, pp.464–72). Whitelocke was convinced that Sir Hugh seriously intended to give up the town and castle, but when he heard of the king's great victory over Essex at Lostwithiel on 2 September he changed his mind and wrote to Prince Rupert pledging his loyalty and asking for reinforcements (Whitelocke, *Memorials* (1732), p.105; BL, Egerton MS 2884, f.47). However, since

the Committee for both kingdomes resident att London carryed thither by Mr Henrie Darley.

1   That the Burgesses and other Inhabitants of the Towne of Scarbrough may enioy all there priviledges which formerly they did before the beginning of these troubles, and have freedome of trade both by sea and land, paying such duties and customes as other places doe under the command of the King and Parliament.

2   That in all chardges the Burgesses and inhabitants of Scarbrough shall beare onelie such part with the country att lardge as was formerlie used in all other assessments.

3   That the Garrison placed heere be att least 2 parts of 3 Yorkshire men.

4   That such officers and soldiors both of horse and foot, and all others whoe shall desire itt, may have libertie to March with there horses and armes, cullers flying, trumpetts sounding, drums beating, matches lighted att both ends, to the Princes Army, or to the next garrison which they shall make choice of, beeing allowed accomodation for there quarters, and not to march above 10 miles a day; and everie soldior to have 12 chardges of powder and bulletts and match parportionable.

5   That all persons whoe have any goods in the Towne or Castle may have libertie to disspose them in what plaice and in whose hands they please with in the Towne, or to carry them to what place they desire with in the Kingdome or beyond the seas, and to have protections and passes for there securitie and better conduct of there said goods. |

(f.13r.) 6   That all and everie person of what quallitie and degree soe ever, which is with in the Towne or Castle att the rendition there of, may have free power and libertie to remove himselfe and family, and to live att his owne house or else where as hee pleaseth, and to pass and travell quietlie about his occasions with out molestations, and to have protections and passes from the three Generalls then att Yorke for his and there better securitie.[41]

7   That all officers, soldiors, Gentlemen, Townesmen and every other person which shall be in the Towne or Castle at the Rendition thereof, may have power and liberty to departe with there armes, and to disspose of there estaites reall and personall as they please, and shall not be chardged with other taxes and payments then is chardged upon the Countrie in generall, and paid in a proportionable way by those which are of the Parliaments side and party.

8   That all and everie person that hath interest in anie Shipp now lying in the harbour or belonging to the towne, may have power and libertie to disspose of the said shipp and ordinance, tackling, and all things belonging to her, as they please to there best advantage.

9   That all Clergie men which are now in the Towne and shall be att the Rendition thereof, and are dispossessed of there spirituall or Temporall estaites and livings by reasons of these troubles, may be restored to them, and enioy there estaites reall and personall and disspose the same as they please, and that they may live quietlie at there own howses and have protections from the three Generalls for that purpose.

10   That noe man with in the towne or Castle att the Rendition thereof be enforced

Cholmley's letter was dated only two days after the battle more than 300 miles away, it is unlikely that he then knew about it. On the other hand, as Sir Hugh himself argued here, some of his articles, particularly the three rejected outright, 10, 12 and 15, were so unreasonable that they invited rejection. There is no doubt that Parliament was so anxious to acquire such a vital port and stronghold before the winter set in and without committing troops that the Committee gave Fairfax and Darley permission to go a long way to meet Cholmley's terms (*CSPD*, 1644, pp.450, 452; BL, Egerton MS 2884, f.43).

[41]   The three Generals were Lords Fairfax, Leven and Manchester; but after the capture of York on 16 July 1644, they separated almost immediately on 20 July. Only Fairfax remained in the city (P. Wenham, *The Great and Close Siege of York, 1644* (Kineton, 1970), pp.101–2.

to take any oath other then such as is settled by act of Parliament, nor be troubled or molested for refusing any oath not settled by act of Parliament.

11 That neither the Governor nor anie under his command be questioned for anie matter or thing that hath beene donn or acted by them or anie of them by sea or land.

12 That the votes passed against the Governor in the house of Commons be revoked, and that hee be put in the same capacitie hee was before they passed.[42]

13 That the Governor may have libertie to pass to what Countrie hee please beyond the seas, and power to disspose his estaite reall and personall as hee pleases, and protections from the three Generalls for himselfe and servants for better security in this point.

14 That the Governors wife may have libertie to live att his house att Whitbie without molestacion, and that the soldiers there may be removed and noe other put in the same.

15 That when the Towne and Castle shall be rendred Sir Henry Cholmeley,[43] Brother to Sir Hugh, may be Governor of the place and have command in cheife.

16 That in caise these articles be agreed on Coll. John Bellasyse[44] be released.

17 That the Governor may have assurance from the Committy for both Kingdomes and the Lord Fairefax that these articles shall be punctually observed without any breach or violation, and that they will promiss to obteine an order in the house of Commons for the confirmation of them with in one fortnight after the surrender of the Towne and Castle. |

18 That betweene this and the 4th of September the Governor may receive (f.13v.) anseweare how farre the Committy for both kingdomes and the Lord Fairefax doe consent to these articles, after the receiving of which the Governor desires and reserves 2 dayes time to consider before hee returnes a conclusive answeare, and after hee shall declaire his assent to the articles which shall be condissended to the Committy and the Lord Fairefax, hee promisseth in the woord of a Gentleman with in 5 dayes to render itt into the hands of such person as the Parliament or the Lord Fairefax shall appoint, and authorise for that purpose, the Towne and Castle of Scarbrough, with all victualls, armes, and ammunition and ordinance but such as was formerly excepted in these articles.

19 And whilst these articles are in agetation theire may be a cessation from all acts of Hostelitie, and under his the Governor subscribed his name.

Mr Darley after some dayes stay att Yorke takes his Iourney to London with these propositions, which hee pursues with more earnestness in hopes to be Governor, and makes soe much expedition as eight dayes before end of the Cessation hee returnes to

---

[42] Cholmley was permanently disabled and to be impeached for high treason (*CJ*, iii, 28).

[43] Sir Henry Cholmley (1608–66), Hugh's younger brother, was MP for New Malton and Colonel of a Yorkshire regiment in Essex's army recruited largely from Ryedale and Pickering Lythe. The regiment, better known as the Bluecoats, disgraced itself by looting in the Midlands and running away from the battlefield at Edgehill (E. Peacock (ed.), *The Army Lists of the Roundheads and Cavaliers* (1874), p.38; P. Young, *Edgehill 1642* (1970), p.116; *CSPD*, 1642, p.387). Sir Henry remained loyal to Parliament after his brother's defection, but the two stayed friends. Henry sent money to his nephew William, Hugh's eldest son, then an exile in Paris, though by this time Henry's estate at West Newton in Ryedale had been plundered by Royalists (*CSPD*, 1644, p.299; *LJ*, vi, 439; *CJ*, iii, 381). At the surrender of Scarborough castle Henry lent his bankrupt brother £200 (Memoirs, f.28r.; see above, p.108).

[44] Colonel John Bellasis had been governor of York and Royalist commander in Yorkshire when he was defeated and captured at Selby in April 1644. Since Bellasis was a Catholic Sir Hugh's particular concern for him is rather surprising. However, the two were first cousins and in 1640–41 had worked closely together in their county and Parliamentary opposition to Strafford. For Bellasis's Civil War record see HMC, *Ormonde MSS*, New Series, II (1903), pp.376–98.

the Lord Fairefax att Yorke with the Committyes answeare to the articles, which is imidiatlie sent to the Governor of Scarbrough and his speedie resolution required.[45] The answeare of the Committy of both Kingdomes to the propesition made by Sir Hugh Cholmeley concerning the Rendition of the Towne and Castle of Scarbrough August the 26th 1644.

1. 2. 3. 4.   First, second, third and fowerth approved of.

5.   Fifth approved of, it beeing provided noe prohibeted goods or commodities be sent beyond seas.

6.   Approved of.

7.   To the seaventh is answered, that all those which have beene in the Towne or Castle since the first of August 1644 shall be used in the same manner and be in the same condition as those that were in Yorke upon delivery thereof.

8.   Approved of, provision beeing made that securitie be given they be not imployed against Parliament, and that such Shipps and Cannon as have beene taken from any persons for there adherence to the cause of both Kingdomes may be restored.

9.   Ninth disaproved, excepting Mr Remmington[46] to whome the proposition is granted.

10.   Disaproved.

11.   Elleventh approved of soe farr as concerneth Sir Hugh Cholmeley and his family, and for what concerneth the officers sufficient is granted in the precedent articles.

12.   Twelth disaproved.

13. 14.   Thirteenth and fowerteenth approved of. |

(f.14r.)   15.   As to the fifteenth the Committy thinkes itt not reasonable Sir Hugh Cholmeley name his successor.

16.   Sixteenth suspended.

17.   As to the 17th it is answeared that the Committie undertakes to use there utmost endeavours for the performance of the articles according to the limitations expressed.

18.   Approved of.

19.   Left to the Lord Fairefax.

Signed in the name and by the warrant of the Committy
of both Kingdomes
Northumberland   Maitland

Though many of these articles were not assented to, yet to speake ingeniouslie there was as much granted as could be expected, espetiall for the Governors owne perticuler, besides a letter was written to him by the close Committy implying Mr Darley had some privaite instructions for his further satisfaction, soe that if enough was not granted probably the Governor might have had more for incissting upon.

The letter to Sir Hugh Cholmeley

Where as this woorthie gentleman Henry Darley Esquier hath brought unto us from you some propositions concerning the Rendition of the Towne and Castle of Scarbrough, which wee have perused and taken into consideration, wee have thought fitt to returne the same with Mr Darley, unto whome wee desire you to give full credence in what hee shall impart unto you from us in answeare to the said propositions.

---

[45] These events are confirmed in *CSPD*, 1644, pp.450–2.

[46] See Memoirs, f.20v., n.266; f.28r., n.393 (see above, pp.91, 108).

> Signed in the name and by the warrant of both Kingdomes
> Northumberland   Maitland

Darbie House
26 August 1644.

But the propositions not beeing fully granted the Governor had a faire oppertunitie to be cleare from the treatie, yet there was a necessitie to keepe itt on to the end of the Cessation, most of the corne designed to be brought into the Garrison beeing still in the field. Now for the Governor to holde on the treatie, with out beeing further ingaiged or not discovering some glimse of his resolution to breake with them in the conclusion (which would have interrupted his provisions), was a verie nise point; yet soe mannaged as itt was kept on foote to the last day. The Governor having in that time got into the Garrison 400 loades of corne and a good quantity of hay with other provisions, then writes to the Lord Fairefax and Mr Darley, that since his propositions were not answered by the Committy according to his demand, nor the exposstulations since uppon them produced ought more to his satisfaction, hee would noe longer continnue the treaty. This did not a little vex the Lord Fairefax, but much more Darlie, soe that order was instantlie given to there horse to fall uppon the Governors, but hee had drawne them into the towne | of Scarbrough the same day (f. 14v.) hee gave his finall answeare. However, the enemies horse advanced neerer the Towne and quartered in all the villages and places convenient adiacent, having alsoe sent to them 500 foote to strengthen the quarters. The small quantity of match formerlie mentioned was now reduced to 40 yards, which was oppertunely supplyed by Captaine Allan,[47] whoe brought as much as served to the end of the siedge, having taken itt from a Parliament shipp which was carryinge itt to there Garrison at Linn.[48] The enemies horse beeing quarterred thus neere the Towne they impeaded all recourse to the Markett, soe that there began to be a great want of coales, salt, and corne, all which were soe seasonably and miraculouslie supplyed, some times by shipps which brought in prises, sometimes by shipps forced into the harbour by Tempest, as man must needes acknowledge the Devine power and providence opperating in itt.[49]

Whilst the enemy quarterred thus neare, 13 of the Governors owne troope breake out, and march above twentie miles into Cleaveland, where many of the Scottish army were quartered after the taking of Newcasstle; they incounter with 15 Scotts, kill two, and returne to Scarbrough bringing each Man a prisoner and there horses with them.

The Scarbrough horse were not above 2 hunderd, but verie good Men and perpetually in action, and grew soe formidable the ennemie durst not stand to looke them in the face under treble the number. About the end of December they had taken Collonel Foulthrop[50] and most of his troope, and brought them into Scarbrough,

---

[47] Captain Allan has not been identified. He was not one of the many Scarborough master mariners who were employed as gun-runners and privateers at this time, but one of the captains who sailed with Bushell was called Thomas Allen (H. Swifen, *History of Yarmouth* (Norwich, 1772), p.559).

[48] King's Lynn was one of the several east coast ports held by Parliament whose trade and shipping were endangered by 'Scarbrough pyrates'.

[49] In 1643–4 Scarborough became a haven of supply and refuge for Royalist privateers (NYCRO, DC/SCB, G11, Account Book Oct. 1643–Mar. 1644). When Meldrum captured the harbour in February 1645 there were said to be 120 ships in it, many of them prizes (BL, *TT*, E258(27): *A Perfect Diurnall*, 17–24 Feb. 1645).

[50] This officer has not been identified.

which together with the prisioners taken att sea (and of which 12[51] or 3 belonging to
Hull) did soe incense the enemie as that in the end of January, though there were frost
and snow upon the ground, Sir John Meldrum,[52] leiutenant generall under the Lord
Fairefax, with 2000 foot and one thousand horse, takes his quarter att a small village
called Falsgrave, not 2 fleete shotts from Scarbrough Town, and possesseth himselfe of
the Mill hill which commands both towne and harbour.[53] The governor understood
well of what consequence the place was, and would not have left itt with out
fortification, but that hee wanted men to maintaine itt, and never intended to holde
the towne in caise any assault should be offered, for 2 thousand men were scarce
sufficient to maintaine the towne and there was not 700 in itt with the Townesmen,
most of which verie wavering. Yet of necessitie it was to be kept till some places for
Magazines with in the Castle were finished, and the provisions in the towne carried
thether, God having soe plentifully and miracoulossly furnished them, that there were
more prises brought into the Harbour in one mounth past, then ever had beene in all
the time Scarbrough was a Garrison.

The Towne was kept 3 weekes, but with soe much paines and dutie that for 10
days together not any soldior stirred from his poast, during which time the enemie
durst never make anie attempt, but played scercelie with there ordnance, which had
(f.15r) dismounted those in a shipp placed to secure that side of the towne towards the | sea.
Those with in the Towne made 2 sallyes, both times beating the enemy out of there
Trenches, and returning with prisoners and armes. Meldrum finding them with in soe
resolute to maintaine the towne, procures Coll. Steward to be sent to him with a
thousand Scotts,[54] and then writes to the Governor in an imperious style to yeild the
towne. The Governor returnes answeare hee verie well understood the towne was
not tenable, that hee would not have kept it soe long against an attempting enemie,
that he held it thus long meerely to gett his provisions into the Castle, which beeing
now donne, hee was resolved to quitt it in few dayes, and that if hee durst make anie
attempt against the Castle, hee should bee received by persons resolute to maintaine
the plaice and the Kings right, whoe hee doubted not but would give him such an
entertainement as should cause him to repent the enterprise. The Governor had then
intelligence that the ennemie on Tuesday following[55] ment to assault the towne, and
therefore the night before draws off all his Cannon except those in the suncke shipp
which could not be removed; and the next morning assoone as the enemie began to

---

[51] This is how the figure appears in the manuscript; in print it became '2' (*EHR*, xxxii, 580).

[52] Sir John Meldrum (1585–1645) was a professional Scottish soldier of great experience, distinction and
courage. Dr Newman believed that he 'had no equal amongst the Parliamentary commanders in the
north, not even Lambert' (thesis, p.473).

[53] Mill hill, or Bracken hill, was a dominating site halfway between Falsgrave village and Newborough Bar,
the main entrance to the town. From the top of the windmill there Meldrum would have had a good
view of the town and harbour below. Today there is still the converted remains of a later windmill on the
hill. Some commentators have assumed that Mill hill must have been Oliver's Mount to the south of
Scarborough, but this was far too distant for contemporary artillery ranges and far too steep-sided for
cannon use. Oliver's Mount is a name not used until more than a century after the Civil War: in 1645 it
was called Weaponness.

[54] Colonel Stewart's regiment was from Galloway (*CSPD*, 1644–45, p.329).

[55] Shrove Tuesday, 18 February 1645. The capture of the town and harbour is fairly well described in the
London press (BL, *TT*, E258(27): *A Perfect Diurnall*, 17–24 Feb. 1645; *Ibid*. (28): *Perfect Occurrences*, 22
Feb. 1645; *Ibid*., E270(2): *The London Post*, no.24; *Ibid*. (9): *Mercurius Civicus*, 13–20 Feb. 1645; *Ibid*. (15):
Mercurius Britanicus, 17–24 Feb. 1645; *Ibid*. (21), *The London Post*, no.25; *Ibid*. (23): *Perfect Passages*, 19–25
Feb. 1645; *Ibid*. (29): *Mercurius Civicus*, 27–27 Feb. 1645; *Ibid*. (30): *A Diary or An Exact Journal*, 20–27
Feb. 1645; *Ibid*. (33): *The Scottish Dove*, 21–28 Feb. 1645; *Ibid*., E271(5): *Mercurius Britanicus*, 24 Feb.–3
Mar. 1645).

appeare, drawes all his Men into the Castle without making the least shew of opposition. Soe that the ennemie, finding the entrance into the towne soe easie, takes the hardiness to advance to the gaite of the Castle, from which they are instantlie repulsed with the loss of many of there lives, and if the Church had not beene neare for there retreate, they had surely suffered much more.[56] At the entring into the Castle most of the Townes men quitt the Governor, except one of the Bailiffes and fower or five others which retyred thither with there familyes.[57] The number of the forces that entered into the Castle were about five hunderd, of which threescore gentlemen and officers, 250 foot, and the rest Troopers most of them having horses, of which there beeing noe use with in the Castle they all betooke themselves to Musketts, and did the dutie of foot soldiors, which they performed verie gallantlie beeing as stoute ressolute Men as was in the worlde.

The first fortnight produced little action, for those with in the Castle hoped for releife (which had beene long and often promised from Oxford); they endeavoured in the interim to make themselves as strong as possible might be, and to that end were imployed in fortifying some places which were most requisite, soe the ennemie having the Church att the foot of the Castle begann to make other places of securitie against attempts from the Castle; and though the Castle could make shotts into the Church and the workes about itt, yett they laid soe lowe the execution was not much, nor the preiudice answerable to the expence of powder.[58] In this time Meldrum writes divers letters to the Governor, some times in milde and plausible, then in menacing and boysterous termes, to invite him to render, which the Governor ever answeared in the Negative, in language according to there severall styles.[59] But finding the Governor not moveable hee writes a letter to all the Gentlemen and officers, offering them plausable conditions, whoe returne answere of there resolution to sticke to the Governor. Then hee shoote[s] arrowes into the Castle yeard with writings affixed to them where hee offers lardgely to all the common soldiers that would come to him, | but that had as little operation, the most of those which were (f.15v.) wavering beeing run away with in 3 or 4 dayes after the entring into the Castle, which were in number of 40. Soe that finding noe hopes to gaine the plaice but by force, hee

[56] That so many of Cholmley's soldiers were able to retreat to the safety of the castle was perhaps due in part to the rearguard action of Sir Jordan Crosland, formerly governor of Helmsley castle, who was again taken prisoner during a fierce encounter near and inside St Mary's parish church.

[57] The bailiff who followed Cholmley into the castle was probably Tristram Fysh, described in 1659 as one of the leading burgesses who had been in arms against Parliament (Ashcroft, *Records*, p.258). Christopher Thompson was the senior bailiff, but there is no indication in the records that he actively fought for the king even though in 1646 he was declared a delinquent and disenfranchised by the Commons (*YRCP, YASRS*, xv (1893), pp.158–60; *CJ*, iv, 528). Other leading townsmen who fled into the castle were William Simpson, vicar of St Mary's, two of his sons, and probably John Hickson, Richard Bilbrough and Francis Sollitt (Ashcroft, *Records*, pp.75, 258). Most of the other Royalist activists, such as Francis Fawether, William Cooper and Browne Bushell were by this date at sea, operating as privateers out of Ostend and Dunkirk (J.R. Powell and E.K. Timings (eds.), *Documents Relating to the Civil War 1642–1648* (1963), pp.203–4).

[58] Here is a suggestion that the major damage inflicted on St Mary's fabric was caused, not by Cholmley's artillery firing from the castle, but by Parliament's cannon firing from and through its structure.

[59] Meldrum's letter of 25 February, demanding Cholmley's surrender of the castle, has not survived. Cholmley's reply to it of 26 February and Meldrum's answer the following day are to be found amongst the manuscripts of Lord Braye (HMC, *Braye MSS*, 10th Report, vi, pp.155–7). It is clear from these two letters and a third intercepted by Meldrum from Sir Hugh to Oxford that the governor had twice appealed to the king on 23 and 24 February for reinforcements or relief (J. Vicars, *England's Parliamentary Chronicle*, iv (1646), p.110). After Cholmley's haughty rejection of Meldrum's summons, the Scotsman threatened him with 'great ordnance', which he promised would break down even the strong walls of the castle.

sends for divers ordinance, of which one was whole cannon which carryed 64lb
bullett, and the rest demy cannon.[60] Beeing to plant these ordnance neere to the sea
cliff for more advantage to batter, Meldrum there in person giving directions about
them, his hatt blowes of his head, and hee catching to save that, the winde beeing
verie great blowes his cloake over his face, and hee falls over the cliff amonst the
rockes and stones att least steeple height. Itt was a miracle his braines were not beaten
out and all his bones broaken, but itt seemed the winde together with the Cloake did
in some sorte beare him up, and lessen the fall. Yet hee is taken up for dead, lyes 3
dayes speachless, his head opened and the bruised blood taken out, though a Man
above threescore yeare old,[61] recovered this soe perfectlie that with in six weekes hee
is on foote againe, and beginns to batter the Castle. Whilst Meldrum lay sicke the
enemie was verie quiett and kept close in there woorkes and the Church, and the
Governor desirous to know the cause, commands Captaine Wickham[62] to sallie out
with 50 Men, whoe falling upon the Scottish garde att the end of the Castle next to
the harbour, made manie of them runne into the sea, whoe thincking thereby to
escaipe fire died by water. This was att noone day, and soe gallantlie performed as hee
returned with above twentie prisoners, left a hunderd killed and wounded. By these
prisoners the besieged had first notice of Meldrums misfortune;[63] whoe noe sooner
recovered but falls to batter soe furiously that in 3 dayes the great Tower splitt in two,
and that side which was battered falls to the ground, the other standing firme beeing
supported by an arch of stone that went through the midst.[64] There were neere 20
personns upon the topp of the tower when itt cleft, yett all gott into the standing
parte, except 2 of Captaine Richard Ledgards[65] servants which were in the Turritt
where there maister lodged. And heere upon I shall a little digress to relaite a strainge
passage. Captaine Richard Ledgard was the first Man that fell sicke after the entrance
into the Castle, and his officers att that time having the maine garde at the gaite house,

[60] A demi-cannon, which had been the Royalist 'queen's pocket-pistol', and since its capture by Parliament
re-named 'Sweet Lips', after a well-known Hull whore, was brought up from York. It weighed $2\frac{1}{2}$ tons
and fired a 36lb. shot (Rushworth, *Collections*, v, p.642; B.N. Reckitt, *Charles the First and Hull, 1639–1645*
(Howden, 1988), pp.117–18). However, the cannon referred to here was the cannon-royal, the largest in
the kingdom, which fired a huge ball of over 60lb. Meldrum placed it in the chancel of St Mary's where
it fired through the east window at point-blank range at the castle keep (J. Schofield, *Guide to Scarborough*,
p.53; B.H.St.J. O'Neil, *Castles and Cannon* (1960), p.xix).

[61] Meldrum was born in 1585. His fall took place on 24 March 1645.

[62] Probably William Wickham of Rowesby (1625–67), second son of Dr Henry Wickham, archdeacon of
York, rector of Bedale and Bolton Percy, by his first wife, Annabella, youngest daughter of Sir Henry
Cholmley, Sir Hugh's grandfather – in short, one of Sir Hugh's many cousins (see Cholmley's Memoirs,
f.5v.; above, p.69). Dr Henry had been one of Sir Hugh's benefactors who had helped to save the
Cholmley estate from bankruptcy (NYCRO, ZPK 13). William's sister, Anthonina, had married Toby
Jenkin of Grimston, Lieutenant-Colonel of Sir Hugh's regiment of horse. Surprisingly, there is no
mention of Jenkin in either the Memoirs or Memorials (*Dugdale's Visitation*, I, p.140; YRCP, ii, *YASRS*
xviii (1895), pp.99–100.).

[63] Both Meldrum's accident and Wickham's successful sally must have taken place at the South Steel battery
on the cliff overlooking the harbour.

[64] Though the Ministry of Works, Department of the Environment and English Heritage, successively
custodians of the castle, have all insisted that the keep was 'slighted' by order of Parliament in 1649 after
the second siege, it is clear from Cholmley's unique description that the cannon-royal reduced the
structure to a state little more than that which now survives. It is also clear from subsequent records that
far from destroying the castle, Parliament spent considerable sums on its repair and that the order to
'slight' was never carried out (*CJ*, iv, 528; *Ibid.*, v, 325; *Ibid.*, vii, 47; *LJ*, x, 247–8; *CSPD*, 1649–50, p.230;
Ibid., 1651, pp.187, 249; *Ibid.*, 1651–2, pp.46–7).

[65] This Richard Legard was probably the second son of Sir Hugh's 'uncle John' Legard of Ganton, and
therefore his first cousin (J. Foster (ed.), *Pedigrees of the County Families of Yorkshire*, 4 vols. (1874–5), iii;
YRCP, ii, *YASRS* xviii, p.7).

beeing to goe the round, apprehended all the walls hung with blacke, but thinccking the light of the plaice might deceive them went into two other courts, where all the walls made the like shew. The men were soe discreete they would not speake of this to the soldiors, but the next morning told it to there Captaine, who would have perswaded them it was onely *deceptio visus*, though they would never be deverted from the realitie and truth of it to there deathes, and they were persons of that Courage as noe one that knew them could iudge any misstake arose through feare and weakeness of spirit; and to those which lived to see the seaquell, this seemed to be a fatall omen of mortalitie to the Garrison in generall, but more perticulerly to that company, for the Lewetenant was shott with a muskett and dyed of the wound, the 2 serjeants killed with shott from the Cannon, and though the Captaine recovered this sickness, yet after hee esscaiped death verie narrowlie, having his hand on another gentlemans shoulder when a | bullett 64lb weight passeth betweene there bodyes, killeth the   (f.16r.) other, and rebounding from the wall not 2 yeards behinde them falls on Ledgards thigh, strucke him to the ground, of which hee recovers not in 12 weekes. His owne 2 servants as you heard fell [from – *crossed out*] with the Tower, and of all the company, which were 50 at the enterring into the Castle, not above 3 left alive att the Render.

The fall of the Tower was a verry terrible spectacle, and more sudden then exspected, att which the enemie gave a great shout, and the besieged nothing dismayed betooke them to there armes, exspecting an assault, by omission of which the enemie lost a faire oppertunitie, the falling parte of the Tower having obstructed the passage to the gaite house soe that the guard there for present could have noe release from there friends. This fall of the Tower put the enemie into such heart and confidence, so that the next day, about six a'clocke in the evening, Meldrum writes to the Governor that hee intended that night to be maister of the Castle and all the woorkes, that if the Governor would Render, hee should have good conditions, but if hee would not, and that anie of his soldiors lost a drop of blood in the entrance, theire should not a person with in the Castle have quarter.

It happened the Governor att the present was verie busie in the ordering some affaires of the Garrison, and soe returned the Drummer with this message, that the next morning hee would returne him his answeare in writing. But Meldrum had made preparation for an assault, and his hott and haughtie spiritt could admitt noe delay, soe that about 9 a clocke that night the enemie beganne to assault the Gaitehouse, and having taken a woorke close with out the gaite,[66] endeavoured to mount the walls, but soe sharplie repulsed they were forced to retire leaving divers dead bodies in the woorke, and having of there partie slaine and wounded above two hundred in that encounter. The stones of the falne tower were throwne freelie amongst them and did the greatest execution.

The fall of the Tower had dislodged the Governor, his Ladie, and most of the gentlemen and officers of qualitie, whoe were forced to betake themselves to poore Cabbins reared against the walls and banckes in the Castle yeard, which though itt was a spatious place conteining 12 acres of ground, yet it was much annoyed and disquieted from the shipps, which was continnuallie playing with their ordnance into itt.

---

[66] Presumably, Cholmley meant Bushell's battery which the captain had built of earth and timber on the plateau outside the barbican wall and over-looking the main entrance to the castle. The new doorway which was cut through the barbican wall to give access to the battery can still be identified. In the London press, Bushell's battery became 'Bushell's Fort' or even 'Bishop's Fort' (e.g. BL, *TT*, E260(36): *Perfect Passages*, 13 May 1645). By 'Gaitehouse' Cholmley meant the barbican defences outside the castle dykes and beyond the drawbridges over them.

Meldrum finding there was noe taking the Castle till the passages were more open, beganne to batter verie furiousslie on all sides, but esspetiall at the gaitehouse, where in a shorte time the walls were so levelled, the besieged were forced to quitt the place, into which Meldrum drawes a hundred men, whoe were twise beaten out att 2 severall sallies (not by a third parte of the number), the first time commanded by Captaine Neueston,[67] the second by Captaine Hugh Cholmeley,[68] and with verie great execution. And though this place was of verie great importance beeing the cheife entrance into the Castle, yet itt laid unpossessed for 10 dayes together, those within the Castle not able to abide the enemies cannon played soe full upon itt, nor durst the enemie enter they had beene soe well knocked. But by the loss of the gaitehouse the besieged were forced to retyre nearer to the Castle, which gave (f.16v.) oppertunitie to the enemie | to draw up two demy Cannon to the ridge of a hill close to the gaite house, which beeing planted commanded the passages and principall woorkes in the Castle;[69] to prevent which the Governor commands Maior Crompton[70] to sallie out with 60 men, whoe beates the enemie out of three severall strong woorkes, fower score men in each woorke, dismounts the two demi Cannon and breakes all there carriages, which was as much as could be donn in that place and soe short a time, and was of soe great consequence as the cannon could not be made serviceable in Ten dayes, in which time the besieged had fortified them selves, and raised up divers new woorkes. Crompton had soe maulled and frighted those upon the guard as the rest with in the towne were readie to runn away, probable if itt had beene a little darker they had donn soe, and as it was the officers had much to doe to keepe the soldiers together. The place which Crompton was possessed of could not be kept, the enemies cannon plaid soe upon itt, and therefore having dismounted the Cannon the Governor commands his retreate. But in this scuffle Meldrum received a shott in att the bellie and out of the backe. Hee had often both in woords and letters protested hee would either take the Casstle or lay his bones before itt, and though hee dyed with in six dayes of this wound, hee before had esscaiped verie great dangers, for [before – *interlineated*] beside that of his fall hee had beene shot through the Codds and perfectlie recovered.[71] This was the last action of consequence not with standing the siedge continued above 12 weekes after;[72] for what by reason of sickness and want of

[67] Possibly Richard Nevinson of Colonel Sir Richard Dacre's horse (Newman, thesis, II, p.56). Cholmley's garrison included a large number of refugee Royalist officers from many different, broken northern regiments.

[68] There is no record elsewhere of a Captain Hugh Cholmley. However, Captains James and Richard Cholmley were with Sir Hugh in Scarborough in 1643 and 1644 (NYCRO, DC/SCB, G11).

[69] Once the walls of the barbican had been levelled by cannon shot, there would have been a clear field of fire from Bushell's battery across the castle dykes and into the approach to the keep.

[70] Major Thomas Crompton of Driffield took the Covenant and compounded in 1646. He was fined £887. According to the composition records, he owned valuable lands in Rimswell, Skerne, Hutton Cranswick, North Frodingham, Nafferton, Wansford and Driffield. He died in 1649 and was buried in York Minster (*Dugdale's Visitation*, iii, p.420; YRCP, ii, YASRS, xviii, p.191).
Crompton's surprise attack on and re-capture of the barbican on the night of 10 May was reported in London as the action of drunken madmen (BL, TT, E260(41): *A Perfect Diurnall*, 19 May 1645; *Ibid.*, TT, E260(39): *Perfect Passages*, 19 May 1645).

[71] Meldrum's corpse was taken to Hull and interred in the parish church there (BL, TT, E286(12): *The True Informer*, 30 May 1645). Earlier the Royalist press had reported that Meldrum had broken off the siege at the beginning of March and died as a result of his wounds the following month (*Mercurius Aulicus*, 8 Mar., 11 Apr. 1645, ORN, I, iii, p.455, iv, p.14).

[72] Meldrum died on 17 May and the surrender took place on 25 July, so the interval was only nine not twelve weeks. Meldrum's successor was Colonel Sir Matthew Boynton (1591–1647). He had fought alongside Sir Hugh at Guisborough and was destined to succeed him as governor of the castle and Member of Parliament of the borough of Scarborough.

poother[73] the besiedged had noe power, and those without, knowing that time must reduce the place, endeavored cheifelie to secure themselves, which they did in soe strong woorkes as itt was as difficult to take them as the Castle, in soe much the soldiors of the Castle would say to the enemie, 'doe you besiedg us or wee you'. The want of poother was a cause those with in could make noe use of there Cannon, which emboldened the enemie to make there approaches verie neare, and though hey did not assault they played verie furiouslie with there Cannon, which kept those with in full imployment to make up there daly breaches. And though the fortefying in Towne and Casstle had beene a great chardge, and the soldiors after there comming had not onelie 12 pence a weeke besides dyett, but sixpence for everie dayes labour, which together with a continnuall supply to the officers even for necessarie accomodations, beeing for above twelve mounthes space, had consumed a good some of monies, yet was theire not one pennie imposed upon any person with in the Garryson for the supporte of this more than 20 weekes billett for the common soldiors whilst they were in the towne. But the Governor boare the greatest parte of itt upon his owne chardge and purse, and att last when hee wanted money, and could not borrowe, having likewise solde the small quantitie of plaite hee had there to defray the publicke chardge, hee made a motion that everie one that had anie plaite in the garrison might contribute some part of it to the releife of soldiors. But those whoe had more them double to what was in the Garrison besides were not onelie unwilling to parte with any themselves, but underhand wrought upon others to be adverse to itt. Soe that rather then to breed the least disquiett by taking any mans goods against his will, the Governor made use of the plaite which belonged to some persons hee had perticuler interest in,[74] | which was cutt in peeces, and passed currant according to there severall weights, some of them had the stampe of a broaken Castle with this inscription *Caroli fortuna resurgam*.[75] By this meanes the officers and soldiors, which beganne to be verie clamourous, were for the present verie well settled, though this was not the last difficulty the governor had to wrastle with before the conclusion. For to speake truth all the actions from the enemie did not soe much trouble him as the pragmaticall practices of some personns with in his owne Garrison, whoe by there cunning and plauseable deportment had gained a good repute amongst the generalitie, making huge shew and pretences of zeale to the Kings cause, though the Governor had cautions from some hee ought to beleeve and give obedience to, not to trust those persons too farre in the businesses concerning the King. Besides whilst they were in the Towne the Governor had severall informations, and reason to beleeve they had beene practising with the enemie against his person, and to betray the towne. And that hee plainelie perceeved they tooke advantage of the straite and necessities the Garrison was in, to infuse discontents into the soldiors upon all occasions. Yet these perticulers beeing more certaine then clearely to be proved, the committing of quesstioning of them would but breed disstirbance or discontent in the Garrison, which was verie unseasonable, esspetiall there having a neere relation to

(f.17r.)

---

[73] [gun]powder.

[74] Some of the silver plate converted into coinage might have come from St Mary's church and been carried up to the castle by the vicar, William Simpson. Though Cholmley never mentioned Simpson by name, we know that he was Sir Hugh's private chaplain and steadfast ally (Ashcroft, *Records*, p.75). Only one piece of St Mary's silver communion plate which pre-dates the Civil Wars has survived them (J. Fawcett, *A Memorial of the Church of St Mary's, Scarboro'* (1850), p.88).

[75] The best examples of Scarborough's siege coins are in the British Museum. All were stamped with an outline of the keep; most of them carried only their face value, ranging from 4*d*. to 5 shillings; and at least one was inscribed 'OBS [*obsidium*] Scarbrough 1645'. Nearly all of the coins were very crudely cut and stamped (Rowntree, *History*, fig.69, opp. p.234).

some whoe had a command, and were really affected to the Kings cause, and soe to exsclude them out of the Garrison were to give more knowledge and advantage to the enemie. Soe that for these 2 reasons the Governor att the quitting the Towne admitted them into the Castle, and att both places connived att manie perticulers hee should not have donn had the enemie beene more remote.[76]

After the battle of Naisbie[77] the enemie sent a Drummer with a relation of itt, thincking thereby to move the Governor to a consideration of Rendering which had soe little influence as that when they solemnised the victory with bone fires, dischardging of Cannon, and drawing there foot close under the Castle walls to give vollies of small shott and making huge acclamations of Joy, those besiedged sounded there Trumpetts, beat up there Drums, shott of there musketts, and made such cryes and hollowing as they caused the enemie to decist from there jolletie. And for 8 weekes[78] after this the besiedged held out in hopes of reliefe, or att least to understand how affaires went with the King, for since there entring into the Castle they had noe intelligence but what came from the enemie, soe strictlie were they guarded both by Land and Sea, where the Shipps did not onelie barr all excess (but in resspect those with in wanted pouder) drew soe neere the shoare they impeaded there fetching of water from under the cliffes, by which they had beene supplyed though with much paines, difficulty, and perrill for divers Mounths past.

At lenght the miseries of the Castle began exceedinglie to multiply, halfe of the soldiors were either slaine or dead of the scurvy, of which disease neare the other halfe laid soe miserable handled they were scarce able to stirr hand or foot. There was but 25 of the common soldiors able to doe dutie, and the gentlemen and officers which (f.17v.) were glad to undertake it in | there roome, were almost tiered out of there skinns. There dyed tenn in a night, and manie layed two dayes unburied for want of helpe to carrie them to the grave. There was corne sufficient, but not hands to make the mills goe, in soe much that most in the Garrison had not eaten a bitt of bread for divers dayes before the render, and the Governor had often in person turned the Mills to gett himselfe bread. There was a well in the Castle but the water it affoorded us nott considerable,[79] and the shipps had now debarred access to that under the cliff, soe that manie horses had beene with out water for seaven dayes together, which occasioned contagion amongst them alsoe. There had not beene above 2 Barrells of poother for 2 Mounthes before,[80] and itt was now reduced to less then halfe a Barrell, soe that in a

[76] Since these traitors or potential defectors were still alive and active, perhaps Cholmley was wise not to name any of them. One leading Royalist townsman who seems to have changed his allegiance was Stephen Thompson, owner of the castle. According to his testimony before the Committee for Compounding, he had used every means he could to persuade the people of Scarborough to lay down their arms and invite Meldrum into the town. Two witnesses said that Stephen had advised Meldrum about the town's defences before he stormed it (*YRCP*, i, *YASRS* xv, pp.3–9). Dr Newman discussed the identity of these 'pragmatticall persons', but could not offer any names (Newman, thesis, i, p.480).
[77] The battle of Naseby took place on 14 June 1645.
[78] Again Cholmley lengthens the time scale, presumably to emphasize his resolution and exaggerate his resistance. After the news of the defeat at Naseby the garrison held out for only another six weeks.
[79] The deep well in the inner bailey near the keep had dried out long before 1645, and the well of Our Lady over by the sea cliff would have been running low by midsummer. It would also have been dangerously exposed to enemy fire from Parliament's warships lying off the headland.
[80] If the garrison had been so short of gunpowder for the past two months, then Boynton might have taken the castle by storm instead of waiting for its surrender. Presumably, either Boynton was ignorant of the weaknesses of the defenders, or he had orders not to spend any more lives on infantry assaults. According to the official report of the surrender, however, the castle yielded 'a great quantitie of Powder' (BL, *TT*, E294(17): *The Copie of a Letter*, 31 July 1645).

manner there was neither bread, water, nor poother, medecine for the sicke or wounded, and in leiu of guards there were not persons with in the walls able to stand sentynells, and in a weeke longer probable there would scarce have beene one able to looke over the walls. In this sad condition the Governor was intreated by divers gentlemen to take into consideration the weake esstaite of the Garrison, where upon hee summons to a meeting all Gentlemen and officers in the Garrison which were able to make appearance, where it is unanimouslie resolved requisite to enter into a treatie touching the Render of the Castle, for which the enemie having made some overtures a few dayes before, the Governor tooke hint there att to shew his inclination to treate. There was three Commissioners agreed on for either partie, whoe concluded upon these ensuing articles, which probable might have beene more for the advantage of the besiedged had not one of there[81] Commissioners (as the enemie confessed after the rendring of the Castle) disclosed the weake esstaite of the besiedged. |

Articles[82] agreed upon the 22th day of Julie 1645 betwixt the ho[noura]ble Sir (f.18r.) Mathew Boynton Knight and Barronett one of the military committee for the Northerne Association, Collonel Francis Lashells, Coll[onel] Simon Needham, commander in cheife of the forces for King and Parliament in Scarbrough, and the Ho[noura]ble Sir Hugh Cholmeley Knight and Barronett Governor of the Castle there concerning the Rendicion there of the persons before named /

1 That the castle be surrendered upon fryday next beeing the 25th day of this instant July, by 12 of the clocke att noone. That all armes, ordnance, ammunition, provisions and goods of what sorte soe ever now in and about the castle (except what is heere [under – *interlineated*] excepted) shall be saifelie delivered to the commander in cheife in Scarbrough, or to whome they shall appoint to the use of the King and Parliament.

2 That all [provisions – *crossed out*] prisoners now in the Castle be sett at libertie within six hours after the sealing of these articles.

3 That the Governor Sir Hugh Cholmeley and those officers, Gentlemen and soldiors who desire itt shall have a saife convoy from hence into holland or be saifelie convoyed to Newarke, whither they shall chuse and if any after there comming to Newarke, shall then resolve to goe to Holland giving notice thereof with in six dayes to the committy for military affaires att Yorke, they shall have passes from then to take shipping att Hull, Scarbrough or Bridlington key, and be accomodated paying usuall[83] raites soe that they take the first opportunitie of winde and shipping; and such other whoe desire them shall have passes from the said committy to goe to the King's army or any of his garrisons w[hi]ch they please not travelling above 20 in a companie, where the Governor or a collonel shall be in person, otherwayes not above 10 in a company the time to be permitted in there severall passes as the distance of the places they goe to shall

---

[81] Surely 'there' is a mistake for 'our'? Cholmley's three commissioners were presumably the same three officers who signed the surrender terms – Lt-Col. Thomas Gower, Major Thomas Crompton and Captain Richard Legard. Curiously, these names of the signatories to the treaty were heavily scored through in the manuscript. There is also a fourth name which seems to read Lieutenant Michael Constable.

[82] Sir Charles Firth chose not to have the Articles of Surrender printed since they were to be found already in Rushworth's *Historical Collections*, v, p.118 (*EHR*, xxxii, p.586). However, the discrepancies between the manuscript terms and Rushworth's are sufficient in number and significance to justify publication of the former for the first time.

[83] 'small' in Rushworth.

require, none of them passing through anie Garrison for King and Parliam[en]t if there be annother way.

4   That noe person what soe ever going from this Castle be plundered arreisted or stayed, uppon any ground or pretence what soe ever and in such caise uppon complaint made to the aforesd committee att Yorke to be speedlie redressed.

5   That the Ladie Cholmeley shall have libertie to live att her owne house att Whitbie, and enjoy such parte of her estate as is allowed by ordnance of Parliament, that shee may have two men servants and two horses to carry her selfe and such necessary things as shall bee granted her. |

(f.18v.)   6   That all Inferior officers, Common soldiers and others who desire to live at home, shall have passes granted them to that end; and shall not bee forced to take up armes against there mindes; that the sicke and wounded shall be provided for untill there recoverie, and then have passes to travell to what place they please [having] sufficient time allowed them for there iourney and two persons permitted to take caire of them.

7   That the Governor march on his owne horse with swoord, Pistoll, Carrabine[84] and defensive armes, and all feild officers on there owne horses with there swoords and Pistolls. All Captaines what soe ever, Leiutenants and Cornetts of horse in like manner three servants of the Governors, and one for everie feild officer aforesd, and all other officers and soldiers what soe ever on foote with out anie other armes but there swoords, and not to be compelled to march above tenn miles a day.

8   That all officers and soldiors may carry upon there personns what is reallie there owne; that nothing be carryed in cloath baggs or knappsackes[85] but there owne wearing apparrell, writings, evidences and bybles.[86]

9   That everie officer, Gentleman and cleargieman may have libertie to buy or lawfullie procure a travelling horse for himself and his servant. That sicke and laime men may enioy the same priviledge.

10 That all gentlemen of quallitie and cleargiemen have libertie to march, Gentlemen with there servants,[87] that none of them carry above 5 pounds in monie or the like value in plaite about there persons and nothing in there cloakebaggs but as is expressed in the eight article.

11 That there be no fraud or deceipt what so ever used in spoyling or imbezeling any thing before mencioned or comprized in these articles; and if anie of them be vyolated the partie of offending shalbe delivered to the commander in cheife where the fact shall be done to give satisfaction for this offence. And his perticuler act shall not be understood as a breach of these articles not be preiudiciall to anie [other][88]

[The next seven lines of the manuscript have been heavily scored through, but presumably they contained the names of Cholmley's senior officers who had subscribed to the articles of surrender. The official notification of the surrender from Major-General Poyntz, Parliament's governor of York, contained a twelfth article: '. . . There were about 200 in the Castle, and 100 came in to the Parliament. There was taken in the Castle of Scarborough viz. Five brasse Peeces of Ordnance, some Field peeces, 1000 Armes, a great quantitie of Powder, Match, Bullets, and other Ammunition, all Cholmleyes bag and baggage.'] |

---

[84] 'Carrabine' was omitted by Rushworth.
[85] 'snapsacks' in Rushworth.
[86] 'bills' in Rushworth.
[87] 'swords' in Rushworth.
[88] '[other]' is printed as 'other' in Rushworth.

Though there were manie hundreds of Cannon shott from land and the shipps,   (f.19r.)
there was not above five men killed with cannon bullett, but the stones which the
cannon beat of from the walls killed verie manie. There was one soldior had his hatt
shott of from his head with a bullett of fower and thirtie pound weight, and the haire
and skinne onelie taken of and noe other harme, but that hee was a little dissie that
night, and the next day upon dutie. Not withstanding this esscaipe hee was after
killed, beeing shoote in the head with a muskett bullett.

At the render of the Castle there was a hundred and fowerscore sicke personns, of
which most of them not able to move, but were carryed out in blancketts, and many
of them dyed before they gott into the Towne. Now as the scurvie which grew to be
as contagious as the Plague reigned amongst the besieged,[89] soe those with out were
nott free from mortalitie in another kinde, for besides the manie common soldiors
that lost there lives in this siedge, Meldrum and nine other officers (the meanest
beeing a Captaine) were slaine heere, and one Captaine Zacherie[90] that commanded
in cheife in the shipps.

Those which had abilitie to march out of the Castle with out helpe, though manie
of them infirme in health, were about threescore, most gentlemen and officers, most
of them had horses, but the entrance into the Castle was soe barracadoed as they were
forced to make passage through the maine wall into the ditch, where the besiedged
passed out, the Governor bringing up the reare.

The articles were verie iustlie observed, and they marched that night to there quarters,
fower miles from Scarbrough, the Governor intending then to go to immediatlie to
his Majestie, but comming to Selbie 10 myles beyond Yorke, hearing the King was
then in the remoatest part of Wales, the Scottish army interposed, and finding himself
in verie ill health, and unfitt either to take soe long a March or to betake himself to
another Garrison, hee committed those personns which desired to continnue in
service to be conducted by Collonel Crossland[91] to Newarke, which was then with in
a dayes march and himselfe with Major Crompton went for France.[92]

---

[89] Cholmley's reference to scurvy is confirmed in other sources (BL, *TT*, E294(15): *An Exact Relation*, 25
July 1645; *Ibid.*, E294(11): *Parliament's Post*, 23–29, July 1645). Before long there was a local and doubtful
claim that Scarborough's spa waters had brought speedy cure to those survivors who had suffered from
scurvy (R. Wittie, *Scarbrough Spaw* (1660), p.204). Like many other towns in the summer of 1645,
Scarborough was visited by the plague.

[90] Captain Zachery's death must have occurred towards the end of the siege, but there is no record of how
he met his death, whether from Cholmley's artillery, or, more likely, as a result of an engagement at sea
with Royalist men-of-war trying unsuccessfully to relieve the castle. In contrast to the second siege of
1648, Parliament's naval blockade of the castle was tight and effective: several Royalist warships were
captured when they attempted to break through it (Powell and Timings (eds.), *Documents Relating to the
Civil War 1642–1648* (Navy Records Society, 1963), p.220).

[91] This is Cholmley's only mention of Colonel Sir Jordan Crosland (1618–70) of Helmsley, who was
released from imprisonment a second time so that he could join a third beleaguered garrison at Newark.
Crosland compounded in 1649 having fought through both wars. After the Restoration, Sir Jordan
became a member of Scarborough's First Twelve and, until his death, one of the borough's Members of
Parliament and governor of the castle there (YRCP, ii, YASRS xviii, p.198; NYCRO, DC/SCB, A2,
Book of Elections 1645–63; *CSPD*, 1660–1, pp.290, 327). Toby Jenkin was also a leader of the party that
went to Newark (Newman, thesis, i, p.482).

[92] In his Memoirs Sir Hugh wrote that he took ship at Bridlington for Holland (ff.28r.–28v.; see above,
pp.108–9) and only later passed on to France.

APPENDICES

Appendix A: Sir Hugh Cholmley 1600–1657: Chronology

1600	Born 22 July at Roxby castle, Thornton-on-the-Hill.
1603–7	At Ganton, home of uncle John Legard.
	At the age of seven survived a riding fall on Pexton Moor.
1608	On his eighth birthday at Whitby saved from a fierce sow by the butler.
1611	Entered Beverley Grammar School as a boarder. His mother died of a fever caught from him at the home of the Hothams at Scorborough.
1613	Went up to Jesus College, Cambridge with his tutor, Mr Petty.
1617	On the death of Sir Henry, his grandfather, he left Cambridge and returned to Yorkshire for a year.
1618–21	Three years spent wastefully at Gray's Inn. Lodgings in Fleet Street.
1622	Marriage arranged with Elizabeth, daughter of Sir William Twysden.
1624	Sat as Scarborough's MP in last Parliament of James I. Richard, his eldest son, born.
1625	Returned again for Scarborough to sit in first Parliament of Charles I. William, his second son, born.
1626	Took over his father's indebted estate and came North to live in Whitby Abbey gatehouse. Re-elected MP for Scarborough. Knighted.
1627	His daughter, the first Elizabeth, born.
1629	Sir Hugh and his family moved into their new home, Fyling Old Hall.
1630	Death of his eldest son, Richard.
1631	Death of his father, Sir Richard.
1632	Became JP for the North Riding. Successful petition for a new west pier at Whitby. Birth of his third son, Hugh, after death of his first daughter, Elizabeth.
1633	Returned to Fyling after winter at Langton on the Wolds.
1634	Sold Fyling Old Hall and deer park to Sir John Hotham. Birth of daughter, Ann. Family moved back to Whitby Abbey gatehouse until main house improvements were finished.
1635	Confrontation at the Malton quarter sessions with Sir Thomas Hoby.
1636	Dunkirkers and Dutchmen at Whitby. Family moved into Abbey House. Sir Hugh became deputy-lieutenant of the North Riding and commissioned colonel of the trained bands of Whitby, Scarborough, Pickering and Ryedale.
1638	Birth of daughter, the second Elizabeth. Family stayed with the Yelvertons at Easton Maudit in Northants.
1639	First Bishops' War. Incident on Pexton Moor.
1640	Elected to Short Parliament as MP for Scarborough. Outspoken protest in the Commons against Ship Money and militia charges. Open quarrel with his former patron, Earl of Strafford. Dismissed from all commissions and summoned before Privy Council. Assigned all Whitby estate except Fyling to trustees. Leading Yorkshire petitioner during second Bishops' War. Elected to sit in Long Parliament.

1641   Sir Hugh's family came south from Whitby to live in London while he attended the House of Commons. Active in the trial and condemnation of Strafford. Voted for the Grand Remonstrance but against root and branch reform of the Church of England. Created first baronet.

1642   One of Parliament's Commissioners to King Charles at York. Accepted Parliament's commission to hold Scarborough. Advanced to Stamford Bridge but refused to join Fairfaxes at Tadcaster.

1643   Won battle at Guisborough, but changed sides and took Scarborough with him after the Queen had landed at Bridlington. Lady Elizabeth and two daughters arrived at Scarborough from London. Cholmley commanded cavalry in the unsuccessful royalist siege of Hull.

1644   Cholmley refused to go into exile with the Marquess of Newcastle after royalist defeat at Marston Moor.

1645   Two daughters sent to safety of Holland. Scarborough town and harbour lost to Parliament's troops under Sir John Meldrum. Cholmley held castle for the king from February until surrender in July.
        After surrender Lady Elizabeth stayed behind in Yorkshire while Sir Hugh went abroad, first to Holland, then to France.
        Young Hugh left St Paul's school to join his father in Paris. William arrived in Paris from Italy.

1646   Sir Hugh moved to Rouen. William returned to Whitby to manage estate.

1647   Whole Cholmley family reunited at Rouen. Sir Hugh wrote his three Memorials on the Civil War for Sir Edward Hyde.

1649   Sir Hugh followed his wife back to London and in the summer returned to Whitby. New alum works opened at Saltwick Bay. Composition fine of £850 paid in full. Sir Hugh arrested at Abbey House on charge of debt but escaped at Malton and travelled to London.

1650   Charges against Sir Hugh dropped. His son William awarded damages for ill-treatment.

1651   Cholmley took up residence with his brother-in-law, Sir Roger Twysden, at Roydon Hall, East Peckham in Kent.
        Eight weeks imprisoned in Leeds castle.

1652–4 Summers spent at Whitby. New Gardens enclosed and planted.

1653   William married Katherine Hotham.

1654   Daughter Ann married Richard Stephens.

1655   Death of Lady Elizabeth. Sir Hugh left Whitby for last time.

1655–6 Sir Hugh wrote his Memoirs at Roydon Hall.

1657   Died 30 November and buried next to Elizabeth in St Michael's at East Peckham.

Appendix B: Writ of Extent for Cholmley Estate,
11 November 1626

The most informative property document concerning the Cholmley estate at the time of Sir Hugh's takeover is a Writ of Extent, dated 11 November 1626 (NYCRO, ZPK 11) (MIC 1628). As the preamble explains, Sir Richard and his son and heir, Hugh, had acknowledged a debt of one thousand pounds to Robert Harrison of London before Sir Henry Hobart, Chief Justice of the Court of Common Pleas, as early as December 1624. Since the debt remained wholly unpaid, the sheriff of Yorkshire, Sir Thomas Wentworth, had been instructed to make inquisition of Cholmley property in October 1626. The property described in the Writ of Extent was then to be delivered to Robert Harrison until the debt to him was settled.

The lengthy original is in Latin. Below is a translated abstract of the property described. For easier identification some spellings of place-names have been modernised.

In WHITBY MANOR John Noble is occupant of a messuage and closes called Heslerton's farm, four closes of pasture called Great Saltwick, and two closes of meadow and two of arable called the Flatts. / Sir Richard Cholmley occupies one close of arable and one pasture called Haggit Howe and Oldstead; three closes of pasture called Moorgate Leas and Horse Close; one meadow called Petlington Field; five closes of pasture and arable called Petlington Field Closes; a meadow called Cliff Close; and a pasture called Alms [House] Close. / Sir Richard also has three mills, of water, wind and horse; and twenty cottages with their gardens. / William Chapman is tenant of Spital Bridge Closes, one meadow and one pasture. / Sir Richard has two pasture closes called Abbey Garths; a meadow and a pasture called Barkerwife's Closes; and a meadow called Baxter's Close. / William Norrison is occupant of three meadows and a pasture close called Stripes. / Henry Sutton and Robert Ricatson have three arable lands called Robin Hood Stones. / Joshua Jackson and Leonard Russell have two pasture closes called Highfield Houses. / Total annual value: £13 6s. 8d.

In HAWSKER fourteen messuages with gardens and thirty bovates of arable, pasture and meadow in the tenure and occupation of: William Browne senior, William Browne junior, Thomas Coward, William Nattris, Robert Munckman, Edward Coverdale, Robert Story, William Fletcher, James Russell, Henry Russell, John Watson, James Russell, William Norrison and Henry Robinson. Total annual value: £4.

In STAINSACRE thirteen messuages with gardens and twenty-six bovates of arable, pasture and meadow in the tenure and occupation of: Leonard Russell, Thomas Aclam, John Sutton, Joshua Jackson, Francis Barker, Jefferson Wife, William Norrison, Sutton Wife, Henry Sutton, John Bolton, Nicholas Ventrods, Christopher Colson and Bolton Wife. Total annual value: £6 6s. 8d.

In FYLING MANOR: In Fyling, Fyling Raw and Fyling Thorpe, fifteen messuages with gardens and twenty bovates of pasture and meadow in the tenure and occupation of: Anthony Potter, William Cockrell, Oliver Robson, Margaret Postgate, Robert

Sheming, Robert Harrison, Thomas Archer, William Harrison, Peter Dale, John Halder, John Stanerig, William Huntrods, Francis Munkman, John Marshall and John Watson.
Total annual value: 40s.

In Fyling, Fyling Raw and Fyling Thorpe and Robin Hood's Bay, forty cottages and gardens in the tenure and occupation of: Richard Lawne, Robert Lawne, Robinson Wife, William Colson, John Booth, Joshua Storme, Robert Farley, William Trot, William Gibson, Leonard Brand, Peter Dale, George Johnson, Russell Wife, James Pearson, Ricatson Wife, Thomas Sharp, William Sharp, William Ricatson, Robert Dobson, Stoope Wife, Foster Wife, Peter Postgate, Hicke Wife, Isabell Hill, William Hill, Edward Dale, Storme Wife, John Carlyle, Thomas Taylor, Henry Storme, Thomas Lyndsly, Joshua Harrison, Gregory Standridge, Francis Cockrill, John Coke, Thomas Pate, William Howetson, Peter Gibson, Thomas Johnson and John Watson.
Total annual value: 40s.

In WHITBY [town] thirty-six cottages and gardens in the tenure and occupation of: Thomas Wood, Thomas Bilcliff, Bagwith Wife, John Sutton, Henry King, Gregory Barker, James Awder, William Chapman, Thomas Smith clerk, John Noble, Russell Wife, Robert Nightingall, Lawrence Hird, Henry Prestman, Gregory Marshall, John Chapman, Christopher Bagwith, Lawrence Haslam, Crosby Wife, William Marten, John Stephenson, Newton Wife, Marmaduke Newton, Linskell Wife, Robert Salmon, John Wood, Christopher Harrison, John Marten, Christopher Sunley, Gawin Noble, Richard Lumberd, Christopher Thackwray, John Hutchenson, William Beck, Henry Spenley and John Boyes.
Total annual value: 36s.

In NORMANBY a messuage and six bovates of land, meadow and pasture in the tenure and occupation of Thomas Stanecliff, Matthew Stanecliff and Richard Stanecliff.
Total annual value: 20s.

In STOUPE BROW and THORNY BROW six messuages and ten bovates of land, meadow and pasture in the tenure and occupation of Robert Gurdon, George Hoggard, William Lowson, Thomas Pate, Thomas Huntrods and Richard Beswick.
Total annual value: 40s.

One messuage with closes in the parish of Fyling called FLASH [FLASK] in the tenure of Sir Richard Cholmley and another with all its closes of meadow and pasture called WRAGBY in the tenure of George Hoggard.
Total annual value: 20s.

In GROSMONT ten messuages with meadow and pasture land in the occupation of Sir Richard and Hugh Cholmley, Robert Milnes, Lawrence Cooke, John Tod, Robert Peycock, Sheming Wife, James Ricatson, Thomas Ricatson, Robert Harland and William Harland.
Total annual value: £6 13s. 4d.

Two water mills in GROSMONT and EGTON in the tenure of Sir Richard Cholmley valued at £2 13s. 4d.

In ROXBY one capital messuage with six closes of pasture and meadow called Westclose, Northclose, Dunkill, Almasse Close, Butgarth and Dunkhill Hill in the tenure of Sir Richard Cholmley and valued a 40s. a year.

One messuage in Roxby called Bensons House and all the closes of meadow and pasture belonging to it.

In the MARISHES of Pickering and Thornton three pasture closes called Moore Close, Midsyke and Agnes Close.

In THORNTON and FARMANBY five bovates of arable, pasture and meadow in the tenure of Sir Richard Cholmley.
Annual value: 40s.

In the manor of KINGTHORPE ten messuages and twenty-two bovates of arable, pasture and meadow in the tenure of Sir Richard Cholmley, Henry Browne, John Kettlewell, Alan Wardall, John Nattris, William Read, Thomas Grayson, George Thomson, Roger Kid, Robert Pearson.

Two closes of meadow in Kingthorpe called Skellamore Closes and two others of wood called Stonegate Banks occupied by Sir Richard Cholmley.
Annual value: £4.

In LOCKTON three cottages and gardens with one bovate of pasture and meadow occupied by Robert Pearson and Robert Merry worth 5s.

In RAMSDALE SIDE in the parish of Fyling four messuages and gardens and four bovates of pasture and meadow occupied by James Woodhouse, Margaret Harrison, Nicholas Coltas, George Law and William Lawnd.
Annual value: 20s.

Three water mills in Fyling occupied by George Conyers and Margaret Harrison valued at 13s. 4d.

Sixteen pasture closes called Intakes on FYLING MOORS in the tenure of Richard Beswick, William Law, Thomas Archer and Robert Gibson.
Annual value: 30s.

One messuage in LARPOOL in Whitby with the following attached closes:
    one meadow called Gallows Close
    one arable called White Leaze
    one meadow called Whitefield
    two pasture called Ox Pasture
    one pastures called Broomfield
    one arable called Hillfield
    one pasture called Lockwoods
    one arable adjoining called [blank]
    one pasture called Henry Nobles
    two meadows called Ingfields
    one arable called [blank]
    one pasture called Long Riggs

All in the occupation of James Lockwood and Henry Noble.
Annual value: 33s. 4d.

[The above account of Larpool has been taken from a Writ of Assignment dated 23 June 1627 (NYCRO, ZPK 13), which in this particular instance provides more detail than ZPK 11.]

In FYLING one close of meadow called Fyling Bottoms occupied by Thomas Archer, Peter Dale and Robert Sheming.
Six bovates of land occupied by William Beachamp, Thomas Allatson, Widow Trewhit, Richard Munkman and William Munkman.
Ten bovates of land in STOUPE BROW and THORNY BROW in the tenure of Francis Cockrell, Matthew Redman, Matthew Watson, Thomas Huntrods and John Huntrods.
Annual value: 20s.

In the manor of WHITBY LATHES one messuage and a pasture called Highfield, another called [blank – called Galings in ZPK 13], a meadow called Jackcroft and a pasture called Butsyke, all in the tenure of Francis Dickinson.
Also in Whitby Lathes another messuage and closes called Beaconfield of pasture, Cottings of meadow, Little Paddock, a meadow, and two closes called Whitby Lathes Close and Turbut Sykes. All in the tenure of Ralph Dickinson.
Annual value: £6 13s. 4d.
Also all those pasture closes called Coatehouse grounds, Matthew Stanecliffs Closes, Highfield and one of meadow called Great Oldstead, and six closes of meadow called Wheeldale Closes in Whitby Lathes in the tenure of Sir Richard and Hugh Cholmley.
And in Whitby, three closes of meadow and pasture called Matthew Whites Closes in the tenure of John White.
Annual value: 50s.

A capital messuage called FYLING HALL and eight other messuages in Fyling with closes called Bownell, Ricatsons Close, Great Cowlecroft, a meadow, one arable called Highfield, and four of pasture called Swallow Head, Horse Close, Aslabyes Moor Close and Barwicks Moore Close.
Five closes of arable, meadow and pasture called Great Park Withes, Little Park Withes, Tods Close, Lamb Field and Low Park.
Two closes called Hagget Wath Closes.
Five closes called Margaret Harrison farm closes.
Two closes called Park Lawn and Park Gate.
All those closes called Park Gate Farm.
One meadow close called Little Cowlecroft.
All the lands, meadow and pasture called Middlewood Fields.
All the land, meadow and pasture called St Iles [Ives?].
All those closes, arable and pasture, called Old Walls and Heslerig.
One close of meadow called High Park or Hither Park.
One close of meadow called New Lands.
All those closes of meadow and pasture called Brockholes.
Two closes of pasture called Hagget Wath and Calfe Close.

All in the tenure of George Conyers, gent.
Annual value: £9.

Four messuages in Fyling called SOUTHWELL HOUSES with all their closes of meadow and pasture in the tenure and occupation of Henry Toutvile, Robert Pate, Robert Fletcher, Stephen Huntrods.
Annual value: £4.

One other messuage called STOUPE FARM with all its closes of land, meadow and pasture in the tenure and occupation of William Lowson and Richard Lowson.
Annual value: £3.

One other messuage called MIDDLEWOOD with all its closes of meadow and pasture in Fyling parish occupied by Marshall Wife, John Marshall and John Booth.
Annual value: £1 6s. 8d.

[Total value of estate: £83 7s. 8d.]

Appendix C: Recovery Deed Listing Cholmley Properties, 5 September 1638

A deed to lead the uses of a recovery, which survives only as a Burnett transcript (Whitby LPS, PB 1784), was endorsed by Sir Hugh Cholmley, 5 September 1638. The following is an abstract of the Burnett transcript, listing some of Sir Hugh's properties and tenants at that time. For easier identification some place-names have been modernised.

WHITBY TOWN: [East Side] Burgage messuages or tenements with back garths on KIRK-GATE occupied by John Wood, Francis Wilkinson, Thomas Lowson, Christopher Sunley, Henry Smithe, James Chapman, Henry Hirde, Gawin Noble, John Sutton, Henry Spenley, William Robinson, William Hobton, Thomas Bilcliffe, Michael Rowsbie [14]

Burgage messuages or tenements with back garths in CROSS-GATE occupied by Henry Linge, George Barker, Henry Watson, Richard Carter, Andrew Craven, James Alder, Robert Grainge [7]
Five wastes or tofts in Crossgate occupied by Marmaduke Hutcheson, one adjoining the land of Christopher Blenkhorne, one adjoining the land of John Leallam, one adjoining the tenement of Andrew Craven, and the coalgarth occupied by William Wigginer

One tenement occupied by Jacob Hudson and a stable by Thomas Bilcliffe in GRAPE LANE

Tenements with garths in BRIDGEGATE occupied by Isaac Newton, William Jackson, Thomasin Potter, William Heron, Alice Russell [5]
One messuage or storehouse with two shops in Bridgegate now occupied by Sir Hugh Cholmley

Tenements with garths in SANDGATE occupied by Marmaduke Newton, Richard Dodds, John Wilkinson, Thomas Stephenson [4]
Two tofts or wastes occupied by Isaac Newton and one called Newgarth Staith [west side of Sandgate]

One messuage occupied by Henry Dickinson in BREWSTER LANE

WHITBY TOWN: [West Side] Burgage messuages or tenements with back garths in BAX-TERGATE occupied by Christopher Bagwith, Jeremy Rotheram, George Meggeson, Robert Carlell, Thomas Ripley, James Potter, Widow Applebie [7]
One toft on Walker Sands in the occupation of Widow Toes

Tenements with back garths in FLOWERGATE occupied by Mathew Yeoman, William Martin, Dionis Raughton, Richard

Jackson (Imployde for the Correction House), Thomas Barnard, Francis Barnard, William Haines, Elizabeth Crosbie, Thomas Shipton [9] / One toft or garth at the higher end of Flowergate occupied by Thomas Barnard

One messuage in the OLD MARKET PLACE occupied by John Glover

On ST ANN'S STAITH messuages occupied by Widow Boyes and Richard Dobson and three shops in the occupation of George Marsingale, John Glover, Henry Sneaton

Messuages with garths in HAGGLESEY GATE [HAGGERSGATE] occupied by John Leedell and John Walker and a stable occupied by John Lumsley
One waste or toft called the Old Coal Garth
One waste or toft called Well Garth in the occupation of William Dodds

On BURTREE [BUTTERY] CRAGGS two wastes or tofts called Burtree Craggs and the Lime Kiln

In ROBIN HOOD'S BAY thirty-two cottages occupied by the following tenants: Thomas Taylor, Edward Robinson, John Ward, John Cockrell, Robert Lotherington, Edward Craven, Christopher Linne, James Robinson, Christopher Montfoot, Robert Trewhitt, George Linne, John Rickeson, Thomas Bedlington, William Linne, Elizabeth Rickeson, William Gibson, William Huntrods, Lawrence Syner, Widow Sander, Widow Mooresome, William Trott, Robert Rickeson, Lawrence Grainge, Mathew Robinson, James Huntrods, John Wilkes, John Hill, Christopher Rickeson, Peter Dale, Widow Booth, John Marshall, John Dodds and two stables occupied by Thomas Taylor.

In FYLING seven cottages with backsides or intakes each in the occupation of: Thomas Newton, Thomas Postgate, Widow Foster, Widow Belt, Widow Hicke, James Helme, Thomas Lindsley and one other with a shop in the occupation of Leonard Willson.

In BONSIDE DALE [also written as BONSIDALE at this time but now obsolete, it probably included Spring Hill, Thorny Brow, Howdale and Cook House] others in the occupation of John Cooke, George Stainrigge, Henry Storme, Henry Rickeson, Edward Daile, Widow Bancke, Widow Storme younger, Christopher Dale, Richard Staincliffe, Thomas Sharpe (2), Robert Monckman, Francis Monckman (with intake), Jeffrey Bayley, William Cockerill

One close in FYLING in the occupation of John Wilkes and five others with the same tenant called Shiminge Close, Inge Close, Shortsie Close, and two others called Causer [Causeway] Closes

In the occupation of Robert Lawe a little intake near NORMANBY and a close called Pitt Close

Appendices D–H: The Cholmley leases

The Cholmley family's long leases granted from the 1630s for periods between 900 and 1000 years, were first recorded on a parchment roll about 17 feet long in 1768. In 1827, after the death of Henrietta Cholmley, the family's clerks copied the contents of this roll into a book and annotated the text to identify the properties and the tenants and terms of the leases. This book is known as the Cholmley Leases Book and is now held in the County Record Office at Northallerton, reference ZCG(W) (MIC 1286).

A few of the originals recorded in the Cholmley Leases Book have survived in bundles of deeds of individual properties and many of their counterparts have survived in the Cholmley-Strickland archives. However, before these documents eventually reached the County Record Office, they had been carefully copied by Percy Burnett at Whitby, and are now to be found amongst his massive collection of transcripts in the library of Whitby's Literary and Philosophical Society at Pannett Park Museum.

Along with the Cholmley Leases Book, Burnett also found an old plan of Whitby town, drawn in diagrammatic form on paper watermarked 1824, which identified the long leases. Burnett made a fair copy of the original (PB 4199), and a tracing of it on a reduced scale may be obtained from the County Record Office, reference DN 184.

The following appendices, D, E, F, G, H and the town maps of Whitby, are therefore derived from these three major sources – the Cholmley Leases Book, Burnett's transcripts of deeds, and the old town plan of Whitby. In Appendices D and E, where no PB reference is given, the source is the Cholmley Leases Book.

Appendix D: Cholmley's pre-war sales of land in Whitby town

PB MS.	Date	Property	Leases Book No.	Price	Purchaser
	1638				
1785	October 13	S. side of Bridgegate	46	£95 os. od.	Wm Jackson, ten.
1381	13	old coalgarth, Haggleseagate	27	—	Isaac Newton, gent.
47	16	wellgarth, Haggleseagate	26	24 0 0	Wm Dodds, boatwright
	18	S. side of Baxtergate	39	80 0 0	Chris. Bagwith, ten.
	29	W. side of Crossgate	24	16 0 0	Hen. Sneaton, tailor
4273	30	W. side of St Ann's Staith	45	86 13 4	Rob. Mason, gent.
	30	N. side of Bridgegate	42	25 0 0	Thomasin Potter, ten.
4159	30	E. side of Sandgate	—	—	Isaac Newton, gent.
	1639				
	January 5	E. side of Southgate	35	40 0 0	James and Wm Lockwood
	February 2	W. side of Southgate	31	40 0 0	Chas Craven
1787	2	E. side of Crossgate	53	30 0 0	Thomas Moon, yeoman
	2	E. side of Southgate	33	30 0 0	Jo. Dunnington
1324	2	E. side of Kirkgate	36	26 13 4	Miles Cosins, gent.
	11	E. side of Crossgate	25	36 0 0	Rob. Norrison

Ref.	Date	Location	No.	Price £ s. d.	Buyer
	.. 16	E. side of Kirkgate	28	25 0 0	Will. Monkman
	.. 18	E. side of Kirkgate	7	86 13 4	Gawin Noble
742	.. 18	S. side of Bagdale beck	–	12 0 0	Hen. Linskill, tanner
966	.. 18	N. side of Flowergate	15	19 0 0	Mat. Sneaton
	.. 18	N. side of Flowergate	10	40 0 0	John Martyn
6037	.. 18	E. side of Kirkgate	38	60 0 0	Rich. Linskel, smith.
6037A	.. 19	E. side of Kirkgate	65	16 0 0	Fran. Repentance
					Wilkinson and Isabel Smales
	.. 23	W. side of Crossgate	37	16 0 0	Rob. Aire
	.. 28	E. side of Crossgate	32	45 0 0	Will. Sneaton, tailor
6036A	March 20	S. side of Baxtergate	48	22 10 0	Rob. Morrell
	.. 21	N. side of Bridgegate	63	—	Thomas Bower
	.. 26	E. side of Sandgate	47	43 0 0	Lawrence Newton
1769	.. 29	W. side of St Ann's Staith	30	61 0 0	Jo. Woodhouse
6028	April 1	W. side of Kirkgate	52	58 0 0	Ralph Rickinson
	October 10	S. side of Flowergate	49	80 0 0	Thomas Cass
	.. 16	S. end of Haggleseagate	44	20 0 0	Will. Pearson
1640	May 20	N. side of old marketplace	50	35 0 0	Rich. Huntroyds
	September 5	W. side of Southgate	29	15 0 0	Roger Huntroyds

total £1183 10s. 0d.

Appendix E: Cholmley's post-war sales of land in Whitby town

PB MS.	Date	Property	Leases Book No.	Price	Purchaser
	1649				
4199	February 19	S. side of Baxtergate	40	—	Hen. Sugisson
294	May 3	waste on S. side of Flowergate	21	—	Thomas Bower
	1653				
753	January 30	S. of new marketplace	6	£45 0s. 0d.	Rich. Sampson, smith
	February 1	E. side of Kirkgate	18	70 0 0	Jo. Wilkinson, tailor
995	.. 2	N. side of Flowergate	—	45 0 0	Wm Linskill, tanner
	.. 15	S. side of Grape Lane	13	60 0 0	Fran. Garland, master mariner
	May 20	W. side of Kirkgate	14	50 0 0	Hen. Dickenson
	1654				
6086	August 26	S. side of Baxtergate	22	41 0 0	Tho. Rogers, mason
	September 6	N. side of Flowergate	5	80 0 0	Sam. Nellist, master mariner

	Date		Location		Amount	Purchaser
	..	9	N. side of Baxtergate	12	25 0 0	Edmd Redman
	..	20	behind Cliff Lane bakehouse	23	36 0 0	Geo. Langtoft and Wm Coates
	..	25	next to Correction Ho. Cliff Lane	2	—	Fran. Wilson
2710	..	25	Correction House in Flowergate	3/4	25 0 0	Wm Martyn, whitesmith
	..	28	bakehouse on Cliff Lane	1	—	Rob. and Joan Breckon
5	..	29	E. side of Southgate	11	50 0 0	Wm Ventriss, labourer
	October 17		N. side of Baxtergate	9	60 0 0	Chris. Bagwith
	November 6		W. side of High Street	34	11 0 0	Sessily Salmon
	..	11	N. side of Flowergate	19	47 0 0	Geo. Vaughan
	..	15	S. side of Brewster Lane	20	44 0 0	Hen. Dickinson
	1656 September 20		Bagdale side	17	28 0 0	Geo. Bennison
1244	1657 October 26		Tentergarth waste, Cliff Lane	8	11 0 0	Wm Peacock, gardener
				total	£728 0s. 0d.	

Appendix F: Cholmley's pre-war sales of land in Robin Hood's Bay, Fyling Thorpe, Raw and Dales

PB MS.	Date	Property	Price	Purchaser
	1628			
5946	February 16	2-acre intake in Fylingthorpe	£6 13s. 0d.	Tho. Taylor, fishmn
	1632			
5985	October 22	2 acres and cott. Fyling Raw	18 0 0	Peter Browne, panymn
	1638			
5962	October 15	cott. and 3 closes Fylingdales	20 0 0	Rich. Harland, husbdmn
5965	.. 16	4 acres (cott. garth and intake) Fyling Raw	13 6 8	Greg. Monkman, yeoman
5970	.. 20	cott., garth, shop, intake Fyling Raw	30 0 0	Leo. Wilson, smith
5948	.. 29	cott., 2 closes RHB and Middlewood	51 0 0	Jo. Watson, yeoman
5974	.. 29	cott. in Fylingthorpe	30 0 0	Tho. Knowles, yeoman
5971	.. 29	2 cotts. in RHB	26 13 4	Rob. Trewhitt, fishmn
5960	November 5	2-acre meadow betwn RHB and Fylingthp	24 0 0	Rob. Stanerigg, panymn
5963	.. 5	Shiming Close, Fylingthorpe	64 0 0	Geo. Conyers, gent.
5984	.. 6	cott. and garth Fyling Raw	16 0 0	Wm Huntrodds, tailor

5969	.. 6	4 cotts. RHB, 1 close Fylingdales	Tho. Taylor, panymn	128 0 0
5987	.. 12	2 cotts. and garths Fylingthorpe	Jo. Harland, yeoman	42 0 0
5967	December 14	2 cotts., plot, stable, garth in RHB	Peter Daile, yeoman	48 0 0
	1639			
5947	February 2	cott. and garth in RHB	Jo. Wilkes, yeoman	20 0 0
5957	.. 2	cott. in Bonsidale	Art. Dickinson, yeoman	29 0 0
5961	March 17	2 closes in Fyling Raw	Wm Law, yeoman.	60 0 0
5959	.. 23	cott., garth, intake, Normanby	Wm Temple, marr.	21 0 0
5986	.. 23	cott., garth, intake in Fyling Raw	Tho. Sharpe, weaver	21 0 0
5983	.. 25	2 closes in Fyling Raw	Wm Watson, yeoman	108 0 0
5969	September 28	cott. and intake at Normanby	Rich. Harland	24 12 6
5966	October 5	cott. in RHB	Rob. Stanerigg, yeoman	10 0 0
5966	.. 5	2 cotts. in RHB	Jo. Marshall, yeoman	10 0 0
	1641			
5958	September 1	close in Fylingdales called Intake	Rich Harland, yeoman	10 0 0
1134	November 11	little house, teafall or kitchen[?]	Tho Wright	—

total £821 5s. 6d.

Appendix G: Cholmley's post-war sales of land in Robin Hood's Bay, Fyling Thorpe, Raw and Dales

PB MS.	Date	Property	Price	Purchaser
	1649			
5993	August 1	2 tens. in Fylingthorpe	£20 os. od.	Rob. Trewhitt, fishmn
	1650			
544	June 15	close and 2 acres of meadow Fylingdales	25 0 0	Jo. Stainrigg, ten.
	1651			
5944	April 1	2 parcels in RHB	10 0 0	Rob. Moorsom, fishmn
5976	May 1	2 cotts. in RHB	20 0 0	La. Grainger, fishmn
5472	.. 11	one parcel for 2 cotts. in RHB	9 0 0	Ja. Helme and Jo. Temple, marriners.
	1653			
5979	March 1	2 cotts. and garths in Fylingthorpe	18 0 0	Mich. Lithe, weaver
5978	August 15	2 cotts. and garths in Fylingthorpe	18 0 0	Ed. Robinson, fishmn

			£ s. d.	
5982	.. 22	2 cotts. and garths in RHB	20 0 0	Jo. Moorsom, fishmn
5995	.. 23	2 cotts. and a house in RHB	20 0 0	Wm Cockerill, fishmn
5973	Sept. 24	2 cotts. and garths in RHB	26 0 0	Rich. Taylor, husbdmn
	1654			
5977	January 14	cott. and garth in RHB	10 0 0	Rob. Lotherington, fishmn
5945	.. 28	ten. and garth in Fylingthorpe	6 0 0	Wm Watson, yeoman
5980	February 4	cott. in Fylingthorpe	6 0 0	Tho. Proddam, cordiner
5952	November 11	house, 4 closes, lane (10 acres) Crossflat in Hawsker	108 0 0	Tho. Knowles, cook
5991	December 29	Gatebeck House, [Hawsker ?]	22 0 0	Tho. White, husbdmn
	1657			
6024	August 31	mess. and close on the moors (Foulsike)	3 0 0	Geo. Cowart, bachlr
5943	Sept. 1	cott. in RHB	7 10 0	Chris. Rickinson, fishmn
5988	.. 6	cott. in Stoupe Brow	7 10 0	Sam. Paycock, labourer
6022	.. 12	cott. in Stoupe Brow	5 0 0	Hen. Dickinson and Ralph Postgate, yeomen
695	November 9	cott. in RHB	25 0 0	Jo. Robson, fishmn
		total	£381 0s. 0d.	

Appendix H: Whitby Town properties recorded in Cholmley leases book (NYCRO, ZCG(W) (MIC 1286)

Number	Property	Date of sale
1	Bakehouse in Cliff Lane	25/9/54
2	Corner of Cliff Lane and Flowergate, three rooms	25/9/54
3	Part of old Correction House in Flowergate	25/9/54
4	Remainder of old Correction House in Flowergate	13/10/58
5	Burgage tenement in north Flowergate	6/9/54
6	Corner of Sandgate and New Market, a burgage tenement	30/1/53
7	East side of Kirkgate, a burgage tenement	18/2/39
8	Tentergarth waste on west side of Cliff Lane	26/10/57
9	North side of Baxtergate, a burgage tenement	17/10/54
10	North side of Flowergate opposite top of Skate Lane	18/2/39
11	East side of Southgate, burgage house and toft	29/9/54
12	Half a toft in north Baxtergate with burgage tenement	9/9/54
13	South side of Grape Lane, burgage tenement on $1\frac{1}{2}$ tofts	15/2/53
14	Half a burgage tenement on west side of Kirkgate	20/5/53
15	North side of Flowergate, next to Stockdale Close	18/2/39
16	West side of High Street, burgage tenement on $\frac{1}{2}$ toft	5/3/64
17	Bagdale garth or toft	20/9/56
18	East side of Kirkgate, a burgage tenement	1/2/53
19	North side of Flowergate, shop, chamber over and 3 houses	11/11/54
20	North side of New Market and south side of Brewster Lane	15/11/54
21	Waste on south side of Flowergate	3/5/49
22	Burgage tenement on south side of Baxtergate	26/8/54
23	North side of Cliff Lane, behind Bakehouse, a house	20/9/54
24	Corner of Grape Lane and Crossgate, burgage tenement on $\frac{1}{2}$ toft	29/10/38
25	East side of Crossgate, burgage tenement	11/2/39
26	Wellgarth, Burtree [Buttery] Crag	16/10/38
27	Old coalgarth, Haggleseagate	13/10/38
28	East side of Kirkgate, a burgage tenement	16/2/39
29	West side of Southgate, a burgage tenement on $\frac{1}{2}$ toft	5/9/40
30	West side of St Ann's Staith, a burgage tenement	29/3/39
31	Two burgage tenements in west Southgate	2/2/39
32	East side of Crossgate, a burgage tenement	28/2/39
33	East side of Southgate, a burgage tenement	2/2/39
34	West side of Highgate, a burgage tenement	6/11/54
35	East side of Southgate, a burgage tenement	5/1/39
36	East side of Kirkgate	2/2/39
37	East side of Crossgate, a burgage tenement on $\frac{1}{2}$ toft	23/2/39
38	East side of Kirkgate, a burgage tenement	18/2/39
39	South side of Baxtergate, a burgage tenement	15/10/38
40	South side of Baxtergate, a burgage tenement	19/2/49
41	East side of Kirkgate, a burgage tenement	1/4/59
42	North side of Bridgegate, a burgage tenement on $\frac{1}{2}$ toft	30/10/38
43	Sandgate	11/11/65

44	South end of Haggleseagate, a stable on $\frac{1}{2}$ toft	16/10/39
45	West side of St Ann's Staith, a burgage tenement	30/10/38
46	South side of Bridgegate, a burgage tenement	13/10/38
47	East side of Sandgate, a burgage tenement	26/3/39
48	South side of Baxtergate, a toft	20/3/39
49	South side of Flowergate, corner of Skate Lane, a burgage tenement	10/10/39
50	North side of old market, a burgage tenement	20/5/40
51	Ruswarp Mills and Salmon Fishery	
52	West side of Kirkgate, a burgage tenement	1/4/39
53	East side of Crossgate, a burgage tenement	2/2/39
54	North side of Flowergate, waste ground	22/7/72
55	West end of Esk Bridge, staith	20/8/66
56	New market place, corner shop	4/10/79
57	Shop on north side of west end of Esk Bridge	16/7/74
58	Shop on south side of east end of Esk Bridge	24/7/74
59	Parcel of ground, on north side of Cliff Lane	9/9/68
60	Waste ground between St Ann's Staith and river	29/8/66
61	Four shops in burgage tenement in Grape Lane	20/3/61
62	Three messuages on east side of Kirkgate	25/11/81
63	A house of Bridgegate, on corner of Sandgate	21/3/39
64	Waste ground between St Ann's Staith and river	12/12/81
65	East side of Kirkgate, a burgage tenement	19/2/39

[N.B. Of the first 65 numbered properties in the Cholmley Lease Book of Whitby town, 52 were sold on long leases by the time of the death of the first Sir Hugh.]

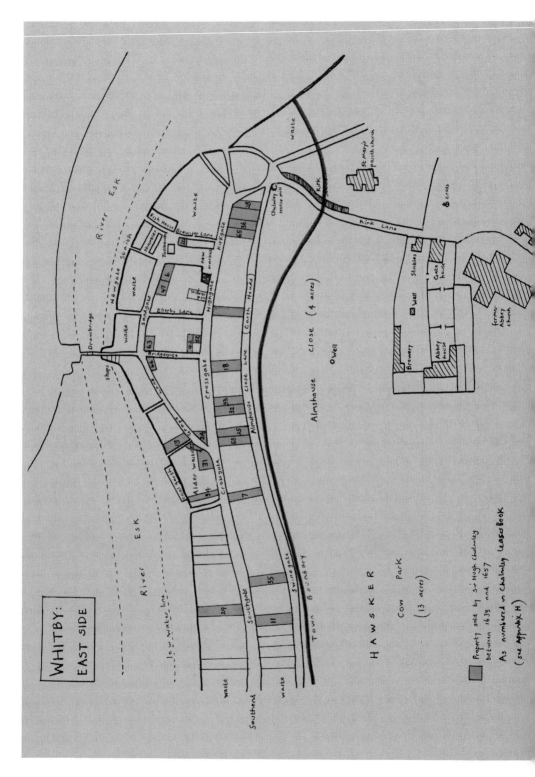

WHITBY: EAST SIDE

□ Property sold by Sir Hugh Cholmley
  between 1638 and 1657

As numbered in Cholmley Lease Book
(see Appendix H)

River ESK

River Esk

low water line

Southend

waste

waste

Town Boundary

Swinegate

Southgate

Crossgate

29   35   11

7   34   31   53   24   55

Aldir water

Kirkgarth

Kirkgate

Almshouse Close Lane (Garth Heads)

Crossgate

18   32   33   35

52   102   63

Bridgegate

shops

Drawbridge

Newgate   Skedith

waste

waste

Sandgate

waste

Killerby Lane

Highgate

Tollbooth

Shambles

Fish House   Brewer Lane

new market

6   47

65   66   28

waste

waste

HAWSKER

Cow Park
(13 acres)

Almshouse Close   (4 acres)

O well

Cholmley
house mill

Kirk

Kirk Lane

St Mary's
Parish church

✝ cross

Brewery

well

Stables

Gate
house

Abbey
house

former
Abbey
church

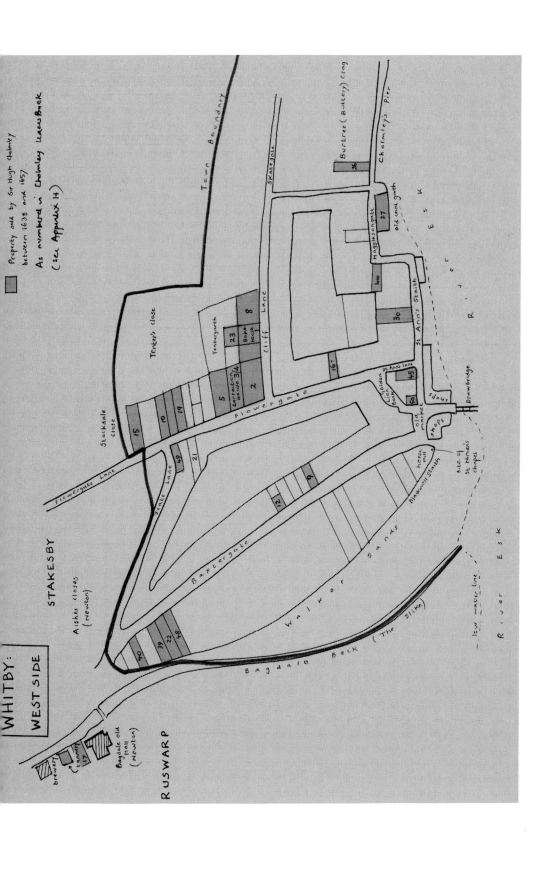

WHITBY: WEST SIDE

Property sold by Sir Hugh Cholmley
between 1635 and 1657.

As numbered in Cholmley viewBook
(see Appendix H)

STAKESBY

RUSWARP

Aisker closes
(Newton)

brewery

tannery

Bagdale old
Hall (Newton)

Flowergate Lane

Scale Lane

Stockdale Close

Tenter's close

Tenebergarth

23

Bake
house

8

Cliff Lane

Skategate

Correction
house 3/4

5

2

19

10

15

40

39

22

48

42

21

Baxtergate

Walker Sands

horse
mill

Blackwall Staith

12

9

site of
St Ninian's
chapel

Flowergate

16

old
market

shops

Golden
Lion
Booth

St Ann Lane

45

50

St Ann's Staith

30

Haggleseagate

27

Burtree (Buttery) Crag

Cholmley's Pier

old coal garth

Town Boundary

Bagdale Beck (The Slike)

low water line

R i v e r   E s k

Drawbridge

St dogs

26

Appendix J: Letter from Sir Hugh Cholmley to Scarborough bailiffs, 1 February 1626 [NYCRO, DC/SCB, B1 General Letters; MIC 1320/524]

To his very worthy freinds the Baliffes of Scarbrough

Mr Baliffes theis
Heareing that Mr Hucheson[1] since his election did not returne to your towne and knowing your intentions and desires to conferre with him about many businesses, I being now goeing towards London (and my occations not permitting a personall visett)[2] I send my footemen purposely to your towne, to bring a perticuler information of all such services as they may implooye mee, to which (god willing) their shall not bee wanting my reall and best endeavoiours; as likewise to informe your towne that this towne[3] and cuntry intending to petetion the Parliament house for some releife towerds the repaireing the Peer, are desirous of my assistance, which I would not give with out acquainting your towne, inrespect there is a flieing report, that it will not give way to that woorke to which I protest I give no beleife, for that I perswade my selfe you would then so much have intimated to mee before this, theis their resolutions being intended (and divoulged) or theis two or three Parlaments late past;[4] nor can I thinke you so inhumaine as not to commiserate a poore towne[5] for want of this peer lately much indamiged and in short tyme like to be absolutely ruined,[6] it being not long since your owne cases.[7] And theirfore I am so farre from iudgeing your towne opposite to so good and publicke a woorke, as I am confident you will afford your best ascistances to the advanceing it; out of which hopes I have perswaded this towne to crave your Certificate, which if you refusse upon any good reasons; doe but let mee know them, and I protest I shall as effectually as I can offer them to the Parlament; but if any mans perticuler or private ends shall divert your towne from showing this neighburly affection, give mee leave to tell you: that obligation which is first and cheifely to your towne, must not tye mee from doeing any publicke and good service to other parts of my cuntry; and so not doubting of a good respect here in, commending my heartyest love to your selfes and the whole Corporation I rest

Whitby / the 1. of February [1626]
Ever a faithfull friend to doe any service Hu. Cholmeley

---

[1] Stephen Hutchinson (1573–1648) of Wykeham Abbey was elected to serve as one of Scarborough's Members of Parliament, along with Hugh Cholmley, in January 1626. (NYCRO, DC/SCB, B1, General Letters, 6, 12, 14, 16, 17 Jan. 1626) He was the same Stephen Hutchinson who, with Hugh's father, Sir Richard (III), and other local gentlemen, had so outrageously abused the hospitality of Sir Thomas Hoby and his wife at Hackness Hall in August 1600. This was the only occasion Hugh was paired with Hutchinson: previously, in 1624 he had sat for Scarborough with William Conyers, and in 1625, with William Thompson.

[2] Since King Charles's second Parliament opened only five days later, 6 February 1626, Hugh seems to have good reason for not breaking his long journey from Whitby to London.

[3] By 'this towne' Cholmley meant Whitby.

[4] When Hugh's father had represented Scarborough in the Parliament of 1621–2, he had made a similar request to the borough to support the erection of a pier at Whitby. However, as Scarborough's Common Hall records make clear, the request was flatly rejected on the ground that 'thinconvenienc therof arising [was] so great and so hurtfull to the state of this towne'. The bailiffs were ordered to tell Sir Richard plainly that 'they would nott give way unto it for him to go about the same eyther in parliament or without' (NYCRO, DC/SCB, Minute Book 1621–49, 7 Nov. 1621).

[5] Aware of Scarborough's long-standing rivalry with and jealousy of Whitby, here Cholmley was trying to

conceal the latter's recent growth and prosperity as a result of the alum industry. He was also trying to conceal his own personal interest in a Whitby pier (see above pp.11–12, 93, n.277).

⁶ This was another deceit: Cholmley's intention was to build a new west pier at Whitby which would greatly enhance the size and security of its harbour, not to repair an old, damaged pier.

⁷ In a vain appeal to Scarborough consciences, here Cholmley referred to the destruction of Scarborough's great pier in the storm of November 1613. This pier was essential to Scarborough's status as a port and its controversial claim to be the only safe haven between the Tyne and the Humber. Fortunately for Scarborough, a Privy Council order of April 1614 had imposed a permanent tax on all East coast colliers which paid for the reconstruction and maintenance of the pier (Ashcroft, *Scarborough Records 1600–1640*, pp.52–6; I.H. Jeayes (ed.), *Copy Translations of Charters* (Scarborough, 1912), pp.153–4). Presumably, Cholmley hoped that a similar grant to Whitby would pay for its new pier.

Needless to say, Cholmley received no support from Scarborough for his pier at Whitby. His project had to wait for several years until it won the backing of his powerful patron, Thomas Wentworth (see above, memoirs MS. 21v., pp.92–3, n.276).

Appendix K: Letter from Sir Hugh Cholmley to Viscount Wentworth, Lord Deputy in Ireland, 18 May 1635 [Sheffield Archives, WWM, Strafford Papers 15(76)]

Whitby May the 18th 1635

My ever honoured Lord[1]

That I may not bee out of your Lordships memory, nor you iudge those humble respects I owe to you, out of mine; I am bold to send my servant purposely to present them by this letter, not knowing whether ether of my former had the hapynes to come to your hand, as allsoe to excuse my not waiteing on your Lordship this spring, according to my promisse, being diverted by importantt busines which drawes mee now to London, and my good Lord I presume your wisdome will iudge him who is not a good servant to his owne occasions, cannot bee one to your Lordship, though to have assurance I am soe in your esteeme is my greatest glory. My Lord I am bold likewise to present to you a few balls of Gascoynes powder, and two playne horses not worthy your acceptance, but that they may bee taken as Hieroglephycall exspressions of my wishes for your Lordships enioyment of health[2] and pleasure, or by your Lordships singuler gift in that knowlidge, receyve a better construction. Your Lordshipe perhaps before this exspected to heare of the proceedings in their Peers,[3] but Sir John Gybson[4] can say wee conceyve the business scarse fitt for your Lordships consideracion, yet because I hold my selfe more obleidged then the other Commissioners to give your Lordship accoumpt their of, I shall be bold to doe it with what brevety I can. The towne findeing the charge great in collecting by theire owne ministers, and much paid in fartheings at the tyme not current, thought fitt to decist before they had dispersed halfe of theire breefes, and many of those not yet returned in, is the greatest cause the Commissioners cannot take a iust accoumpt of the Collections, and with it (I hope before Michelmas) will bee finished halfe of the west Peer, and if it please my Lord Keeper[5] to renew the breefes (for those Countyes not yet collected) and with that favour others have had for disperseing them. It is thought the mony aryseing that way will finish the said west Peer, which in this place will ever bee a Monument to your Lordships honour and glory, the towne allredy by this little findeing soe much benefitt and good, as the whole Inhabitants are your daly Orrators, and by Mychelmas I hope all things will bee in such a posture as a more perfect and full accoumpt may bee renderd to your Lordship:[6] my paper restreines mee from being more trublesome to your Lordship though nothing can from sayeing I am ever

Your Lordships most faythfull servant
Hu Cholmley

[1] Cholmley's letter was addressed to Thomas, Viscount Wentworth (1593–1641), then Lord Deputy of Ireland and subsequently Earl of Strafford.

[2] No doubt Sir Hugh was aware that Wentworth suffered badly from rheumatism, gout, insomnia, migraine and fainting fits, all of which had grown worse in Ireland's damp weather (C.V. Wedgwood, *Thomas Wentworth. A Revaluation* (pbk. edn. 1964), p.166).

[3] In fact, Cholmley's building project was a single pier on the west side of Whitby's outer harbour. For other references to this work see the Memoirs MS, f.21v. (above pp.92–3).

[4] Sir John Gibson of Welburn Hall near Kirkbymoorside in the North Riding was one of the commissioners who, like Cholmley, were engaged in raising the money for and carrying out the construction of Whitby's new pier. Sir John was a friend and business associate of Wentworth, and his interest in Whitby probably dated from 1630 when, acting on behalf of the viscount, he bought a future

lease on the Crown's alum works (*CSPD* 1629–31, p.291; R.B. Turton, *The Alum Farm* (Whitby, 1938), pp.161, 164, 170–1).

[5] Lord Coventry, Lord Keeper from 1625 until 1640, was another close friend and admirer of Wentworth. Together they had secured the briefs which authorised a national collection for Whitby's new pier in 1632.

[6] Cholmley's contemporary account in this letter of the difficulties and delays encountered in raising funds for the west pier should be compared with his retrospective treatment of the matter in his Memoirs, MS f.21v. (see above, pp.92–3).

Appendix L: Copy of Sir Hugh Cholmley's last will, 19 November 1657 [HUL, DCY/19/2]

A Copy of my Father Sir Hugh Cholmeley his will dated Nov 19 1657[1]
In the name of God Amen. the nineteenth day of November in the year of our Lord God according to the Computation of the church of England one thousand sixe hundred fifty and seven. I Sr Hugh Cholmeley of London Knt and Baronett being in some indisposition of health, but of sound and disposing memory (thanks bee to god). Considering the certainty of death, and the uncertainty when it may happen,[2] doe therefore for the better quieting my mind, and setling of my estate, make and ordaine this my last will, and testament in manner and forme following. that is to say. First I beequiathe my soule to almighty god my creator, hopeing and beelieving to bee sound by the merritts, and satisfaction of Jesus Christ my only Saviour and redeemer. And my body to bee buryed without pompe, or more then necessary charge, in the Quier belonging to the family of the Twysdens, in the church of great Peckham in Kent, as neare as conveniently may bee to the place where my deer wife lyeth interred, between her, and the chancell belonging to the saide church.[3] And whereas I lately purchased the mannor and Lordship of Aslaby, alias Asilby, alias Haselby in the parish of Whitby in the County of Yorks,[4] which said mannor and lordship of Aslaby I have passed to my brother Sr Henry Cholmeley Knight, my brother in Law Francys Twysden Esq, and my deare sonne in Lawe Richard Stephens Esq by Indenture bearing date the sixteenth day of November in the yeare of our Lord one thousand six hundred fifty seven, upon trust and for such consideration as is therein exprest, as relation being thereunto had, more plainly doth and may appeare. And whereas by indenture bearing date the fifth day of May, in the yeare of our Lord one thousand six hundred and fifty five, I have granted to the above named Sr Henry Cholmeley Francys Twysden and Richard Stephens, the mannor and Lordshipp of Daleton in the County of Yorke aforesaid,[5] first for the payment of eight Hundred pounds principall debt, with the Consideration then due to my good brother in Law John Twysden Dr of physicke, and the remainder to my daughter Elizabeth Cholmeley for her portion (to be payde at her day of marriage, or age of twenty and one years, and in the meanetime the profitts and use of the mony, for her present maintenance[6]) as by the saide Indenture relation being thereunto had more at Large doth and may appeare. Now in case my said trustees doe find that the saide mannor and Lordship of Daleton will not satisfye the saide debt of eight hundred pounds to my saide brother in Law Dr John Twysden and also rayse two thousand five hundred pounds for the portion of my said daughter Elizabeth, My desire and meaning is, that my saide trustees shall out of the mannor and Lordshipp of Aslaby aforesaide, rayse and pay to my said daughter Elizabeth, so much mony as shall make the remaynder of Daleton (eight hundred pounds being first payde to my saide brother in Law Dr Twysden) the summe of two thousand five hundred pounds, which I give and intend as her portion in full discharge of all other claims, and demands whatsoever. And the aforesaid debt of eight hundred pounds, and portion of two thousand five hundred pounds being fully satisfyed and payde, if there should happen to remaine any surplus, and advantage out of the sale of it or otherwise, my desire and meaning is, it shall be disposed and given to my sonne Hugh Cholmeley and his heyers. And my farther will and meaning is that in case my said daughter Elizabeth should dy before shee bee marryed or attain the age of twenty and one years, that notwithstanding shee shall have power and

liberty, to dispose of two hundred pounds of it. And that of the remaining two thousand three hundred pounds, my desire and will is that my daughter Anne Stephens should have one hundred pounds of it. And that the remaining two thousand two hundred should be equally divided betweene my two sonns William Cholmeley and Hugh Cholmeley and ther heyers.[7] And for and Concerning my personall estate, I doe give and bequeath the severall legacyes hereafter mentioned to bee payde by my executors. That is to say I give to my deare Brother Sr Henry Cholmeley my bay Bald Barbary mare Called Spanker. Item I give to my deare sonne in Law Richard Stephens my young Stone Colt comming three years old, now or late going at grass in the parke or paddock of Whitby (manor house) aforesaide. Item I give to my deare brother in Law Francys Twysden aforesaide, my chestnut guelding. Item I give to my sonnes William and Hugh, and my two daughters Ann and Elizabeth, and to the two children of my brother Sr Henry Cholmeley, and likewise to the two daughters of my deare brother Sir Richard Cholmeley (deceased)[8] Margarett and Ursula, to each of these a plaine gold ring with this posy or motto (*Ex eadem radice*) each ring to bee of thirteene shillings price. Item I give to my sonne Hugh Cholmeley aforesaid all my bookes, as well those that are at London as else where in the Countrye. Item I give to my deare daughter in Lawe wife of my sonne William Cholmeley, the greene cloath hangings, wrought with needle worke which I desire her to esteeme, because they were wrought by my deare wife and her servants, when wee were first house keepers. Item I give to my three deare grand children, Nat, Dick and Betty Stephens to each of them five pounds to bee disposed of on something for a remembrance as their mother, my deare daughter Anne Stephens, shall like best, to whom I beeseech the Lord make them a Comfort. Item I give to my very good Ant Mrs Dorothy Bushell widdow[9] five pounds. Item I give to my deare sister Mrs Jane Twysden wife to my Brother serjeant Twysden a little gold pott of tenn pounds price, with hearty thanks and acknowledgements for her many favors and kindnesses to my selfe and children. Item I give to my Cosin Francys Comyn[10] my dunn mare. Item I give to my trusty servant George Coward fourty pounds and my will is if hee desire to live at Aselby aforesaide, that hee may have the house was Robert Knaggs and his farme at the yearly value or rent of sixteene pounds, for so long time as hee shall live there. Item I give ten pounds to Thomas Huntrods to bound him prentice, providing hee bee not prentice when I dye. Item I give to Mr Crosby minister of Whitby five pounds to bee disposed in buying a gowne for him. I give to the poore of the parish of Whitby twenty nobles to bee disposed by my sonne William Cholmeley. And to the poore of the parish of Great Peckham in Kent five pounds to bee distributed as my deare brother in Lawe Sir Roger Twysden shall thinke fitt and appoint. And I ordaine my before mentioned loving friends Sr Henry Cholmeley, and Richard Stephens to bee the sole executors of this my last will and testament (revoking hereby all former wills and dispositions of this kind whatsoever) to whom I give the remaynder of all my goods and chatells. And my interest in the lease and tearme yet to come in the parsonage or rectory of Whitby in the County of Yorke aforesaide. Neverthelesse upon this farther trust and confidence, that after my funerall expences discharged, my debts and legacys paide, they give and dispose the remaynder to the sole use and beehaafe of my sonne Hugh Cholmeley. Neverthelesse my intent and meaning is that my sonne William Cholmeley (if hee desire it) should have all my household stuffe and Lumber in Whitby house, and the Gatehouse (paying to my executors one hundred pounds of Lawfull mony for the same). Item I nominate and desire my four Brothers in Lawe Sr Roger Twysden Knight and Baronett, Thomas Twysden Esq Serjant at Lawe, John Twysden Dr in physicke and

Francys Twysden Esq to bee supervisors of this my last will and testament, referring all or any scruple or difference that may arise upon the same, to bee determined by them or any two of them, of which my brother serjant to bee one so long as hee lives. And to each of my said Brothers I give a gold ring of twenty shillings price for a Legacy. And lastly I doe declare this to bee my last will and Testament, and have sealed and subscribed and made severall duplicates to bee produced, as there shall bee occasion. Signed, sealed, published and declared by the said Sr Hugh Cholmeley to bee his last will and testament in the presence of Thomas Twysden: Tho. Williams: Tho. Rasell: John Watson: George Covart.

Hu Cholmeley

[1] This is a copy of the will kept by the Cholmley family amongst their Howsham Hall papers; the original is to be found in the London Probate Act Book, Register Nobbs, 8 November 1660, f.206. An abstract of the original will was published in *YASRS* ix, no.248, pp.163–4.

[2] Sir Hugh died eleven days later, 30 November 1657.

[3] His body was buried as described here near the south wall of the chancel in St Michael's church, East Peckham, Kent, next to that of his wife. The inscription on their joint tomb reads: 'Heer also lyes the body of Sir Hugh Cholmeley her husband who for the great love he bore the virtue and worth he found in the said Elizabeth declined the being interred in his own country among his ancestors, and chose to be laid heer beside her, by whom he had six children Richard and Elizabeth deceased young, William, Hugh, Ann and Elizabeth did survive at his death which happened the 30th of November 1667 [*sic*] in the 57th yeare of his age.' St Michael's is now a redundant church.

[4] For references to Aislaby in Eskdale see Memoirs MS, ff.21r., 22r. (above, pp.92, 94).

[5] For references to Daletown in Hawnby see Memoirs MS, ff.21r., 22r. (above, pp.92, 94).

[6] Sir Hugh's younger daughter, Elizabeth, was then only 19 years old. She never married and died in 1699. She was also buried in St Michael's.

[7] Two months after Sir Hugh's death, his brother, Sir Henry, brother-in-law, Francis Twysden, and son-in-law, Richard Stephens, sold Daletown in Hawnby to Lord Fauconberg for £2,950.

[8] This Sir Richard Cholmeley of Grosmont (1617–44) was Sir Hugh's half-brother, the son of his father's second wife, Margaret Cobb. That Sir Hugh had a great regard for his half-brother is evident in his Memoirs MS, 11r. (see above, pp.77–8).

[9] Dorothy Cholmley, sister of Sir Richard (III), had married Nicholas Bushell of Bagdale Old Hall, Whitby, in 1601, when she was only 14 years old. Their eldest son became Captain Browne Bushell (1609–51), Sir Hugh's cousin and comrade in arms. By 1657 Aunt Dorothy had been a widow for 25 years. There are several references to 'Ant Bushell' in Sir Hugh's Memoirs.

[10] Francis Comyn was the son of Timothy Comyn of Durham, second husband of Margaret Cholmley, one of the seven sisters of Sir Hugh's father.

Index

Spellings in brackets are Sir Hugh Cholmley's variants; alphabetical order is word by word.

INDEX   197

Holland, departs for 108
honesty of 29
Hotham, Sir John, defended by 123, 131
Hull, siege of and 106, 146 fn. 26
illness claimed by 99
impeachment ordered 105
imprisoned in Leeds Castle 113
as JP 13, 95, 100
King Charles, declares for 105, 144
King Charles rebukes 102
and kinship 39–40
knighted 7
land sales 7, 10–11, 176–85
in Long Parliament 16–17, 103
marriage 7, 52–3, 55, 74, 84
Militia Ordinance opposed by 19
MP for Scarborough 5, 7, 16, 85, 99,
    103
nurse's son pretends to be his son 92,
    94
nutrition poor in infancy 40, 80, 81
Parliament:
    attachment to, nature of 21
    conscience about serving 14–15, 145
    reasons for deserting 22–5, 142–3
    support for 20–4, 140, 142, 145
Parliament's criticism of 23, 142, 145
Parliament's orders to 22, 23, 142
personal life 18–19
petition to king 102–3
petition to Privy Council 100–1
political career 14–21
portraits of 99 fn. 324
pride in ancestors 40
privateers steal goods of 86, 110
property sales 7, 10–11, 12, 176–85
property transferred to trustees 13, 14,
    16, 109, 192
Queen, meets at York 24, 25, 143, 145
religious views 18, 19, 47
Royal family, concern for 17–18
Royalists, defection to 24–5, 105, 142–3
Royalists, successes for 146 fn. 26
Roydon Hall, lives at 54
Scarborough:
    effect of defence of 28
    Governor of 105
    requested to secure for Parliament
        104–5, 141–2
    siege of castle 28, 148–3
    surrender of castle by Sir Hugh 28,
        108, 160–63
    taken over by Sir Hugh 22, 140, 142
Scarborough Memorials commented on
    19, 21, 123, 124

Scarborough Memorials mentioned in the
    Memoirs 105
Scots, dislike of 103 fn. 352
Scots, wars against 15, 98–9, 101
Ship Money and 15, 16, 17, 100, 103
in Short Parliament 16, 17, 99
soldier struck by 99
sports 82–3
Strafford and 11–12, 14, 15, 16, 93, 189,
    190–1
    rift with 16, 21, 99–100, 101–2
succeeds father as manager 6, 85–6
succeeds to estate 7, 80
takes up Parliament's commission at
    Scarborough 16, 104–5, 140
Taylor (Tayler) and 111–13
tenant farmers' assistance to 10
trained bands and 15–16, 22, 96, 98, 101,
    102, 104, 140
virtues 28–9
wet-nurse 80, 81
Whitby and 11–12, 13
    pier 11–12, 51, 188–9, 190
wife, first meeting 52–3, 84
wife's death, grief at 51, 53–4, 115–22
will 192–4
on writing the Memoirs 39, 79–80
Yelverton, Sir Christopher attended by
    59, 98
see also Memoirs; Memorials; for relations
    with other people, see under names of
    people concerned
Cholmley, Sir Hugh (Sir Hugh's son):
    'Account of Tangier' 12, 42
    autobiography 41
    baptism 46, 48, 91, 94
    birth 41, 52, 91, 93
    born at Fyling Old Hall 41, 93
    born with damaged finger 93
    father's exile and 13, 41, 109, 110
    joins family abroad 41
    Memoirs dedicated to 40, 61
    public life 41
    wet-nurse for 56–7
    writings published with father's memoirs
        41–2
    youth 41
Cholmley, Jane/Ann (Sir Hugh's great-great
    aunt) 62
Cholmley, Joan/Jane (Sir Hugh's half-great
    aunt) 3–4, 54–5, 64, 65, 66, 67
Cholmley, John (Sir Hugh's brother) 72,
    77
Cholmley, John (Sir Hugh's great-great
    uncle) 62